Robert Frost

ROBERT FROST
A Living Voice
by Reginald Cook

The University of Massachusetts Press Amherst, 1974

Grateful acknowledgment is made to the following publishers and institutions for material reprinted with permission.

Holt, Rinehart and Winston, Inc. and Jonathan Cape Ltd, for material from *The Poetry of Robert Frost* edited by Edward Connery Lathem. Copyright 1916, 1923, 1928, 1930, 1934, 1939, 1947, © 1969 by Holt, Rinehart and Winston, Inc. Copyright 1936, 1942, 1944, 1947, 1951, 1953, 1954, © 1956, 1958, 1962 by Robert Frost. Copyright © 1964, 1967, 1970 by Lesley Frost Ballantine. Reprinted by permission of Holt, Rinehart and Winston, Inc., and by permission of Jonathan Cape Ltd.

Holt, Rinehart and Winston, Inc., for material from *Selected Letters* of Robert Frost edited by Lawrance Thompson. Copyright © 1964 by Holt, Rinehart and Winston, Inc. and the Estate of Robert Frost; for material from *Selected Prose of Robert Frost* edited by Hyde Cox and Edward Connery Lathem. Copyright 1949, 1954, © 1966 by Holt, Rinehart and Winston, Inc. Copyright 1946, © 1959 by Robert Frost. Copyright © 1956 by the Estate of Robert Frost; for material from *Robert Frost: The Trial by Existence* by Elizabeth Shepley Sergeant. Copyright © 1960 by Elizabeth Shepley Sergeant; for material from *Fire and Ice: The Art and Thought of Robert Frost* by Lawrance Thompson. Copyright, 1942, by Henry Holt and Company.

Macmillan Publishing Co., Inc., for material reprinted with permission of Macmillan Publishing Co., Inc. from *Collected Poems* by William Butler Yeats. Copyright © 1928 by Macmillan Publishing Co., Inc. Renewed 1956 by Georgie Yeats.

The Viking Press, Inc., for material from *Writers at Work* The Paris Review Interviews, Second Series, Copyright © 1963 by The Paris Review, Inc. Reprinted by permission of The Viking Press, Inc.

Harvard University Press, for material reprinted by permission of the publishers and the Trustees of Amherst College from Thomas H. Johnson, Editor, *The Poems of Emily Dickinson*, Cambridge, Mass.: The Belknap Press of Harvard University Press, Copyright, 1951, 1955, by The President and Fellows of Harvard College.

Charles Scribner's Sons, for material from *The American Scene*, by Henry James (1946).

University of Oklahoma Press, for material from *Robert Frost: Life and Talks—Walking*, by Louis Mertins. Copyright 1965 by the University of Oklahoma Press.

National Broadcasting Company, Inc., for an excerpt from the March 22, 1959, *Meet the Press* program.

Cowles Communications, Inc., for material from "A Visit with Robert Frost," by Chester Morrison, *Look*, March 31, 1959. Copyright © 1959 by Cowles Communications, Inc.

The Estate of Robert Frost, Alfred C. Edwards, Executor, for permission to use the transcriptions of the recordings of Robert Frost's lectures at the Bread Loaf School of English.

Any who seek him seek in him the seeker.
"Escapist-Never"

What would not a man give if he might converse
with Orpheus and Musaeus and Hesiod and Homer?
Socrates, *Apology*

This book is warmly dedicated
to my friend
John Hicks

Contents

PART III
Surmisings

Preface

In the original draft, *Robert Frost: A Living Voice* was entitled *Viva Voce*, now the heading of part II. The chapters in parts I and III appear serially, but this is not the order in which they were first written. My underlying idea in this book is to introduce Robert Frost as an extraordinary talker, to present transcribed evidences of his flexible expression, and to reflect on the resonance of his voice in poetic skill. If I had wanted to attempt one more biographical record, part I could well have been extended. Or if I had decided to make an omnium-gatherum without commentary, the second part could readily have been enlarged. And, if I had thought chiefly of a critical interpretation, the third part might have been greatly amplified. In lieu of such possibilities, I hope that an idiosyncratic voice, illuminating impressions of a complex man, and interpretive insights in reading the poetry will draw readers deeper in Frost.

Forty years of thinking about Frost alter one's perspective. I am aware of a danger in the soft focus, but I am equally aware of a compensating sympathetic detachment. Once, when inscribing an original couplet in a copy of *A Further Range,* Frost wrote: "They say the truth will make you free. / My truth will chain you slave to me." This is perhaps the ultimate Frostian paradox in an Emersonian doctrine of compensation.

If Middlebury College had not given me the opportunity to direct the Bread Loaf School of English, I should never have been in a position to make the Robert Frost recordings which compose the second part of this volume. My first debt of gratitude is, therefore, to Middlebury College, and especially to the president, Dr. James I.

Armstrong, who, with grace and alacrity, arranged for the institutional permission to use these personal tape recordings.

In the initial preparation of the recordings, Professor Erie Volkert, director of the theaters at Middlebury College and at Bread Loaf School of English during my directorship, gave unstintingly in time and assistance. On various occasions the following also gave yeoman service in preparing the recordings: George W. Smith, Jr., John Cotter, Professor William Meredith of Connecticut College, John Anderson, Brian Pendleton, and Joyce Higley. To each of these, my thanks.

In the preparation of the several manuscripts, my wife, Nita, always patient and devoted, assisted expertly in typing, suggesting emendations, and attention to details. Only she knows how grateful I am. My deep appreciation also to Kenneth Walker, a brilliant and sympathetic editor; to Barbara Palmer, an incomparable copy editor and proofreader; to the staff of the University of Massachusetts Press for great service in the book's publication; to the exacting manuscript readers, Professor John Hicks, editor of *The Massachusetts Review,* Professor Benjamin L. Reid of Mount Holyoke College, and Professor Francis Murphy of Smith College, all of whom have assisted me far beyond the call of professional duty. They have been wise in judgment and watchful in details. To say that I am grateful to each only scratches the surface of my appreciation.

I have also leaned heavily upon the library staff and publications offices at Middlebury College. Special thanks go to George H. Huban, Sr., editor of Middlebury College Publications, Max P. Petersen, editor of the College News Services, and Gregor Hileman, editor of the College *News Letter.* John R. McKenna, librarian at the Egbert Starr Library of Middlebury College, the assistant librarian, John B. Rothrock, and Robert Buckeye, curator of the Abernethy Library of American Literature at Middlebury College, have helped greatly.

In securing special information, I was assisted immeasurably by Professor Carlos H. Baker at Princeton University, Professor George Anderson at Brown University, and Edwin Way Teale at Trail Wood, Hampton, Connecticut. In using the facilities of the American Literature department at Middlebury College, my thanks to Dr. Howard M. Munford. And in various ways I am grateful to Egbert C. Hadley; Walter E. Brooker, Vice President and Director of Development of Middlebury College; Dr. Paul M. Cubeta, Academic Vice President of Middlebury College and Director of the Bread Loaf School of English; and notably to Mrs. Kathleen Morrison, who helped in many ways, both directly and indirectly.

Robert Frost

PART ONE
Of Poet and Place

CHAPTER 1
Introduction

1.

Why, it might legitimately be asked, should anything more be added to the already numerous recordings of Robert Frost's table talk? Haven't we already in hand the accounts of Lawrance Thompson and Elizabeth Shepley Sergeant, Louis Untermeyer and John Bartlett, Sidney Cox, Daniel Smythe and Louis Mertins, and a host of reminiscences like those of Robert Francis, Stearns Morse, Wilbert Snow, and Melville Cane? Indeed, it would be sheer presumption on my part to attempt another elaborate discourse on Frost's *ars poetica*. And who wants further to get entangled in the ambiguities of the Frost legend to which the first volumes of the three-volume official biography have already subjected readers?

Instead, I have chosen in this series of interrelated essays, based on notes continuing from 1925 until 1963 and on a number of tape recordings of the 1950s and early 1960s, to clarify directly by quotation and indirectly by personal insight what Frost's poetry meant to him and to those who receive it. In effect, the stress will be equally upon what Frost said and the way he said it. If there are some happy hits like those Maxim Gorky made in the *Reminiscences of Tolstoy, Chekhov, and Andreyev,* which enable us to see and feel the unique separate self beneath the public figure, I shall be satisfied. But the personal record and the aperçus have one intent: to illuminate the poetry in which the wisdom of Yankee runes, the craft of verse, the unmistakable tone, and unique vision of the essential Frost are to be found. His views on the nature and purpose of poetry in relation to the mimetic theory of Aristotle and the cultural primitivism of the romantic revival of the nineteenth century have been noted. And so, too, changes in attitude and form, the breadth and depth in range of expression, the climate of his time, the native myth of the American

3

dream, the writer's relationship to a technological society, personal aspects of belief, and inescapably the lessons learned from success and failure are considered in varying degrees.

Since his death in 1963, there has been more candor in discussing Frost's egotism and cantankerousness and the jealousy of his professional rivalry. The stubbornness, self-distrust, and laziness attributed to him can be taken in human stride, but the accusations of arrogance and vindictiveness call for more study in psychological depth. His long life and the remarkable recognition that he received toward its close, especially at President John F. Kennedy's inauguration, alerted a nation. Here, it seemed, was a living example of genius in one's own time. By his gregariousness, he contributed to the popular image. What poet has ever appeared in a more public context than Frost—as a personality before the millions on the TV screen, as an identifiable voice heard on the radio, as an unusual master of the higher revels in the lecture room, as companionable house guest, and even as an amiable purchaser of groceries in the local markets or grazer of horses on leash at his farm in Ripton? The sedulous grubbers will yet be digging up another remembered interview, and the anglers will catch this side or that one. Whatever was quirky, jesting, idiosyncratic, will be remembered, and he well may be the hapless victim of total recall. But we certainly may apply to Frost, Robert F. Sayre's remark on Franklin, "The man behind the actor was always bigger than the single part."

Detractors have emphasized, as I have mentioned, Frost's particularly sensitive sense of jealous rivalry, and they have criticized his egotism. Partisans, who are just as fervent, have remarked compassionately on his intense personal loyalty and the great show of courage in his long struggle for recognition. What a granitic Yankee outcrop this man really is, some have thought. What a vulnerable human being, others have contended. At least originality in craftsmanship and a compelling sensibility enabled him to attain recognition. Yet a poet's place in literature is hardly secured by critical initiative alone, no matter how vigorously urged or cunningly defended the particular genius is. Only in time is there likely to be anything approaching tacit agreement about a poet's quality. "So our virtues," says Aufidius in *Coriolanus,* "lie in th' interpretation of the time."

Critical interpreters are less often at odds with the characteristic elements in a poet's natural genius—Frost's sound of sense or handling of what is common in thought-felt experience—than they are with the way each poet has arrived at his view and with the particular evidence he has adduced to embody it. There is also the more subtle complexity of human nature which makes the image of every genius a disputed territory. Naturally the partisans of Yeats and Stevens will approve of anything that diminishes the popular image of Frost. And naturally the adherents of the household poet will settle for nothing less than their exaggerated claims. When critics cry up one major poet at the expense of another, I think Whitman's insight is sure. "One supreme," he said sensibly, "does not contradict another supreme." The New Criticism of the 1940s prompted critics to ascribe the merit of originality to *The Waste Land* and the *Cantos* and to deny it to the poetry of Frost because the subtleties of Eliot and Pound could only be unmasked by clever scholars in *explication des textes*. A cultivation of tolerance might better have been urged. For while cryptic poetry may test an advanced reader with his guard up while seated in the window "behind the *Encyclopaedia Britannica*," the discerningly witty and deceptively simple poet might sharply test the flexibility of the same reader with his guard down. At any rate, the disparagement by the New Critics seems justifiably to have rankled in Frost.

In the following interpretive essays, which compose parts I and III, I have had the advantage not only of the transcribed tapes making up part II but also of vis-à-vis meetings with Frost, usually at Ripton and Middlebury and occasionally at South Shaftsbury, Amherst, Cambridge, wherever. For obvious reasons, these personal meetings were not taped, so the direct quotations from the poet must stand on their own recognizance. I have never used a word, phrase, or sentence in preparing this record of personal meetings except as I heard it on Frost's lips. No words which appear here have been invented as substitutes for his. Self-suppression is not always a virtue, but it can be when a poet of Frost's stature is quoted. When I met with him he talked frankly and freely and nowhere more memorably than in the relaxed comfort—at stretch in his old Morris chair —of the cabin on the Homer Noble farm in Ripton. Since we met at his appointment, I never found him impatient, offish, or distracted. Nor did I find him—as we often heard it said in the later years —adjusting masks. If this, as it was assumed, was an occupational hazard, whom was he fooling and why? He could be indirect, I noticed, but without being devious. The only show of belligerence I ever saw was demonstrated in dramatizing the reenactment of an episode. He was remarkably attentive. Carefully, I tried not to presume in extending these meetings beyond the hours of common courtesy; but he was a hard man to get away from when he was wound up.

The difference between Frost as poet and Frost as talker is more a

5

matter of method than of style. In the run of his talk I heard passages in cadences as moving as any of those in his poetry. The idiomatic style was unmistakably the same in poetry and conversation. But the wholly relaxed conversation found a tauter discipline imposed upon it in the poems, and although it was basically equivalent to the poetry, where there is a difference between the two, attribute it to the magic of art. The art was no cutting off of pieces from the whole cloth of talk and describing the result as poems; it represented a complex process during which poems as thought-felt substance came to life.

His visitors were like trackers, beaters, and whippers-in. They helped him drive ideas into the open. In a public lecture he would refer to this or that idea picked up from one of the marathon talks. Hearing Frost perform many times publicly at the Bread Loaf School of English from 1946 to 1962 was like eavesdropping at the sessions in the Ripton cabin. The story would be retold in a different context; the idea would be released in a new shape; a familiar thought was freshly rephrased.

Another thing: Frost betrayed neither confidences nor his own reticence. He kept intruders off his unposted personal boundaries, commonly, as I discovered, by taking the initiative in the talks or, in public, by sallies of wit, a tactic reminiscent of Socrates in the *Symposium*. When Aristodemus was awakened toward daybreak by the crowing of the Athenian cocks only Socrates, Aristophanes, and Agathon were still awake and drinking out of a large goblet, "which," according to Plato, "they passed around and Socrates was discoursing to them." There are those who remember sharing similar all-night sessions with Frost, sans the large wine-filled goblet, as he talked in a slow, steady, engaging flow of commentary, allusion, quotation, paradox, and occasional eloquence, until the Ripton cocks celebrated another upland dawn in the Green Mountains. And none of us ever beat Frost because none of us could outtalk him.

Once, in a newspaper, someone remarked that if Frost only prepared a laundry list or itemized a grocery list it would be unmistakably his style. This is true enough. Everything about him was self-identifying, uniquely expressing his individuality. I hope these commentaries carry his unforgettable earmark. Even when he chose to be noncommunicative during those intervals before a reading or talk, which he called characteristically "the silences," these occasions were as expressive of his natural genius as volubility. Wherever the voice is heard, his presence is forever felt.

CHAPTER 2
Four Meetings

Robert Frost, like America, is hard to see. Nor is it going to grow any easier to see him more clearly in the lengthening perspective of the years. The mode I have chosen to project these four images of Robert Frost as I saw him was suggested by an autobiographical essay by H. G. Wells. Once, when preparing a statement of his philosophy, Wells looked over several pictures of himself taken at different times in his life and attempted to reconcile them with his changing views. Similarly, I have several pictures of Frost in mind, and by identifying each one it is hoped, first, that a sense of life as a changing process will be suggested and, secondly, that each of these meetings will stand significantly on its own. I have selected four from several hundred meetings: a first meeting when I was a young college graduate, and Frost at midcareer, having consolidated a hardwon recognition, extended the hand of encouragement and friendship to one of many; a second meeting ten years later at "The Gully" in South Shaftsbury, Vermont; a third, an afternoon walk with Frost on the Long Trail in Vermont; and, finally, Frost at eighty-six, a master talker in action. Over a stretch of thirty-five years I had a chance to see him as preceptor, paterfamilias, outdoorsman, and performer.

JULY 15, 1925

At the Bread Loaf School of English, Bread Loaf, Vermont, Professor Wilfred E. Davison, dean of the school, took me over to Maple Cottage with its pumpkin yellow, Mississippi-riverboat balconies and, after introducing Frost, left us alone for more than an hour. We sat together on an old-fashioned stuffed sofa, and Frost immediately began to talk about the idea of progress and illustrated a particular theory by spiral motions with his eloquent hands. Later, I was to see a great deal of these manual gestures, especially of the index finger of the right hand wagging dramatically at Bread Loaf audiences. Over the years I often heard that inflected voice, pitched low and intimately persuasive, rally ideas by nearly total recall. What a memory! Apposite references to support his views were like stout armor and sharp swords produced readily from a well-supplied trophy room. Today he cited Nietzsche, then Einstein, and finally, to clinch his point, he referred to Parmenides.

His tactic was not Socratic. He did not attempt a subtle inquiry to draw me out; there was no dialectic; it was, rather, an ingratiating monologue. But throughout the meeting he was evoking, opening up, suggesting points of view. The monologue divagated without hitch or embarrassing pause from comment to counterstatement and included cautious qualification. What made this apparent skimble-skamble congenial was the lack of condescension and the vigorous thrust of ideas. He talked to me as a friendly preceptor with no edging away, completely relaxed and composed, his legs stretched out, his clothes rumpled

An imaginative and resourceful talker, he recalled his early experience in teaching when he sat on a wood box with his right arm resting on a window ledge instructing fifteen children in the eighth grade in the public school at Methuen, Massachusetts, in the spring of 1893. While he used himself as the object lesson, it was obvious he was thinking of my literary interests and what lay before me. Having a great deal to share, he shared it generously and uneffusively. As I learned later his preceptorial instinct was one of the most compulsive. What was he up to at twenty? Well, for one thing, he wasn't going inside himself introspectively; he was more interested in studying nature—"botanizing," he called it. He was also interested in writing some of the poetry that later went into *A Boy's Will*. Autobiographical references to Dartmouth College episodes and to Methuen days were regarded simply as things done. The least of pedants, he must have been a very relaxed teacher. When he talked about people his interest quickened perceptibly, and each reference to writers like Sherwood Anderson and Ben Hecht, and to friends like Raymond Holden and Louise Bogan, scored a point. He was concerned with what friends and acquaintances were trying to do —their hard-won successes, their way of facing difficulties, their peculiarities. Not one cutting thing was said.

When he talked about writing, he was critical of notebook keeping and recommended reading mainly as a way for a writer to acquire a sense of literary form. Self-consciousness with its mannerisms and early sophistication were phases, he thought, every would-be writer had to live through. Independence was the thing. Emphatically and colloquially, he asserted: "What the hell's the use of thinking about what other people think you are doing as long as you are in the way of knowing what you are to follow through?" Since he had four published books of original poetry behind him, he could say this with some authority. An encouraging preceptor, a brightly lighted intelligence, he was still fighting on the way up. Once, much later, he said: "A student is an orange pip between my fingers; if I pinch him he'll go far." Distance is deceiving; I only felt pinched.

SEPTEMBER 28, 1935

Four of us—Robert and Elinor Frost, my wife and I—sat in the kitchen of the white farmhouse called The Gully in South Shaftsbury, Vermont. It had been a miserably rainy day, and after the eighty-mile trip from Middlebury we were trying to dry off and get warm in front of the kitchen range in midafternoon. Frost sat in the corner with his chair tilted back, and Mrs. Frost was seated close by. Mrs. Frost, an animated talker, had as pleasant a voice as I have ever listened to, and her warm, friendly smile quickly overcame any constraint we might have felt. The Frosts' hospitality was disarmingly genuine. We stopped in for an hour; we were persuaded to stay the night.

Our gambit was the reading we had heard Frost give at the Art Museum in Santa Fe on August fifth. During the next few hours Frost's talk was just as good off as on the rostrum. It was the same man of course and the same voice, but I began to catch different inflections—a greater variability in banter and quip, in seriousness and in ironic twittering—when directed at people he knew. Here, as paterfamilias, he was on home ground after diversions into alien territory. When a reference was made to the Santa Fe "colony," both the Frosts were critical. The inebriated Witter Bynner, leader of the colony and rather a bad boy, I gathered, had poured beer over Frost's head as a well-intentioned libation. This had not endeared the New Mexican poet to the New England Yankee.

Then it was time to drive over to his son's house, where Carol and his wife Lillian and their son William Prescott awaited us for supper. In a few minutes we arrived at the Peleg Cole house, timbered at the

9

top but with a stout stone lower story, situated a mile away on the main highway, U.S. 7, leading to Bennington.

What interested me was how quickly the poet took charge. The hospitable Carol was a bit daunted (I felt) by his father. The poet, quite as much as Mrs. Frost, arranged tea, sandwiches, and ice cream. It was he who reprimanded the inattentive Prescott, and it was he who fanned the conversation now this way, now that. One thing led to another—a digressive twist led into a gossipy turn, a rambling pursuit of a point came to an epigrammatic conclusion. I saw another side of Frost with which I was at the time little acquainted.

Many who commonly met the poet in casual exchange were often either mesmerized by his presence or confused by their assumptions. They had heard how quick he was to take offense, how tetchy and mocking. What I now felt was not an overbearing oppressiveness but certainly a dominance of personality. He was no tyrant but he was clearly of a mind. What should be done was to be done, according to his way of looking at it. He was hardly a man to be crossed with impunity.

When, later in the evening, we drove back to The Gully, Mrs. Frost begged off. Once more we sat close to the kitchen range, listening to Frost talk about Amherst under Dr. Stanley King; sports, both tennis and prizefighting; lecturing, which scared him as much as it attracted him; teaching, which he considered "performance"; politics—mainly the New Deal and its brain trusters; and literature, with references to Shakespeare, Hardy, Howells, and Thomas Wolfe.

The poet had with him a small Boston bag from which he took a brown commonplace blotting book like those commonly used in grade school. It contained the introduction in longhand that Frost had prepared for the Macmillan edition of Robinson's *King Jasper* (1935). He read it well, with the light from a kerosene lamp falling upon the manuscript. After several pages the introduction continued on separate sheets of paper. Since he had these in order there was little hesitation. His full, strong, well-pitched voice drew out the rhythms of the prose as though he might be reading poetry. The light from the lamp accentuated his face and head—the deep-set eyes, the brow and wide forehead, the gray hair on top, the white on the side. During the reading I heard several times in the pause of his voice a pheasant squawk out in the rain-soaked fields of the night.

After he finished reading the introduction, he lingered over some of the ideas, summarized the main points, suggested where he might have written much more, and clarified here and there. Then he turned to some manuscript poems of *A Further Range* (1936)—"The White-Tailed Hornet," "A Leaf-Treader," "To a Thinker," and "The Vindictives"—and read them without comment. It was long after midnight before he was ready to be driven back to the Peleg Cole house.

JUNE 30, 1950

Frost and I drove up to the Middlebury Gap (elevation 2,149 ft.) on Route 125, and, accompanied by Gillie, Frost's companionable Border collie, we walked slowly along the Long Trail, heading for a high mountain swamp where we might find some orchids. Bordering the first sharp pitch, Frost was not enthusiastic about the ferns we encountered. He dismissed them: "Oh, they're all the common ones, the hay-scented and the ladies' ferns." What did engage his attention were the numerous plants: oxalis, baneberry, true and false Solomon's seal, bunchberry, cohosh, saxifrage, patches of clintonia, hobblebush, and mountain ash. Tracking one plant up the rise, he was stumped; so he broke off one of the tender runlets and stuck it in his loose blue jumper pocket to examine at leisure back in the cabin at the Homer Noble farm where he had botanical books.

He inspected trees carefully as we went along—one where an activist woodpecker had fretted the bark, another where torsion writhed the bole. With a geologist's instinct he knocked off a piece of quartz from a rock seam, substituting a tenpenny nail and a flat stone for a geologist's hammer. So insatiable was his curiosity we were long in reaching the swamp. At its border he took off his blue sneakers but kept his socks on, rolled up his baggy overalls to the knees, and waded in about twenty-five yards, going directly to a spot where we came upon a grand display—a whole bog full of queen slipper orchids *(Cypripedium reginae)*. This alone might have been enough to make the flower hunt worth the strenuous effort. But Frost didn't stop. Poking into all the nooks—and even a relatively small mountain swamp has many—he discovered some spring ladies' tresses *(Spiranthes lucida)* and then, for a bonus, some stalks with flowers of the Northern Green bog orchid *(Habenaria hyperborea)*. Nearby there were bunchberry sepals to inspect and a variety of other flowers. Once we caught the repeated bell-like note of a bird—not a thrush—which we could not place. As we stood there listening, Frost told of the invitation he had received from a wealthy wild-flower gatherer to fly to an island off the Newfoundland coast to look for some rare flowers. "I'd like to see the island," he said dryly, and then

11

added, "I'm casual. I see what I see." He would do his own flower hunting right here in Ripton.

At the edge of the swamp Frost paused to tell of a scholar friend who had gone to Widener Library in Cambridge to look over a copy of Schopenhauer which Melville had owned. Melville's comments, the scholar decided, might throw light on *Billy Budd*. Frost thought if one wanted to know Melville he should read "Bartleby." When I praised Hawthorne's "Young Goodman Brown," Frost was quick to point out that each writer was important in his own way. "Let us be fair to both writers," he seemed to say. He recalled how difficult it had been when his scholar friend lectured on Emerson in a large university classroom. When the lecture was over, the friend remarked to a student in the front row, "Well, I guess it didn't go," and the student nodded in agreement. Perhaps with too much show of bravado, I said, "I'd try to convince the students." Frost replied wryly: "I don't try to convince anyone. I let them perish in their own sin."

When we got back to the log where we had left our shoes, we washed off the mud, and Frost, after wringing out his socks, put on his sneakers, and we pushed on toward Silent Cliff, stopping frequently to talk. Walking, looking, speculating are inseparable in the poet who might be described as an inquiring "miscellaneous Botanophilist," a term Henry Thoreau used to describe himself.

Had poetry been his only career? "No, it wasn't a matter of any forced choice. I didn't take a stand to die or fall by poetry. I simply turned from one thing to another. There was nothing heroic in my attitude. It was a catch-on-as-catch-can, take your chance, try this and try that." He had made a point, he said, of moving away from professions or occupations before they swallowed him up.

Nor had he attitudinized, rebelling against "a world I never made." "I say: here it is. I make my place in it; I am part of it. I take it as it is; I try to make little bits of clarity in it as I see them." He quoted, as his preferred view, from Thomas Gray's "Ode on the Death of a Favourite Cat Drowned in a Tub of Gold Fishes": "And be with caution bold." Reinhold Niebuhr's guilt-consciousness and worry about "the other world" was deprecated. Right *here* is where he was expected to swing his load. Once he said pretty emphatically: "I don't want to know what I can't swing. I learned that reading *Middlemarch*, reading about Casaubon. You've got to be able to swing your wit." Before we got off the mountain he told half a dozen anecdotes to support his points, directed a shot at the squabbles among the poets during the early years of the New Movement in poetry (ca. 1925), talked a little about Edward Thomas as a soldier, discussed truffle hunting, and in a euphoric burst praised Emerson. "One of the freest of them all in my sense of freedom," he said, "in his wit to make unexpected connections."

A seventy-six-year-old man, he was as quick on his feet as a cat, completely absorbed in what he was doing, and always turning things over in his mind—speculating—every bit of the way. On this fine day—a warm seventy-six degrees in the mountains, with a strong sun in a clear blue sky—I expected he might be early fatigued. He was not; he was only pleasantly tired as we parted at the Homer Noble farm. "I've still got the sight of them [the orchids] in my eyes," he said feelingly.

What I had discovered in this afternoon on the mountain was something I associated with Thomas Hardy. Whenever I stopped at the cabin to talk with Frost about local matters—flowers, trees, birds, streams, mountains—he had been informed. His replies were like annotations to the poems. When friends sat before the hearth at Max Gate, Thomas Hardy, too, talked about simple country things—the habits of owls and Wessex weather. His comments could serve as footnotes for chapters of the alfresco Frost, an outdoorsman too: "He was a man who used to notice such things." Natural things, for instance.

JULY 27, 1960

At eighty-six what more is to be expected from a man who has been through as many personal crises as Robert Frost? In reply—and augmenting the views of the poet as preceptor, as paterfamilias, as nature walker—there was a remarkable occasion which showed his consummate skill as a talker.

It was Frost's custom, a magnanimous gesture far beyond the call of duty, to visit the English School at Bread Loaf, Vermont, a second time following his special lecture-reading. The visit customarily took place toward the close of the session. He might visit a Chaucer class, and once he talked about the Masques to the drama group, but usually he met the students assembled in the recreation room at the Barn, where the open area invited informality.

This particular evening the group gathered at nine o'clock. Written questions had been prepared by the students, and the first question might well have ended the evening right then and there. "From a mile or so down the road, how does the Bread Loaf brand of education seem to be going?" was the brash question. Annoyed by the question, Frost rallied. "It insults me. I won't answer that," he said sternly. Then, to play along with his audience, he said: "I say: going to hell." There was a burst of laughter. Immediately, he asked reprovingly, "What kind of a question is that?" The group squirmed uneasily.

If Frost had been annoyed, it was only for a moment. His audience had at once been captivated by his taunting reply. Here he had assumed a moral obligation—and what a man he was to keep his commitments!—and here he would talk it out if it took all night. He treated some of the slighter questions as cavalierly as they deserved; he replied to the interesting ones with such skill that one would have had to be acquainted with such an occasion to grasp fully how cleverly, wittily, and knowledgeably he was handling what could have been a difficult situation. The success of the evening, I thought, was a twofold one. It consisted in his attitude of play, detected in the shifting tones of voice, and in the remarkable display of memory.

An inquiry about metrics launched him into an animated discussion of poetic technique in which he used Shakespeare and Keats as examples. He quoted a line here, a verse there, and he lingered over a phrase, returning after five or ten minutes to quote again a key passage, like holding up a picture for close scrutiny. The poetry quoted stayed in the ear. (And he convinced me he had been the truly knowledgeable one when two years later—in 1962—at the National Poetry Festival he alone had taken a stand to define poetry: "It's tone I'm in love with; that's what poetry is, tone.") He kept on unfolding and developing his point about what he called "numbers." "I'm reveling in technique," he said, and revel he did, moving over into a discussion of Gerard Manley Hopkins and "sprung" rhythm, then into Wilfred Owen's poetry. "There's sprung rhythm and there's scansion," he asserted. It was apparent he sided with scansion, and to illustrate he quoted Shakespeare's sonnet, "Let me not to the marriage of true minds," repeating the first four lines for emphasis and telling us: "I'm hearing the metronome all the time. I couldn't read it without the sense of it."

When a question directed at the teaching of literature—particularly poetry—was raised, he supported his position by quoting Milton, Tennyson, and Emily Dickinson and by referring to Darwin and Thoreau. But his point of departure in the discussion was really I. A. Richards's notion of Basic English. Frost always returned to what was central in his mind, the point to be made—that a teacher ought not to be too studious of poetry. "That's the teacher's place," he would say, "to *ease* it [the poem] to him. Temper it to him. Show him around. He ought to learn something for the ear and the play and the beat of it and the swing of it. Don't, don't, don't, don't let him study [it] until he's ready—until he's got some of that. The approach to it ought to be through *Mother Goose*. It ought to begin there."

He next discussed philosophical matters. He told his audience of a recent TV appearance (September 29, 1959) during which Dr. Julian Huxley and he had a sharp exchange on the origin of things. It started as one might expect with a reference to monkeys. "But I said, 'We've come up?'" the poet reported. "He [Huxley] said, 'Yes, up! up!' He thought 'up!' He thought we'd come *up,* not down," Frost underscored emphatically. "I just wanted to know," he added dryly. "And I said, 'What do you suppose steered us up?' He [Huxley] was very vague about that. Then, in that kind of a corner, just sort of out of indignation, in patient indignation, I just said: 'Wouldn't it be possible to say that it was passionate preference —preference—passionate preference?'" This was an example of his mental agility at its most acute—of a shrewd tough-minded poet, who recognized that basic in humanity was the great original procreative drive, standing off the quizzical scientist wrapped up in his theoretical opinions. From philosophic matters Frost moved into politics, and toward the close of the two-hour session he returned to pedagogy and poetry, playing originally every bit of the way to the final distinction. How would he explain tragedy and comedy? The former—tragedy—is a "kind of conflict *without* villainy"; the latter—comedy—is the same thing, "only you're laughing at it."

If Dr. Johnson is right—and he is a good deal of the time—"he only is the master who keeps the mind in pleasing captivity." In Dr. Johnson's terms Robert Frost was one of the master spirits of our time. This evening we had a convincing demonstration of "pleasing captivity." Clear to the end of his life Frost cast his spell, as that immense crowd jam-packing an auditorium at the University of Detroit on November 12, 1962, testified. Here at Bread Loaf, on this particular evening, he did with apparent ease what he had done so many times before, gave "a performance."

When he stopped at Fritz Cottage afterward to autograph copies of his books for the students at the school, he was still teased by a reference to Conrad Aiken who had asserted Emily Dickinson was superior to Henry Thoreau. What did Aiken mean by this statement? Wasn't it an "invidious distinction"? Sipping from a glass of ginger ale laced with rum to which a spoonful of sugar had been added, he autographed volume after volume holding his fountain pen high up on the barrel and pressing down firmly. We talked about an orchid with tufts on the stalk that bent down, not up, and about the wild cucumber the Indians used for food. When I thanked

15

him for a fine evening—a matchless performance, full of fun and sharp insights—he said disconcertingly: "You know I get an awful lot of guff." I wondered if I should have said nothing. I remembered a few years before when he had said pointedly: "You don't thank a friend."

His replies always kept one on guard. To a well-wisher asking of his health, he would answer curtly: "Cut out the therapeutic." When I had to return to my teaching assignment after a long night's talk in his Cambridge home at 35 Brewster Street, he said crossly: "Well, go back to the woods." He played with society and solitude a little more casually than most of us.

I early noticed you could make the mistake just once in his presence of forgetting what he remembered. And there were always questions occurring to you that should be asked. "Now is the time," I would say to myself; "no man lives forever." Yet as soon as I met him there never seemed to be the right moment. Meanwhile, he was already talking. But the best of it all is perhaps the fact that as I listened he was already answering the important questions, anyway. He was his own shrewdest interpreter.

One certain shot rings out and reverberates through the years. Although it was late in his life that I heard it, the echo carries back and back to other similar shots. The shot compounds Frost's sanguinity and aggressive courage. Moreover, it expresses his two-way passionate belief in the forward thrust of his country—what it had done, what it could do—expressed in "The Gift Outright." During the celebration of July 4, 1953, President Eisenhower issued a statement from the White House in which a reference was made to doing "penance for the day." Frost's indignation flared and he remarked derisively of the President's attitude: "What does he think we should do, crawl on our knees from Yorktown to Appomattox? It's a day of triumph, not a day of humiliation." He added vigorously, "It's a great country and it can stand a lot." It could stand a lot of just such nonsensical guff; it could stand a lot of setbacks. But it would endure.

If his belief in his country was affirmative, so too was his belief in the effort of the human spirit. You might have thought the well-beaten path from the Homer Noble farm to the cabin on the rising ground in a bowl of the Green Mountains at Ripton, Vermont, suggested a capitulation to popularity. Not so anyone would notice it. Inside the cabin or outside in the fields, there appeared to be only an invaded man, there was never a victimized one. He was always there swinging *his* load.

CHAPTER 3
A Sense of Place

Did they make something lonesome go through you?
"In the Home Stretch"

The focus of Frost's vision of place is New England. The specific locality in the early poems is far to the north of Boston in the intervales of the White Mountains and the Derry countryside of southern New Hampshire. In the later poems, the specific localities are the Taconic Mountains around Shaftsbury and the Green Mountains around Ripton in Vermont's heartland. A view of place must reflect comprehensively both time and the custom of the country.

To a mid-twentieth-century New England Yankee, Frost's early poems, say, the first four books and some of the poems in the later ones, strike the legendary note of "once upon a time." What meaning, for example, would mending wall have to farmers who now string up electrified fences? Rotary plows and mechanical hay balers drawn by tractors have replaced work horses and the hay wagon, and milking machines have transformed the lives of dairy farmers. It is even likely that those who might once have been hired hands are now unionized factory workers in busy industrial centers. One has to look hard nowadays to find any farm folk driving little Morgans along snowy roads of a winter evening, or, in season, driving on "a highway where the slow wheel pours the sand." One almost looks in vain for buggy, gig, or democrat wagon. What was once common in Frost's experience has now become memory to an older generation.

When Henry James revisited the New Hampshire country around Chocorua late in his life, he recorded the vivid impression it made upon him. "The history was there in its degree," he wrote of the countryside in *The American Scene,* "and one came upon it, on sunny afternoons, in the form of classic abandoned farms of the rural forefather who had lost patience with his fate. These scenes of old, hard New England effort, defeated by the soil and climate and reclaimed by nature and time—the crumbled, lonely chimney-stack, the overgrown threshold, the dried-up well, the cart-track vague and lost—these seemed the only notes to interfere, in their meagerness, with the queer *other,* the larger eloquence that one kept reading into the picture." We find in *North of Boston* or *Mountain Interval* all of Henry James's items—above all, "the larger eloquence," which I take to be a poet's overtone, one of the most cherishable characteristics of poetry.

In "Ghost House," "The Black Cottage," "The Generations of Men," "The Census-Taker," "A Fountain, a Bottle, a Donkey's Ears and Some Books," "The Need of Being Versed in Country Things," "The Old Barn at the Bottom of the Fogs," "Closed for Good," and "Directive," the recurrent image is the melancholy one of decline by defeat and abandonment by default. The image of back-country New England with its old cellar holes, moss-covered gravestones, and tree-choked clearings is a moving and nonsentimental one. Henry James has reported accurately, candidly, and feelingly. All honest Yankees must admit these direct evidences of the decline and fall of one phase in New England's history.

Frost's poetry dramatizes what James saw—the passing of the solitary house and its half-remembered inmates. Consider, for example, "Ghost House" as an early lyric:

> I dwell in a lonely house I know
> That vanished many a summer ago,
>   And left no trace but the cellar walls,
>   And a cellar in which the daylight falls,
> And the purple-stemmed wild raspberries grow.
>
> O'er ruined fences the grapevines shield
> The woods come back to the mowing field;
>   The orchard tree has grown one copse
>   Of new wood and old where the woodpecker chops;
> The footpath down to the well is healed.
>
> I dwell with a strangely aching heart
> In that vanished abode there far apart
>   On that disused and forgotten road
>   That has no dust-bath now for the toad.
> Night comes; the black bats tumble and dart;
>
> The whippoorwill is coming to shout
> And hush and cluck and flutter about:
>   I hear him begin far enough away

Full many a time to say his say
Before he arrives to say it out.

It is under the small, dim, summer star.
I know not who these mute folk are
    Who share the unlit place with me—
    Those stones out under the low-limbed tree
Doubtless bear names that the mosses mar.

They are tireless folk, but slow and sad,
Though two, close-keeping, are lass and lad—
    With none among them that ever sings,
    And yet, in view of how many things,
As sweet companions as might be had.

This poem grows out of the poet's experience of place and time. It seems psychologically true, suggesting how deeply and genuinely Frost feels about the lonely house and its former inhabitants. We see also that the poet's vision of place is specific even in memory. He lingers lovingly on little details, observing them precisely ("The footpath down to the well is healed") and realistically ("The woods come back to the mowing field"). Although it is a little archaic in diction, rural in setting, and has as its subject matter country things, "Ghost House" is neither sentimentally quaint nor countrified. But emphatically, Frost's elegy on a deserted farm is a self-contained poem reflecting turn-of-the-century New England without editorial comment. It is a "thought-felt" whole. The feeling for a traditional way of life is evoked in the suppressed melancholy of its quietly resonant, cumulative, and affecting tone.

Loneliness is a central spring in Frost's poetic impulse. Rooted in the country north of Boston, it amounts to one of "the blighting inhibitions of New England," to use Henry Adams's phrase. In the early poems loneliness is not only a token of place, it is an attribution of the Yankee condition. Whether it has the cosmic overtones of "An Old Man's Winter Night," where in this big drafty universe the faceless silence of "All out-of-doors looked darkly in at him," or the more intimate loneliness of country folk who experience the attendant fear that goes with solitary places, Frost felt it deeply, as in "House Fear" in "The Hill Wife."

Always—I tell you this they learned—
Always at night when they returned
To the lonely house from far away
To lamps unlighted and fire gone gray,

19

They learned to rattle the lock and key
To give whatever might chance to be
Warning and time to be off in flight:
And preferring the out- to the in-door night,
They learned to leave the house-door wide
Until they had lit the lamp inside.

Later, much later, in his life when reading one of the early poems, he referred to the early New Hampshire days feelingly. "Back in those lonely days," he said, as much as to say, back in those days of bereftness and anxiety. Significantly, though, unlike Henry James, he never strikes a renunciatory note. Loneliness was an experience like any other to be lived through.

•

"Unless you have geography, background, you have nothing. You have a dramatic vacuum," Hemingway once wrote. Yet a prevalence of geography guarantees neither a sense of place nor poetry. It is for other reasons than a catalog of names on the land that Walt Whitman's *Leaves of Grass* has a claim on our attention. What is true of Whitman is similarly true of Frost. Granted, as Frost says convincingly, "the land is always in my bones." We must then ask in what particular way he felt it in his bones. How did he relate it to himself?

There is, first of all, a special feeling he has for the objects in his poems—the birches, the spring pools, the dark woods—that is characteristic. Call it honesty of feeling. It shows in correctly identifying what is observed. He does not betray the thing seen by fulsome "Ohs" and "Ahs." Rather he understates, and if he praises, he praises reticently. He says simply and disarmingly of a young birch, "It was a thing of beauty. . . ." "I dislike calling the common birch what it is commonly called—gray birch," he will say. "That's not white enough for me." Or, while traveling by rail from Boston to New York, he takes pains to notice if the birches he sees are his kind of swinging birches bending to left and right. The spring pools of which he writes while in Michigan, he points out to a Vermont audience, are "not as full of water as they were usually, right now." He had been up in the mountain woods to see for himself. The dark woods in "Stopping by Woods" are alders—"snow falling among the alders," he tells us. These are specific evidences of scrupulous attention. Birch, spring pool, and dark woods are accurately identified.

There is also a quality of feeling—*restrained* feeling—in Frost's relationship to place. If we were to substitute "poet" for "novelist" in another Hemingway statement, it would do no violence to him.

Hemingway's point of view is valid for Frost: "The country that a novelist writes about is the country he knows, and the country that he knows is in his heart." The quality of restrained feeling in Frost's vision of place eliminates all threat of callousness. In the emblematic "Hyla Brook" he reminds us that "We love the things we love for what they are." Elsewhere he sees the "sun-shaped and jewel-small" meadow, smells the air stifling sweet with the breath of all those rose pogonias, hears the country brook with its note "as from a single place," leans on the sunburned hillside which sets his face aglow so close his breathing "shakes the bluet like a breeze," feels at night the "shadowy presence" of a nearby mountain, revels in the exuberant southwester, our thawing wind which flutters the poet's papers and drives him outdoors. And finally he exclaims feelingly (in "A Hillside Thaw") of a spring thaw:

> To think to know the country and not know
> The hillside on the day the sun lets go
> Ten million silver lizards out of snow!

A strong, restrained feeling for the land, reinforcing an attachment accurately identified, characterizes the relationship to place in the slow-pulsed poetry of Frost. But at the very center of his vision of place is a third characteristic—sympathetic detachment, which is well illustrated in "The Need of Being Versed in Country Things." When the poet comes upon a farm where the house has burned and where the phoebes are now building their nest in the abandoned barn, he writes of the birds with a depth of implied feeling but with no sentimentalism:

> For them there was really nothing sad.
> But though they rejoiced in the nest they kept,
> One had to be versed in country things
> Not to believe the phoebes wept.

Frost's relationship to place is not unlike Thoreau's. It is not only the natural setting with which he is primarily concerned, it is also the human condition. But if, like Thoreau, he goes and comes with a strange liberty in nature, it is also his concern to give us insights into natural as well as human predicaments. In recognition of the vigorous force of nature everlastingly at work, he compresses a convincing fact in a dramatically understated line: "The woods come back to the mowing field." Or, in another poem ("The Birthplace"), he says with minimal expansiveness: "The mountain pushed us off her knees. / And now her lap is full of trees." Yet he also evokes the human predicament. In "The Code," the pride of a hired man, challenged in the hay field, asserts itself in the hay barn. Frost sums up the bucolic crisis in one strong poetic sentence: "The hand that knows his business won't be told / To do work better or faster—those two things." This pride, native to the Yankee grain, has not changed; it never will. And the climactic statement in the rollicking "Brown's Descent"—"Yankees are what they always were"—is still as true and ambiguous as ever. The poet may be saluting the tough, straight-up-and-down Yankee character, or, tongue-in-cheek, he may be having a little fun with the odd and quirky but not graceless, rugged and resourceful New England breed.

At least Frost is not a regional apologist, either for the behavior of its people or for the vagaries of its natural phenomena. He gives us insights into lonely hill wives who suffer in their loneliness "finalities / Besides the grave" and hired men who have "nothing to look backward to with pride, / And nothing to look forward to with hope." The grimmer side of New England life appears in "The Housekeeper" and in "A Servant to Servants." But there is also the comic side, the humorous twist Frost catches in the New England scene, whether in the habits of its native creatures as in "The Cow in Apple Time," in its temperamental weather in "Two Tramps in Mud Time," in its crotchety character in "The Gold Hesperidee," or in himself in what he called "my most Vermontly poem," "A Drumlin Woodchuck."

What meaning does Frost's vision of place have for us? Frost really is not studying out the land, as Walt Whitman urged upon the American people. He is not primarily a regionalist. Had he remained in California, or settled in Virginia or Nebraska, he might well have written as characteristically. He is natively American and regional only by circumstance. This is not to say, of course, that he fails of a deep and abiding attachment to the particular locality he feels in his bones. Strenuously, he played down regional attachments. He was a regionalist only in posture. As Emily Dickinson reminds us, "And Place was where the Presence was." He called himself "a realmist," "a pursuitist." So he was, each in its own way. But C. P. Snow *(Variety of Men)*. recognized "the locative" as central to his art. Rooted in the particularities of place and expressed in a common language, he has long been associated with the rural. Yet except as his subject matter reflects local color, I think it is a serious critical lapse to stress the prominence of the rural tradition in a poet whose "ulteriorities" have so much more to do with a sophisticated world of human knowledge than with a bucolic tradition concerned primarily with scenery. Only in the way Robinson's Tilbury Town or

Faulkner's Yoknapatawpha have imaginary geographic location is Frost's north of Boston pastorally located. How much less he has to offer in the sense of place than a local-color poet like Whittier or a short-story writer like Sarah Orne Jewett.

As a poet he is concerned with the universal in scope. I think the scope of his poetry is as wide and deep as his intellect and emotions can make it. Birch stands and wandering strips of stone wall, sugar bushes and mountain intervals, little Morgan horses and ovenbirds, rose pogonias and apple orchards, old logging camps, and the folk in the back-country villages and their rural occupations are all-important items in his subject matter. But the significant point will always be what Frost has done with these. The truth of the matter is that, although Frost writes *from* New England, he also writes inescapably *about* New England. The effect of the scene upon him is quite as important as his detachment. In a characteristic exchange with C. P. Snow, he contended, *against* the British novelist and scientist, that the only art that meant anything was "locative" and rooted in the singularities of a place. For his evidence he might have cited *Walden* or *The Adventures of Huckleberry Finn*.

It might be contended that Frost, exulting in a self-imposed limitation of subject matter, is a poet of the New England past in both place *and* time. If this is so, how can we reconcile such a limitation with his ability to release his material to general significance? A writer's compensation in sticking to one place—whether his native heath is Concord or Amherst, Sligo or Carmel, Haworth or Hannibal, Wessex or the Long Valley, the Lake Country or North of Boston—is knowledgeability. When the local is fully realized, knowledgeability strengthens the conscious impulse of controlled art. The language which expresses deeply felt experience assumes symbolical significance. This is what the poet himself means when he refers to poetry as "thought-felt substance." His poems often do double duty because he has what Ortega calls proximate and distant vision. In "The Gift Outright" the far vision extends beyond region into the nation's continental sweep, just as "The Vindictives" and "The Bearer of Evil Tidings" take us into the Andes and the Himalayas, not only spatially but spiritually.

Frost's attitude should never be confused with what Allen Tate called "aggressive provincialism." On the contrary, in universality of scope Frost is *above* his region quite as much as he is a part of it. Once, Frost explained, he suggested to his publisher that with the appearance of *Mountain Interval* a note be added to the effect "that I talk of universals in terms of New England." Then he added, "I talk about the whole world in terms of New England." What the careful reader feels in *Complete Poems* is the effect of the region working in the poems, yet not dominating the poet. Surely it is more than regionalism that identifies his uniqueness. As a matter of fact, he is not creating but renewing a tradition in which Bryant, Emerson, Whittier, and Dickinson are predecessors and Robinson is a contemporary. His capacity to renew this local tradition in poems acutely of the region (in idiom and manner no less than in atmosphere and tone) has more to do with an art of sympathetic detachment than with rugged Yankee traits in his temperament. The fact is that Frost is as little place-bound as any major poet in the great tradition. Place is the fulcrum for the lever by which he raises the world a little, the better to see and know it.

Frost, who happens to live in New England, is not primarily concerned with identifying that region or with evoking its picturesqueness or yet in enumerating its homely pieties. He is as aware as the next fellow that the weakness of regional poetry is its inability to rise above the level of the parochial, a weakness that is almost as negative as provincialism. When the vision of place has scope and intensity, as in Hardy's poetry or in Emily Brontë's *Wuthering Heights,* the writer escapes the parochial and provincial. Yet it is precisely the enabling grace of such native traits as independence and self-reliance, shrewdness and resourcefulness, courage and energy, reserve and pride that identifies Frost with his region.

As becomes a poet with a philosophic mind, Frost, too, escapes the parochial and provincial. He is much more concerned with the circulation of ideas in natural analogues, parables, and poetic anecdotes. These ideas take their origin, have their prevalence, and are tested in human experience. Frost does start with place but this is not where he leaves us. New England serves as the background setting; the foreground is the poet's ideas and reflections. We hardly need to be reminded that Frost himself has written: "Because I wrote my novels in New Hampshire / Is no proof that I aimed them at New Hampshire."

William Carlos Williams once referred to a classic as "the local, fully realized, words marked by a place." Williams evokes the special quality in our literature of native books like *Walden; Winesburg, Ohio; The Country of the Pointed Firs;* and *The Adventures of Huckleberry Finn.* In Williams's terms, Frost's *Complete Poems* is also classic. In it the local in person, place, and thing is intensely realized, and the idiomatic language identifies the voice tones of place. Frost, who is certainly not the first to give the country north of Boston a local habitation, has succeeded in doing considerably more than New England's local colorists who preceded him. He not only gives us a local assertion, he makes the region a microcosm for ideas and feelings that, in transcending the local, share the spectrum of universal emotion and thought. I think we would have to say, as George Santayana said of Virgil (substituting Frost for Virgil and American for Roman): "[Frost] has not written a line in forgetfulness that he was [an American]."

PART TWO
Viva Voce

CHAPTER 4
Viva Voce

1.

While I was director at the Bread Loaf School of English from 1946 to 1964, Robert Frost appeared before the school audience at each session, and occasionally he appeared informally in the recreation room in the Barn later in the session. Usually he led off our formal lectures, the first Monday evening following the opening. He would talk for a half hour and read from the poems the remainder of the hour or hour and a half. When he appeared later in the session, he sat by an open fireplace and talked from nine o'clock until eleven. On at least two occasions his appearance in the Barn was a remarkable display of memory and agility in handling questions. Both the formal and the less formal appearances are represented in the following transcriptions.

Frost usually read his own poems; the exception would be the poems he quoted from other poets illustrating the points he was making in the introductory part of the more formal appearance and throughout the less formal one in the Barn. He quoted with care and taste, using the resources of British literature and the Roman to anchor ideas to other cultures, other traditions. But I never heard him use Spanish or French or German poetry in the native tongue. He was hardly a linguist except in his knowledge of Latin.

The way he handled poetry had a definite relationship to poetry generally. He was distressed and indignant when he found someone "outraging the poem," an outrage that extended to the defense of other poets. He showed us that what the indelicate reader did to "Stopping by Woods" he would also do to other poems.

In focusing attention on the art of the poem—its metaphor, imagery, rhyme, meter, and cadence—he did poetry a great service. He showed us both how to read a poem and how to listen to one. In view of the increased reading of poetry in public today before live audiences, on TV or radio, and in stereo recordings—one thinks of the fine Caedmon records—Frost gave poetry a lien on our attention during these disturbing years of social and political change.

2.

The following transcripts are from Frost's voice on magnetic tape, recorded in the Little Theatre and the recreation room in the Barn at the Bread Loaf School of English, the summer campus of Middlebury College. After recording the talks, I studied at leisure the nuances of Frost's voice in tempo, pitch, and volume, and the first thing I noticed when I prepared a typescript was how the public readings and comments *without* the accompanying tones of voice flatten out. Invariably the lectures *sound* better than they read. The voice on the sound track, with its pauses, hesitancies, repetitions, and stresses, enlivens the talk and evokes a remarkable presence. Luckily, through instrumentalities of technology—tape recorders, microphones, and television—we have the validating voice. We can always test the typescript against the recorded voice. However, such summaries of Frost's talks as we find in Louis Mertins's *Robert Frost: Life and Talks-Walking* (1965) are apparently carefully prepared abridgments. When compared with the tape recordings of the poet's talks at the Bread Loaf School of English, a difference can be detected between the literal and the essential statement. Mertins's summaries satisfy the latter. No doubt Mertins has caught the essence of Frost's thought. The phrasing sounds right, and the accuracy of the passages is hardly challengeable.

I also found the response of the audience, especially the pouncing applause, the unexpected silences, a delayed reaction, and even those times when an apparent gesture—a wagging finger or movement of the head—drew a ripple of laughter, illuminating of the poet's manner. An attentive ear will catch the heavy-duty words like *say* and *see*, *play* and *pretty*, the dry humor, the gay bonhomie, a cavalier lightness of mood; and, just as apparent, there are the times when Frost had a severe cold and froggy voice. On such evenings he pulled a stoneboat of heavy drift boulders. After these agonizing appearances when he seemed old and frail, he would redoubtably make a return appearance at the Barn and give a fine performance. Only on those evenings when from vanity he would try to read without glasses and had great difficulty, stumbling badly, was he his own worst enemy.

Frost's captive audiences at the English School were good ones. They stimulated him so he felt at home and confident. The crowded hall, the air of expectation, and the enthusiastic auditors were an excitant to Frost, who so much depended upon the listener. Consequently, what was most rewarding were the revelations into the secrets of his craft and the disclosures on how to take the poems. Even when an old-fashioned New England thunderstorm came roaring up the mountain pass and the rain detonated on the tin roof, he was not greatly put off his pace. By recruiting personal resources of agile wit and vigorous play of ideas, his talks never stiffened with moral purpose. A teacher by gift, he was hardly ever morally didactic. Amused and amusing, he rambled among the contents of the green hard-bound *Complete Poems* of 1949, entertaining his audience by flicking its imagination.

After listening to the almost constant laughter, I sometimes wondered if his auditors ever took him for anything more than an entertainer. Serious things were said as though in joking and jesting things were said as though he was his own straight man. As one studies the pauses, it becomes apparent he was at times a little taken aback by the hair-trigger response. And just as apparent are the times Frost was being subtly ironic and few seemed to have caught it audibly. Occasionally he was confounded. Once, in real perplexity, he stopped to inquire in what way he was expected to present himself before his audience—as a reader of poems, an entertainer, a critic of education—what? "I've heard it said that everybody knows what I'm going to say," he told us, and added, self-defensively, "I'm always wondering if you know what I'm going to say next."

At the English School, he was usually concerned with playing variations on the theme of education through poetry. At the Writers' Conference, he talked about poetry and craftsmanship. Since early in his experience William James had demonstrated that thinking was a present act rather than a prepared or "canned" performance, the line of direction in his "formal" talks is less dependent on concatenation of logic than on a sequence of associational ideas, thoughts, remembrances. Invariably, his views on institutionalized education were provocatively caustic. Undoubtedly the necessity to earn his living outside a protective tenure system, so solidly a part of institutionalized education, greatly influenced these biting views. And, of course, he was never much impressed with conformism and not at all allured by the rigidity of orthodoxy.

Of the several problems encountered in preparing a transcription of the Frost tapes, the first and the most persistently recurrent has been syntactical. He started sentences and left them dangling when intrusive thought deflected the original intention. Secondly, he was repetitious, which made necessary judicious excision. Thirdly, and certainly the most frustrating was the occasional word murmured unintelligibly in low register, which will forevermore remain unclear. These three problems—syntax, repetition, and unintelligibility—have been in part obviated by emendations. Since his sentences, like those in relaxed conversation, tend to trail into one another, divisions had to be made. I assumed the responsibility of punctuating the sentences and organizing the paragraphs according to the apparent central thought. I have cut some repeated phrases but added nothing not indicated by inserted brackets. One has to imagine the sound of the poet's voice; it is precisely this voice which gave a measure of meaning to a simple statement through its stress and inflection. Frost, more than most people, had a remarkably idiosyncratic sound track.

To illustrate the difficulties, consider the problem of words. Frost, in referring to the right kind of people "taking" his poetry, said: "There's a good deal of sway in [the poetry]. There's a certain *deftness, definiteness*, but it sways at its anchor" (my italics). The difference between *deftness* and *definiteness* is apparent. But in the context, which, exactly, did he mean to use? Did he, by chance, mean both? I included both words in the quotation, odd though the sentence appears. In the same talk (June 30, 1955), when noting a reader's tendency to interpret his poetry personally, Frost's meaning in the following sentence is clear but the jumbled statement is incomplete. "The aesthetic moral is: that if you can go any poem one better, for all of me if you do it one better—not one worse—and if you don't chew it, take it all to pieces; just get another poetic something going—one step more poetic anywhere." The close of the statement seems more incoherent than, in actuality, it is. To resolve this dilemma I deleted "that" and ended with the first "better." Thus, "The aesthetic moral is: to go any poem one better." This slight revision does violence neither to Frost's intent nor to his phrasing. In loose, repetitious statements, I also exercised judgment. "And this is a free and loose thing—the association—the beauties of the association are always something you didn't know you were going to have," Frost said. By omitting the first clause and starting with "the beauties of the association," the statement clearly stands on its own.

3.

Frost's statements were direct, spontaneous, and unabashed. Although he often repeated himself, he freshly improvised much of the time. What is also apparent is Frost's undiminished devotion to his art—a craftsman's great and unremitting love of his labors. How well this showed when Frost explicated "The Tuft of Flowers," frequently referred to in his talks. "One cannot derive the biographical in factual statement from any poem, but one can say what absorbed and evoked the life of these fusions in the poet." What Muriel Rukeyser says of Thomas Hariot is also true of Frost. I have little doubt a careful reading of the poems will give us a biography of the imagination. They tell us something about the poet, surely. For example, on July 30, 1955, when Frost referred to Dr. Cohen's interview with Einstein, which he had lately read in *Scientific American* (July 1955), it was, as he mentioned, the great bursts of Einstein's laughter and then the way the great scientist talked about another scientist's book—Immanuel Velikovsky's *Worlds in Collision* (1950) —without patronizing him that impressed Frost. Apparently he had this view in mind when he "teased," to use his word, science in his poem, "Why Wait for Science."

I find myself equally impressed with Frost's handling of his own poems, specifically how he wanted to be received, cunningly focusing the attention of his audience on the poem *as a poem* in which technique counts. "You see," he would say, "I prefer in reading the poems ordinarily a great deal better not to go on with them into anything beyond" (June 30, 1955). But, as he showed in "The Tuft of Flowers," the simplicity was most deceptive. A reader could readily miss the point from inattention. The only requirements in reading Frost were innate. They were the same traits he brought the writing: concentration and attention.

These transcriptions do not have the benefit of Frost's ordering of the punctuation and paragraphing, let alone the attention to phrase or sentence. The responsibilities for the ordering are entirely personal. I have in some of these transcriptions preferred to leave an occasional awkwardness, an ellipsis, repetition, where these reflect a mannerism in tone or manner.

Commonly, Frost's discursive talks were improvised from a few leading ideas. Even in those talks where his main view was developed in a logical sequence of ideas, as in the talk on June 29, 1959, when he used Emerson's "cherub scorn" to set the mood, free association was the usual manner of his maneuvering. In these talks his devices—repetition, alliteration, word play, suspended phrases, verbal indecisiveness, digressive spin-offs, spontaneous asides, and audience interrogation—were those of practiced platform speakers. What holds the talks together is the intonation of the voice in its deliberate rhythm, low pitched and varying from precise to slurring inflection. The familiar diction lapsed occasionally into the collo-quial idiom of an upland countryman but without syntactical oddity.

Obviously Frost didn't prepare these talks to be either cross-examined for their logic or scrutinized for the subtleties inherent in sudden shifts of mood. If, in retrospect and by virtue of his emi-nence as a poet, we view them as semantic exercises, I don't think the poet did so. They served him in a three-fold way. (1) Personally, they served as a warming-up before he read from his poems. "They're not prefaces," as he told us once, on June 30, 1958; they were "just," in his phrasing, "my little preliminary indulgence." In fact, some-times he drew his listeners into the reading of the poems so casually they got the impression the poems were the precipitating effect of self-indulgent delight. (2) Psychologically, the introductory remarks served as an opportunity to put the audience in a receptive mood, as-sisting them in becoming acquainted with his voice and manner, the better to understand how the poems should be taken. And (3) ideologically, they served as an anvil on which to beat out the impli-cations of his ideas. The ruminative theorizing on July 3, 1961, with its base in some autobiographical reference is exemplary. It shows us that Frost, unlike Whitman filled with wonder at mundane miracles, didn't circle around ideas but nudged them in order to take advan-tage of their implications. So these talks reflect his reactions to scientific discoveries, as in his reference to Foucault's pendulum on July 3, 1961; the changes in ethical fashion in his topical boast on July 4, 1960, that he had written a whole book without the word *sex* in it; his sense of privately experienced reality, which appears in his comments on the poems; and the convictions of an old man that grew out of a lot seen and a lot thought about, like his reaction to bravery, honor, and glory, "that I go with in all my heart, all my days," which he mentioned on August 2, 1954, or his reference to "heroism of magnanimity" on June 30, 1955.

Listening to these tapes and remembering the particular occasion, I hear Frost's live voice saying so much more than I do when silently I read these transcripts. The difference is startling. His voice was not only an animator, it was an interpreter, discriminating among the semantic possibilities in the casual ready-made phrasing. It gave a single tone to these mental monologues. For example, he would say, "great stuff, insubordination," and the listener became aware of the very high level of approach on which Frost operated. He was think-ing of Lucretius's defiance of religion in book 1 (lines 52-73) of *On the Nature of Things*. "And," remarked Frost in his talk on July 3, 1957, "you can throw away religion, and you can throw away education, and you throw away all you can of it and see what you have got left."

In its pitch and intonation Frost summoned his words into direct oral action. What is lost therefore in the absence of the speaking voice is immeasurably more than what is sacrificed by Frost's not having had the opportunity to hear these transcripts and perhaps rigorously revise them. If the transcripts read banally, it is surely because they lack the vitalizing force and energy of the Frostian voice in all its great flexibility of pitch, intonation, tempo, and volume, and capacity to dramatize an idea and make it seem as important as it really is.

Yet what is gained in the spontaneity of free association and a poet's discursive rambling may in some part more than compensate for the absence of the poet's voice on the sound track. No firmer assurance do we have that "all the fun's in how you say a thing" than in noting here that all the meaning's in the inflection Frost gave what he said. More than in many speakers his voice is the rare communicant. And although the listener may have assumed he was hardly accountable for anything more than a skimming of the surface—the remembrance of a joke, anecdote, wisecrack, or aphoristic sentence—the results were notable ones. First, those attending the readings who came to be amused remained to be edified by truths that were often more psychological than pedagogical, more general than professional. Secondly, these transcripts are as accurate a notation of Frost's speech habits as we are likely to find and are only limited by the proficiency of the mechanical instrument and the ear of the transcriber. And thirdly, they reveal the poet's essential inquiring and speculative mind, turning things over in a vastly poetic and ruminative way.

CHAPTER 5
On Being Let in on Symbols
June 25, 1953

The following talk and reading was given by Frost at the Bread Loaf School of English, and although it is a relatively short talk, it is in several respects an important one. Frost's concern about symbols was very much on his mind, early and late. In part, this concern originated in his sensitivity to the New Criticism, the analysis of poems, and symbol reading. Eliot and Yeats were closely read because, it was thought, there was more to find and comment on in their cryptic poetry. Frost's poems, it was assumed, were simpler and clearer; consequently, there was only a modest need of explication. This seemed to diminish the depth and lessen the significance of his poems. And he was aware of this critical view.

Also significant in this talk is the reference to Saint Mark. In "Directive," Frost mentioned a broken drinking goblet, which was under a spell "so the wrong ones can't find it, / So can't get saved, as Saint Mark says they mustn't," and over the years at Bread Loaf we were to hear repeatedly the name of Saint Mark in context. The stanza he quoted from Thompson's "The Hound of Heaven" reminded him of an episode in his early life. As in Proust, particular details in and out of poetry evoked associative memories, and usually, as in this instance, when Frost pointed up the meaning of the poem he added something fresh in the recollection.

What I had in mind to talk about a few minutes, before I began to read to you the poems that I've read so often, was another word that people have been using a great deal and using too much for me, away beyond my love for it—it's the word *symbol, symbolism.* I was shocked a little while ago to have a young grandchild of mine[1] told

1. Probably Robin Fraser, whose mother was Frost's daughter Marjorie and whose father was Willard Fraser, onetime mayor of Billings, Montana. When Robin, now Mrs. David Hudnut, completed her education at Smith

by a college teacher that when she got the hang of the college teacher's symbolism she would do better. [*Laughter*] And that scared me because I had always thought everybody was supposed to get the hang of everybody's symbolism or else we couldn't communicate. Because we're always trying to communicate with each other with double tongues. We say one thing. to mean that and another beside—always do, always have, in [the] Bible and everywhere else. A parable is a story that means what it says and something besides. And according to the New Testament the something besides is the more important of the two. It's *that* the nonelect are supposed to miss and so not go to heaven. Saint Mark says so and somebody else says so; it occurs twice in the New Testament.[2] And these things are said so as to leave the wrong people out. I love that because it sounds so un-democratic. That's not because I'm smart either, but I just love to be shocked, don't you? I like to come right up against something like that.

Now then, the confusion, the trouble, in our time with teachers and students comes from two things. One thing is the ordinary thing: to have been let in on somebody's symbols. And that, you think, is what is going on mainly in the college. People are there to get let in on so-and-so's symbols. And also somebody else's symbols. That is something I hadn't thought about until I had grown up to the present age. I always supposed I was good at symbols without being let in on them. I'm always annoyed when a word baffles me. I've been bothered about one for the last week. Somebody brought it up: logrolling. We all know the symbol that that stands for, the political logrolling. We use it. But where did it come from?[3] But I always think I can get at something like that. Let's leave it for a minute.

I see a frustum. Pronounced in English, "frustum." And I have the word *frustrate.* And because I'm a kind of free and easy person, I like to think I can get those [*frustum* and *frustrate*] together, but I can't. I think I'm just figurative enough to make a connection. But I didn't notice the spelling when I was younger. I wish it were frustrum—*f-r-u-s-t-r-u-m*—but it isn't; it's just frustum. That means in Latin a bit, a piece, a piece of a cone. And I wish it was a frustrated cone! [*Laughter*] Like that! That's my figurativeness.

But now take this logrolling—I've puzzled over it and puzzled over it until I got something out of it. I wonder what you make of it?

College her grandfather gave the commencement address.

2. Mark 4:11, 12; 7:17, 18.

3. The first recorded reference to scheming with other politicians so that legislation is passed, called logrolling, is to be found in *An Account of Col. Crockett's Tour to the North and Down East* (1835).

See! That's the fun of it. I hardly ever come across a fresh word or two in poetry but that I do something to them as I go. I'm a slow reader for that reason. I don't stop there but [use] deliberate speed at handling the words that way as I go. Always was [like that]. Take it in anything like this. Are you good at it, or have you been let in on it? It's only if you are good at it that I'm talking to you. I don't want you to be let in on anything I ever made. I don't want any teacher to let you in on it, if you aren't good at it so that I needn't say to you, "Do you get it?" Just the same when I crack a joke—if I ever crack one. Serious question. When I crack a joke I'd hate to say, "Do you get it?" Worse to have somebody nearby say, "He means . . . " [*Laughter*] Well, the logrolling. Leave that. Frustum. See. I went wrong on that. But the logrolling—I think I got to the bottom of it today—thinking about it. You know we have what they call spelling bees and sewing bees. You know what those are. People get together and sew together for the church or something, and get together for a game for amusement now and then. There used to be a house-raising bee where everybody turned out and put the frame of a building up together, and they used to be—way before my time. The figure is kind of lost but I can't rest until I get back to where it came from. There were bees like that in clearing the land. Everybody turned out and logrolled together. They got what they called a burn—a good burn; but the thing that was done in company in a bee that way—all helping each other with every work—just as they do in Washington now, I'm sure. [*Laughter*]

And I wouldn't be writing poetry now unless I thought I was some good at it. When I was very young, and in Boston, one day I was in a bookstore, I flipped open a square-shaped, thick book, and this is what I read:

> I fled Him, down the nights and down the days;
> I fled Him, down the arches of the years;
> I fled Him, down the labyrinthine ways
> Of my own mind; and in the mist of tears
> I hid from Him, and under running laughter.

And I bought the book and walked home twenty-five miles just on those [lines].[4] I thought every one of them I got instantly—no one

4. See Beverly M. Bowie, "New England, a Modern Pilgrim's Pride," *National Geographic*, June 1955, p. 774.

Not far from the Athenaeum stands the Old Corner Bookstore. I can never pass it now without thinking of the story Robert Frost told me as we were driving through the Vermont rain one night. He had been had to tell me about them—and the meaning of the poem itself, although it was entirely strange to me, entirely strange. I always thought of my seeking goodness. See. This is called "The Hound of Heaven." It is goodness chasing me. Running me down. See, that was a new one to me. But I got it. That by Francis Thompson.

Now the other thing. It says in other places in the Bible, it says: "Though you understand mysteries."[5] Mysteries. Very interesting to me that the word *mysteries* occurs so much. In the Corinthians, that is. He was talking to the people of Corinth, Paul was. And the people of Corinth were all fooling with ancient mysteries—Eleusinian and things like that. All those cities were full of it, and the word keeps occurring so that you wonder if there isn't black magic alluded to. And it is something like that—ancient rites and things you wouldn't be able to guess unless you were initiated—unless you've been to a graduate school. No matter how good you are at that sort of thing, how you fancy yourself as quick in taking it, you can't do much with mysteries—the real mysteries. And that's so with some people's poetry. They want it to be mysterious. And if they want it to be—if they've got some secrets, let them keep them. [*Laughter*]

It's a fair field, see, it's a fair field, that's what poetry is; for people—a fair field—that have come up from *Mother Goose*, you know, and its figurativeness into the general figurativeness of grown-up people. That's all. And the poetry is the height of it, isn't it? That's why poetry is *the* liberal art.

Take Mr. Einstein right now on his birthday. He's up against it. Seventy-five years old and he has a little formula, a little equation. Four terms, you might call it. One term is zero. And there it is. And he's sure that's it. But he can't solve it. So then what does he do? He turns to poetry and tries to tell us. I think he never said for himself—I think people said for him—that his was a mystery that only twelve people were in on, and the rest of us couldn't expect to be

only 17, he said, a bobbin-cart pusher in the textile mills at Lawrence, when he rode to Boston on the train. Stopping at the Old Corner, he picked up a copy of Francis Thompson's *The Hound of Heaven*.

From the first on-rushing line—"I fled Him, down the nights and down the days"—young Frost was caught, bemused. In his pocket he had only enough money for his return ticket. He pulled it out, paid for the book—and walked the 25 miles back to Lawrence, reading it over and over.

"If I could meet that poem again for the first time, I'd walk the same miles and find them easy underfoot," said Frost.

5. 1 Cor. 13:2.

39

good at it. He wants to say things that people like us can understand. And so what does he say? He says in desperation: "I'm in the same fix that Newton was in when he had to invent a new mathematics. He invented one and I can't seem to." Touching. Metaphor. Analogy. Very touching. And then he says, "I have sometimes wondered if I got away on the wrong assumption." This is in his letter to the *Christian Science Monitor,* of all places![6] Touching. Some people are angry at him for having attempted what he has attempted. And like Prometheus, you know, they seem to resent him, but no, it's touching, dramatic and tragic, almost. Then he says—going way, way back in the thinking of the world—he says: "I'm not sure but the universe is made of jelly or sand." That! About the continuity, discontinuity or continuity, and that's come all the way down with the philosophies to him. And he said it in those simple, nice terms. Jelly or sand. Discontinuous. And then he says another—a rather pretty one: "Here I'm asked to describe the universe." Nobody asked him but himself but it's nice he said it. [*Laughter*] "It's as if I was given two bones and asked to describe the megatherium." Pretty. But you see—again—all the things, up and down, slight, trivial, plain. Now take the one about the jelly and the sand. That has a long, long history. That's a very deep, deep consideration. But that's the place to get hold of it—start there and go back to the Greeks with it. Just as well. Better to pick them up anywhere, if you're good at it. If you are not good at it, you're out; better go to college.

Now let me show you something that's hopeless for you. Say some Spaniards came to Yucatan and they found what looked like a cross to them there and their minds picked that right up as something they were already let in on. Religious symbol. But they were wrong. They thought Saint Thomas or somebody must have been there. They were wrong. Nobody had been there. It was another symbol. You might have guessed—anyone good at it might have thought of the four winds or the four directions. You might have worked on it that way. That! Altogether different. Ours is a long story that we've all been let in on by religious education. That's one thing.

Now for the fun of it, I'll take you to Tibet. That's where all the mysteries are. Most people who are full of it—the new mysteries —have just been to Tibet. I've been reading some of the poets, you know—Sanskrit. Can you handle these? I offer them to you because you can't. I've been let in on them. There are three things—three things called the three poisons—that keep us from attaining nirvana

6. The library staff at the *Christian Science Monitor* was unable to locate any letter written by Einstein and published in the *Monitor* in 1953.

and so getting out of the round of existence. Three things known as the poisons. The round of existence. You have to be careful about that in translation. It's often translated, the wheel of existence. Wheel isn't good. That's been chucked. It's the round of existence. But you want to get out of that. Your object [is] to get out of that; [it] keeps going round until you get dizzy being born into so many different things. Angels. Human beings. Animals. Purgatorians. Titans. And Yidags. That's all. Angels. Even when you are an angel you have to get out. You can't still be going round and round in that. And the three poisons that keep you out are the pig—know what the pig means?—and the cock and the snake. Make anything of them? Probably not. In Chesterton's poem it says—I think it says:

> There was a young wife of Antigua
> Who said to her spouse: "What a pig you are."
> He answered, "My queen, is it manners you mean,
> Or do you refer to my figua?"[7]

Does it mean gluttonous or fattenous? It doesn't mean that in my religion—in my newfound religion. You'll have to guess hard. You wouldn't get it. Anybody make anything of it? Want to tell me? It just means ignorance. See? You aren't in on it. You'll have to be told. The pig is a very bright animal in my understanding. Now the cock means ambition, desire, and cockiness. I guess we get a little there, but it may have more to do with desire than with anything else—and appetite, ambition, all that. And the snake—you know what your snake means. Some of my rather immediate ancestors were called Copperheads.[8] Civil War history. And we know what that means,

Now I'm just enough so made that when I look at a thing, like —want to bring in a poem about the coronation, you'd say, I remember "Pussy cat, pussy cat, where have you been?" (I pronounce *been* to rhyme with *queen*.) "I have been to London to see the queen. / Pussy cat, pussy cat, what did you see there? / I didn't see anything that I mightn't have seen had I stayed at home and seen a little mouse run under a chair." And if I wasn't good at that I'd better not have been brought up on *Mother Goose*. And you wonder how those things go. I've been to the Colorado Canyon, and what did I see there? Or, I've been to Niagara Falls, and what did I see there? I saw a lot of water falling, just what I've seen falling out of the faucet many, many times. And so on.

7. Gilbert Chesterton's limerick is unlocated.
8. Frost's father, William Prescott Frost, was a Copperhead and gave his poet-son the name of Robert Lee in recognition of his southern sympathies.

The thing is: there's no story written that has any value at all, however straightforward it looks and free from doubleness, double entendre, and duplicity and double play, that you'd value at all if it didn't have intimations of something more [special] than itself. It almost always comes under the head of synecdoche, a part, a hem of the garment, a part for the whole, a hem of the garment; touch the hem of the garment for the whole garment.[9] And that's what it's about all the time. The only difference—my only quarrel with anybody—is that they seem to think there must be something beautiful in having it so that you have to be told. And I hate to be told. After all these years I'm sorry when I'm caught unready for somebody's figure of speech—somebody's metaphor. The symbol will do for it all. But metaphor, parable, allegory, synecdoche—all the same thing!

I remember people—some of them narrower—people very good at their subject, narrow in the classics. They had an idea there were eight or ten different kinds of figures. And that's one of the things I think helped to kill Latin as a general subject, because all the figures are one figure. It's a live thing that keeps the mind rising into poetry. There are two things about it: good at it or being let in on it. Let me say this about my Latin. I had a lot of Latin and I never was good at it. I don't call it I was good at it. I can read what I read before rather easily. [Laughter] I worked at and got in on it—looked in on [it]. But as for [a] new stretch of Latin poetry, I don't have a good time with it. I'm not fast enough with it.

Shall I read you for the fun of it this little paper? [Picks up a little scrap of paper] I have a Christmas poem every year. It hasn't been sent out, my Christmas poem, this year.[10] It's mostly because I'm lazy. But I have to find a better reason than that, of course, to present to the world. So I've had a little slip printed to be put into it, and this is what the printing [says]: "This Christmas poem, though not isolationist, is so dangerously near isolationist it was thought better to send it out for Independence Day instead of Christmas." [Laughter] See the figure I'm playing with there. The devil of it is it's

9. Frost called himself "a synecdochist." In *Modern American Poetry*, 5th ed. rev. (Harcourt, Brace and Co., 1936), Louis Untermeyer quoted Frost as saying, "If I must be classified as a poet, I might be called a Synecdochist; for I prefer the synecdoche in poetry—that figure of speech in which we use a part for the whole."

10. Frost's Christmas poem for 1952, "Does No One but Me at All Ever Feel This Way in the Least?," was included in *In the Clearing*, where Frost omitted "but Me" in the title.

getting nearer to July fourth than I thought. It's [his procrastination] getting something awful.

After talking this serious way, the way I do, half fooling about it but somewhat serious, I'm always afraid that for the first poem or two I read afterward everybody will be straining too much. 'Tisn't like that. The first surface meaning, the anecdote, the parable, the surface meaning has got to be good and got to be sufficient in itself. If you don't want any more you can leave it at that. Suppose I try one that has a great deal of that in it. Some of them have got more, some less. This is called "The White-Tailed Hornet." In blank verse it is. [*Reads "The White-Tailed Hornet"*]

[He introduced "The Lost Follower" by saying that it was about "one of the best I've known in my time," a student he had known at Amherst, and it was about another also, a student at Bryn Mawr.][11] Both of them forsook poetry to do something for the next election. They thought one good election and the world would be saved. They tried three or four. This is about them. It's called "The Lost Follower." You can see it's anything but condescension. [*Reads "The Lost Follower." Stops at line, "By grace of state-manipulated pelf"*] This [line] is one whole period, isn't it? [*Repeats*] This has been poetry's great antilure.

He [one of the two about whom the poem was written] says it every day in the Lord's Prayer, if he uses the Lord's Prayer. Most do; those didn't. They are what they call Marxists. They were friends of mine, and still are, you know. If they recognize themselves [in the poem]—I doubt if they would. All the importance [is] just that one thing—all my resentment, all my hurt, hurt.

[*Reads "Not Quite Social"*] It goes with that ["The Lost Follower"], I suppose. Suppose I take something else, far away from those intimations.

[*Reads "The Witch of Coös"; "The Road Not Taken"; "Desert Places"; "The Runaway"*]

You see, just for the fun of it I was asked to give a poem to this college magazine by one of the people in "The Lost Follower" and I gave him that poem because it was about him. I didn't tell him that it got around about years afterwards. Somebody else told him.

Here's one about California where I was born in on a rainy morning. In New England, you know, we say we all must eat our peck of

---

11. The two young people to whom Frost refers are Jean Flexner (at Bryn Mawr) and Carter Goodrich (at Amherst College). See *Selected Letters of Robert Frost*, ed. Lawrance Thompson (New York: Holt, Rinehart and Winston, 1964), p. 591.

dirt. When you drop a slice of bread butter-side down you get dirt on the butter [but] you eat it just the same and say, we've got to eat it. That's what they call philosophy. [*Laughter*] Well, out in California it's different. In New England they say it's dirt; out in California they say something different. This is my memory of California. [*Reads "A Peck of Gold." Reads "Once by the Pacific"; repeats the poem. Reads "Come In"*]

I've been told by a birdman, somebody who knows a lot about birds, that birds never shift their perch at night, and I've felt corrected somewhat. I made a generalization out of having made birds shift and I've distressed myself about them. One of the amusing things was I used to walk in the night along a thatched roof—a very old thatched roof that came clear down from way up, came down to my shoulder—and I used to scare the birds out of that in the night if they lived in the thatch. Do you know? Did you ever see them? And I'd scare them out. It bothered me a lot because I didn't know where they went when they roosted on the ground the rest of the night, and I was in distress myself but I was sorrier to distress the birds. And that's always been with me—the notion of what becomes of a bird that is scared off its perch. Just that line, that little thing I don't get credit for.

[*Reads "Spring Pools"*]

CHAPTER 6
Poetry and Education
July 5, 1954

Despite Robert Frost's statement that he hadn't talked about either poetry or education "regularly" before the Bread Loaf School of English audience, it would appear on the record that he had talked about little else. This evening, however, he was determined to focus without slippage precisely on poetry and education.

One particular theme of the talk is Frost's deprecation of a scholarly approach to poetry at the introductory level. But it is also to be noted that he was not generally indicting scholarship. He made it clear he loved scholarship, but it was "not of the first importance to what they call poesy pure—pure poetry." Nor, of course, is it.

Frost read fifteen poems this evening, and some of his more pertinent comments on "The Ax-Helve," "Birches," "Acquainted with the Night," "Why Wait for Science," and "Stopping by Woods on a Snowy Evening" have been included. Although he was in good voice, and in very good humor, Frost did not preface the reading of his poems with a long introductory talk. He appeared more interested in scoring his nonsubversive point about "the deadly thing" he wanted to say. So he made emphatic his view that the scholarly graduate-school approach to poetry should never be introduced in either the high school or the college classroom.

I ought to say something tonight about both poetry and education, it seems to me under these circumstances. And I've done that regularly . . . I haven't usually talked about either poetry or education. I've talked about everything under the sun. I can remember some of the subjects and they were far from poetry and from education. But I've been accused lately of having said something in print very subversive. That's a funny word, isn't it? It has other connotations than I mean, hasn't it? But I told a story of my relation through ıxty years to a particular poem of Emerson's.[1] A fellow teacher of mine said the other day, "I see through you." He said, "I suppose others have. They don't like to tell you. But I'm going to tell you. That's a very subversive piece of writing. It undermines education [and] the teaching of poetry." He said, "I won't tell anybody else on you." I said to him: "I've been telling people on me for the last forty years. So you needn't think you've been telling anything special. I've been trying to tell on myself but I haven't been able to phrase it, I suppose." He seemed surprised to find it in that article—thought he had done quite a thing to see it himself. He said, "I guess you mean you don't want your poetry taught in schools. Is that right?" I said, "By the wrong people, yes." [*Laughter*]

Now it seems to me a chance for a little demarcation about these things. Suppose I'm thinking of the top of poetry—not my own, but the top of poetry—the *Oxford Book of Verse* [and] the Palgrave.[2] I've been long puzzled and you've been puzzled by what to do with that in school. Most of you are teachers. What would you do with the Palgrave? It was published without a single note, if I'm not mistaken. I have a very early edition of it. And what is there to be said about poetry like that? Me, myself, I read Shakespeare out of my hip pockets when I was working in the mills.[3] I never touched him in reading until then. Never really read him through. Some people tried to scare me. They said there are some of the words in that that look as if they meant the same as they do now but they didn't then. There are about fifty of those. And you ought to go to college for four years to get those, you know. [*Laughter*] Very terrible threat!

Let's go back. In the eighteenth and nineteenth centuries all education—all college education and some high school education—was pre-pulpit and pre-parliament. All of it was. Everybody was thinking of being either a preacher or a member of Congress. They spouted a great deal. Something of that spirit still lingers in us. There's some of that. The spouting has almost disappeared. I wish

1. See Frost's explication of Emerson's "Brahma" in the lead essay, "The Prerequisites," in the *New York Times Book Review,* March 21, 1954.

2. The two anthologies referred to were among his favorites, especially Francis T. Palgrave's *The Golden Treasury* (1861). It was published, as Frost rightly contended, *without* a note and with the unabridged text of *The Rubaiyat of Omar Khayyam.*

3. Frost, at aged nineteen, was a light fixer in the dynamo room of the Arlington Mill, located between Methuen and Lawrence, Massachusetts. This was the summer of 1893, and in the slack periods he would climb into a hideout under the belts and read Shakespeare, as he said, from the hip pocket.

there was a little of it left: the reciting of poetry by heart
—things like that—Shakespeare by heart. We have the word *pre* with
us everywhere: premedical; prescience; prescientific; and prelaw; I
suppose you could say some of it is. But anyway I think that nearly all
poetry that is handled in the high school and colleges today is pre-
graduate schools. That's the deadly thing I wanted to say. Now that's
not the least thing subversive. That's not the least thing against the
graduate school. It's just that it is pre-graduate-school training—not
education. See. The college and the high school should be kept as
free as possible from all that. It's hard that it should be so because
nearly all of the teachers who are out of graduate schools have
doctor's degrees. It is very hard for them to forget the methods of
the graduate school, the scholarly methods. And most of the students that you have in the high school and college are not going to be
scholars, and why should you handle them as if they were going to be
scholars? Only maybe you could say: only so they shall respect scholars, and remember to respect them when they get down into Wall
Street, and send plenty of money up to support them. Maybe that's
the justification. But something's gone wrong. The graduate school
has backed up into the college and even into the high school. There's
nothing to be said against handling Shakespeare in the scholarly
fashion, but that's all pre-graduate school where it's handled that
way.

I remember years ago the head of the educational system in New
Hampshire told me that he came into a class in the high school
visiting—in Concord, I think it was, or Manchester—and he found
the children reading a play of Shakespeare.[4] They were translating
it word by word into other and worse English to prove that they understood it—everything being gone into in little details. And he said
to the teacher—I ought to tell you the kind of man he was: he was a
great education bully; he ran the whole state of New Hampshire. He
once took out his watch and said to me: "I can tell you what every
teacher in New Hampshire is saying." [*Laughter*] He said, "That's because I have to supply what they shall say because they don't know
what to say themselves." He said to the teacher: "Now that isn't the
way to read a play. This is a play, something to which you might go in
the evening that might take two or three hours to see it acted. When I
might sit up of a night at home reading when I'm not busy, I might

4. Henry Clinton Morrison, Dartmouth 1895, Superintendent of Public
Instruction for the State of New Hampshire. Morrison had helped secure
Frost's appointment to the teaching faculty at New Hampshire State Nor-
mal School in Plymouth for the year 1911–12.

47

read a play by Marlowe or Webster or Shakespeare, one that I had not read before and I'd read it the whole evening. It's very readable. Strangely readable. Of course if you've been swept through it in high school you might come back to it for parts you like to dwell on; some of them have charmed you especially; and then if there's little difficulties, you know. A play will bear so much, only so much. A little poem will bear only so much of teaching, you know. There's little things to look into; you might do that, you know—anachronisms and such things." Next year he was back there, he said, and looked in on her again. She [the teacher] said: "I'm going to open up a play for you today. We're going to read *Julius Caesar* for rapid reading." She said that in just the accent of cant. I heard that said once. I was crossing a campus. I heard two teachers [who] were crossing the campus, and I heard one say, "It's a rapid reading book." Rapid reading book! I guess it was *Walden* or something. [*Laughter*] First we'll read it for rapid reading. Then we'll read for beauty. Then we'll tend to things like anachronisms. And he said: "What can you do with anyone like that?"

All I say is, that I'd like to come up here sometime, another year maybe, and give four or five lectures on how to treat poems in a high school.[5] I won't bother with a college. That can take care of itself. But in a high school. Doesn't matter who the poet is. Take in Chaucer: that's what you might call a somewhat foreign language, a slightly foreign language that can be got over very quickly. That part of it is study, of course. You're going to get over that. And then the way the words are pronounced—a few weeks and you're in there. Just the same as in Shakespeare. Suitable for rapid reading. [*Satirically*] Now look. I never ask anybody to write anything down. (But I'm going to.) I start the lecture by asking everybody to write down one sentence for me. And I'd make my four or five lectures out of the different words in the sentence; they're these: "Our object [speaking for the poets] is to entertain you by making play (symbol and metaphor) with things we trust you already know." By making play! That's the height of it—the apex. Now in one of the lectures I'll modify that last—just for the fun of it—that you almost entirely know. There's a

5. Frost's suggestion about giving a special group of lectures on "how to treat poems in a high school" was considered as a possibility, and even his giving a course at the English School during one of the sessions was talked over. But there were problems involved—financial and methodological —which could not be obviated. So Frost, never a member of the faculty at the English School, remained a special lecturer throughout the many years of his association with Bread Loaf.

little something there always. When you write or read a poem as I am tonight, there are parts of it that one person hears and another person is missing. I've been often asked over the years: "How do you make children like poetry?" The answer is: you don't. You don't do it in that sweeping way. There will be a lot who stay indifferent to poetry. I'm not here to whoop it up for poetry. I said to my friend Clifford Lyons—he's going back to give up his deanship to teach Shakespeare again—I said, "What are you going back to do, going back to exaggerate Shakespeare, whooping up Shakespeare?[6] He's been advertised too much. Advertise some of us others." But that's what I'm going to do. And it's largely to sort of cleanse the high school of the graduate-school approach.

Now the great, great, greatest scholarship, see—the greatest scholarship I venerate. I've had a good many adventures in education. I remember once hearing Nichols—he was president of Dartmouth a short time, a Nobel Prize man on the weight of light and a very distinguished scholar who was not a very successful president—I remember his saying to a lot of teachers that he wished, speaking as a scholar-scientist, [that] they would let science alone in the high school; it's just prophylactic teaching.[7] He says they take the wonder all out of it so there's nothing to astonish them. He might have gone on to say it's almost as bad as the comic strips, it takes all the wonder out of everything. What would I have them do in the high school? Well, there's Latin. Then there's Greek. They might have four years of Greek. Then he thought hard and said, "A little mathematics. And I wished they'd let other things alone." Said, "French and German, the equivalent for Latin and Greek." He just wished they'd let all that stuff alone. That's an extreme way of putting that.

I'd like to see "what might be done" for the sake of the top level of poetry. Can you think of anything to say of what research there is for the lyric? For instance, there's a lyric that begins:

> The glories of our blood and state
> Are shadows, not substantial things;
> There is no armour against fate;
> Death lays his icy hand on kings:

6. Clifford Lyons, professor of English at the University of North Carolina, was a member of the faculty at Bread Loaf School of English in 1954.

7. Ernest Fox Nichols (1869–1924), a physicist who became president of Dartmouth College in 1909. Later, ill health forced him to decline the presidency of M.I.T.

Sceptre and crown
Must tumble down,
And in the dust be equal made
With the poor crooked scythe and spade.

Now at the head of that poem in one of the books it says "Death the Leveller." And me, myself, you see, I can say that it occurred to me after years of thinking, if that was a poem in Shirley's play where it occurs or whether there was any title at all.[8] This is speaking (a little) as a scholar. See, those things have an interest to me. I love the scholarship of it. But it's not of the first importance to what they call poesy pure—pure poetry. That's what I'm speaking for. The plays are all like that. They've all got a first quality of entertainment: making play of things we can trust you largely know. And if I have to say too much to prepare you for the poem—say anything to prepare you for the poem before you read it—too bad. If I have to say anything to you while the poem is going on, it's worse. And if I have to say anything after it—well, I hope you will have gone home.

I'm going to read a poem, for instance, tonight that [has] got a little French Canadian dialect in it, at which I'm not very good. I never read [it] before for that reason. I read it once years ago at a Phi Beta Kappa place and always let it alone a little.[9] And I've always let it alone for that reason. Sorry I can't say the French very well. It's English French, American French. My years of experience in reading have convinced me that I can entertain people more when I have a person in my poem. See, that's odd. I read two poems on the occasion I speak of years ago. One of them had no persons at all and the other had these French people in it. And somebody afterward said to me—the editor of the *Atlantic* said afterward, "We don't like that first one you said, but give us that second one with the Frenchman in it."[10] I've been more and more aware of that—of people, of characters. It's called "The Ax-Helve."

I ought to have brought with me tonight a paragraph in an eighteenth-century book I read, a paragraph with ten words in it about what expenses a man is at to harvest a crop of rice in India. And there are all sorts of expenses—there are ten expenses, all with

8. James Shirley (1596–1666) included a final dirge in which this stanza appears in *The Contention of Ajax and Ulysses* (1659), a semidramatic play.

9. "The Ax-Helve," read in June 1916 before the Phi Beta Kappa Society at Harvard during commencement. The other poem read at the Phi Beta Kappa dinner was "The Bonfire."

10. The editor of the *Atlantic Monthly* from 1908 to 1938 was Ellery Sedgwick, who once miffed Frost by rejecting three of his poems.

the strangest names. And I ought to have read them to you. I didn't know what a single one of them [meant], and you wouldn't know and there wouldn't be anybody here who would know. I don't care how many graduate schools [he attended]. But I wouldn't do that to anybody, naturally—naturally—except to high-hat them.

[*Reads "The Ax-Helve"*] But now, I could go a lot into that. And some of you perhaps don't know about an ax, some of you don't know the word *helve,* but I'll leave it to you to find out in some other poem. I always look at it that way, too, that I come upon the word, "Smooth-sliding Mincius, crown'd with vocal reeds!"[11] I come on the word *Mincius* in history. And I come upon the word *Mincius* in Napoleon's campaigns. And by the time I've come on it two or three times, I've pretty well known that it's a stream. I don't need very much more than that about it.

[*Reads "Birches"*] The line that means the most to me: "when I'm weary of considerations." That's when you get older. It didn't mean so much to me when I wrote it as it does now. I've made some of the worst psychological mistakes in the world, so don't listen to anything I say. That is true. I'm just thinking of one I made—a terrible one —an educational one. Almost fatal to many people. Maybe tonight, too, you know. There's another thing about little noticings—what you call scholarly noticing. You like to come along with that in the graduate schools and do something of that for yourself. It says in Keats, "Thy hair soft-lifted by the winnowing wind"; I happened to think when I was reading it one day—someone didn't tell me—there ought to be a hyphen in there.[12] If you say "winnowing wind" it means it's winnowing her hair, and if you say "winnowing-wind" it's the regular wind that winnows the grain. The hyphen makes all the difference in the world there. I'm telling you. Little things you notice like that. The same kind of a thing happened in one of my poems- —ought to be a hyphen in it [e.g., "Mending Wall"; cf. "old-stone savage," a Paleolithic savage]. You've got to notice. The most noticing man that ever lived maybe was Thoreau, wasn't he? He noticed some things wrong, they like to point out. But he was a very noticing man. That's why we're celebrating the hundredth anniversary of the publication of *Walden*—that great, great book, that sacred book to all Thorosians. There'll be a word in the dictionary—*Thorosian.* I'm going to say on the celebration the word *Thorosian* along with some other words. I don't think it's in yet. Transcending transcendentalism. [*Ironically*]

11. John Milton, *Lycidas,* line 86.
12. John Keats, "To Autumn," line 16.

Take all this matter of anyone's symbols. What did I hear someone say today?—an interesting thing—a symbolic thing. Now everything symbolic has to be true on two planes. I have to thank a young lady for that. Two young people were walking hand-in-hand in a thunderstorm, and just after they let go their hands and separated a little the lightning struck the ground right between them, which goes to show that we're safer apart than we are together. Anyway, it's a nice symbol whether it happened or not, you say; but it ought to have happened. But I kind of doubt that. But it's such a nice symbol, it's too bad it isn't true, because it goes with my doctrine. I'm always talking that. It's a very Thorosian tale. I'm going to keep it. I go around saying: the separateness of the parts is at least as important as the connection. But I'm going to say after this, it's more important. If you all keep getting together it'll end in statism. That's what they mean.

You know, what is there left for the person who listens to a poem? You know, what is it to him? It's just his agility—to show his agility—in handling the things; it's things he knows played with and his agility in keeping up with the little game. That's all there is to it. If there's anything I have to explain about understanding it, that's absolutely fatal.

[*Reads "Acquainted with the Night"*] There's a pun in that I made for a friend of mine. His name was "A. E."—George Russell. He was always saying: "The time is not right."

[*Reads "Why Wait for Science"*] One of the interesting things about science to me, always, is that it seems to be seeking first things—that is, in its largest aspects; all it is seeking [is] first things through the ages. I didn't say that loud enough—[it has] never got within millions of miles of first things; still as far [away] as ever. The nearest [scientists] have [come] today is to say we can't tell substance from form; we can't tell—this thing that seems to be coming in on you—[whether it is] substance or form, form-substance, substance-form. Anybody knows that's nothing. They haven't got anywhere yet. I don't mean that it isn't great fun—pushing back that way.

A companion piece to the one ["Come In"] about the thrush—but in a different tune. [*Reads "Stopping by Woods"*] That one I've been more bothered with than anybody has ever been with any poem in just the pressing it for more than it should be pressed for. It means enough without its being pressed. That's all right, you know. I don't say that somebody shouldn't press it, but I don't want to be there.

52

CHAPTER 7
A Session in the Barn on Poetry August 2, 1954

This talk was given in the recreation room of the Barn at the Bread Loaf School of English on the evening of August 2, 1954. Frost, as usual, had prepared nothing formally. He came to answer questions on or about poetry, and the recording follows the sequence of questions. Typically, it was an uninhibited performance in which the vagaries of memory are reflected in the rambling talk. Such talk often led to important personal revelations about the poet's relationship to his craft; and the following record is no exception. As a matter of fact, it was a rewarding evening.

A large audience had gathered, and as the questions came, written or by voice from the floor, they were relayed to Frost. He started off on translations to warm up his inquisitors, referring to Leonard Bacon's work in this field, turned to the question of metaphor and allegory and allowed, "a parable is about my length. I can stand a parable. Beyond parable, no." And as for metaphor: "As much metaphor as there is in a little poem. Not too long." Then he launched out on "the question of the parable," which he thought, addressing his audience, "might interest you." Throughout the evening Frost was careful to qualify some of his most decisive statements. He explained: "I'm talking my own way, more or less for your entertainment, tonight. There's nothing so entertaining as each other's attitudes." His remarks were directed mainly to the audience of teachers and to their classroom practices.

I've been talking about symbols and parables and metaphors one way and another, and somebody wrote me a rather rebuking letter—somebody who thought he knew the Bible better than I did—and he told me: "Did you realize that the parables in the New Testament were written not to be understood? They were deliberate mystification; deliberately esoteric." I had spoken against the esoteric in art in a talk I gave somewhere, and he picked that up.

He'd heard it on the radio or somewhere, and I thought I'd made some fun out of that. It says in the New Testament: These things are said in parable so the wrong people can't understand them and so get saved.[1] I said that, and I'd just been reading Tom Paine who didn't think any Bible was good.[2] But that's good Bible. And then the question [is]: Is that aristocratic or is it esoteric? What is it? Well, I said, I'll tell you what it is, it's plain. It means by the wrong people —professors, scribes and pharisees. It means except you come as little children. It says [that] somewhere else.[3] They [children] understand stories. They naturally do. It [the story or parable] is a natural ꞁutburst. I made fun out of it that way, and this fellow got after me ꞁnd said the parables had been accepted as esoteric long since by the Church. OK!

I was talking with Rabbi Reichert before he went away, and he had a nice quotation from Hosea.[4] Just the same [as the parables]. But there's no talk of mystification. It's just that these things are conveyed in similitudes—the same word [as parable or simile]. My similitude. There are things you can't convey except in similitudes. That's the way we get from one thing to another—from one place [in thought] to another; by similitudes, of course. [Our] whole thinking is that. When Schopenhauer says, "the world as will," he just gives his whole life and that can get very tiresome.[5] He gives his whole life to one big book about the world being likened unto that trait in man which we call will and not likened unto what Plato said. He was making a distinction. Plato's metaphor would be that all of creation might be likened unto that trait in man which is called reason. Just a metaphor. [A] sustained metaphor. After you've got a hint of it, you can do the rest yourself, if you're any good.

Q. What do you like in prose? What about the popularity of Charles Dickens right now?

1. Mark 4:11, 12.

2. Thomas Paine (1737–1809), in *The Age of Reason* (1794–96), wrote, "In fine, do we want to know what God is? Search not the book called the Scripture, which any human hand might make, but the scripture called the Creation."

3. Mark 10:15.

4. Dr. Victor E. Reichert, rabbi for many years at the Rockdale Avenue Temple, Cincinnati, Ohio. A likely passage from Hosea would seem to be 12:10, "I have also spoken by the prophets, and I have multiplied visions, and used similitudes, by the ministry of the prophets."

5. Arthur Schopenhauer (1788–1860); *Die Welt als Wille und Vorstellung* (The World as Will and Idea), his principal work, appeared in 1819.

A. That [i.e., prose] comes in another department. That's all right. I don't have that kind of opinion very much, you know. I'm not an evaluator. Dickens is all right. I remember. I've just been over the French Revolution in two different authors, and as I read [in *The Tale of Two Cities*] I distinguished in Sidney Carton some of it. I haven't read much of Dickens to any extent since 1891. There isn't any reason why I shouldn't start again.

Q. Will Mr. Frost illustrate the use of parables in his own poetry?

A. The metaphor, as I say—the most of them [his poems] are no longer than a metaphor—but you mean name them? One of mine that is very much taken as a parable is called "Mending Wall." There are intimations in that, you know, hints. And then another at the other end of that same book, *North of Boston,* is a little one about the same length called "The Wood-Pile." And "The Grindstone" is one. Over and over again some of the little ones [e.g., "Hyla Brook"] are little metaphors. Some of them clinch their own little metaphors at the end, like "We love the things we love for what they are." That is, as you get it [the brook] when it's worn out at the end of summer, when it's dried up, dead leaves stuck together by the heat; and then it says at the end, "We love the things we love for what they are"—whether they're young or old, fresh or spent. See! That's easy enough! That's what it's doing. Then, I think all of them are. ["Brown's Descent"?] Yeh! That's so easy. Some of them are just for the fun of it. Some very open and some are less veiled, you know.

Q. What do you think of the people today who say there is nothing left to say about nature that is not trite?

A. Ah! I've just been noticing Whitehead quoted by Lucien Price on how [there] can be fresh little observations about man and nature.[6] Those can all be new. The basic things like the world as will, the world as reason, the world as mathematics, or science, or something like that—those are all spent, according to Whitehead, according to Lucien Price. And that may be so. We might never get another vast philosophy. When you think of that, you wonder. But about nature: I should think anyone might always be noticing little fresh things. If my book isn't sprinkled with it I don't know what it is —sprinkled with them. I'm not going to search my own book, but in an early one [i.e., "A Prayer in Spring"] [a] hummingbird "thrusts in with needle bill / And off a blossom in mid-air stands still." That's the kind of thing you mean. That isn't anywhere else. Somebody else noticed—since—not on top of mine, but I noticed someone saying

6. Lucien Price, *Dialogues of Whitehead* (New York: Mentor Books, 1956), p. 62.

the other day: the hummingbird is the only bird that can fly backward. They were first. That's interesting—very interesting! That's
what you mean by fresh observation. Lots of things are reduced to
statistics, and there are still little things that you notice: something
about people and people's [ways]. You have to, all the time, live with
people.

The nature part of it! Talking about Thoreau the other day. I
have a friend in Amherst, Massachusetts—a real-estate dealer who,
if I wrote novels, would be in one.[7] He's one of the characters of my
lifetime, and he has read every word that Thoreau ever wrote and
not only read it forward but backward and sideways. It's common
criticism that Thoreau made mistakes in his observations, acute as he
was and close to things, and it's in all the books about Thoreau that
he did make some mistakes. That's the old cocksure one and, as my
friend Brown says, "They [the Thoreau critics] are so stupid; they
just give a little list of the few that he made and they keep making the
same list down the years. Nobody's made a fresh observation of any
of the mistakes Thoreau made. [*Laughter*] The old stale crowd."

Q. Here's another question. What is the ultimate value of the
study of poetry?

A. I'm not in favor of studying it very hard. I just picked this up
for the fun of it.[8] I had no intentions of using this on you in any way.
It's called *Parnassus.* Do you know whose it is? Raise your hand. [*No
one did*] *Parnassus*! It was an anthology made about the same time that
Palgrave's was.[9] Made by Ralph Waldo Emerson. And you had an
anthologist around here the other night.[10]

But the study of poetry isn't anything, you know. Goodness' sakes.
The beauty of those poems, at the top of everything, is that some of
them must be in your nature, you know, in your head. You can't hear
them without their catching on to you without being studied.

[*Interjected question:* Is that primarily what makes a poem survive,
would you say?] Yeh! Yeh! Yeh! You know when you think of it: how
hard does it want to be? How hard is hard enough? It wants to be
some test of your nimbleness and also of your experience—what
you've lived with other poems and where you've lived—some test of

---

7. Warren R. Brown; see numerous references to him in Lawrance
Thompson's *Robert Frost: The Years of Triumph* (New York: Holt, Rinehart
and Winston, 1970).

8. Ralph Waldo Emerson, *Parnassus* (1871).

9. Palgrave, *The Golden Treasury.*

10. Oscar Williams, *A Little Treasury of Modern Poetry* (New York: Charles
Scribner's Sons, 1948).

that. But the main test is your nimbleness. Are you up to this? "He can do little who can't do this." See! Come on, catch on. That's what the beauty of it is.

Amherst in my head, a little. I lived—I've been in and out of Amherst so many years—and lived through the last part of the bitter war down there between the Emily Dickinson niece and Emily Dickinson's brother's mistress.[11] I've got to get that all straight. That was a very bitter, bitter thing. It still lives a little. And there's one left—the daughter of the mistress still lives in Washington, and she still burns with this thing.[12] The great question in Amherst for years was: Who did Emily like best—her brother's mistress or her brother's wife? And there were trials and things and everything went to court, you know—property involved. Practically all gone but a daughter of the mistress. Friend of mine. And it was so bitter when I think of it.

Think of a little poem. How could all this rise from someone's having written a poem like this? Let's see. "My life closed twice before its close; / It yet remains to see / If Immortality unveil / A third event to me, / So huge, so hopeless to conceive / As these that twice befell. / Parting is all we know of heaven, / And all we need of hell."[13] I've mauled it a little calling it up. Now when you stop to look at that, does anything more than the thing itself occur to you? One can say always that some days nothing more than the thing itself occurs to you. It's huge [enough] just in itself to take. Sometimes something extra occurs to you. I remember one of the bitter ones in Amherst saying that "nobody in the whole life of America made a line like 'If Immortality unveil / A third event to me.' " And what did he mean by that? He's gone. He's not there any more. But he said: "None of you folks can write like this: 'If Immortality unveil / A third event to me.' " The beauty of that, it occurs to me, is that she said, "My life closed twice before its close; / It yet remains to see." Now she doesn't say "death" in there. It's the way—it's the curious use, the brilliant use of, the high poetic use of the word *immortality*. I agree to that. That's very high. Then the last two lines—"Parting is all we know of heaven, / And all we need of hell"— are wonderful epigrams. But

11. Emily Dickinson's niece was Martha Dickinson Bianchi, and her brother Austin's mistress was Mable Loomis Todd.

12. The daughter of Austin's mistress, living in Washington, is Millicent Todd Bingham.

13. Emily Dickinson, *Complete Poems*, ed. Thomas H. Johnson (Boston: Little, Brown and Co., 1900), p. 702 (# 1732, "My life closed twice before its close"). I have corrected Frost's presentation against Johnson's definitive reading of the poem.

did you ever notice as you said it that parting is all we know of heaven? What do you know of heaven? You only know that some people go there. She means *knows*. "And all we *need* of hell." That's another word, you see. She doesn't say "know" of hell; she says "need." Wonderful that "need" in there. Sometimes you get a thing like that in your head and it dawns on you. You don't want somebody to tell you about it.

Somebody said: "Don't you think you need any note about anything?" Any note is a hell of a note. [*Laughter*] No! I don't want to be too sweeping. Here's the top of all poetry, you see. He [Emerson] made an anthology. Henry Dana made an anthology.[14] Goldsmith made an anthology.[15] Did you ever see it? There've been anthologizing right down. Taking the top of poetry—interesting—there isn't anything in any of them that needs a note when you get up to that height of poetry. There is a poem that begins: "The glories of our blood and state / Are shadows, not substantial things." Now at the head of that it says in the Palgrave, if I remember rightly—haven't looked in that for many years—"Death the Leveller." It's only occurred to me lately that that name might not have been on the poem at all—in Shirley's play. Palgrave just added that—a smart addition. I got a little suspicious about that title. It comes from thinking and knowing a lot about levelers.[16]

Q. Would you comment on T. S. Eliot in this respect [i.e., with reference to the use of footnotes]?[17]

A. Before, during, and after [the poem]. Well, I don't think he thinks you would need [footnotes]. He hasn't met you; he doesn't know what you're up to, see; he's used to a lot of people who talk Sanskrit. [*Laughter*] He isn't putting on any airs; he isn't high-hatting us or anything—just the way he's got educated by scribes and pharisees. It's carried him a little off there, and then come and see us in a democratic world [where we are] all asking him to please let us into his meaning. That's what we go to college for, [to] say: "Please, Mr. Eliot, let us in on this, and if you haven't time some of your friends will do it for you."

Q. Here is another Eliot question. Do you agree with Eliot's proposition that poetry in a complex civilization must necessarily be com-

14. Does Frost mean Charles Anderson Dana, city editor of the *New York Tribune*, who compiled *The Household Book of Poetry* (1857)?

15. Oliver Goldsmith (1728–74), *Beauties of English Poesy* (1766?).

16. Frost was accurate in the title Palgrave gave James Shirley's poem.

17. T. S. Eliot, *Collected Poems* (New York: Harcourt, Brace and Co., 1936); see "Notes on *The Waste Land*," pp. 91-98. The tone of Frost's comment was, of course, ironic and the audience responded accordingly.

plex and be involved to express that civilization?

A. You know, they used to tell us back in Dreiser's day, speaking of novels—I've read a few of them—that in a confused age the most representative art would be a confused artist. And it's very dangerous, that doctrine is, because a very brilliant person can think he's got to talk confused and, frankly, say, you know, [a] tale told by an idiot. Write it out—a title: "All storm and noise"—then add, "signifying nothing." Why not? Don't want it to signify. Is there anything more tiresome than sense? [*Ironic tone of voice*] We get so tired of meaning. I want something that hasn't any meaning; I'm sick of meaning. It's like a disease, that is; could be a disease like that, in time, decadence. Sure. There may be some happiness for some to give way to it; say, just let us revel in no meaning at all, storm and noise, tale told by an idiot, signifying nothing. If it signified anything I'd be sorry. And I might for one hour, you know, one day, lend myself [to it]. That's the gift you've got to have in this world. That's the gift to the liberal—being able to lend himself for the duration of the peace to almost any nonsense.

Now look, speaking of Dreiser—I want somebody else—I want Mirabeau. See, Mirabeau had a doctrine of hostility toward all society that Dreiser spoke [of] once in a speech [I] read when I was in Indiana. That's how I happened to notice it once. He [Dreiser] came down to where Dillinger lay buried—Dillinger was a killer—and laid a wreath on his grave, and he said that [it] was for this reason. He said: If you're going to hate society and all of it, hate it. The boys who've gone to college and have got words to do it with, let them talk. And a poor boy who hasn't been to college, let him shoot. And Mirabeau said almost the same thing: that in order to be a real revolutionary he had to go live with criminals awhile so he'd learn disrespect and contempt of all laws and order. That's in his history.[18] Ah, you can listen to that. Sure. I can see how I might feel that way for a few minutes, a little while.

And how far down will you go in this thing? How far will you go into disorder, into chaos? Out of chaos we rise to those points. You rise to insight, to points; and then there are moods. One of the relaxations must be back into chaos. Call it relaxation; that's all right. That's just me talking. I'm only entertaining you. I said recently I was going to come up and make good on this one sentence. I don't know what I'm going to talk about down in Brazil.[19] Somebody just

18. Comte de Mirabeau, *Histoire secrète de la cour de Berlin* (1789).

19. Frost was appointed a delegate to the World Congress of Writers at São Paulo, Brazil by the U.S. Department of State. He was in attendance from August 4 to August 19, 1954.

sent me a little book that shows me that all those movements that we talk about here or in Paris or anywhere swept the whole civilized world. I won't need anything different down there. The names are strange to me—the writers' names—but I'll see somebody down there that's called a sculptor because he's bent a wire a queer way. That'll probably be one of the first things [I'll see]. I hope the wire will be thick enough so I'll see it. [*Sarcastic tone*]

Q. Here is a related question. What do you think of the trend of modern, that is to say, contemporary poetry written by poets born after 1910? Is it getting more complex or less? Does this cut into feeling, into emotion? Is the intellect riding over the emotion, I suppose is meant by the question.

A. A poem is a thought-felt thing, isn't it? You can make a hyphenated word out of it: a thought-felt thing, and I don't know about the balance of it. More wildness, you know; the wildness comes, must be something wild [in it]. We know about all that. It's got to come to something—the wildness. It isn't so wild that you're nowhere or you're back to chaos. Oh, that's all right. Sure, a little chaos goes a long way with me. I've lived all through this thing. I remember the first of all [of] it coming along—Sorel's book on violence, and Marinetti coming up from Italy to talk.[20] Marinetti said that "the day is done of all argument but the blow in the face." That's a good saying. Hit them again, hit them again, rip, slap, set them up again right in the middle of a two-cent pie. That's all right. It's part of it; it's off to one side—short distance down. It isn't where the things [are] mainly going. We're going right after meaning and point and more, and always after it, catching it, and happy when we catch [it] and less happy when we lose it; that's all—and a part of the battle. Just the same as good and evil. We have bad days and good days. We have all that.

Look, this is what I said [I would like] to make good in: "Our object [as poets or novelists] is to entertain you by making play (have to look out for that), by making play with things we trust you already know." Now the emphasis is on "making play." No! I'm going to make the emphasis right in the beginning. Who are we that we should talk about our object? Well, we are troubadours. Somebody said that to me yesterday. Said there'd never be such a troubadourlike time as there is right now in America with all you fellows [poets] barding around. And there's something to that. And a good excuse. Our object is to entertain you. Now the word *entertain* becomes the

20. Georges Sorel, *Reflections on Violence* (New York: P. Smith, 1941). Emilio Marinetti (1876–1944), founder of the Futurist movement in 1911, joined the Fascist party in 1919.

difficulty. Monkeyshines? Flippancy? Frivolity? No. By making play! The word metaphor comes right in there that will test your agility, your knowledge—way up high! "With things we trust you already know." That's the least part of it. "We trust you already know." We do it on a percentage basis. There will be some of it you don't know.

Take farming in the day of Keats. I saw some early primitive farming when I was younger. But, of course, I never saw a threshing floor [in use]. I've seen the floor and I've seen the flail, but I have never seen the flail in use. But what do I do about that? The poet for my information says—he addresses Autumn—"To Autumn":

> Who hath not seen thee oft amid thy store?
> Sometimes whoever seeks abroad may find
> Thee sitting careless on a granary floor,
> Thy hair soft-lifted by the winnowing wind;

He's [the poet's] talking about the wind that doesn't winnow her hair. I know that very well because her hair doesn't need winnowing. But he means the winnowing-wind—the wind that has just been used to winnow the wheat.

> Thy hair soft-lifted by the winnowing wind;
> Or on a half-reap'd furrow sound asleep,
> Drows'd with the fume of poppies, while thy hook
> Spares the next swath and all its twined flowers.

See, this is another picture. In the first one she's sitting on a granary floor with the wind going through her hair. Am I getting information out of this? What am I getting out of it? Somebody will say: don't you need notes on that?—"Thy hair soft-lifted by the winnowing wind." Didn't you get this without notes, without my saying anything?

> Or on a half-reap'd furrow sound asleep,
> Drows'd with the fume of poppies, while thy hook
> Spares the next swath and all its twined flowers.
> And sometimes like a gleaner thou dost keep
> Steady thy laden head across a brook;
> Or by a cyder-press, with patient look,
> Thy watchest the last oozings hours by hours.

See, there are four Burne-Jones pictures there. Pre-Raphaelite pictures. They're stock-in-trade for all the Pre-Raphaelites right in those four pictures there. Hear me saying that. I'm saying that for fun. You go write that in the next examination. But look at it.

61

There's not a thing there [except what we know]. I have pressed some cider a little. I've been at a cider mill and watched the last oozings hour by hour. I happen to know that in the old world the poppies are in the wheat—the flowers in [the] wheat—very beautiful, but they're really like the mustard in the wheat over here that makes them burn up. [They] throw a whole harvest away if there's more than a certain amount of it [mustard]. All that's in there. Enough of information.

Somebody said [to me], "You're too contemptuous of what anyone can learn from a poem." Yeh! I expect you to come to the poem with enough knowledge to get the poem. You'll pick up a little extra. I don't want to be too contemptuous about it. But if I've got to be told—take a little scrap like, let us see—

> I strove with none; for none was worth my strife.
> Nature I loved, and, next to Nature, Art;
> I warmed both hands before the fire of life;
> It sinks, and I am ready to depart.[21]

That's one of the richest lines anywhere. Just the very richness beats anything in the Greek anthology. But look at it. Look at the items in it. Anything there that you aren't prepared to handle? "I strove with none; for none was worth my strife." President Wilson got a whole doctrine out of that. [22] [He was] going to keep us out of war because nobody was worth fighting. Didn't keep us out, but he used it a lot. Too proud to fight. "I strove with none; for none was worth my strife. / Nature I loved, and, next to Nature, Art." Here was one of the most artful men; he put nature first—a little observation like that. They [Whitehead] say we can't have any more. "Nature I loved, and, next to Nature, Art." And then, the little simple metaphor, "I warmed both hands before the fire of life." And that's a pretty one. "It sinks, and I am ready to depart." And what information did you need to have for that? I'll tell you some information about it. It always amuses me when he says, "I strove with none; for none was worth my strife." He was a very quarrelsome man, and this is "information, please." Once his gardener offended him, and he threw the gardener out the window and rushed to the window to see

21. Walter Savage Landor, "On His Seventy-fifth Birthday."
22. Woodrow Wilson believed in "neutrality in thought and deed," but one summer morning in 1915 when Colonel House, Wilson's confidential adviser, stepped out on a London street he saw a newspaper headline that read: "Wilson too proud to fight." See John Dos Passos, *Mr. Wilson's War* (New York: Doubleday and Co., 1962), p. 135.

if he'd fallen into the violet bed. That's why he didn't fight with anybody—even the gardener. This sort of spoils the poem. All right, any more [questions]?

Q. Somebody would like to know if you would be willing to comment on Gerard Manley Hopkins.

A. Yes, somebody want to recite one of his poems for me? [*Mischievously*] There's not much to say. A very fine poet, and one of our poets. There'll always be some of him in the anthology, speaking of him that way—[in] the English anthology. His difficulty for me is not in any obscurity. His difficulty for me is the slight hysteric sound some of it has—too throaty. I think Thoreau says somewhere that all poetry is a feminine thing but at its best in men. That's a good one. That's a little bit too feminine for me—a little—too throaty. That would bar some of it from me, but, of course, everybody has the defect of his virtues, as they used to say in France.

Q. Mr. Frost, you wrote a nice piece about a poem of Emerson's recently, and it occurred to me when you were talking about the need of footnoting that maybe you would have got that poem about thirty years sooner if you'd had a footnote to help you out at the start.[23]

A. Yes, what would I have gained by getting it thirty years earlier? [*Laughter*] That's what I thought somebody might say. What's the all-fired rush? Let it ripen. Let it happen to me in its slow way. He's referring to my having told about running on to Emerson. Speaking of Emerson and Thoreau again, I talked on the BBC the other day and it amused me to say that Thoreau wasn't so much interested in liberty in a big *L* or freedom in a big *F* as in the liberties he took. Doc and I gave the talk together on the BBC and we mentioned the loon on the lake. I remarked that I wished we had time to read it into the interview.[24]

Q. Are there some other questions?

Q. Would you express an opinion about your own clear line and the clear line in Hemingway as you find it in *The Old Man and the Sea?* Clear line—clear short line—a living line.

A. I don't know; I hope so. Emerson said that these sentences

23. The reference was to the foreword, entitled "The Prerequisites," in *Aforesaid* (New York: Henry Holt and Co., 1951), which also appeared in the *New York Times Book Section*, March 21, 1954.

24. Discussion on Thoreau, tape recorded at Ripton and broadcast by BBC on July 16, 1954, to commemorate the centennial of the publication of Thoreau's *Walden.* The text appeared in the *Listener*, August 26, 1954.

bleed when you cut them.[25] That was a good sentence to say, wasn't it? He was always [doing it]—every single sentence. Interesting thing about him—and his living line: it is as if many of us had been influenced by Emerson, not by his thinking, you know, [not] in his transcendentalism especially, but in just that way, in the line, you know. The lines all look the same lengths—funny thing—and they're all said differently. I remember talking that over with John Erskine forty years ago.[26] How monotonous they look to the eye, but how various they are when you say them aloud, and think them. [Take a] little line like "Give all to love." You've got to say that just a certain way—"Give all to love." Begins the poem. Some people begin with a dead statement to get started, and some get dramatic instantly. Always dramatic; always alive.

Interesting thing about Thoreau: Thoreau said that prose was better than poetry.[27] So few dare to say it. He thought it was—had a wider compass. Got more in it. I don't agree with that, but he said that, you know. It might have been sour grapes to him. He couldn't write poetry very well. But other times he talked rather large about poetry. I think he thought poetry in prose was better than poetry in verse. That's what he meant—he couldn't write poetry. It's very second-rate. He read poetry; he knew poetry. One of his limitations—looking back over him—I found him praising Ossian along with Chaucer.[28] Isn't that a terrible error? Could you do worse than that? It makes you forgive yourself for any errors you ever made.

Q. Could we come back a minute to that remark you made about the two books—*Walden* and *Robinson Crusoe*? You said once—I think

25. Of Montaigne's writing, Emerson said: "Cut these words and they would bleed; they are vascular and alive; they walk and run." *Journals*, June 24, 1840.

26. John Erskine (1879–1951), professor in the English department at Columbia University from 1909 until 1937 and author of many books, including the popular *The Private Life of Helen of Troy* (1925).

27. "Great prose, of equal elevation, commands our respect more than great verse," wrote Thoreau in *A Week on the Concord and Merrimack Rivers* (1849), "since it implies a more permanent and level height, a life more pervaded with the grandeur of the thought. The poet often only makes an irruption, like a Parthian, and is off, again, shooting while he retreats; but the prose writer has conquered like a Roman, and settled colonies." *The Writings of Thoreau* (New York: Modern Library, 1937), p. 421.

28. "The genuine remains of Ossian . . . though of less fame and extent, are, in many respects, of the same stamp with the *Iliad* itself." Thoreau, *A Week on the Concord and Merrimack Rivers* (New York: Rinehart, 1963), p. 291.

it was you who said it—that the thing that pulled those two books together was the idea of making yourself snug in the infinite.[29]

A. In the world. It's almost as if they were both metaphors for that.

Q. How about that as a theme in your own poetry?

A. Well, I wonder; never thought of that. This time on the BBC I put three books together. I said—rather wantonly, the way I do things—I said, *Robinson Crusoe*, *Walden*, and *The Voyage of the "Beagle"*—another dandy. When these people who think they're making a list of the hundred best books make a list, they put in Darwin's *On the Origin of Species*. This other one—*Voyage of the "Beagle"*—this is where he thought of it [*On the Origin of Species*]—on that enterprise.[30] That's the beauty of it. A beautiful story—people and things and animals and observations, great world travel. It's one of the wonder books. I set those three on a special shelf of mine. The thing that comes oftenest into my mind [in *Walden*] is the loon, and the Canadian woodchopper that ate woodchucks.

The question is: When you've got somebody like that to imitate, what will you imitate him in? Will you go and live by Walden Pond? You can't; there's too much of a crowd there now. What will you do—to be [like] unto him? Some people think you have to go somewhere and hunt loons. And it's very like the imitation of all the great—Christ or anybody—imitation of Christ—what will you do in the imitation of Christ? What will be an imitation? It's interesting to think. He was a very brave man. You've got to be brave; you've got to be independent; you've got to be cranky like him. He was a little cranky. Got to think that out for yourself.

Q. Do you agree with Shelley that the poets are the unacknowledged legislators of the world?[31]

A. "We are the music makers." And "We are the dreamers of dreams"—world forsaken—and so on.[32] No! That's a pretty thing to

29. In the list of favorite books compiled for the Massachusetts Library Association published in *Books We Like* (Boston, 1936), pp. 141-42, Frost wrote of *Robinson Crusoe*: "I never tire of being shown how the limited can make snug in the limitless." See Lawrance Thompson, *Robert Frost: The Early Years, 1874–1915* (New York: Holt, Rinehart and Winston, 1966), p. 549.

30. It was while on the surveying voyages of H.M.S. *Beagle* between 1831 and 1836 that Darwin made the observations which later led to the famous evolutionary theory published in *On the Origin of Species* (1859).

31. Percy Bysshe Shelley, *A Defence of Poetry* (1824), "Poets are the unacknowledged legislators of the world."

32. Arthur O'Shaughnessy, "Ode."

say; I like that. All these things are pretty things to say. Doc [Cook] was saying he'd been out to walk this afternoon, and I said, "Did you have anybody with you?" And he said, "No!" That's why I call him a Thorosian. Thoreau said once, "I have no walks to waste on company." That's a dandy. What's the finality in anything? Are these definitive, they say, when they write somebody's life—only to have it written again by the next generation. Definitive. That's a funny word. Definitive life of Christ, for instance. No, Shelley.

Did you ever notice—a little observation like this—speaking of Shelley. He's always talking about delight. "Rarely, rarely comest thou / Spirit of Delight!"[33] And then he says—there's a poem that goes "O World! O life! O time! / On whose last steps I climb, / Trembling at that where I had stood before." That's what I was thinking of—"Trembling at that where I had stood before." How many years I had known that poem before that struck in. "Trembling at that where I had stood before." Never mind the rest of the poem. And then he uses *delight*—the word *delight*—in there.

> When will return the glory of your prime?
> No more—Oh, never more!
>
> Out of the day and night
> A joy has taken flight;
> Fresh spring, and summer, and winter hoar,
> Move my faint heart with grief, but with delight
> No more—Oh, never more!

You'd think he was a hundred years old, wouldn't you? Very fine poem. But you'd think he was a hundred years old—"No more—Oh, never more!" He was in the twenties when he was talking that way, and he's always saying "come soon, come soon." Always waiting for that moment that makes poems. He is the kind of person who raises the question for you about love and inspiration and the trueness of inspiration. Can you feign inspiration? Can you feign love? Why can't you? He raises the question. He didn't pretend. . . .

Q. Here's a very personal question. You mentioned that poetry must contain a certain amount of defined knowledge beforehand. Is not feeling or emotion the essence of poetry?

A. Oh, yes! That's what I've been saying—that's the knowledge so assumed—see, the general knowledge is so assumed—that I don't want to talk about it. I don't want it in notes. I assume you've been to college. Do you know the difference between the graduate school

33. Shelley, "A Lament."

66

and the college? It lies right there. You're getting trained in the graduate school; it's a training in scholarship. That's a training for a profession. And then the other; there must be no suspicion of training at all. It must be a spreading of this kind of general knowledge that makes you so you can handle the poetry of the world without straining yourself. The knowledge shouldn't be the strain; the strain is how you catch it. I talk[ed] about it the other night. When I don't catch it, when I don't get the joke in a joke, you know, the picture in a picture, the point in a poem, I'm always cast down. If anyone has to tell me, if anyone is right there threatening to tell me, I say, "Don't tell me; let me alone; give me a chance to see what good I am." And the whole of these—the top of it—is kept that way—pure. Palgrave didn't put any notes in his book.[34] And Tennyson didn't with his —oh dear, [it's] the whole question of training.

The old college in the last century, as I was saying, was nothing. It was pre-pulpit. Now some of the colleges are pre-med; and I heard a girl say, the one she went to was pre-wed. There's a lot to pre- to it. What I complain of is so much of the college education is pre-grad school. The minute training creeps into it, you've got to watch it; you're not being trained. This is the very thing you're getting ready for, so you can take the poetry. And all you have to show in it is that you've had the experience of poetry, you've lived with poetry, and you're good at getting the ideas. You've seen others who have beat you at it, and it makes you so jealous you tried to catch up.

I told an amusing one. Irwin Edman down in New York, when I was in a crowd a little while ago down there, came up to me and said to me in the crowd: "I tell Robert that good fences make good burglars."[35] I was disturbed; I wasn't my best self. I said: "Oh, Irwin means that what makes crime is law. Some people think that bad stuff. If there were no laws there wouldn't be any crime. Of course not." He went away, and pretty soon he came back and said: "I tell Robert, good fences make good burglars." He wasn't satisfied with what I said: "Oh, get along with that immorality." And you know it was away into the night before I saw what he meant. And wasn't I sick of myself when I saw how slow I was to get that? And yet, the words are perfectly good words. I had all the material. I knew what a fence is and how he handles stolen goods for robbers, and I didn't catch it. I nearly committed suicide.

34. Palgrave, *The Golden Treasury*.
35. Irwin Edman (1896–1954), a professor of philosophy at Columbia University.

If I had any excuse, you see, for not having the material, but I didn't have an excuse. "Trembling at that where I had stood before." Well, anybody who's climbed mountains, you know, at the top looks back at places where he was. It's all right. You might miss. And if you do miss something and see it years later—all right! You're missing some, of course. Take Keats again:

> No stir of air was there,
> Not so much life as on a summer's day
> Robs not one light seed from the feather'd grass,
> But where the dead leaf fell, there did it rest.
> A stream went voiceless by, still deaden'd more
> By reason of his fallen divinity
> Spreading a shade: the Naiad 'mid her reeds
> Press'd her cold finger closer to her lips.[36]

See, that's just taking a little observation out of a little spot in the opening of "Hyperion." Then he said, "the chill." He gives the chill in that one, you know. Fancy sitting there. Then he says, "the Naiad 'mid her reeds / Press'd her cold finger closer to her lips." Dandy! He's [Keats] full of it.

Funny thing about Masefield, you know. There's much of that in Masefield—only so much careless writing and sloppy stuff, too. But there's always that very Keatsian line in some of the poems. I'm not condescending toward him. But that's his difficulty—that he's careless; anyway to get the rhyme; slops his way along sometimes.

> Oh some that's good and godly ones they hold that it's a sin
> To troll the jolly bowl around and let the dollars spin;
> But I'm for toleration and for drinking at the inn,
>   Says the old bold mate of Henry Morgan.[37]

Don't you wish you'd written that? What does it in there? The magic word is the strange word "toleration" in that fellow talking. The rhyme "toleration and drinking at the inn, / Says the old bold mate of Henry Morgan." That's one of the best poems he ever wrote, but there are two or three stanzas in it you could dispense with. They're carelessly made; they aren't as good as that.

Q. Here's one [a question] that's relevant. You say it's the poet's duty to make play with things we trust you already know. Is this why poetry must be taught to high school students?

36. John Keats, "Hyperion," 1: 7-14.
37. John Masefield, "Captain Stratton's Fancy."

A. No.

Q. Because they know so little?

A. No! No, they ought to be increasing their knowledge, not using the poetry to get the knowledge out of it. No! Right there. A-way back. "A wet sheet and a flowing sea," and "A wind that follows fast."[38] There are endless fine poems in the anthologies that you don't have to use for knowledge at all, just for the entertainment of poetry. And the higher the play, the lower the play, down in the ballads, anywhere the range, to increase their range by first the poems and then the knowledge is in all sorts of ways—geography, history, philosophy, economics, sociology, all that stuff.

Q. Keats could get them all wrong, couldn't he, in "stout Cortez"?[39]

A. Yes, that wouldn't matter. I always felt sorry for Balboa.[40] Poor Balboa. Too bad to treat him badly in a sonnet, because he got hanged, anyway, to add to his troubles. Do you know he was hanged? Sad, ain't it? Hanged! Someone of those—the discoverer of the Pacific Ocean was hanged—discoverer of the Pacific Ocean.

No, the knowledge part of it is very general. Pick up some, for instance. I often think I learn how to pronounce the word from the way it occurs in the poem. The accent—you've got to look out for that because sometimes the poet didn't know how to pronounce it himself. Meter's taught me a lot of pronunciation; the rhymes, also. Again, you've got to look out for those. A century or two ago they were pronouncing the word in English the same as they do in Ireland now. That mixes you up. But the knowledge is very incidental.

If I wanted the knowledge, we've got two great magazines in the United States. I don't take either of them. One of them is the *New Yorker*, and I don't like it very well because of the terrible advertisements in it. If they were only out. But it is our one literary magazine. The others are so overloaded with economics and sociology and politics and everything. I don't count them any more. And then the other is *Scientific American*. That's a beautiful magazine—and beautifully written and beautifully edited. And there's one of the great places for information. 'Cause you get it in gossip and every way. Some we pick up from poems; for instance, does it startle you to hear "Spares the next swath and all its twined flowers"? I wonder how

38. Allan Cunningham (1784–1842), "A Wet Sheet and a Flowing Sea," stanza 1.

39. Keats, "On First Looking into Chapman's Homer."

40. Vasco de Balboa (ca. 1475–1519) was arrested by Pedrarias Dávila, governor of the Colony of the Isthmus of Panama, on the charge of treason against the king and beheaded.

much our younger people will take that—"while thy hook / Spares the next swath and all its twined flowers, / And sometimes like a gleaner thou dost keep / Steady thy laden head across a brook." Evidently it's a real hook, not the big scythe she falls asleep over, "Drows'd with the fume of poppies." That's stretching it a little. Does the fume of poppies put you to sleep? No, but opium will and opium comes from poppies. Encyclopedia. So you know a lot of things.

Socrates says that you can only know things in two ways in the *Ion*. He says, either by experiencing them—doing them—or by inspiration.[41] And he leaves out what I call common knowledge. Newspapers, gossip, and everything else, he leaves all that out. That's the way you get most of it—out of what you call current knowledge. Everybody's talking, everybody's writing editorials, everybody's reading. Pick up a lot. I almost know about the H-bomb now. Too late to do any good about it. No, that's one of these things. I don't settle it. I'm talking my own way, more or less for your entertainment tonight. There's nothing so entertaining as each other's attitudes. There's nothing so composing as composition.

Q. Here's a stumper. Would you please say "Directive" as an example of traits you discussed in 1952? It's a memory question.

A. I don't know "Directive." And I haven't got it with me.

Q. And someone asks for "The Witch of Coös."

A. I didn't bring my book with me. I don't believe I can say "The Witch of Coös." I can almost say it, long as it is, but I wouldn't trust myself. I've read it a number of times.

Q. Would you speak about traits?[42] Concrete language?

A. I don't know what I could have said about [traits].

Q. The use of words like *lovely* and *beautiful*.

A. I probably said it speaking of *beauty*, boasting that I never allowed myself the use of it [beauty] more than two or three times in a lifetime. It's the same story with *love*. I've never used *glamor* in a lifetime. Very economical I am. I heard a funny story about that the other day. Tell anyone it's funny and they're sure to be let down. Make it funny. I always wonder at a person writing who describes a remarkable character and keeps calling him remarkable and witty and all this in a book, you know, and never gives you a real example of anything he ever said. Very easy to get out of it that way. Just say

41. Plato, *Ion*. But Socrates stresses inspiration: "For all good poets, epic as well as lyric, compose their beautiful poems not by art, but because they are inspired and possessed."

42. On July 28, 1952, Frost had said: "If you want to be a writer, never exclaim. I have never used the words *beautiful, lovely, wonderful, marvelous, glamorous*."

"remarkable—remarkable—remarkable." I don't know just what you mean by traits. What are they?

Q. Would Mr. Frost comment on Tolstoy's reference to Shakespeare as a third-rate writer?

A. It [Ossian] was the dullest stuff ever written. I suppose it had some foundation, but it's been long since exploded. And Thoreau came at a time when everybody was saying, "Have you read Ossian?" That's the way you get in the time you are living. Have you read something?—and you pretend that you have. You ought not to pretend—you never feign emotion. Robert Louis Stevenson said that's the greatest crime of all—feigning emotion. That's one of those questions—you just expect Tolstoy to say that. He was lost in his intensities. No humor at all. Nothing to save his soul with. [In] Chaucer and Shakespeare you see right away the breadth of it—just the opposite of what Thoreau said: that there was something narrowing about humor. It's broadening. Funny thing, both of these are in it, but sometimes I doubt I've known what that means. I think some of the great saints, people, martyrs—I wonder what Charles I was doing there when he tried the ax's edge, whether he was rising above the situation. I don't believe he was. "Nothing common or mean upon that memorable scene."[43]

I'm not decisive about that any more, but the sense of humor might spoil a saint. Did you ever notice in the last fifty or hundred years there've been attempts made to give Christ a sense of humor? And somebody has written about him as a backslapper. Rotarian. Can't do that, can you? There's no glimmer of humor in it. Not a glimmer. All another sort of thing; all noble. That's all right. I'm not saying which, but there you are. You get these people with a kind of high, saintly, passionate way of taking life. I saw a Spaniard like that—I've seen glimpses of him—I won't name him—he's reckoned a very great poet in Spain.[44] He's had to live out of Spain a long time—very handsome, dark person and understanding English well, and nothing but a sustained gloom, perfectly sustained—pale, pale features, black hair, very striking—but at least if you make play with anything and you leave him out of it, that's all, he might even understand it enough to disapprove of it but I doubt it. Reckoned a very great man, down—I've heard—in Spanish America—and in Spain. And he can go home now; things have eased off. But in

43. Andrew Marvell of King Charles I, "Horatian Ode upon Cromwell's Return from Ireland" (1650): "He nothing common did or mean / Upon that memorable scene."

44. Probably Juan Ramón Jiminez (1881–1958), a Spanish poet, Nobel Prize winner for literature in 1956.

Buenos Aires there was more. I've heard that he was received with more noise and ticker tape than Lindbergh was in New York. We don't know him that way. He lived a long time in Washington—in and out. Guess he taught a little while and lectured some little while at Maryland, the University of Maryland. Very fine person.

But there are those two things: Chaucer—just look at him—I notice they're quoting this speech about our life and our ideas. It comes to you this way—some of the traits, if that's what you mean —like honor. You know that simple poem:

> So strength first made a way,
> Then beauty flow'd, then wisdom, honour, pleasure.[45]

You might linger over those [lines] to wonder why he put them [in that order]. He made strength first. God gave us gifts: first he gave us strength, then he gave us beauty, then he gave us wisdom, then he gave us honor, then he gave us pleasure. Are these intended? Is that an intentional order? I'll have to think about that. Those are all things that haven't anything to do with society, utopia. Honor. Can you idealize ideality—satisfy it, see, in those personal things—or has it got to get up and make a better world?

Those are the two idealisms. I understand Faulkner favors the first—not the better world but the honor and all that, bravery and honor and glory. [46] That I go with in all my heart, all my days. Glory, bravery, honor. People, some people, make fun of it. Tom Paine made fun of people bowing courteously to each other—and then shot each other dead. He thinks that's terrible. He didn't know what honor was. He was no gentleman. That's what Gouverneur Morris thought, anyway. But he [Paine] didn't know about that. I had a friend who died in the First World War—a poet, he went out to die—left his family and all that, children and all, and went out to die.[47] Said to me: "I can stand it or fall if there is no blackguarding." You don't have to blackguard the Germans. Some, he said, can't fight unless they blackguard the other fellow. I always treasured that memory that he knew that—died without blackguarding the Ger-

45. George Herbert, "The Pulley."

46. William Faulkner, in the Nobel address delivered in Stockholm on December 10, 1950, spoke for "the old verities and truths of the heart, the old universal truths lacking which any story is ephemeral and doomed —love and honor and pity and pride and compassion and sacrifice."

47. Edward Thomas (1878–1917), a warm friend whom he met while living at Little Iddens in the Dymock region of Gloucestershire, England, and who was killed in World War I on Easter Monday, April 9, 1917, at Vimy

mans. All right, have we had enough of me?

Q. Are there any other questions?

A. [*Quotes George Herbert's "The Pulley"*]

> When God at first made man,
> Having a glass of blessings standing by—
> "Let us," said He, "pour on him all we can;
> Let the world's riches, which dispersèd lie,
>   Contract into a span."
>
> So strength first made a way,
> Then beauty flow'd, then wisdom, honour, pleasure:
> When almost all was out, God made a stay,
> Perceiving that, alone of all His treasure,
>   Rest in the bottom lay.
>
> "For if I should," said He,
> "Bestow this jewel also on my creature,
> He would adore my gifts instead of Me,
> And rest in Nature, not the God of Nature:
>   So both should losers be.
>
> "Yet let him keep the rest,
> But keep them with repining restlessness;
> Let him be rich and weary, that at least,
> If goodness bring him not, yet weariness
>   May toss him to my breast."

I got one word in there wrong, didn't I? Do you know which one? "Goodness bring" [should be "lead him not"]. That's the idea. Pretty little thing, isn't it? Is there any novelty in it? No! What's the charm of it—the form of it? That it's a whole statement of religion—the whole story? Just a pretty idea—"a glass of blessings standing by" and all that? It's a very religious poem, and also it's very deep, you know. First, strength led the way—the basis of it all. That was the great gift—strength. May be many kinds of strength—spiritual; then beauty and wisdom, honor, pleasure. "Yet let him keep the

---

Ridge. See "To E.T." in *The Poetry of Robert Frost,* ed. Edward Connery Lathem (New York: Holt, Rinehart and Winston, 1969). Frost said "The Road Not Taken" was written about himself and Edward Thomas. Thomas rented a cottage for August 1914 next door to Frost, near Wilfred W. Gibson at the Old Nailshop out of Dymock and Lascelles Abercrombie at the Gallows in the nearby village of Ryton.

rest, / But keep them with repining restlessness." That's the formula for many novels: "keep them with repining restlessness"! That's the stress they talk about. I'm getting weary of that. Sometimes you wonder about what the sense of original sin is—"repining restlessness." If you were a good Buddhist I wouldn't believe there was any such thing as original sin. All you have to do is move over into that religion and you're out of that bother.

CHAPTER 8
On Taking Poetry
June 30, 1955

This talk of Frost's, like so many of the others given at the English School, did not have a specific title. But from the context it is apparent that Frost was thinking again of how he wanted an audience of teachers to respond to his poems and communicate them to others. In spite of his characteristic divagating approach to his poems, he scores important points.

Wherever feasible I have annotated the talk, and, as one can well imagine, there were some difficulties, especially with an occasional phrase. For example, when Frost referred to Comus, *at first I thought he said: "We that are a purifier," which didn't make sense. The phrase was checked and Frost was actually quoting Milton's line in* Comus: *"We that are of purer fire." I have also corrected the title of Ignatius Donnelly's book in a note. Like any other mortal, Frost had to be watched closely when he quoted and made allusions. He tended to phrase them idiosyncratically.*

Frost's performance on this particular night was a good one. His voice was strong, the audience was responsive, and there were no meteorological interruptions from our strenuous, untimely thunderstorms. The indicated audience response provides a sense of the way the English School audience "took" their poet's teasing and flouting, taunting and dryly sarcastic comments.

Since Frost was interested in commenting on the poems he read this evening, I have given the full text of the talk. Poems like "To an Ancient," "Paul's Wife," and "Directive," he did not commonly read, and this added to the audience's interest and appreciative response.

I've been thinking about a good many things lately because I've been at a good many places. I have to say something wherever I go. I get into a good deal. What's been on my mind mostly of late is something that comes round, I suppose, to how people take a poem—how they take anything written—how they take a poem particularly.[1]

I suppose a poem is a kind of fooling. I've just been reading in a sermon by a great Unitarian friend of mine about "the foolishness of God"![2] The foolishness of God. God's foolish, you know, and God's fooling. And I've just been reading about the last days of Einstein, the old man, by somebody who knows his science and who knew his philosophy because he was a great philosopher among great scientists.[3] And the thing about him was that every few minutes it was a burst of laughter about something philosophical or something [about] God, relativity, or something about Newton. He got a great laugh over his little quarrel with Newton. He once said something in print, something we've seen: "Forgive me, Newton. Forgive me, Newton." Of course, if the height of everything is fooling—God's foolishness—then poetry mounts somewhere into a kind of fooling. It's something hard to get. It's what you spend a good deal of education on—just getting it right.

I thought if I came up again some evening, I'd like to talk about Puritanism—in Greek, Roman, Early Roman, New England, and Later Roman—and right out of the head, not out of my books. I'm one of these people who read some. You can see how little I depend on books for anything I do. They [his books] are in such disorder that they're very fresh to me whenever I happen on one that I've been looking for. [*Laughter*] *A Pleasant Night:*[4] I haven't seen that for twenty years. I'll have to get that down and read it. But I can't get a talk out of it. I'll just have to come up and talk off the cuff, as they say, about Puritanism and the greatest poem that it produced: *Comus.* You thought I was going to say something else, I see. Shall I say that Puritanism didn't repent, you know? It relented a little and became Unitarianism. I've found it relenting. [*Laughter*] I'll come up and talk about that.[5]

But this thing that I've brought up before here. I've quoted it, I think, in a couple of places, and it's always coming into my head: that

1. How to take a poem is certainly one of the perennial themes in Frost's talks. On May 27, 1936, he gave a talk and reading at Middlebury College on this topic and returned to it often in his talks before the students at the graduate School of English at Bread Loaf.

2. Unidentified Unitarian friend.

3. A reference to I. Bernard Cohen's "An Interview with Einstein" in one of Frost's favorite magazines, *Scientific American,* July 1955.

4. Author of *A Pleasant Night* unidentified.

5. Good as his word, he came up from his cabin on the Homer Noble farm in Ripton on the night of July 28, 1955, and talked informally for a couple of hours on Puritanism in the recreation room at the Bread Loaf Barn.

these things are said in parable so the wrong people can't understand them and so get saved. It says that twice in the New Testament.[6] It seems very harsh and undemocratic, doesn't it? Sounds esoteric. And one of my good friends went forth from my saying that to say that I was esoteric—that my thinking was esoteric. But not at all. Because it also says in the New Testament that except you become as little children, you know.[7] That meant that so professors won't understand it. It's so simple and so foolish that only little children can understand it. We try too hard—we strike too hard—that's the danger of it. Now take God's foolishness as the question. And you've got to be in an awfully easy mental state. That's the thing you acquire through the years of poetry—from *Mother Goose* on—easy does it. And you've got to know that it's being played with—it's said—as I say: I can say and you can take it a good deal your own way—that's for conversation. You don't have to contradict it. But make it a rule almost. I was saying that over at Dartmouth:[8] make it a rule, almost, never to contradict anybody. Just say: "Let them have their say and then take it your way."

That comes to this question of who has a right to do what he pleases with my poetry—the right kind of people that can take it their way. There's a good deal of sway in it. There's a certain deftness, definiteness, but it sways at its anchor. It swings at its anchor tow. And of course that's the fun of it. Of course, now I go through a good deal about that, and there's a common laugh you can get among students about the right of teachers to go on with a poem and carry it their way a little. It can be wrong; it can be utterly wrong. This matter of getting it right and wrong. That's what you grow up in, getting it right and wrong, in and out, trial and error with it—in this spirit of the thing. And there's such a thing as throwing dust in the eye, you know—a person can write so that he's insulting. He is just throwing dust in the eyes. And that's again just going a little over the edge about this play, this fooling. To tease people is all right but to insult them is going too far. It's always one of my concerns.

I'll start saying some of my poems. I thought as I came in that I ought to bring somebody else's poems. I'll bring Shelley or Milton or somebody, you know. Forever me, you know, and it's just because people want to hear the way I say them. They probably know how to say them better than I do. They just want to know out of curiosity

6. This is a key idea in *A Masque of Mercy* (1947) and is alluded to in "Directive," *The Poetry of Robert Frost*, p. 379. See Mark 4:11, 12; 7:17, 18.

7. Mark 10:15.

8. At Dartmouth College, Hanover, N.H., on June 12, 1955.

how I say them. [*Laughter*] That's all they want, some association with it.

You see, one of the great things about it all, the depth of it all, is where if you were reading aloud—it has to be something rather new. I've been a reader aloud all of my life, probably. I was at home. I was the one that did the reading aloud. And I've read in school, and then I've got to reading this way, more and more. Done a good deal of it. And the question, when reading a new thing at home [or] sitting around with anyone, is where do I have to hide it when I am having almost too hard a time with my emotions. Where do I [let] on? I never let on; I try to hide it—but [it] will move me almost to breaking in the voice. Well, it's never anything ever sad—never! It's a strange thing. You can kill all the babies you want to and it won't make me cry. And it isn't about bombs and things; nothing like that. It's always magnanimity—the heroism of magnanimity. See. Always that I can hardly keep my voice right about. Always. My own poetry of course is too much accustomed with me now. It's always something about the largeness, something about the greatness of spirit [that affects him].

I have just been thinking about Einstein a little. Just saw a very pretty thing about him that almost moved me to tears.[9] I couldn't read it to you—probably couldn't—without pretending I was not seeing the page or the light wasn't right or something like that. But it was about this. There was a book, and there are a lot of professors in this country—noted liberals—who threatened a publisher. If he didn't stop printing it, they wouldn't buy his textbooks any more. And they were noted liberals. One was a noted Red, you'd almost call him. He used to go to Moscow and come back and say they were the only people who knew how to treat a great man like him right. [*Laughter*] But he was supposed to be of the free modern world, and he led this attack on Macmillan's. He was one of the kind of people who talk about burning books. They wanted to burn that book, and old Einstein just happened to speak of it casually, you know, and he

9. In the interview referred to above in note 3, Einstein mentioned "a fairly recent and controversial book" that had received rough critical treatment from fellow scientists. Frost, considerably moved by Einstein's sympathetic statement in deference to the "charmingly crazy book," almost certainly had in mind Immanuel Velikovsky's *Worlds in Collision*, published by Macmillan in 1950. The paragraph in which Einstein referred to the suspect book prompted an exchange of letters on the rights of privacy between the executor of Einstein's estate, Otto Nathan, and me. Bernard Cohen, author of the Einstein interview. See *Scientific American*, Sept. 1955, pp. 12, 14, 16.

didn't name the book, but you could tell what it was from the description of it. He didn't name the publishing house. He didn't name the suppressors. He just said what a charmingly crazy book it was. I've got some on the shelf of my library. Just as charming as Ignatius Donnelly's *Lost Atlantis*.[10] That's another wonderful book. And the books about Shakespeare who didn't write Shakespeare. What's all this severity about back over these years? The old man Einstein made a laugh about it—that crazy book. How charming! And terrible—with passion, he said: "How terrible suppressing any book!" That's too much for me. Well, I'll leave that. But you can almost judge yourself by how deep you go into things. It's what you call compassion. But I think this is more than compassion—this magnanimity.[11]

Compassion is almost as tiresome a word critically used nowadays, as threadbare a word, as the word *escape*. "Why do children look at television?" I was reading. Why do they look at it? A scientific person in the psychology department of one of the great colleges has found out that children of the upper middle class (which doesn't exist, of course) look at movies more if they've been too much disciplined. See. This is a complicated thing. And children of the lower middle class (that doesn't exist), they look at movies a little more than children of the upper middle class, but they look at it the same whether they've been overdisciplined or not. [*Laughter*] This is what you call holy smoke. [*Laughter*] Of course the word *escape* I came on this way made me think of it. The whole question was one of escape. I talked about that in the old days. It is a long time since I've talked about escape and made it out that life was a pursuit of a pursuit of a pursuit of a pursuit.[12] You know, one person pursuing something else and he pursuing something else, and this modern psychological idea

10. Ignatius Donnelly (1836–1901), American writer and political reformer who helped found the Populist party, is the author of *Atlantis: The Antediluvian World* (1882). He argued that the lost Atlantis was the seat of the world's original civilization.

11. The ascendancy of magnanimity in Frost's thinking was given an international slant when, in September 1962, on his visit with Nikita Khrushchev in Gagra on the Black Sea, he urged upon the premier of the powerful Soviet Union his concept of "mutual magnanimity" in the "noble rivalry" between two great countries. Stewart L. Udall, secretary of the interior in the Kennedy administration, discussed the meeting of the poet and the premier in "Robert Frost's Last Adventure," *New York Times Magazine*, June 11, 1972.

12. See "Escapist-Never" in *In the Clearing* (New York: Holt, Rinehart and Winston, 1962), p. 27.

seems to be that everybody is escaping from something or somebody. So you're an escape from an escape from an escape from an escape until you get to hell. [*Laughter*] But this word *compassion—escape*—[are] rather tiresome critical words. I remember saying to a professor friend of mine fifty years ago nearly—no, forty; no, thirty—that I was sick of that word then and I don't want to hear it any more, and he said, "You're going to have to." And I have.

Well, take one of my poems to begin with, a little poem. And I'm not going to dwell on what I've been saying except for one or two poems. Suppose I say ["The Gift Outright"]: this is what I was talking about—our Revolutionary War, you know. Was it an escape or a pursuit? Pursuit of nationality—as simple as could be. Not an escape at all. One person understood it one way, one another. Tom Paine understood it as the beginning of a world revolution. That's wrong. It wasn't that; it was a pursuit of nationality. Wanting to be, feeling that we were, something. Tom Paine was one of the first to see that [and to] speak of the continent as something; something with the meaning of the land and it all. This one [poem] of mine is about the Revolutionary War. [*Reads "The Gift Outright"*]

That's a whole story of just that—the realization that we've got to belong to what belonged to us. That's all. We had a big part of it. It's as simple a statement as that. Interesting in it, too, that it's a pursuit, you know, artless, unstoried, vaguely realizing westward but still unstoried, artless, unenhanced—all to be storied and enhanced. See. A vague aspiration as much as anything that made it. Not an escape from anything. Pursuit, pursuit. And that was in the nature of the best people in it. See. Just that thing. Leave that there.

Now let's take another one. There's nothing very dubious about that one. Not much play that you can make with it in the sense of that I spoke of first. I'll say this little one. I've got to say old ones, familiar ones, to some of you, for what I've heard people make of it. [*Reads "Stopping by Woods"*]

Now, you see, the first thing about that is to take it right between the eyes just as it is, and that's the ability to do that: to take it right between the eyes like a little blow and not, you know, take it in neuter sort of. And then, you know, the next thing is your inclinations with it. I never read anything, in Latin, say, without a constant expectation of meaning that I'm either getting justified in or corrected. See. Confirmed in or corrected. I've got that going on all the time or else I'd be a dead translator. I've got to have something that's a little aggressive to it, but that's so with a poem. Right away you begin to take it your way. And you can almost say in a poem that you see in it the place where it begins to be ulterior, you know, where it goes a little with you, carries you on somewhere. And if you're very strong about it—of course, it may not be the same day. I know that's the way with me. I hear a talk like this from somebody else, see, and I may not be able to hold my own with it—not then. I think to myself that when this is over I'll get going again. [*Laughter*] My own stream-of-consciousness will get going again. I'll be all right. I'll be all right on Monday after hearing it on Sunday. Many a time I thought that. This is putting it all over but I'm still there, you know. I'll resume my thread, and no matter what's said to me I want to be sure if I differ with it a little that I know what it is that I'm differing with.

Now this little thing ["Stopping by Woods"] you see very simply as I wrote it—night, evening, snowstorm, woods, dark, late, snow falling among the alders, and trees, and with a little poetic exaggeration, you know (to see the woods fill up with snow). Did they fill up? How high? See. You want to know. Don't ask me. [*Laughter*] And I've been asked such things, you know. [*Laughter*] I've had people say —somebody who ought to know better—quote me as saying [in] that poem, "the coldest evening of the year." See. Now that's getting a thermometer into it. [*Laughter*] And "The darkest evening of the year" 's better—more poetical some way. Never mind why. I don't know. More foolish. That's where the foolishness comes in. Got to be a little foolish or a good deal foolish. But then it goes on and says "The woods are lovely, dark and deep," and then if I were reading it for somebody else, I'd begin to wonder what he's up to. See. Not what he means but what he's up to.

> The woods are lovely, dark and deep.
> But I have promises to keep,
> And miles to go before I sleep.

There are so many things that have happened, too, that way. People have come to me to ask me what were the promises [to keep], and I've joined in on that. Let them have their say, and I took it my way. I remember telling one committee that came to me about that from a college—committee of students—and I said, promises may be divided into two kinds: those that I myself make for myself and those that my ancestors made for me, known as the social contract. [*Laughter*] Now did I think of that when I wrote it? You know better. I've just got to say something. Just take it. [*Laughter*] They take it their way and I take it my way. But this is the thing I finally said about it—partly in self-defense; I said: What does it say there? "The woods are lovely, dark and deep." That's just as I might be getting along. That's all. That's the nicest way out of it—if you've got to get out of it.

Now take another old one and then I'll drop this. What's the moral of it? The aesthetic moral is: to go any poem one better, not one worse, and you just don't chew it, take it all to pieces; just get another poetic something going—one step more poetic anywhere. "We that are of purer fire." [13] You know that I'll come up to talk about it. "We that are of purer fire." The best statement of the great rout of Comus—of the anti-Puritans—the Episcopalians—is the ultimate. We sit up all night and that's the gayer way. I seem to shock 'em. Shock 'em gently. Wait until you hear me on the subject. Come up and I'll really shock you, going away back to the Greeks—Attis and all that sort of thing.[14]

Then this one. It's about walls that Doc Cook [has] been telling about. [15] It's about a spring occupation in my day. When I was farming seriously we had to set the wall up every year. You don't do that any more. You run a strand of barbed wire along it and let it go at that. We used to set the wall up. If you see a wall well set up you know it's owned by a lawyer in New York [laughter]—not a real farmer. This is just about that spring occupation, but of course all sorts of things have been done with it and I've done something with it myself in self-defense. I've gone it one better—more than once in different ways for the Ned of it—just for the foolishness of it. [Reads "Mending Wall"]

Now, you can see the first person that ever spoke to me about it was at that time becoming the president of Rollins College—making Rollins College over—and he took both my hands to tell me I had written a true international poem. [16] And just to tease him I said: "How do you get that?" You know. I said I thought I'd been fair to both sides—both national [and international]. "Oh, no," he said, "I could see what side you were on." And I said: "The more I say I the more I always mean somebody else."[Laughter] That's objectivity, I told him. That's the way we talked about it, kidding. That's where the great fooling comes in. But my latest way out of it is to say: I've got a man there; he's both [of those people but he's man—both of

13. Milton, *Comus*, line 111; thought by Scott Elledge to allude to Plato's *Timaeus* 40, where the heavenly gods are said to be created out of fire and to wheel in a dance that measures all time. See John Milton's *Complete Poems and Major Prose*, ed. Merritt Y. Hughes (New York: Odyssey Press, 1957), p. 92.

14. See above, note 5.

15. A reference was no doubt made to walls in introducing Frost.

16. Hamilton Holt (1872–1931), owner and editor of the *Independent* from 1913 to 1921. In 1925 he became president of Rollins College at Winter Park, Fla.

them, he's] a wall builder and a wall toppler. He makes boundaries and he breaks boundaries. That's man. And all human life is cellular, outside or inside. In my body every seven years I'm made out of different cells and all my cell walls have been changed. I'm cellular within and life outside is cellular. Even the Communists have cells. [*Laughter*] That's where I've arrived at that.

Now we go away from those things. That's what's going on it ["Mending Wall"]. I'm always distressed when I find somebody being ugly about it, outraging the poem, going some way, especially if it's on some theory I can see their applying to everything. See, this is a loose thing, just as my library is. I don't want it in order. I'm not organized that way. And this is a free and loose thing—the association—the beauties of the association are always something you didn't know you were going to have. If you're going to think of something, study them [the poems] out, grind them, nothing much to it. When it gets so that something doesn't come into my head that I never thought of before, you know, in connection with the emergency of the moment—the emergency of reading or talking, something I never thought of them—when I get that way I'm done. I don't want to go any more.

You sit listening to a lecture in class, and you always ought to be unhappy if it's just being put all over you. Ought to be some unhappiness in it—just that sort of mood of I'll know what to do with it before tomorrow, you know, if it crosses me up. I talked about that over at Dartmouth, about just the one little item I might mention.[17] I remember when I was very young. I didn't go into the details when I was young; my mother, I suppose, was getting somewhat distressed about evolution—not very much—she was a very faithful Christian and very assured about all that and a kind of a Presbyterian-Unitarian-Swedenborgian. [*Laughter*] And she was all right. But still it bothered her a little about evolution and it was supposed to bother me, but I got old enough to say to her one day: I don't see that this makes any difference at all. I don't know how old—in high school, it was. I said I didn't see that it made any difference at all. "Your idea was that God made man out of mud; the new idea is that God made man out of prepared mud."[18] [*Laughter*] You've still got God, you see—nothing very disturbing about it. You've got to have something to say to it—that's all—to the Sphinx. That's what the Sphinx is there for. And you don't have to do it with presence of mind. And it's nice

17. See above, note 8.
18. This is a witticism Frost never tired of repeating before the Bread Loaf audiences.

when you do—when you can sass it right back. Some of us are slower than others. I always want something a long, long time. For instance, about the tendency to smear: what [are] you going to say to smear? I don't think I ever heard the word until '32 or somewhere near that. I wasn't used to the thought of smearing. And now it's regular. So that I'm out when I ever hear anything about anybody on our side or the other side or any side; I think, "I wonder how much is smear in that," and again I'm saved from it to tears by somebody's largeness that takes that out of it, you know, gets you back to what is partly so, you know. And I've just been going through it lately, always going through it—it's the day's news to me always—somebody straightening something out that way and doing it for myself.

All right, now I've got to read to you a little and I'm superstitious to this extent. Religion is one thing, you know, and superstition is another. I always [like] to read out of my latest book a little, and that doesn't give you much hope because my latest book is just made out of my old books. [*Laughter*] But I made the selections. Let's see what I've got here. I'm going to read you one—nice light tonight, thanks be. [19] This is called "Directive." And I'll do it slow and you take it straight. But it's all full of dangers, sideways, off, and all that, you know. [*Reads "Directive"*]

Here's another little curious one beside that I see here: "To an Ancient"—ancient, ancient. [*Reads "To an Ancient"*] That's an archaeological one. Doesn't get quoted enough. Then here's one more, familiar again. [*Reads "Desert Places"*]

You see, I prefer in reading the poems ordinarily a great deal better not to go on with them into anything beyond. But that's somebody else's business. I did that just for the fun of it.

Now something else for a change. See what I've got in this little book here. [20] [*Reads "Reluctance"*] That's one of the early ones.

And another early one that I want to read to you. This is one I think I handed in in English A at Harvard. [*Laughter*] It's called "The Tuft of Flowers." And it's about this subject—another one that you get awfully tired of—the subject of togetherness. There's a word [that has] been coined—togetherness. And it turns up everywhere nowadays. As if everybody hadn't thought about that. Some people say, "You know why that crowd's in a crowd? Because they're

19. The light on the lectern at the English School Little Theatre was always a source of concern to him. Sometimes he would fidget with it, turn it off, then turn it on, or ask for the house lights to be turned on so he could see his audience.

20. *Selected Poems* (London: Penguin Books, 1955). It includes 186 poems and a preface by C. Day Lewis.

lonely." The question of loneliness: Oppenheimer seems to think he's the only person who was ever lonely because he had deep thoughts.[21] One thing I couldn't stand. This is what I was thinking about in the nineties. This is what I might be thinking about now if I were out helping in the haying. "I went to turn . . . before the sun." And I might just say that in the old days we mowed by hand a great deal—more than we do now. We do some of that now. There was always a boy or somebody—some fellow around like me—to toss the grass, open it up, let the sun at it. The mowing was apt to be done in the dew of the morning for better mowing, but it left the grass wet and had to be scattered. We called it—the word for it was "turning" the grass. I went to turn the grass once more. [*Reads "The Tuft of Flowers"*]

See. I said it both ways in the middle nineties — early in my life. I got over with that, but I get into trouble about it today. Some people think I don't believe in togetherliness. I don't like the word. Terrible about that. But then, one of the interesting things again is I keep running onto this idea of what's your pose. See. What's your pose? Who do you think you are? See. Now there's a nice way of saying that: who the hell do you think you are? [*Laughter*] That's a nicer way to say it. That just means you know you aren't so much. But when you say, what is your pose? Yeats says somewhere you have a choice of one of seven poses. Only seven poses possible—which is yours? Are you putting on airs as a don or a teacher, you know, or are you putting on airs as what—as a farmer, or as a common man, see? That's one of the horrible ones. And that kind of stuff. And what would you do if you got a choice of poses and you were afraid you weren't keeping out of the seven? What would you do? The only thing I can see is, do nothing. Commit suicide or something. Get out of it. Isn't it terrible to think that that's all it is? And I said that there. [*Quotes*] "Nor yet to draw . . . not for us . . . to flourish." These words are all in it for me, my life. Leave something to flourish, "not for us / Nor yet to draw one thought of ours to him." No self-consciousness about it. "But from sheer morning gladness at the brim." See. That's the height of it all. That's clear out of the posing: "sheer morning gladness at the brim." Butterfly and I lit upon as a poem, you know, too: "butterfly and I had lit upon, / Nevertheless, a message from the dawn." Just as if I had seen that all about poetry then; that I had thought about it all. I hadn't. Seeing it there, you

21. Reference to J. Robert Oppenheimer, American physicist, who served as director of the Institute for Advanced Study at Princeton, N.J., for many years. From 1943 to 1945 he was director of the laboratory at Santa Fé, N.M., that perfected the atomic bomb.

know about it before you know it. Let me see what time we're getting to. [*Looks at watch*]

I ought to read you one of the character ones, should I? This little book—I'm not used to. [22] Here's another. Let me see just a minute. Suppose I do "Paul's Wife." It's a lumber-camp one. And you might be interested to hear that I wrote a book called *North of Boston* and I liked the name so well—the luck of the name. [23] I got it out of the advertisements in the *Boston Globe* years and years ago. It came back to me far from the *Boston Globe*. I was away off in England, and all of a sudden I just remembered that constantly in the advertisements that I used to read with interest—and still do—this phrase "north of Boston" popped into my head—just the name. And I got a dozen poems together—a dozen or fifteen, I think it was—that hadn't been written toward that name and hadn't been written toward any particular ideas. They had been scattered among lyrics. They were blank-verse things scattered through twenty years. Then, all of a sudden, I put them together with some little dim notion of their belonging together—swept them together. They're not organic. Then I got that name on them. Just as I didn't write that toward any name or toward any idea—I refused to go on and do some more of the same kind at the time. I was asked to go on and urged to go on, by friends and by publishers, but I refused to have anything to do with it. Then I forgot myself entirely about it and now, lately, looking back I see I did it. I went on scattering some more around. And so now I'm going to have for my literary pleasure—I'm going to have a book called "North of Boston" and subtitled "Twice Over," and then put fifteen-fifteen, like two baskets, you know, on each side of the donkey. This is one of those. I went on. I never thought about it. Little more than fifteen. But I think I'll try to balance it—just have them equal weight. That'll give me a little chance to select.

One of the important ones in it is that "Directive" that I read you and also the one called "The Witch of Coös" that's too long to go into tonight. And then several—quite a number—like this. [*Reads "Paul's Wife"*]

Now, one or two little ones. I brought this little book [Penguin edition] up, and it's so much smaller print than my other ones that it's bothered me a little. I hadn't looked at it very closely. It's nice

22. *Selected Poems.*

23. In Lawrance Thompson's *Robert Frost: The Early Years*, chap. 31, entitled "England: North of Boston," is devoted to a discussion of Frost's second book of poems. On pp. 433 and 434, Thompson refers to Frost's choice among titles, but in this revealing note during his talk at the English School, Frost discloses the source of his title.

print but it's real small for my eyes. [*Reads "Acquainted with the Night"*]

You know, so many things are packed into one little place like that. "One luminary clock against the sky . . . right." That's out of years when I remember a friend of mine who constantly said from reading Henry Adams and people like that—constantly said—"the times are not right."[24] "The times are not right." No times are right. No times are otherwise than right. They're all bad. All bad; all bad.

Let's see if I can think of something else. [*Reads "Take Something Like a Star"*] [25]

I've got another new one here—a new book—very small one for a cent. Never been on the market. And I guess I'll read that and one little lyric. This one's about a dog. It's called "One More Brevity." [*Reads "One More Brevity"*]

That's that. Then I'll say one of the old ones Doc Cook asked me to say. [*Reads "Come In"*]

24. As Frost has told us before, the friend who said "the times are not right" was the Irish poet "A. E." or George Russell. The allusion to "Henry Adams and people like that" was a Frostian sarcasm.

25. "Choose Something Like a Star" was later changed by Frost to "Take Something Like a Star"; the title may be referred to either way in these pages.

CHAPTER 9
On Puritanism, Darwin, Marx, Freud, and Einstein
July 28, 1955

Frost had "threatened" his Bread Loaf School of English audience at the opening talk on June 30, 1955, that he would return later in the session and talk on Puritanism. "Wait until you hear me on the subject," he said to whet our interest. "Come up and I'll really shock you." On the evening of July 28 he came up from the Homer Noble farm, and the students sat around in the large recreation room at the Barn to hear Frost talk informally about Puritanism and anything else that interested the students. Only a few additional questions were asked. Frost did most of the talking, and he was (I think) in the rarest form I had ever seen him. Not only did he talk provocatively about Puritanism, he finally reached out and talked about some of the greatest architects of the twentieth century—Darwin, Marx, Freud, and Einstein. Ironically, when he was in the middle of the talk about those great men, the tape recorder failed us temporarily.

At these meetings in the Barn, Frost was always in a most responsive mood, and, although he made no attempt to answer the questions asked of him in any crisp or definitive way, he gave us an impressive performance, especially in the faculty of his memory to recall, and in his idiosyncratic way of thinking by connecting disparate things, and by exfoliating an idea or elaborating a thought.

Ask me anything you think you're likely to be asked about. I'll tell you. I wish you would ask me some things. A pleasant thing happens to me at Dartmouth every year. I go over there to talk in the evening and I get questions the next morning about my talk by six hundred boys, six hundred questions. Mr. Jensen knows all about it. [1] I see

1. Prof. Arthur Jensen, on the Bread Loaf School of English instructoral staff, was a professor of English at Dartmouth and, later, dean of the faculty.

him back there. I talk about religion, politics, history, Tom Paine —anything that comes into my head. And then they ask me why I write poetry. And they wonder why and I wonder why.

I noticed Einstein saying the other day, just before he died, to a friend of his—very interesting talk—he said that it was very hard to tell anybody about why he thought of anything. [2] He says somebody else could after you're dead probably tell better why you thought anything. That means something like what Dr. Johnson says about the insincerity of letter writing. You see, you'd think he [the letter writer] would get nearer anybody in his letters that he wrote in his lifetime than in any other way. Dr. Johnson said not. You're always fixing yourself up to be nice—especially if you ever get the idea they're going to be published. He talks about the various poses—Pope's pose of hating his poetry. Pope didn't mean that. All Pope thought about was his poetry. Had a writing table on his bed all the time. He woke up to a writing table. Went into fits when somebody didn't like what he'd said. Passionate, passionate hater of his critics. Didn't care at all—all that sort of stuff people get to talking. I just thought about the letter writing. I don't like to write letters but I get a good excuse now I came on that. [3]

While you're thinking about getting ready to ask me questions, I said I'll say a little about the Puritans tonight. I've let myself in for that. I haven't gone into that. You know, a schoolboy may be defined as a person who can tell you everything he knows in the order in which he learned it and never gets loose from that. [4] All his life, taking it that way. What he wants to get—if he can be broken—is to know that some day he's got to get loose and get what they call sweep-

---

He supervised the Great Issues course at Dartmouth, at which Frost spoke each year.

2. Cohen, "An Interview with Einstein."

3. In his essay on Pope in *Lives of the Poets* (Everyman, n.d.), 2: 182-84, 207, Dr. Johnson states: "If the letters of Pope are considered merely as compositions, they seem to be premeditated and artificial." And of Pope's prose, he wrote: "One of his favourite topics is contempt of his own poetry." As for Pope's writing box, Johnson says, "It was punctually required that his writing-box should be set upon his bed before he rose." As for the "fits" to which Frost refers, in Boswell's *Life of Samuel Johnson* (Everyman, 1925), 1: 81, Boswell describes Pope's infirmity as "of the nature of that distemper called St. Vitus's dance."

4. Frost expressed this view nearly the same way in a talk he gave at Wesleyan University in December 1926. See Gorham Munson, *Robert Frost* (New York: George H. Doran Co., 1927), p. 127, app. C. Frost seldom forgot any effective quip like this.

ing, run over things according to his own feelings and what's survived, you know, and what he's liked and disliked and making his sweeping, no matter how, if it's a little, you know, a little twisted, like a picture, like a painting that isn't nature, better than nature. That's what a schoolboy is. And then a teacher is a person who enjoys leading the conversation where you don't show up well—the opposite of a lady or hostess in polite society—the very opposite of that.

Now, I've been in this sort of thing, you see. I'm emancipated. I've been left free for many years, and I can talk about the Puritans without any obligations at all. For instance, the first thing that comes into my mind is how many years I've thought of the puritanism of Greeks and Romans before it dawned on me that other people had conceived that, too. I hadn't had that called to my attention. I thought there was no such thing as pagan puritanism. I just thought I was the only one that thought of it. Of course, everything about Diana and Minerva had something to do with chastity and all that—and restraint.

And then I remember when I first came in Catullus on the story of Attis who from sheer hatred of love—it said in there "sheer hatred of love," you know—destroyed himself and then was sorry, went to the shore and wept at the shore, and then the goddess chased him back off the shore right to the undertombs. Purity, purity, purity. Then, skipping around: "Milton, thou shouldst be living at this hour." [5] I wonder how many times that will be said in the history of England, in the history of America? "Milton! thou shouldst be living at this hour: / England hath need of thee; she is a fen / Of stagnant waters: altar, sword, and pen, / Fireside, the heroic wealth of hall and bower, / Have forfeited their ancient English dower / Of inward happiness. / We are selfish men."

When you say the name Milton you name the name that will be forever Puritanism—the great poet of Puritanism; not only the political one but the thinking one, too. You have to get those two things separated. Most people are very narrowminded about it, you know. They just think about the Puritans that landed here in America and the political thing that executed a king. And all that. But it's a whole way of thinking. You began to see it in the mockery of Chaucer—that light way he took it. And in the severity of Langland, you saw it rising there, something that happened to the corruption of the Church. But that's not the thing. I always think of it this way. Two things I think about in connection with it: one is—it is that in you that fears your own pleasure, that distrusts your own pleasure.

5. William Wordsworth, *National Liberty and Independence,* 1. 14.

We've had that way of talking about that. I can remember my mother had a way of talking about it when things were going too well, you know—that you were too happy. She wouldn't say what because she was religious. It would spoil your luck, the Greeks would have said. You better throw something away that you value and that you better be careful. That's in it: fear of your own pleasure. And then—more than that—that's almost like superstition in it, that gets down to that level, you've always got that around you, I've got it around me. And then the other one is—the greater one—that there ought to be in you something that forbids yourself. Somebody who knew Hull very well—who just died—and who saw a lot of him said that once when he was talking with him—and with [F. D.] Roosevelt in the next room—he said, "There's a man in there I'm very fond of but he needs somebody to hold him." [6] He would have taken the presidency as many times as you would give it to him in contradistinction to George Washington who had checks within himself. There were no checks in Roosevelt. He wasn't that much of a Puritan. You'll hear people say that: "Oh, get all you can and let others get all they can and you'll hold each other in balance." There ought to be something in you that hates to be checked—that you better not need to be checked—that ought to be self-checked. That's Puritanism too.

I should have brought Milton with me but I didn't have one. I should have read some little places that I remembered, but it's just as well to take it that way. *Comus* is the great poem of [Puritanism]. You don't need anything else. You don't need *Paradise Lost*. It all lies in that—the ideas of the two things—in the rout of Comus and the Puritan family—the Puritan girl and the Puritan boy and brothers, and things are said over and over again. It's interesting in there to think what stays with me. . . . Did you ever notice this about your memory—that in the course of years you corrupt a line in a pretty fair way until it's got to be something else with you entirely? I remember thinking years ago that it was in one line in Milton: "Shall I go on? Or have I said enough?" See, that makes a line: "Shall I go on? Or have I said enough"? [7] I like to think of it as two such lovely tones of inquiry. "Shall I go on? Or have I said enough?" And that's what I think makes poetry, you know. That's a very high line of poetry. It's half in one line and half in the other, I saw. I made it into one line and put it on the blackboard once. It's on the iambic meter. "Shall I go on? Or have I said enough?" [*Repeats it*] See, pretty! And the other

6. Cordell Hull (1871–1955), secretary of state from 1932 until 1944.

7. *Comus*, lines 779, 780. In *Comus* the sentences break as follows: ". . . Shall I go on? / Or have I said enough? . . ."

lines in it I think of—in the rout of Comus. You get "We that are of purer fire / Imitate the Starry Choir."[8] We sit up all night and tipsy. I can't go on with that but there are two lines. I always think of the rout of Comus as a purer fire because they stay up all night and sleep all day in the court of King Charles II, in Hollywood and Las Vegas. All that. That's the rout of Comus.

I knew of a very puritanical lady—Louise Imogene Guiney[9]—who adored Charles II and some way she straightened that all out for herself. He was pure—in his way. She lived in England on his account. She was the poet who said:

> To fear not sensible failure,
> Nor covet the game at all,
> But fighting, fighting, fighting,
> Die, driven against the wall!

Then let's see if I remember something else. I misquoted that, I'm sure. "None but the good can give good things." And that isn't quite right. I shall have to look that up. I was thinking about that this afternoon. "None but the good can give good gifts" is the way I remembered it. But I know it's "things," and I know that "none" is in the wrong lines. I've got a picture of it; it's in the other line. "None, but such as are good." I can't get that. But, anyway, that's the idea. "None but the good can give good things."[10] That thing I got into when I was very young. It's bothered me all the years that a man may be a rotter and yet give good things—give great poetry, give good thoughts, noble thoughts, though he's a terrible person like Verlaine or some of these drug fiends. People like that. It's a very Socratic sentiment. Socrates gave me that idea a good deal. Only out of the good can good come. And that isn't true. Emerson says, "Out of the good of evil born."[11] He found it out. But the great man—the president of the United States—might be the son of a criminal, and in fact I knew a great judge of the Supreme Court (the Supreme Court is one of my greatest admirations, one of the greatest things in the world of all the world's institutions). I knew Cardozo very well—was with him alone some—one of the greatest, gentlest, noblest people, son of a

8. *Comus*, lines 111-12.

9. Louise Imogene Guiney (1861–1920), American Catholic poet and essayist, whom Sir Edmund Gosse described as "only at ease in a chivalrous and antique dreamland," published *Songs at the Start* in 1884. The lines Frost quotes are from her poem "The Kings" (stanza 9).

10. *Comus*, lines 702-3. ("None / But such as are good men can give good things.")

11. In "Uriel," Emerson writes: "Or out of the good of evil born."

political criminal, and it's thought that that isolated him somewhat, made him a quiet, solitary man.[12] He lived just for the law and his book. But he was saddened by that, by his father's faults. I don't know but he [the father] was associated with Tammany Hall. I've known of other cases like that. I've known one very recently. A friend of mine who was born in an interesting city—part of his education was political—he was some sort of thief or something like that, I'm thinking of—I won't go into names—a fine administration and was talked about. Very attractive man.

Then you've got all this—the court, the rout, the love in the woods, you know, and you think of Silenus again—Silenus and Falstaff. See, that's the other thing. And very attractive. That very fact. One of the kind of laughs we give that kind of person—it's a special laugh—a wicked laugh—a laugh. You do it with little children, the first sign of a kind of cunning, not a cute but a cunning craftiness in a little boy, somebody being shrewd beyond his years in the grocery store or somewhere and hear him speak up and you see them all exchange glances—he's a comer, he's a good one.

Then—let's see what else I've been thinking about Puritanism. So many people, you see, don't look at it large enough. What's the name of the Italian historian? Someone who wrote a book on the Romans. We get it all narrowed down to a certain kind of people that came late to America, and we kind of like to have something on the Plymouth Rock people and the Mayflower people; so they like to talk about witchcraft and Salem. And they think they've got something on them. They had a little something but it's awfully little. There were ninety thousand people executed in Europe for witchcraft, according to Voltaire—ninety thousand—while we were doing it to twenty or thirty in Boston. It was a form of intellectuality, you see —very, very sophisticated people thinking about witches at that time. It didn't get over here except in the very cultivated Boston where there were more college-educated people. Did you know that? Sam Morison is my authority for that.[13] It [New England] was the most collegiate community the world ever saw. And they picked up this thing.

Somebody asked me if I believed in God. They're asking that

12. Benjamin N. Cardozo (1870–1938), nominated to the Supreme Court by President Hoover in 1932 when Justice Oliver Wendell Holmes resigned, wrote *The Nature of the Judicial Process* (1921), *The Growth of the Law* (1924), and *The Paradoxes of the Legal Science* (1928).

13. Samuel Eliot Morison (1897–), American historian and professor at Harvard. Frost probably had in mind *Builders of the Bay Colony* (1930) or *Puritan Pronaos* (1936).

question around. I didn't answer. I could have said: I believe in God but I don't believe in what he told the Jews to do to the witches. He told them, but that was very intellectual at that time—thinking about the question of witchcraft. It's always haunting you a little bit. What are these mysteries? Are you incapable of believing in any mysteries? Did you ever see a witch? And I often said: I could name twenty that I have known. A friend of mine on the *Boston Post*—editorial writer—a great friend of mine,[14] he was out visiting another friend of mine near Gloucester and they—both of them—noticed and pointed to a spiritualist church in the woods. And they noticed that [church] several times. And they said: "Let's go in and see it. What is this place?" They went in looking for it, and a very sturdy sort of fishwife sort of person came out and spoke to them—out of a kind of hovel or little house—and they said what they were looking for. And she said, "I'm it." And she said, "I don't go for any of this crowd that comes out from Boston. I don't know who they were." And she said right off: "Are you on the *Boston Post?*" Startled him. And she said: "Your papers won't carry my advertisements." Just like that. She was supernatural without any question. [*Laughter*] And you're always coming on those things. What do you say to them? Do you have a sort of shrug for all that? You quote Shakespeare: "So I've heard and do in part believe."[15] When I came on that it relieved me a great deal to say that.

Well, I think that's enough of that about it all. I could go along with more. For instance, what's the history of it? Let's stop and think a minute. Suppose it's gone. Suppose the political movement's gone. Well, the first thing it did was execute a king with great dignity on both sides.[16] Then the other party in the rout of Comus—they executed a couple of queens like that. But the Puritan movement executed just one king. Then it started this thing here, this New England thing that scattered teachers like you all over the United States. I remember a couple of senators in Washington talking together once—one from New England and one from Virginia. And the Virginian said: "See those mules? Are they from New England?" And the New Englander said: "Yes, they're New Englanders

14. Unidentified editor of the *Boston Post,* to whom Frost later refers feelingly.

15. *Hamlet;* act 1, sc. 1, line 165 (*Horatio:* "So have I heard, and do in part believe it").

16. A reference to the beheading of Charles I in 1649 at Whiteside, London, after the regicides convicted him of treason for his part in the English Civil War.

[schoolteachers] going down to teach school in Virginia." That's part of the Puritan movement—that schoolteacherism.

I had a visit the other day from a very distinguished judge —Learned Hand—who said to me that he rather had his doubts about what the Supreme Court had just done.[17] I said: "I haven't." And he said: "My people were antiabolitionists." And I said, "My people were worse than that: they were Copperheads. They were wrong and your people were wrong." An antiabolitionist is a person who couldn't stand the abolitionist, the reformer. I had something in my bones that I find hard to get rid of, you know—fanatics like that—and I know the kind of needling that that kind of people do to the world; that needling had something to do [with] the Civil War. It made the Supreme Court do unanimously what it did the other day, from needling of that kind. My friends in the South that I'm very fond of think they could have done it all themselves without being needled. I hate to be disagreeable but it's a puritanical thing. So it's been a great story.

I don't belong enough to any church, but historically I should be a Congregationalist. My people were all Congregationalists, and the history—my people were here, early that way—and I never see a Congregational church but that I think I must declare myself. I haven't declared myself yet, but I'll do it yet. Prettiest little one. See if I can't do something about it. History of the family. We were Congregationalists, I guess. My mother was a Swedenborgian.

There's a place in there [i.e., Comus], and I wish I had those words—where Milton says that evil will become scum on the surface and settle into dregs, and goodness will no longer be mixed with it.[18] That's esoteric; that's regular purification. That's one thing in there. Then another interesting thing is he talks like a Socialist. You can go and see that. That's a kind of Puritanism, I think. And I'm going to say something else: Marx is a Puritan, Karl Marx. And he says—as I remember it—Comus is saying that you've got to enjoy all things in the world and not be as if you were nature's bastard rather than nature's son. "And live like Nature's bastards, not her sons."[19] We'd be just overwhelmed with wheat and everything, you know, if we don't eat it. The answer to that is that if things were properly distributed so that everybody had as much as was good for

17. Judge Learned Hand (1872–1961). In 1954 the Supreme Court in *Brown* v. *Board of Education at Topeka* had outlawed racial segregation in public schools as "inherently unequal" and in 1955 ordered desegregation to proceed "with all deliberate speed."

18. *Comus,* lines 594-98.

19. *Comus,* line 727.

him there wouldn't be too much. The trouble with the time was the rich had everything and the court had everything. All that. Terribly democratic. Terribly socialistic. The socialistic problem is always the panacea, and the panacea is somebody turns up with a new way to manage the distribution so we'll all have the same culture, and all have the same food, and all have the same everything. Get the distribution right—that's right in Milton there—right in *Comus*. Should have brought the book. Somebody sees that. Another thing about a schoolboy—I noticed this when I taught high school. Sometimes I trained the debating club that went out to debate, and I told them never to say an idea is your own, because that doesn't count anything with the judges. Always say, as so-and-so said it. You find that out.[20]

Nice to go on reminiscing. I put on plays sometimes. I put on *Comus* once. And I had a puritanical venture with that. I didn't ask for anything. I went to the city and bought some masks—horrible masks, swines' heads and things like that—for the rout of Comus. Rented them—didn't buy them. Did this all on my own. And I put on the play without permission of the head of the school—a gray old member of the church and an old scholar.[21] And I hadn't thought of asking his permission to do this. I sold tickets without getting permission. I was thoughtless. And I met him on the street one day, and he said to me: "I understand you're giving a play." I said, "Yes, sir!" He said, "Milton's *Comus*?" And I said, "I haven't much of anything." And he said, "Don't you want the church silver service for that?" This is Puritanism, isn't it? You're always looking for illiberality. And I'm always moved by that. Tears came to my eyes. We used it. We set out a great scene. All the silver service—communion service. Nobody made any trouble.

Some of the lines almost come back to me. I probably missed both of them as some of the girls and boys said it. I had quite a sinister-looking boy with dark, deep eyes that I used for Comus. I haven't seen him all these years. I'd like to see how Comus came out, whether to the top of the scum or the bottom of the dregs. "Out of good is evil born . . . Cherub Scorn."[22] Now that's my part of it.

20. This example of Frost's shrewd insight into human nature has its counterpart in the episode in Benjamin Franklin's *Autobiography* where he discovered, in Xenophon's *Memorable Things of Socrates*, the Socratic method of "modest diffidence" in disputation. Rather than embarrassing anyone by giving "the air of positiveness to an opinion," he would substitute "I conceive" or "I apprehend" for "certainly" or "undoubtedly."

21. The head of the school was Rev. George W. Bingham.

22. Frost is again quoting from Emerson's "Uriel."

Anybody that wants to speak up, or doesn't want to speak up and has something to make himself speak up?

Q. Sounds to me as though you make these Puritans real humanists with that second point about the self-check. Irving Babbitt would feel pretty good about that, wouldn't he?

A. Yes, he was a Puritan.

Your conscience is related to you as your eyes are related to your sense of touch, you know. They reach further; they're an extension of touch so you can know long before you bump into anything. So this sort of fear—this puritanical fear of being rebuked—is ahead of it, you know; anticipates anybody else's rebuke—rather being self-rebuked—that's what your conscience is. It rebukes you before anybody else has a chance to rebuke you; rebukes you with a gallows, with a shotgun.

You know, again one of the very Puritan things, classical things, is the way every single election we have in this country is a sort of libration, of balancing of scales between freedom and equality. The equality is the mercy thing, and freedom is the justice thing. Freedom means, you know, freedom to achieve, win, freedom to win, and that has to be checked by mercy and equality. Every election is about that, and sometimes one party is from the mercy side. For instance, the Republican party gave us the Sherman Antitrust Law, which is an equalitarian thing; and then the New Deal time—from Wilson [the Democratic party] on—was more on the mercy side, the equalitarian side. But it's always about that. We want to be as equal as we can without checking ability too much. We want to be as equal as we can be in school without checking ability too much. We don't want to give everybody *A.* And some people stay in school that ought not to be there. We don't have the courage to fire them out, but because of equalitarian mercy we keep them—until people begin to say the schools are beginning to deteriorate from mercy.

Another thing, of course, the Puritans gave us is the great counterrevolution—Loyola and all that. They pass out of history just that same sort of thing—this fear—this political thing gave way to that time. We all may go back to the Roman church in the end. I'm not saying we won't. The tremendous blow Puritanism struck over three or four or five hundred years there in history—that'll be forgotten. It's just historical; it's people there I'm talking about. It's always people. Sometimes when I don't think I know any good Puritans in the Protestant church I go see my Catholic Puritans. And they're there. The one I'm speaking of—the amusing one, on the *Boston Post*—one of the most learned people, with his Irish wit—he's the one that was recognized by the spiritualist woman as an editor of the *Post*. He is an old Puritan. For instance, I often heard him use the word *prudence*. He said, as Saint Thomas says, "The virtue of all virtues is prudence." And that's in it. This state between freedom and equality—the prudent thing. The Supreme Court doesn't have something to do about it, but we all have something to do about it. Voting every so often. That will be librating, not vibrating—librating. Prudence. Exercise of prudence.

I have heard—someone else put three words together. Interesting words. Prudence was one of those. Courage, prudence, and justice. See. That's a nice trio. Prudence has something to do with it. "And now the matchless deed's achieved, / Determined, dared, and done." That's a pretty trio in that poem of Smart's.[23] What are the three parts of it?

> Thou that stupendous truth believ'd,
> And now the matchless deed's achiev'd,
> Determined, dared, and done.

Now you can ask me anything.

Q. What kind of flower was it you didn't see from that railroad train [in "A Passing Glimpse"]?

A. I think it was probably lupine. I never looked back. That's the point of that. That's the trouble with cars. You get carried by things you want to look at.

Q. I thought you might have seen it when you weren't looking for it.

A. No, it was a strange place I happened to be passing. That brings you to a kind of thing that shows the difference between me and the scholars. If I'd been a real scholar I'd have gone back —thoroughness, you know. I miss some things. I miss some words—and now and then a classical reference in Milton. But I don't like them unless I know them, you know. Score by the sentence, not score by looking it up. I don't like anything I have to look up. And there are things in *Comus*. It's terribly readable. I know Sabrina chiefly at Amherst College. [24]

[*Talks about great men of the last hundred years —Darwin, Marx, Freud, Einstein*]

And everybody misuses the word *relative*, you know. Everything is relatively so, you know. What I say about Puritanism is only relatively

23. Christopher Smart's "Song to David."
24. Sabrina, goddess of the river Severn, is mentioned in *Comus*, line 840. At Amherst College a statue of the goddess was the object of a struggle for possession between the odd and even classes.

so. The only trouble with Marx was that he used the word *capital*, and he didn't know what capital was. All capital is the dollar ahead or the tool ahead—hammer—or anything ahead. That's all it is. And the whole question—he just gets you all at sea about that—he never just gets clear who should be the keeper of the tool. But he thought he knew something different about capital. All it is is that simple matter. Fifty cents I've got in my pocket is capital. I've got something ahead; that's capital. That's security.

And then, let's see, who else is there? Freud. Oh, yes, as I said, that's like a man minding each other's business. Sex is in that. That's a small part of it. We watch each other. We like to say that our private life is nobody's business. We protect ourselves, always screening, we say, our private life. It's nobody's business. It doesn't make any difference how many wives and mistresses we have. That's just about your money and everything. The income-tax people—seems now they're going to open up our income-tax reports again. For awhile they shut them off. Everybody's business. That's the ruling passion in Freud. That's what holds us together. That's fraternity.

Q. What about Sir James Frazer and *The Golden Bough*?

A. Those are minor people. They're down in the bush leagues. That kind of stuff all comes under the Darwinian thing. There's a whole string of those people like Huxley. And one of them wrote a book on the evolution of God—where it started from—whole big book. Another on the idea of the evolution of Love. That other —Grant Allen was the name of one.[25] I saw those around when I was young. Didn't bother me any. The thing I was saying is, what do you think of these people who come along? All very well. There is evolution. Things are relative. Did you notice? Science gets into the newspaper as it never did years ago. Very thorough article: light is apparently going ten miles a second faster than it used to go. Somebody's just found that out. That was supposed to be the only absolute there was—the speed of light. Apparently lately it's been going a little faster—ten miles a second out of 187,000 miles—but the speed of light Einstein treated as an absolute. Einstein knocked that into a cocked hat.

If you want to read a very pretty thing about a charming man, go to the last number but one of the *Scientific American*: there's an inter-

25. Grant Allen (1848–99), born in Canada, died in England, was a novelist, poet, essayist, scientist, and philosopher. Frost probably had in mind *Colin Clout's Calendar: The Record of a Summer* (1883), which was also praised by Huxley and Darwin; and also *Force and Energy* (1888) and *Evolution of the Idea of God* (1897).

view with him just before his death by a man in it all.[26] Very beautiful thing. Very moving thing. Very lofty person. Even his uncertainty is very attractive. This little formula, you know, for everything. He just felt this way about it: he hoped he had something. One of his friends that I happened to know, I said to him: "You all happy about him and what he concluded?" He said: "We think he got away on the wrong foot." And that's what Einstein said in this article. He says that Planck—that other greatest man that he had admired so much —right in the middle of his career got afraid that he had got away on the wrong foot and changed his whole life and went off on another tack entirely. You find that kind of a mind there.

You know what I've been talking lately about that might interest you? I've just made up my mind that I wouldn't clash with anybody if I could help it, either from cowardice or from whatever you call it. I never ran a class that way. I knew a reputedly great teacher who threw one apple of discord into the class per day. He would start a row. But it was for ten boys out of fifty. The others looked solemn most of the time. I peeked in once in awhile. A lot of the students took right hold of it and loved it, but I always noticed that I would rather not clash with the Jews or anybody else. I always say this to myself, that I hope that I'm broad enough and large enough so that I can listen to almost anything without losing my temper or my self-confidence. I said that over in Dartmouth.[27] And then my next step is, I say: I'll accept anybody's say-so—anybody's premises. I'll let them have their say, and then I take it my way. Give me time and I can without hurting anyone, yes, yes, yeh! For instance, when I heard that God made man, I wondered if my mother was greatly disturbed by all that Darwinian[ism]. And I remember saying to her (I don't remember how old I was; it's easy to lie about those things, but somewhere around fourteen or fifteen or sixteen)—I said to her: "You think, don't you? It doesn't make any great difference—to give up saying that God made [man] out of mud. All you have to say is that God made him out of prepared mud—worked it up from animal life." So it comes to the same thing—it's a Darwinian thing. It's the same about many things.[28]

I know something lately. For instance, all the best people left New England when the Revolution started. Went to Canada. Never quarrel with the premises. They all went to Canada. [*Pause*] Haven't been

26. Cohen, "An Interview with Einstein."
27. Remarks at Dartmouth College commencement, June 12, 1955.
28. Frost often repeated this anecdote from his youth, indicating not only his early quipping but a seriously held point of view.

heard of since. [*Laughter*] You know what happens to them? If they naturally drift to England and Australia—just the same—and New Zealand, they have a hard time. I had a visit from a man named Ian Donelly, editor of a big newspaper out of New Zealand, and he just said that there's always something out there. "Home is England." As Kipling says, "We learn from our English mothers to call old England home."[29] Generation after generation, they say "home." That may be nice. I haven't even said it's best.

Then the other possibility is that nothing good ever comes of the best people. Now that's me talking. The best usually comes from the worst. Somebody said to me the other day how some boy [was] singing on the street selling cookies in Saint Petersburg (maybe it was built then, I guess) and Peter the Great heard him singing—a sweet voice. He became one of his great men, had never been educated; lifted him up, took him home, and he became one of the great men of the empire. Somebody said you mustn't tell this kind of a story. Tell me how some rich man amounted to something. I said, "I often do—[F. D.] Roosevelt." Don't you think it fun to think about those things? How many disadvantages does a man have to have to become great? He has to be born in a log cabin. I think it's a great disadvantage to be born too rich. Here's a man born very rich—only son —very domineering mother. There's three disadvantages he's got already. Then he goes to Groton. [*Laughter*] Then he goes to Harvard. That's five disadvantages. [*Laughter*] Then he goes and hangs around Washington for some years and up in Albany and all that, and they all get used to him. And that's a great disadvantage. Everybody gets to say he's an old story. And God said to himself, you know, then: "What can I do for that man to make him great? I've set my heart on making something of that boy. I've given him all of these disadvantages and there's nothing to it yet." And he gives him polio and he becomes one of the world's great men. That's the other kind of story. Log cabin. Don't want to confuse you.

Q. You know, someone was interested in what happened down in South America, Mr. Frost. Maybe it's too long a story.[30]

A. Not too long. I got back to the farm just as fast as I could. [*Laughter*] I flew, say, fourteen or fifteen thousand miles, they tell me, all told. I didn't want to fly. I was afraid to fly—very heroic

29. Note also Mary Howitt (1799–1888) who, in "Old England is Our Home," wrote: "Old England is our home, and Englishmen are we; / Our tongue is known in every clime, our flag in every sea."

30. From August 4 to August 19, 1954, Frost was in South America as a delegate to the World Congress of Writers, who met at São Paulo, Brazil. He had been sent to the congress by the U.S. Department of State.

—except when I was taking off and landing. Then I got down there among them all and saw a little bit of a revolution. I saw a few cars tipped over in the street, burned, you know, and the night I spoke down there everybody was warned on my part—burned, you know—to keep off the street. I took it to heart. [*Laughter*] Speeches were dangerous to make. So I didn't have a very good audience.

The thing I went for was not that; that was an incidental talk. I went for a convention of intellectuals. I was supposed to be there the week before among the literary people, and the writers, but I got belated in some way and I got among the intellectuals. They were all worried about the United States—from all the countries south of a certain line. Let's see: Italy was there; Spain was there; Portugal and South American countries. And nobody from England, nobody from Germany. Let me see. And the person I liked best—the one that talked some English, that I could communicate with best and had ideas nearer mine—was a count from Portugal. A very nice man. Some of them were too remote from me. I can understand some French but I can't talk with them much. But everybody was despairing of—putting their hands up this way and moving their heads—despairing of the materialism that America was to lead the world in. They were just sorry about it, anxious about it. I read their speeches. Had them interpreted to me. A girl from Donald Davidson's classes out in Tennessee was an interpreter down there.[31] She lives down there, educated up here. She did pretty well but I had an idea that some of it I wasn't misunderstanding, you know—America! Materialism! How can you save the world from materialism?

I didn't go with any written address. I talked about our materialism as long as they wanted to talk about it. I accepted the premises as usual. I didn't quarrel with anybody. I just said I was sure we were anxious about it too, because in everybody's bathroom wherever I went there were scales to weigh yourself. [*Laughter*] Pleasure of food, pleasure of not weighing too much. Saint Thomas is right. They talk about us a little this way. That old Rivet—great old French anthropologist, so learned, so attractive, so handsome, so aged, very splendid man.[32] After we'd done all this, he did it too —put his arms around me French-style, you know, just as nice—no acrimony in any of it. That Rivet—he's the man I'll remember

31. Donald Davidson, poet and teacher, a member of the English faculty at Vanderbilt University in Nashville, Tenn., was also a long-time teacher at the Bread Loaf School of English.
32. Prof. Paul Rivet, honorary director of the Musee de l'homme in Paris.

longest. The Italian, I didn't like him very well.[33] Didn't like his style. Very brilliant. But he had a formula for combining—to save the world from American materialism—combining Marxism and the Roman church. Amazing person. That's not new. Didn't astonish me enough. You see, you change your emphasis from Saint Thomas Aquinas to Saint Augustine. Enough.of that casuistry.

Saw a little—didn't need to see Rio. I'd seen so many pictures of Rio in my life, it looked really stale to me—mountains sticking right up out of the water like that. And I felt I didn't get anything out of that, but I got a good deal out of São Paulo. They were both cities of about three million. Big cities. And São Paulo is just like Chicago or Dallas; it's a huge humming city, tall buildings over it all, and I could point to that too. It was where this [convention] went on. And over that great city was a four-letter word in neon lights—four-letter word, right over the whole city, at night—Gulf. [*Laughter*]

I didn't go to see anything. Then, because I was there, they said you might as well come over and see Lima. Might as well. Just seven or eight or nine hours of flying over the highest mountains on the continent. And I said: "Are you going to do that in the night?" A lot of the flying had been in the night. I hadn't seen anything. Hadn't seen the Amazon River or anything. They said: "Oh no. You can't do this in the night, it's dangerous." They had to see where they were going. [*Laughter*] I liked the cities, you know, to see them. I should have gone — getting that far in the government's expense [I] might as well go see something. I kept saying that to myself, but I kept thinking whether the deer got into my garden. [*Laughter*] I'm not a traveler.

I saw the whole [view] underneath. I saw the wild parts of Brazil that I'd never dreamed of seeing. You see unbroken wilderness. You couldn't tell whether it was trees or what it was, or just nothing. And then there'd be a little thing that looked like a loaf of bread—shaped like a loaf of bread—and you could interpret that into a community house where savages lived, and the trodden ground around it marked it and you could see little threads of path off from it. They looked just like threads. Nothing there; no animals; that is, no pack animals. There'd be just human feet. And then we came to—we saw—a path down below us. Saw someone in an automobile scooting along. Not so very high, we were very near it. And then we almost touched the volcano tops that we crossed. We went and looked into them. They tipped the plane around so we could look down. Then I thought of the joke—the boner—you know, the boy said: "If you

33. Unidentified Italian, probably the same individual to whom Frost referred earlier as an Italian historian who wrote about the Romans.

look into a volcano you can see the creator smoking." [*Laughter*] We looked into two volcanoes. We were right up among glaciers and peaks, and all of this country was nothing but glaciers and peaks. Two were misty, and the other we looked down into. And we were very near this city—it's where the poetess lives—what is the name of this city? [34] It's a very famous little marble city. You could see that. Well, I'm not going to be able to remember that now. Then we went down into Lima, and Lima's a beautiful city, under clouds all the time. We had to make that kind of landing there, right down through clouds. But it's a very interesting city. Never rains there, but it's cloudy all the time. And you go out ten miles to nightclubs and places like that, and you go out to day clubs where the sun is—just up the mountains a little way and you're up above the clouds rising from Humboldt Current. Went to one of the places. Had a half an afternoon in an ancient city that probably had a half a million inhabitants [and] all in adobe, and the graves all around—mounds, you know —and I saw a skirt, the edge of a skirt, the cloth flutter in the wind, and I pulled it and pulled it and pulled more and more skirt, and pretty soon I pulled a lady. [*Laughter*] I found a few pieces of things to stick in my pocket. I didn't do much of that.

I had an unlawful adventure, I think. I said to an archaeologist there who was a very, very fine man: "What I would like out of this country is a little piece of gold, you know, Inca gold." I said, "I suppose that never gets out." And he said, "Sometimes it does." Nothing else was said. And I got in the mail, without anything to mark it in any way from whom it came or anything, a little thin piece of gold ornament—a little bit of gold ornament—thin gold—must have come from him. Didn't say a word. Not a word. Not a word. But it's very tiny. Sent it as a joke. So that's all there was about that.

I saw Dulles when I came back and was supposed to tell him what to do. [35] And he said he would do all he could. Well, you know what I told him to do? I told him to be nicer to the cultural relations people in those places. They haven't diplomatic standing. They can't go through red lights. [*Laughter*] That's enough of me—unless you've got something serious to ask.

Q. You ought to tell them to take that Gulf sign down.

A. No, we couldn't do that. The other sign that was over everything—was sprinkled over every building, every store, and everything—was Coca-Cola. There wasn't a car on the street; it was

34. Gabriela Mistral (1889–1957), Chilean poet who received the Nobel Prize for Literature in 1945. Frost probably had Vicuña in mind.

35. John Foster Dulles (1888–1959), who was U.S. secretary of state from 1953 to 1959 and the architect of the "containing Communism" policy.

crowded with cars! You ran for your life down there. Those cities are rich—terribly rich—and someone said: "Did you go slumming?" No, I didn't have time to go slumming. There are slums down there, I've heard. Cars, and all American—all ours—more ours than continental and British cars—just swarming with cars—Cadillacs.

Then, one more story before I go. A boy came to me at Amherst College. His name was Adcock—Bruce Adcock. He had known me there. He told me he was now at Harvard studying philosophy. And he asked me what I thought of the philosophy department at Harvard, and I said I didn't know how to judge it. It had been my favorite department when I was there. "Well," he said, "I can't stand it. They're nothing but a lot of epistemologists. There isn't, I mean, a philosopher there." And I said: "Is that so? Why do you stand it then?" And he said: "I don't want to be a quitter, do I?" And I said: "Well, the Bible says, 'quit ye like men.'" [*Laughter*] And he said: "Well, where would I go?" "Anywhere." This was a long while before Brazil—two years ago, three years ago, four years ago. I said: "Anywhere. Brazil." [*Pause*] And I found him in Brazil. [*Laughter*] And already he'd given up philosophy and was a great authority on precious and semiprecious stones. He gave me a few. Rewarded me for sending him to Brazil. All right, shall we quit?

CHAPTER 10
On Surmising
July 2, 1956

No matter how carefully the reader follows the transcription of a Frost talk, he can never quite get the full thrust of it, for the latter is the result of an attendant atmosphere and the inimitable play of the poet's voice. Strictly speaking, a Frost appearance was not a reading, it was a performance. Subtract the voice, omit the gestures—the waggling forefinger, the roguish or chiding sotto voce aside, the nod of the head, the glance of the eye, the raised eyebrow, even an idiosyncratic jab of a finger against the blade of the nose—and the poetry of the occasion is nearly reduced to a literal verbalization. How Frost said everything enhanced the saying in a rare and often remarkable way.

One thing to notice in the following talk runs counter to the general consensus concerning Frost's talks. It was often said—even by those who should know better—that he simply appeared and, as it were, talked off the top of his head. While he did not come with a talk all thought out, to be recited from his unusual memory, I do think he always had a theme in mind. Here he carries you from the first part of his talk into the poems used as illustrations. The spontaneity and freshness of his talks, the tendency to ramble and divagate, are all of a piece and reflect the positive as well as the negative sides to his method.

What am I anxious about? I know I'm a great equalitarian. I spend most of my time with my equals. And I've been saying lately that I'd vote the Democratic ticket again if they'd run a plebeian. [*Laughter*] I'm sick of all these aristocratic Democrats—from Jefferson on down. I want a plebeian. We've had a few of them. I won't go into that. But I was thinking of it in literature too. I suppose Thoreau was a plebeian. And I suppose one of my favorite plebeians was William Cobbett, that awful British plebeian that you ought to take a look at on my account.[1] And another one—I suppose George Borrow was one.[2] That's the kind of person I mean. And we've had them in literature. I'd like to get them together sometime in a course—teach a course in real plebeians. Not just Democrats—I'm sick of that word. Everybody is a democrat in one sense of the word, except on election day, and then it's divided into Democrats and Republicans. But I'd like to be with people that were at ease; you know, that weren't bothered when I made play with something in literature like Cobbett, let us say, or Thoreau.

This is what I've been thinking of before I got here, before Doc Cook diverted me.[3] Been thinking when I say, "once more, O ye laurels," see, introducing myself like that [*laughter*], I want you to get it, you know. Then when I say that I think all my writing, all my writing, has been never wild surmise but a mild surmise: no one has ever understood me who doesn't know what the play is there —what a mild surmise is. I've been talking all sorts of things this winter. One of them [the lecture readings] comes round to that so often. They all come round to that. It's a kind of a summary of what I've been through with friends in the fall and winter, especially this spring. A wild surmise and a mild surmise—surmise!

I've been saying the three greats in our life—the three greats—are

1. William Cobbett (1762–1835), English author and journalist, whose *Rural Rides* (1830) was one of Frost's favorites. Cobbett's description of the life and agricultural conditions in the English countryside delighted the poet. In using the epithet "awful British plebeian," is Frost here reminded of the pro-British pamphlets, written in the United States under the pseudonym of "Peter Porcupine"? That is, Cobbett's plebeianism was distinctly national and didn't extend to the experiment in American democratic plebeianism.

2. George Borrow (1803–81) is known to readers of travel and adventure books as the English writer who recounted his experiences while touring Europe as a Bible agent and newspaper correspondent. Among his books, *Lavengro* (1851) was referred to often by Frost, and it was included on the list of readings for his course when teaching at Amherst College, 1923–24. See Thompson, *Robert Frost: The Years of Triumph,* p. 603.

3. Obviously Frost came to the Little Theatre with his mind focused on a special topic, and the introduction occasionally put him off his topic. In introducing him, I used a quotation from Thoreau's *A Week on the Concord and Merrimack Rivers* to anchor the introduction: "After all," wrote Thoreau, "the truly efficient laborer will not crowd his day with work, but will saunter to his task surrounded by a wide halo of ease and leisure, and then do what he loves best." For some reason, Frost was reminded of Milton's *Lycidas,* his favorite poem, whose opening line is, "Yet once more, O ye laurels, and once more."

religion and science and gossip.[4] And the greatest of these is gossip because it is both a wild and a mild surmise. It's our guessing at each other all day long and all our lives; guessing at each other—and sometimes, you know, what it ought not to be and sometimes what it's got to be and sometimes what it ought to be. And it rises from the ordinary daily gossip into the columns of the newspapers and then into literature, drama; and all the time you get nearer what I mean by the mild surmise. It gets away from too much prejudice, gets away from the fanatical and the hatred. It gets larger and larger, but it's still gossip, still surmise, guessing at each other. Then in our insecurity about it, and our fear for it, we think there may be some help from one of the other two: from science [and from religion]. They figure there may be a little scientific help in our gossip, and they call that psychology. I like to say of science that all science is domestic science, it all has to do with our domestication in the universe and on the planet. And all its laboratories are glorified kitchens, you know.

This thing I care most about is surmise, surmise, so that you're going to be misunderstood in it if you don't get the tone of it. There's no word so dreadful I wouldn't dare to say it to you, if you were my equal and knew how to take the tone in which I said it.[5] And I rely on verse more than anything else on the height of literature, where the play is, up there.[6] I rely on that for conveying the poem in which I say I make my surmises about God and man.

And the teacher has one advantage that I've lost. I used to have it when I was a regular teacher. I could say something, anything I pleased, the first lesson of the year and trust the rest of the year to make you understand it. But when it's just like in passing with me now, as it is most of the time now, much depends on my getting the right tone and being with other people who can catch the tone: my equals. And you see, your guessing gets a little surer as it sublimates, as it mounts. You can say of a certain character in a play, you know,

4. "The three greats" were much upon his mind at this time, and references to this theme will be found in *Interviews with Robert Frost,* ed. Edward Connery Lathem (New York: Holt, Rinehart and Winston, 1966), p. 176; and also in another Bread Loaf talk on June 29, 1959, which indicates the topic was of continuing interest to him.

5. Frost never got far away from this view in the entire range of his poetry. "But all the fun's in how you say a thing," he told us early in "The Mountain" (*The Poetry of Robert Frost,* p. 44).

6. Play was another basic in his ars poetica. In fact, he said in his talk before the Bread Loaf audience on July 5, 1954: "Our object [speaking of the poets] is to entertain you by making play with things we trust you already know."

that he might be drawn from somebody you know, and you could be wrong about the person you know; but there is such a thing, see, you get up, see, you get up where there is such a thing—you're up where you're safer, surer, greater, and better, and nobler, and everything else. I'm not going to make so much of that.

A momentary illustration comes into my head. We have to guess. We still guess what made World War I. We're guessing now what's going to make World War III. Amusing after the First World War how many books were written of the guesswork kind on where the World War came from. Some went clear back to Greece and Rome for it; some went into the Teutoburg Forest—dug it up out of the Teutoburg Forest with the help of Tacitus, I suppose. And some knew all about the immediate German. And one of my surmises was that the Germans looked with envy for years on the British on top of the world; and it wasn't that they couldn't get on top of the world—to sit on top of the world or stand on top of the world—by sheer force, but what they envied was the serenity with which the British reclined on top of the world.[7] [*Laughter*] And they could buy Eton jackets and they could buy pipes and they could do all that, but they couldn't get that, and so they made a war about it. Didn't get them anywhere, did it? Still where they were.

We're in the same position now. We may be on top of the world. I don't know, it's just one of my guesses. I've heard some people guess that way. It's not my guess especially. I've heard it guessed: that we were on top of the world. But are we at ease on top of the world? We won't be happy unless we are. And that means, will we write what I think is the height of it all for me? I might sum it up in the word *Golden Treasury*—lyric poetry.[8] A book almost without animus; all up in the spirit of high poetry; a book all the way up in the high guesses.

I must have been asked once years ago what I was doing in England, and I had forgotten what I was doing. I have all sorts of theories about that. That's always the way when I'm retrospective. I get up different things. Somebody said: "Where did you learn to write?" Why, I tell them I learned from one person and then from another. I have a different one every time I'm interviewed.[9] I said to

7. A good illustration of Frost's original play, whimsical as it might seem to the historians, is a perceptive insight.

8. Palgrave's *The Golden Treasury* was, as indicated, another of Frost's favorite books, to which he referred and from which he quoted often. See *Selected Letters*, p. 20, for a reference to the early impact of Palgrave.

9. A revealing statement in view of the dust Frost learned strategically to scatter in the eyes of those who peered too closely into the private trade secrets of his craft.

somebody—I saw it in print somewhere—that I said that I had come to the land of *The Golden Treasury.* That's what I went for. One of my theories was that I went to live under thatch. I said that once [about *The Golden Treasury*], but that [i.e., the thatch rejoinder] stays with me some way among my guesses. I'm guessing at myself, you know; guessing at ourselves. The beauty of it is the lambent way the mind plays over that guessing.

I am looking for a particular poem. I wonder if I went and lost the place. This is about a different part of the country from New England. I was just as much out of my native heath as I was when I went to England. Out of the Ozarks. I don't know how I happened to write this poem, but it is (I guess it was) at somebody I saw looking out of the train window. Another poem—I guess I had almost forgotten that—in another poem, "On the Heart's Beginning to Cloud the Mind," I was looking out of a train window away out in Utah and way in the night, and I saw one lonely light way off, you know, far from any other all around. I made a whole poem out of that. Footnote people, be prepared. And this kind of country I was going through. [*Reads "The Figure in the Doorway"*]

It might not be true of him [the figure in the doorway] at all, but there is such a thing. [*Laughter*] I might have been all wrong about him. He might have been a candidate for the Democratic party. [*Laughter*] That varies a little. I read that poem first here years ago. I don't think I've read it in public since. But that is some democratic guessing.

Then I'm going to read another guess. This is closer rhyming. There are four rhymes to a stanza in this one. This is out of twenty years of my life, living with the people, some of whom have to take refuge in the Fifth Amendment now. Friends of mine, all sorts and kinds, but that was the period, and I did my little mocking and they did theirs back at me, and this is about two of them, one in particular, but two of them that I was fondest of, two young people. One of them, as a matter of fact—if you need to be specific—one was at Amherst and another was at Bryn Mawr.[10] And the time was about 1917, and this is my—I've introduced it all right. [*Reads "The Lost Follower"*]

I ought to say this of them: that they were two whom I had set my heart on for the poetry they were going to write, and both of them

10. The two young people are Jean Flexner and Carter Goodrich; See *Selected Letters,* p. 591.

left the poetry to do social work. Both of them. I call it "The Lost Follower."

Now, you see how much I'm surmising. Now let me read the end again. [*Rereads the last stanza*] I'm simply going to use those [lines] and then leave my theme, just to show you how we do it all the time in our talk and writing. How deep that thing always was to me! Two words in Keats were terribly deep to me, and I get to suspecting one of them as a word that had dominated English literature for a hundred years after it. "She stood in tears amid the *alien* corn" [italics added]. [11] And that is such a high poetic use of that word *alien* that it just got to all the poets that wrote for a hundred years. You'll find them doing it, trying something with that word for a hundred years there. And I said the only way I got away from it was remembering it was the name for Ellis Island people. Get back to Ellis Island. This "wild surmise" is another wonder. How deep that goes! I suppose I never said that word, ran through that [sonnet]—"Look'd at each other with a wild surmise—/ Silent, upon a peak in Darien"—without something so beyond any symbolism or anything like that, or echoes, just as over some deep hollow in my nature. [12]

Another one that I haven't read much of any is a recent one. [*Reads "One More Brevity"*]

Shall I say one more thing and start that one over again? So it won't have to be a footnote, you know. [*Laughter*] Sure, my crowd—my equals—are those I don't have to write footnotes to. The footnotes, if I used them, would be a condescension to the people that can't keep up with me. [13] Humanitarian. [*Laughter*] This is one now, for instance, this making play with Sirius. I've known somebody of Amherst College who walked nights with me a great deal who had never seen northern lights. [14] We walked in the city, as it happened, and the city lights kept him from seeing anything. And he didn't know stars, and the sky never bothered him. We talked about other things we found in our way. [*Continues the reading of "One More Brevity"*]

Then some of the little ones—the older ones—that I say. This word *surmise*. I never used it in talking about it [poetry] before.

11. John Keats, "Ode to a Nightingale."

12. Keats, "On First Looking into Chapman's Homer."

13. At the risk of belatedly patronizing Frost, let it be said that in his denunciation of footnotes he is indirectly attacking T. S. Eliot's elaborate footnotes in *The Waste Land*. See T. S. Eliot, *Collected Poems, 1909–1935*, pp. 91-98, "Notes on *The Waste Land*."

14. Frost's friend was George F. Whicher, professor of English at Amherst College.

That's brand new for me tonight. I trotted that out of Keats. But, for instance, two or three times this winter in public places—down in Washington—I've been asked to say a particular poem, and it has to do with my guess about the Revolutionary War. That's why I was asked to do it. The word *guess* wasn't used. People were interested in my guess. Some people guessed that the Revolution—that the British were to blame for the Revolutionary War, and others guessed that we were. That fellow in Maine—I always forget his name—he guessed that we were.[15] He writes history novels. He concludes that we were to blame for the Revolutionary War. This ["The Gift Outright"] is my guess. It's a simple matter. It begins in the first line; it's the whole business. [*Reads "The Gift Outright"*]

Many deeds of war, little deeds of war—Bennington, one more, Kings Mountain. Named after a king. Down in North Carolina. Went by that within a year in a fast train. That's when I get most of my knowledge these days—looking out a train window. Went by a little empty station. There wasn't a truck there. There was nobody there. There wasn't anything. I just happened to look up from a book or magazine or something and it said on the station "Kings Mountain." One of those great little battles. Before the French had anything to do with that.[16] Something else. [*Reads "The Road Not Taken"*] See, the tone of that is absolutely saving. You've got to look out for it, though. See. "I shall be telling this with a sigh."

See if I can't find something else. [*Reads "Haec Fabula Docet"*] The only political poem I ever wrote. A wicked one. I wouldn't have written that if it hadn't been for my own badness. I behaved very badly all through this and I look like the blind man in the poem. Another one [i.e., similar to "Haec Fabula Docet" in wickedness]. [*Reads "An Importer"*]

Let's read some of these old ones. Let me just read a little stanza of a village evening. [*Reads from "Good Hours"*]

> I had for my winter evening walk—
> No one at all with whom to talk,
> But I had the cottages in a row
> Up to their shining eyes in snow.

15. Kenneth Roberts (1885–1957).

16. At Kings Mountain, in York County, S.C., on October 7, 1780, the Americans under Sevier, Shelby, Campbell, and others defeated the British under Ferguson, who was killed.

An old memory of Plymouth [N.H.].

[*Reads "After Apple-Picking"*] I'll read one of the longer ones. Let me read one or two of the little ones. Like this. I heard this word the other day. [*Reads "The Oven Bird"*]

Here's a cruder, a cruder old time, of a memory many years ago. I really had in mind the giant animals on the monument—the Prince Albert Memorial in London.[17] It's supposed to be done in the heroic vein. [*Reads "The Cow in Apple Time"*]

Well, I guess I'll read "The Death of the Hired Man." "The Tuft of Flowers" is one of the earliest I ever wrote. In rhymed couplets. One of the farming ones. And it has in it a line I used to think from. I didn't see it when I wrote it but I've thought a good deal about it since—"from sheer morning gladness at the brim." [*Repeats the line*] Just notice that as we go by it. Has a lot to do with it [his vocation as a poet] all. That's where the poetry transcends sociology and reform and everything like that. I met the other day in my travels a William Lloyd Garrison, trustee of a noted college. It's strange—I'd never been so close to the abolition world as I was then. A handsome man, old-time New England face. I didn't go into politics with him. [*Reads "The Tuft of Flowers"*]

I wrote that back in the nineties and I was thinking both ways: together and alone. Some people make a business of talking lonely; get a great deal of sympathy from doing that, scientists as well as poets.

All right now. I guess I'll read you "The Death of the Hired Man." [*Reads "The Death of the Hired Man"*] But then, I won't leave it on that. [*Reads "Desert Places"*] Then, for another sound altogether; that's what I'm always looking for—and the tone of it. [*Reads "Provide, Provide"*] That's another sound. [*Reads "Etherealizing"*]

You can put people in jail for not believing in evolution now. You can suppress a book because it isn't sound on the subject of evolution. You can make a publisher stop selling it on the threat that if he sells that any more, see, if he sells that bad science any more, the colleges of this country won't buy the textbooks of that firm any more. And some of the most noted people entered into that to suppress a

17. "The Cow in Apple Time" was written in England and first published in *Poetry and Drama,* December 1914. *His* cow reminded him of the bronze animals on the Albert Memorial in Hyde Park, London, and, according to Thompson, he tended to take his cow seriously. See Thompson's *Robert Frost: The Early Years,* p. 605.

book that was unsound on the subject of science.[18] Just as bad as the Middle Ages, you know.

One more. Something else. Don't ask me afterwards why didn't I "say" something. Tell me now. What is the last one I'll say? See if I know it.

[I called out "Come In" and "Directive."] Everybody ought to smile when Doc Cook asks for "Come In." That's his speciality, isn't it? Doc and the thrushes. [*Sarcastically*]

One of my diffidences is about poems like this ["Directive"] to read aloud. I'm not afraid to, but I'm a little diffident about it. Some of them, you know, are more open work and this is a little more closed. [*Reads "Directive"*] I'd like to read this one. [*Rereads the first lines*] The prelude is in this. See, I don't read it with the same certainty that I should. I feel a little afraid of it. But there are things in it that I like. Shall this be the end of it? Shall I say a little one? [*Reads "Come In"*]

Will I say just this about the symbol that you're working at all the time? Every single one of the poems has its design symbol, see; but there are some people who want to know what's eating you. That's what they mean by symbol. See, what do you mean that you didn't know you meant? That's what's eating you.[19]

[*Reads "Birches"*] You see, did you notice the emphasis laid on "weary of considerations"? See. It just means you're getting weary of all things that pair off—loneliness, togetherness, lone-wolfness. I'm sick of having to consider the lone-wolfness and the togetherness. Those horrible words! Somebody manufactured one, and I manufactured the other.

18. A reference to the controversy which erupted when, in 1950, Macmillan published Immanuel Velikovsky's *Worlds in Collision*. When speaking at the English School on June 30, 1955, about "An Interview with Einstein," Frost had talked about this furor. Now it is clear he sided with Einstein against those scientists who sought to suppress it. The idea of suppressing the voice of the imagination, whether in science or poetry, aroused Frost.

19. Frost was very sensitive about the reading of symbols. He had heard that some of the instructors at the English School tended to slight his poetry, feeling that, unlike Yeats, Eliot, and Pound, he didn't require reading in depth because of the absence of symbols. On June 25, 1953, Frost talked at length before the Bread Loaf English School audience on what might be described as his definitive word on symbolism in poetry.

CHAPTER 11
On English Departments and Poetry
June 30, 1958

What goes on in education was increasingly on Frost's mind. As an institu-
tion, it was among his bêtes noires, and the teaching of literature especially
disturbed him. Since he had been "barding around" a great deal, as he called
it, I got firsthand glimpses into what was going on within the various English
departments. Moreover, since Bread Loaf School of English drew largely
upon teachers from high schools and preparatory schools for its enrollment,
speaking there gave him an opportunity to strike out to some purpose. And he
did, as the following talk makes clear.

The usual repetitions, false starts, and awkward spots have mainly been
eliminated. I have, however, left in a few interjectory statements when they
seemed to add to the tone of the discussion. Since the injunction "see" often
appears, it can be taken for one of Frost's more specific locutionary man-
nerisms. "See" is his signature. "Mehr licht," demanded Goethe; "see," Frost
urged. The title—a banal one for which Frost is not responsible—at least has the
merit of describing what Frost was talking about.

Another important idiosyncratic matter is the poet's reaction to his "little
preliminary indulgences." He didn't want—at least on this particular
occasion—to establish any sense of interrelationship between the generaliza-
tions in the opening talk and the poems he read. On June 2, 1956, however,
while talking on mild and wild surmises, he had integrated the opening talk
with the reading. True to a poet's prerogative, he did exactly what he felt like
doing and justified it with his own poetic logic. He had a precedent in his
favorite Emerson. "I would write on the lintels of the door-post, Whim." In
the reading Frost was all for insisting upon the form in his poems, especially
the rhymes: "And just let's take the little rhymes for the fun of it." In talking he
rambled with impunity; in writing, he was all for neatness, order, form.

That's a kind of tall order; something to live up to, I suppose. [1] It has been my luck to kick around in education as much as in anything. I don't see why I shouldn't say a word about education tonight. The word *integration* has a special meaning in education, hasn't it? And I suppose that since the very beginning of my curious career in teaching I've been in every department there is. I'm a living, walking case of integration. [*Laughter*] I've taught Latin, taught solid geometry, and I've taught all the rest of things. [2] It always amuses me. I'm a terrible critic of schools and school people.

I said to somebody once that I'd taught philosophy. [3] "What philosophy did you teach?" See. You'd know a school person would say that. [*Laughter*] I said: "My philosophy!" See. They meant Spinoza, Plato, or what—you know—the history of philosophy they thought [meant]. See. That's what it means most of the time, doesn't it?—the history of philosophy. I had one teacher in philosophy—two that might be said to teaching their own philosophy. [4] Nobody asked them whose philosophy they taught. Then, I've been in it so long. That's a very significant [thing] to me that I should be asked that. Whose philosophy did I teach? What philosophy? Whose, they meant.

Another curious thing is I find girls and boys, as they talk to me around in all those colleges and places, seem to me to be reciting. They can only tell me what they know in the order in which they learned it. See. And the object of this integration should be to scatter a person all through departments—majoring and minoring and subminoring or whatever you call it; it ought to be a very mixed thing. And out of that mixture he ought to run a little change, a little concatenation of thought. And that ought to be the text. In the little poem it ought to be—even in a short one, you know—that you can put your finger on five or six items that come from different quar-

1. He was introduced as an old pro, whose playing fields are nationwide classes and forms, chapels and auditoriums, the nub of whose play is education by poetry.

2. In view of the considerable range in early curricula, this is an amusing exaggeration.

3. Teaching at Amherst College in 1923, Frost straddled two departments: a course in selected readings from American, English, and European literature in the English department, and one on judgment in history, literature, and religion in the philosophy department. See Thompson's *Robert Frost: The Years of Triumph*, pp. 250-52.

4. One philosopher was George Santayana, with whom Frost studied at Harvard University, 1897–99. The other philosopher to whom Frost refers is William James, but he did not study under him while at Harvard.

ters of the universe in it [the poem]. Not out of any department. There ought to be that. That's the satisfaction you have as you write the poem or the essay, that you match the things you didn't know you had with the feeling that you've taken another step. I summon something I almost didn't know I had. I have a command.

I went out to Pittsburgh about education on a condition. I said I'd go only—see—if I was going to be able to holler near the pile—that meant the pile, you know, that's out there. And I hollered near the pile and I seemed to make some impression on everybody but the pile. There were editorials about it and all that, but I haven't heard of any money yet. [5] Not for me, you know, but where I want it in the educational world. I don't want it for the damned colleges, you know; I want it for the high schools. I want it where it belongs—for the American high schools. I tell them just one thing about that —one of these little things today—one little thing: that I sit around with in town and gown all over the United States graduating teachers, and in the last year I've only met (this is town and gown, mind you, both school and town that I'm in)—I've only met in these beautiful towns, college towns, I've only met one high-school teacher in the year invited in. They're not of our class. Something wrong. If you go to Exeter or Andover, they're all on the college level, the teachers are. I meet them—the whole business. But I've only met one high-school teacher in the year. Something. Just that.

I hear Barzun talking—criticizing our system, as if it ought to be like the French. [6] That's his point of view, really. It's good, it's brilliant. But it's all that one thing. He wants to speed up [the system] and harden it up. But I'm not interested in speeding it up or hardening it up; I'm interested in toning it up. See. And the way I'd tone it up is to elevate the high school in some way—socially—or in some way. And I went out [to Pittsburgh] with a plan to do something

5. Frost was referring colloquially to "the pile" of the wealthy Mellon family in Pittsburgh, and particularly to Paul Mellon who had, on occasion, given generously to the arts. What the poet wanted was some wealthy person or foundation to endow a permanent chair for outstanding teachers of literature in high school, and I understand this was done at Allegheny High School in Pittsburgh in memory of Willa Cather, who taught there from 1903 to 1906.

6. Jacques Barzun (1907–), professor of modern European history at Columbia University and sometime dean of faculties and provost of the university, is of French birth. Among his publications are: *Darwin, Marx, Wagner: Critique of a Heritage* (1941), *Teacher in America* (1945), *Berlioz and the Romantic Century* (1950), *God's Country and Mine* (1954), *The Energies of Art* (1956), and *The House of Intellect* (1959).

about that, and we'll see what comes of it. Nothing will, probably. They just like to hear me talk.

I was once asked to lecture at Chicago, I remember, years ago when Manley and a lot of them were there—a great gang, the great days. [7] And, as I was put on the train in the night—this was many years ago, thirty or forty years ago—the president's secretary said to me: "You know you weren't asked out here for your poetry. These old-timers here—Manley and all of them—like to hear you rail about education. That's all." I went to bed on that. I didn't sleep. [*Laughter*] They were all western, you know; they hadn't accepted me as a westerner yet; and it isn't railing exactly.

I know what I want. For instance, I could have a whole plan of integration. See. Get it right while you wait. See. The first thing of all is that the aim is the ability to generalize—not to be afraid to be an unscrupulous generalizer; that is, the one that doesn't stick at trifles, you know—to learn to be sweeping about history and art and everything you know and have things to say. There are two things about that. What you call general education is now run as if all the generalizing is to be done by certain heroes in the faculty. They do all the generalizing. And now that's all right if it sets the example to all the graduate students and everybody else: that what their end in life is [is] to do some of their own generalizing and to resent a little group being given all the generalizations. I'd just as soon have a thousand of brick backed up and dumped onto me and let me put it into the shape I want, you know. It's mine to shape. It's my shaping. The shaping is mine. And I remember I early felt that. But I could admire a great generalizer, and there are some fine ones going, you know. But it seems to me they steal the whole show, and they make us forget that the object is to set others generalizing. Let's hear you generalize.

Now I've heard people sitting around say that all generalizing is unsafe. There's a tone of that in good society. But what are you doing but saying things, you know, at the risk of your judgment and your taste? You're venturing in taste and judgment—the extent, you know, of your resource, where you get it. You get it in life. You get it looking out the windows. You get it looking in the bookcase. You get it in school. And you get it in business, and you get it in the news-

---

7. John Matthews Manley (1865–1940) was professor and head of the English department at the University of Chicago (1898–1933). An outstanding Chaucerian scholar, he published *Specimens of the Pre-Shakespearean Drama* (1897), *Chaucer* (1928), *Some New Light on Chaucer* (1926), and *Chaucer and the Rhetoricians* (1926).

paper. There was a gay time in education when real professors didn't read the newspaper. I used to hear that back when I was younger. "No, I don't know what goes on in the newspaper!" That sort of thing. Then the next you know some of these sociologists hung a newspaper on the wall and lectured from it. [*Laughter*] And so it went.

But the integration might be like this. Suppose I claim for the English department that it might be the clearinghouse, the place where everything came tumbling together that way and [was] put in order by the orderly mind in the English department. Then let the other departments be a little narrow—a little down-to-the-mere-thousand-of-bricks that I've been talking about. Let them be. And then how would you manage it? You'd say: You're supposed to be generalizing in what you write, whether you write stories, essays, or poems. There ought to be in everything you write some sign that you come from almost everywhere. Nobody can tell where you got it, who you have been reading. They say to me: "Who've you been reading?" And that follows you through your life. Somebody will say, "Have you been reading Browning?" You never get anything out of me that way. I wouldn't even show resentment, I would feel it so deeply. I don't want to be pressable.

But now suppose the English departments were run that way—as a place where the writing was supposed to show that you were all over the college and all over the world, you know, outside athletics and everything. You would always find your figures unexpected and out of different levels and out of different times in your life. See. A long time ago I got a college president to agree with me that we would do this if I'd come and do it with him: [8] that we would treat the English department as a kind of clearinghouse where everything showed, and various departments could put in their claim and have something to say about it—a little of me, a little of somebody else. But I'd go so far as to say that there ought to be an English department with a policeman's right to go and take papers out of any department and mark them for not talking anybody's jargon—any departmental jargon.

Well, that's all. I'm not going to talk too much about that, about any of it. But I'm sure that—oh, dear! These hurried-up judgments

8. After the dismissal of Alexander Meiklejohn, George Daniel Olds, professor of Greek and Latin literature at Amherst, was appointed president of Amherst College and in 1923 he persuaded Frost to return to teach in the English and philosophy departments, according to Thompson, *Robert Frost: The Years of Triumph,* pp. 228-29. See also note 3, above.

they're making now, the reports on education are just absolutely worthless. I haven't seen anything that excited me at all. The root of it all is that: are you getting young people to the point, somewhere before college ends, of valuing themselves on an occasional generalization they make of their own? And keep that word for me. I'd rest it on that. I said down at Smith College once at one of these raids, you know—Miss Drew, I think, was there. [9] My speech was on how can you tell when you're thinking. And that's the way you can tell when you're thinking—one of the ways. Do you ever make a generalization that's a little concatenation of things you picked up, God knows where, you know? Did you ever make one? A little song-and-dance, you know; a little rigmarole, you know. Do you have them? Sometimes they don't go very deep.

On the last one, I talked on the two great towers—Babel and anti-Babel. Where did I get those? Got one out of the Bible and I got one down in New York—the Rockefeller belt—the tower of anti-Babel, to undo what Babel did. [10] Babel scattered us all into the various languages, and I advocated this. But everything ends up in favor of the English departments. I said, "Let us strengthen the English department so that if the world comes to the undoing of Babel—and if we have just one language—let's have it so that it'll be English. See. So my poetry won't have to be translated." [*Prolonged laughter and applause*] Well, you see, that's just a rigmarole. You can't expect to have things done about that. You would expect to annoy somebody and please somebody else. That's all.

And then I was thinking the other day how sick I was of the word *evolution*. I have to report that it's subsiding somewhat—you don't hear it as much as you used to. I never was satisfied with the evolution talk in all the years by the Huxleys—the three generations of Huxleys; I never was satisfied that there wasn't a terrible gap still between animal life and human. See. Still unsatisfied. There's something, you know, about us. And my theory is—just casually, this way, a little rigmarole—my theory is that when the meat and the vegetables were ready we arrived on a saucer. And this saucer thing is in our instincts, you know. We want to go saucering now to the next place. And all the early country people I lived with drank their tea out of saucers. There's something about saucers the same as there is about us. See. Well. I don't set that up to make any difference to you.

9. Elizabeth Drew, professor of English at Smith College, was a long-time member of the instructoral staff at the Bread Loaf School of English, offering courses in modern poetry, drama, and the English novel.
10. Rockefeller Center in New York City is Frost's symbol of anti-Babel.

It will offend some of you and please some of you fundamentalists from Tennessee.

But what's all this got to do with poetry? Well, just this. I think poetry, again, is the great clearinghouse. It's where you don't want to just recite it or set [it] to verse, as people did at one time, you know. They tried to write the great evolutionary poem. Attempts were made. They think: "Well, Lucretius did it; why shouldn't we have ours with just Darwin in it?" I used to look at them. Dreadful things. But the whole thing was already worked out. You see, the generalization was done in a few minutes by Darwin on the voyage of the *Beagle* where he got the seasickness that he never got over.[11] Just that one little gleam he had. One of these things. And he scattered it, making everything come tumbling into it, you know, the way I'm saying, out of everywhere. He [Darwin] never rested from it. He didn't have much more, did he? He seemed to think it was necessary to fasten that on people.

Well, now I'm going to say poems to you. And I've always had to say, after these talks, that they've got nothing to do with the poems. They don't lead up to the poems anyway; they're not prefaces. They're just my little preliminary indulgence. I want to have a little fun out of this; don't want to keep repeating the same poems. Now I've said enough. But sometimes they [the opening remarks] are very deep and serious [to] me; for instance, my annoyance with some words sets me off on one of these rigmaroles, frame-ups, and one I've thought a great deal of is my antipathy to the word *agnostic*. I know what's the matter with that. I thought just the other day —someone said to me—a beautiful lady said to me not so very long ago—we were all saying what we all were. I was saying, historically speaking I'm a Congregationalist. And we were carrying on and she said she was an atheist. I said: "Well, thank God, you're not an agnostic!" And she said: "I had a suspicion you'd feel that way about agnostics." I won't go into that, it would take all the rest of the evening.

All right. Here goes for the poems. Too bad you can't retaliate. I have a notion to go way back and just say some of the early ones and

11. One of Frost's three favorite books—the other two were *Robinson Crusoe* and *Walden*—was *The Voyage of the "Beagle"*(1840). But in the decidedly curious dissatisfaction with the Huxleys (Thomas Henry Huxley and Sir Julian Huxley), Frost's semiwhimsical play on saucers will give pause to those who might think of him as a free-thinking opponent of religious orthodoxy.

wander down through my poems. Isn't it strange that, at the other end of this—the thought part of it that seems to be so important to me, that goes on all the time wherever I am, wherever I walk, wherever I read, that's almost as bad as revery, the aimless sort of always going on—at the other extreme of that must be my love of neatness, of a little poem, you know, and the rhymes of it and the little bits. I made some people angry by talking about that entirely of an evening. I have a little ivory box that I had in San Francisco many years ago.[12] It was a Japanese box—a couple of inches—a little box with a slide cover, carved, and in it two layers of pieces and they fitted together—a little puzzle; it's not much of a puzzle, but the lower layer is two pieces that make the square, and the next one is four pieces that make the square. And you see what the two would have to be, and the others you'd have to think about a little. But they're very like a poem to me, with two sentences in one stanza and four sentences in the other stanza but different stanzas, and the poem is the box.

And I talked about that once on one of those occasions and somebody got very angry and said, "That's all poetry is to you!" And I said, "Yeh!" [*Emphatic*] And the little rhymes. I saw a very pretty poem by a little girl the other day—a really pretty little poem—about wishing on a star and a cloudy night and how was she going to find a star to wish on with when it was too cloudy and no star to wish on. But the first little stanza of it set you to hoping that she was going to get out of the two stanzas all right. But she didn't. The last stanza she had to give up on. Very lucky little rhymes in the first one, and then the little one she couldn't quite get. And she knew it. She was a nice young girl. I said, "I wish you had the same luck with the second stanza that you had with the first." A pretty little idea it was—a poem—one of the little frame-ups. And she said yes, she didn't have the same luck. Luck. Superstition. That's why I'm not an agnostic.

Suppose I said a little one to you. Our friend Ciardi is coming here soon.[13] I've seen him so we've made our peace with each other. He'll be on the scene pretty soon. Ciardi's been making a public spectacle of me. [*Laughter*] That's all right. It's very fine—what he did

12. I recall hearing Frost analogize about a poem and this little ivory Japanese puzzle-box in the mid-1920s at the Bread Loaf School of English.

13. John Ciardi, director of the Bread Loaf Writers' Conference, had published an interpretive essay entitled "The Way to a Poem" in the *Saturday Review*, April 12, 1958, in which he associated "Stopping by Woods" with a death wish. Frost has this in mind and here rebuts the friend who has been making "a public spectacle" of him.

—but it's amusing what he thinks of my little poem, "Stopping by Woods." [Reads "Stopping by Woods"]

Now, you see, we won't go into that, but you'd hardly call such a slight thing an orgy. [Laughter and applause]And the little rhymes. He calls that—I believe Ciardi and others have said—some people have said—it's a suicide poem. That's going some. But he thinks it's a death poem. And you can see how you could say: "Life is lovely, dark and deep." See. "But I have promises to keep. I have heaven to go to, you know." Like that. You could do that. That analogy's in it. Many others. You say, just as I could right now: this is a lovely dark and deep situation, but I've got something [else], I ought to teach a class tomorrow, or something like that. Promises to keep. Company of an evening. One o'clock in the morning—two o'clock. An appropriate thing to say—that stanza is lovely, dark and deep, but I've got to be getting along. And it doesn't mean that you're going to do anything bad. Sounds rather good to me. I can see that someone might turn it the other way, like the old saying, "I used to be afraid to go home in the dark, but now I'm afraid to go home at all." [Laughter] They think it's like that. And all this metaphorical play and all!

But here's a little death [poem]—just for the fun of it. This is a real death poem. It's called—I guess I call it "Away"—"Away"—"Away." [Giving the word different intonations] That would make you suspicious to begin with. And just let's take the little rhymes for the fun of it for me. [Reads "Away!"] Now every step of that is the fun for me of the rhymes. I'll say it again just so you can see how guilty I am—but a slave of the rhyme. [Repeats "Away!"] That's the moment—that one is. That's unmistakably a death poem. [Laughter] All right.

Then, these lyrics, "The Road Not Taken": you can go along over these rhymes just as if you didn't know that they were there—as if you all but forget they were there—like this. [Reads "The Road Not Taken"] You see, that talks past the rhymes and almost hides them as it takes them. That's the kind of thing that you'd like to feel complimented to have anyone say to you: "When I read that I can just hear you talking." I wish they could.

All right. There, way back very early, this little one—not in the meters I usually use but just in talk. [Reads "Mowing"] Now, you see that one line in there again—there's always one line —something—"The fact is the sweetest dream that labor knows." That had a lot to do with my career. Just my wish—my satisfaction —in gloating. The fact. Gloating. The poetry is gloating. It's not getting up fanciful things. I had no business to mention fay and elf in it. I always feel sorry about that. But that's—"Anything more than the truth would have seemed too weak /To the earnest love," etcetera.

[*Repeats "The fact is the sweetest dream" as "the fact is the dream"*] I've just seen a whole essay to disprove that: the fact is the sweetest, etcetera. That's all right, you see.

Then: [*Reads "Tree at My Window"*] See the rhythm again in that last stanza. No matter what I think it means, I'm infatuated with the way the rhymes come off there. [*Laughter*] And then of another kind—"Once by the Pacific." It was before either of the world wars that I wrote this. This is a memory of the Cliff House beach—outside San Francisco. [*Reads "Once by the Pacific"; repeats last line*] I didn't say that quite right. You know one of the things that comes over you once in awhile is how much can you say in poetry without being at all expressive in the tones? Can you write poems poker-face—the tones of which will be poker-face? Is there some object in doing that? I think there is in the way things are going. They've got a poker-face sound—so many of them. Sometimes they're very good at saying but they don't set up for me. And then you get it—there's a danger of acting up too [much]. You're between the devil and the deep sea, all right.

Browsing around—see—then going back again to that earliest book of all [*A Boy's Will*] that I had my beginnings with. Things like this. Here's one in which, if you want me to tell you something personal about the poem, I was very much aware that I was giving it a prayer sound. See. "Oh hushed October morning mild." I wouldn't have put that "mild" to that if I hadn't been prayerful. [*Reads "October"*]

That's one of the very earliest I ever wrote—way, way back. And then I wrote one called "Reluctance." Most of these I'm saying to you have been all strung through my books. They're all in that last one—the "Away!" one I said—the same thread down through the years, the same play. [*Reads "Reluctance"*]

That was one of my first fortunes. I remember my old friend—I made a friendship out of that with a famous pirate, Thomas Bird Mosher, some of you may know.[14] He pirated European poetry and published it in America and paid the poets over there in England but went over the heads of their publishers and was much disliked by the publishers. But he was quite a friend of mine. And he once said, sitting down beside me—he printed that ["Reluctance"] once way back early in my time—but he sat down by me after I had three books, and he said, "Robert, you're going to tell me frankly—have you written

14. Thomas Bird Mosher (1852–1923), a Maine man, founded the Bibelot in 1895, which reprinted little-known literary masterpieces and printed a series of small volumes in excellent taste.

more than that one poem?" [*Murmur of laughter*] He died pretty soon—I didn't have to kill him. [*Loud laughter*] Then, I'd like to stir up old ones like that tonight. The new ones—the same thing—let's just see for the tone. This reminds me a little of "October" in the address that it has. [*Reads "Choose Something Like a Star"*]

That's different. And then, here's the beginning. I won't read all of this—just this nice, amusing beginning. It's called "The Broken Drought." [*Reads first two lines*] We won't go into that tonight. And then—this one shouldn't be in the book necessarily, but it was out of the irritation of a certain time when people were talking, you know, the kind of other thing—it's "A Case for Jefferson," I call it. [*Reads "A Case for Jefferson"*]

See, that's the period poem. [*Laughter*] That's what they call dated. We won't insist on that. But it's just as true as the gun. These fellows are all denying it, but they've all gone to cover about it. Just so sure. I said to a person high up in the government lately, I said, "As long as all my educated friends and Mrs. Roosevelt [*laughter*] think that socialism is inevitable and can't be avoided and has got to come that way, why don't you and I join in and hurry it up and get it over with? It couldn't last." And he said, "I wouldn't favor that policy." His policy is to drag his feet. Those things I've cared about, but not cared about the way I care about rhyme and meter. Here's a little more recent one, too, in the book, but it's one of the last ones in the book, I guess. It's called "Closed for Good." It's just about a road that's been abandoned—an abandoned road. Again, watch the rhymes for my sake—to please me. [*Reads "Closed for Good"*]

Now it's nice to get that chance to use that tone for the last line. That's what you're writing about, too. Well, haven't I been about long enough? Much talk tonight. Let's see, what shall I say, Doc [Cook]? I haven't said a line of blank verse—blankety-blank. [*Laughter*] Now, take one like this (let's see if I can lay my hand on it), just, again, for something I do with a rhyme that nobody would get at all except seeing it. It isn't where I thought it was. [*Fumbling through the book*] I would like to find it. I've forgotten its name. I guess I'll give it up. Take this one. It's another one people have bothered around about—the meaning of—and I'm glad to have them get more out of it than I put in. [*Laughter*] That's all right. I do that myself. I get more out of them as the years go on. The very first line strikes this note. [*Reads "The Most of It"*]

To get literary again in parting: I met a critic [Kenneth Burke] the other night out in California who said to me, "All people's writing, prose or verse, will be found an effort of their inner nature to get their own name into the writing. Now, for instance, in that poem of yours ["The Most of It"]—'forced the underbrush.' " See, this deer forced the underbrush.[15] That looks innocent enough to me. But he said that the name Frost tried to get in. [*Laughter*] This is the subconscious, you know. And then he went on, to our amusement, to show how all words could become another word while you waited. He wrote out two words with eleven or twelve letters in them, two of them. He said, thoughtfully, "You know, we treat them as an equation." Said that one there cancels that one there. By Grimm's law we can dismiss that one; and when he got through, [he] grinned and said, "See, that's the same word. They didn't start the same but they ended up the same. You know who that is." I said to him, "Ah-h-h, you know. I've been reading you." And he said, "I think you're trying to sound grim." And I said, "It's a grim piece, you know, one of Hawthorne's things."[16] "Oh," he said, "I've done worse things than that. I can darken everything." He smiled—a pleasant fellow. You know him—some of you. One more poem—blank verse—I always get chided for not saying "Birches." Take this one. You always like to say to young people that there's no sharp line between good and evil. "You didn't think it was the good over the bad, did you?" you ask. And they admit they didn't. Poor things. This poem is one of the most interest in this respect—"There Are Roughly Zones." There are roughly zones between falling to sleep and not falling to sleep. [*Reads "There Are Roughly Zones"; prolonged applause*]

Shall I read some more or sit down? Maybe a couple of poems—"After Apple-Picking" or "Design." I'll say "After Apple-Picking."

Now this is one that I wrote and forgot I had—years ago. And someone turned it up and it began to get said about and I put it in the book. It's one of those that is very undramatic in the speech entirely. It's a kind of poker-face piece. [*Reads "Design"*]

Shall I say that twice so you can look at it, the better to look at it? [*Rereads "Design"*] This is the kind of poem I am never sure of because I am too observing. See. How observing do you want to be? And I always wanted to be very observing, but I have always been af-

15. Kenneth Burke (1897–), one of the more original literary critics of our time, is the author of *The White Oxen* (1924), *Counterstatement* (1931), *Permanence and Change* (1935), *Attitudes toward History* (1937), *The Philosophy of Literary Form* (1937), *A Grammar of Motives* (1945), and *A Rhetoric of Motives* (1950).

16. Burke's essay, to which Frost refers, appeared in *Hopkins' Review* (5: 45-65) in 1952 and was entitled "Ethan Brand: A Preparatory Investigation."

raid of my own observations. I'd rather be observing psychologically, rather seeing into people, seeing into what's the matter with agnostics. This one is a very special piece of observation.[17] [*Reads "Design" again*]

This is called "After Apple-Picking." It's one of the observing [poems]. [*Reads "After Apple-Picking"; applause*]

17. Frost's reaction to "Design" is self-revelatory. He tended, first, to classify it as among his nondramatic poems, implying perhaps a preference for the dramatic ones. Secondly, he deprecated close observation as Thoreau did when the latter found he became narrowly preoccupied with details in nature. "Man," Thoreau decided finally in the *Journal*, "cannot afford to be a naturalist, to look at Nature directly, but only with the side of his eye"(*Journal*, 5:45). Frost also was sensitively disturbed by extreme preoccupation with details, stating a preference for the psychological over "a very special piece of [impersonal] observation."

CHAPTER 12
Cherubic Scorn
June 29, 1959

When this talk was given, Frost was eighty-four years old. He was in good health, his voice was strong, he kept to his subject, and appeared to let the poems he chose to read ramify thematically from the Emerson reference. I have emended this talk a little, chiefly adding explanatory words where necessary for logical progression and a few explanatory phrases for clarity. I have thought it best to include the repetitions and interjections, but I have omitted the audience response. This is, literally, a viva voce reproduction—all, that is, except the most important projector, the poet's voice. I have indicated the poems presented and have distinguished between those "said" (without the book) and those read (from the book). One reason for giving the verbatim transcript is to show Frost's spontaneous and revealing reactions to the poems read or said. Among Frost's performances at the school, this talk was representative. And it happened to be given on the occasion of the fortieth anniversary of its founding.

The introduction to which Frost refers included (1) reference to Frost as a poet speaking to friends; (2) recognition of him as one of the great teachers who has taught us by metaphor; and (3) the remark that his influence casts a good shadow–buena sombra–not a "terrifying one."

For his subject he chose a phrase from the third line to the last in Emerson's "Uriel." The line reads: "Came Uriel's voice of cherub scorn." What Frost did with "cherub scorn" throughout the evening performance tells as much about Frost as it does about Emerson in the latter's great poem. In A Masque of Reason *(1945), Frost had referred to "Uriel" as "the greatest Western poem yet." (See* The Poetry of Robert Frost, *ed. Edward Connery Lathem (New York: Holt, Rinehart and Winston, 1969), p. 485.)*

Well, I heard the introduction that time. It was talking right to me. So I can start there. It throws me off my intentions a little. Suppose I assume an air of scholarly authority and start with a subject like this: "cherub scorn." Know where you are? "Cherub scorn." We don't approve usually in my intellectual hideout—Apalachin, places like that—we don't approve of a noun used as an adjective.[1] But it seems to be necessary there. It's Emerson speaking, you know. That's the whole of Emerson—"cherub scorn."

Now you're all here to catch up with something, or keep up with something, or get ahead of something, I suppose. And so you've probably heard I have helped found this whatever-it-is.[2] You've probably heard of the new college we're starting up at Lake Itasca, the source of the Mississippi River, the source of everything. And I won't go into it too fully. Some of us happened to get together—nine of us—and we started voting furiously, see, getting 5-4 results all the time. And as we voted, this new college gradually took form. And the first novelty of it, you may have heard, is that sometimes we made a decision by minority vote. See. Sometimes by the majority; some-times by the minority. And we decided that by lot. See. We thought that after using all our brains we ought to leave something to God. And so a lot of it grew out of that. Just a word or two about it.

The first thing, the first slogan, the first phrase, to remember is it was a college that was to be all head and no overhead. See. We were to get along without the foundations at all. We were to go un-founded. The next thing was we were going to have no one admitted to it who didn't come with a proposal or a suggestion for the college, for the country, for the world, for life. Come with a proposal. See. I have this to propose; or, wouldn't it be a good idea to think this? See. No one was to be admitted [who didn't come with a proposal].

Two or three more things you may have heard. The three de-partments only—it is to be very simple—first, superstition; second,

---

1. Apalachin, a reference to the high summitry meeting of La Cosa Nostra or the Mafia in 1957 at Apalachin, N.Y., where the *capos,* or head men, were raided and their undercover operations surfaced briefly.

2. I do not think Frost is here referring to the Bread Loaf School of Eng-lish of which he has been erroneously numbered among the founders; his first association with the school began in the summer of 1921, a year after its beginning. He refers in the next sentences to a lifelong dissatisfaction with conventional institutions of education and, concomitantly, to his penchant for founding new colleges, theoretical or otherwise. I do not know who the eight other "founders" of a new college "up at Lake Itasca" were. Presuma-bly, they were like his other friends, George Whicher of Amherst and Wal-ter Hendricks, originally of Marlboro, who had ideas about fresh educa-tional ventures at the college level.

science; and third, gossip.[3] I myself have teachers for all three. I myself assume the science one. I have such a respect for science that I want it to behave itself. See. I want to take care of science. We won't go into this too much. Sometime perhaps I'll see you later and tell you more about it.

Then the teachers that come to it are to be warned of one particular thing: that they must bear with it [cherubic scorn]. We don't want anybody who hasn't a proposal or suggestion for the school, for the country, for life in general, for the world, and for the UN. [*The latter said slyly, with tongue in cheek*] Everything like that [i.e., a proposal]. But we don't want anyone around who hasn't, at the age, say, of eighteen or twenty-five or so—right around there, in those years, you know—who isn't a case of cherubic scorn.

Now cherubic scorn is the scorn a really eager spirit has for people who are older people, the old guard, older people who are lost in the difficulty of betterness. Betterness is hard, you know, and the old guard are all people who have given up on it, you know. And they deserve cherubic scorn, Emersonian scorn. He stayed cherubic all his days; he knew it; he knew that he had the feeling of contempt for a person that had aged to the point where he had given up newness, betterness, you know. Now I don't have to go into that too much, but I've lived with it. It begins, cherubic scorn begins, for the old guard when the old guard gets to be about thirty. And you have to stand it. I've lived through it a good many years and always enjoyed it and all that. I just thought I'd tell you about that and be a little Emersonian to begin with. You know, in Emerson, just those two words are the heart of all the Emerson writing. Cherubic scorn! Surprise subject!

Now you aren't here to listen to me talk this way. I just thought I'd open something for you to think of while I'm reading to you. Isn't it strange that you've read that "Uriel" poem so many times and never stopped there as the very heart of it all and the heart of all of Emerson? Cherubic scorn! Isn't it strange? And all the courses you've had and everything. I just wanted to show you a little cherubic scorn of my own. That's it. See. Along comes a new idea like communism with its cherubic scorn—I lived through all that in the early twenties at

3. Frost frequently made references to the "story" implied in "gossip" while being interviewed by the British author-critic Cecil Day Lewis on September 13, 1957. Religion, science, and "friendly gossip" were "the three great things" (see *Interviews with Robert Frost*, p. 176). In the opening talk and reading at the Bread Loaf School of English on July 2, 1956, Frost had scored the same point about "the three greats in our life." For superstition, substitute religion, and his view clarifies.

Amherst College. I was just surrounded by young people who scorned me for not seeing this new hope, you know. The whole school [Amherst] was full of them. It was a new hope to them. And it was very attractive in some of them. Some of them gave it up. They're old guard now. Worse than I am. Right.

●

I have a long poem that I shan't read you tonight. It ["Kitty Hawk"] will be in my next book.[4] It's a good deal about flight. Flight. And it's the reason why I'm going to take the second department —science—the science department in this new college. So you're listening to realities, you know. And it begins with my visit when young—I shan't read the poem to you—Kitty Hawk, long before the Wright brothers were there. And it ends with its dawning on me that all science—that I used to think was domestic science only; it took some time for me to get over that, domestic science—is our hold on the planet. It's domestic, you see. It has been that all the time. It might look as if it was going to be a kind of interplanetary tourism next, you know. That question is up.

But it dawned on me at the point that all, the whole, the great enterprise of life, of the world, the great enterprise of our race, is our penetration into matter, deeper and deeper; carrying the spirit deeper into matter. And though it looks like something different out into space, that's just deeper into matter, that's material penetration of the spirit—of the ethereal into the material. Put it that way. And that is our destiny—that is why science is our greatness. It's got to do with our penetration into the material. And how did I get there? Through reading a good many pages—but I reach the point where I say, "God's own descent / Into flesh was meant / As a demonstration / That the supreme merit / Lay in risking spirit / In substantiation" and in going into material. That's what our religion means. That's what the Christian religion means—God's own descent into flesh in substantiation. And that's just the same if you're writing a doctor's thesis. See. You're risking spirit in substantiation. And usually the spirit gets lost. But we've got to take the risk. Sometimes it doesn't, you know. Sometimes it fails. Sometimes in the byproduct of science we lose the spirit entirely; but not in the act of scientific penetration—deeper, deeper, deeper, further, further, further. "We cannot look out far. / We cannot look in deep." But —as far as we can and as deep as we can, as far out as we can—still we penetrate into matter, further into matter. That outlines a poem I

4. "Kitty Hawk" appears in *In the Clearing*, pp. 41-58.

131

won't read. I quoted a part of it—a part of it I wanted you to hear: "But God's own descent / Into flesh was meant / As a demonstration / That the supreme merit / Lay in risking spirit / In substantiation."

•

Suppose I begin with something I have in my head—some offhand ones. I joke about science. We all do. This is a real field day for comic-strip teasing, you know. Everyone can make his own comic strip, that is to say, one like this I made:

I once had a cow that jumped over the moon.
Not on to the moon but over.
I don't know what made her so lunar a loon;
All she'd been having was clover.

That was back in the days of my godmother Goose.
But though we are goosier now,
And all tanked up with mineral juice,
We haven't caught up with my cow.[5]

Now you'd think that I was bothered by science and things like that. We have a right to tease those people till they get somewheres. Why don't they go? I notice that Mr. Killian was warning us not to get too excited about getting into space, that we'd better attend to some other things, too.[6] Licking the Russians, I believe he meant. Better lick the Russians than explore the moon.

Then, see, one of the things you have in my school, in the gossip department, is to learn to distinguish between a vice and a propensity. It's quite necessary. And to do that, now, take this as a propensity. Jealousy is a propensity; it isn't a vice. And this is one—I don't know the name of this one [i.e., propensity]—"The Objection to Being Stepped On." You ought not to mind that if you're a good liberal, you know. But you can't help it.

[Says "The Objection to Being Stepped On"] And that all has to do with this question of back and forwards. You have to be reminded that the Hungarian Revolution that occurred just before my time, that I heard a lot about when I was young, was all fought, nearly, with farm tools—the poor peasants—pitchforks and flails and anything they

5. See "Lines Written in Dejection," *In the Clearing,* p. 85
6. Dr. James R. Killian, Jr., president of Massachusetts Institute of Technology, 1948-59, was reacting to the chagrin of our taking a back seat in the space race following the Soviet's launching of Sputnik I, the first man-made satellite, in 1957.

could lay hands on. Weapons go to tools and tools go to weapons—it's back and forth. That's what that poem's about. It's deeper than you think.

Then, turning to this sort of place up here, this sort of lap—this little one, too, is almost a lap in the mountain. [*Reads "The Birthplace"*] That's one I never read before. I thought I'd look around in *Complete Poems* a little tonight. See.

Then another one that I have read many times, and I often read it the same as you sing "The Star-Spangled Banner" when you get through an occasion. This is called "The Gift Outright." It doesn't sing like "The Star-Spangled Banner." I didn't mean that. I'm not comparing it with "The Star-Spangled Banner." [*Says "The Gift Outright."*]

Another—here's one I haven't read much. This is a harder one to read. [*Reads "A Young Birch"*] That's away down late among them [the poems]. Let's take something away back early: "To the Thawing Wind." This is what we waited for in the spring in the days when we were shut in on the farm. [*Reads "To the Thawing Wind"*]

Here's another. This one is called "Mowing." [*Reads "Mowing"*] I often think in these poems that one line in them—nearly every one of them, one line in them—has something to do with my own philosophy of art; not philosophy, but philosophy of art. Take that line there, "The fact is the sweetest dream that labor knows." Doting on things, gloating on things, just dwelling on things. Not getting up things, not exaggerating things, not whooping things up, but just gloating.

And here's a California one—a memory of California—the climate of San Francisco. "A Peck of Gold," this is called. This is a child's one, really. [*Reads "A Peck of Gold"*] I didn't say beforehand that I was changed from saying that when I got East. In the East I found everybody saying, "We all must eat our peck of dirt." I was a Californian. Here's another California one. I can't see you. It's getting dark, isn't it? Isn't there any light? Just a little light. [*Light turned on*] That's it.

This one is called "Once by the Pacific." This is out at the Cliff House beach when I was young. I left there when I was very young, but one evening I felt as if I was alone out there. I probably wasn't. Probably my parents were somewhere near. [*Says "Once by the Pacific"*]

I mustn't just try to get away from those I've been reading. I've got to say this one to you: "Provide, Provide." Wait a second. That isn't what I'm going to say. [*Reads "Triple Bronze"*] Some more politics.

And this is called [reads *"It Is Almost the Year Two Thousand"*; reads *"The Secret Sits"*]

Then, I've some more like that, haven't I? That are going to be in the new book [*In the Clearing*, 1962]. Like this one.

> Forgive, O Lord, my little jokes on Thee
> And I'll forgive Thy great big one on me.

I saw Aldous Huxley speaking about our dubious human existence, our dubious position in the universe. Dubious—isn't it terrible?[7] We must all feel that way or you wouldn't be released in a laugh about that, you know. What is it? What is it?

Then one that isn't so funny as that or deep as that is. Gets you down to thinking of elementary things. See. I spoke of the older people that get lost in the difficulty of attaining oneness and pureness and all that sort of thing, and on what terms do they give it up? That's what they call philosophy, I suppose. Something like that, I suppose. That's what they call Buddhism. One of the dreams, of course, is that there is some sort of an element—hydrogen or something—that is the one thing we could all be, you know, that there is some oneness somewhere. Far as you get, there is none—the amoeba, you think of, and the amoeba while you're looking at it needs a psychiatrist; it's got something going on, another person, going on inside it. See. It's barely containing itself. It's a doubleness right there.

Then this little couplet I made once from looking at a lump of iron that was supposed to be perfectly pure and meant to be the oneness that we could all attain—the purity.[8] And I said:

> Nature within her inmost self divides
> To trouble men with having to take sides.

7. Is this a confusion of Sir Julian Huxley with Aldous Huxley? See *Interviews with Robert Frost*, pp. 207-13.

8. According to the poet, the source of the couplet "From Iron" (which appears in *In the Clearing*, p. 95) was the lump of iron located at the United Nations building in New York City (see *Interviews with Robert Frost*, pp. 178, 196, 198). The couplet "From Iron" is dedicated to a Pakistani friend, Ahmed S. Bokhari, an assistant secretary at the UN, who had approached Frost "to put something in my head." The "something" was the great lump of iron ore weighing many tons from one of the most famous mines in the world, which the king of Sweden had sent to the UN. Placed in what is called the Meditation Room at the UN, it rested on the bedrock of Manhattan.

The lump of iron—the purest iron—is at once tools and weapons as in that poem ["The Objection to Being Stepped On"] that I told you about. It's tools and weapons right while you're looking at it. Everything's like that.

Then I'll read you a longer one. I didn't say the other one I was going to say, did I? Just for turning on a different note. [*Reads "Provide, Provide"*] It's funny, isn't it, how prophetic poetry is! I wasn't thinking of any American beauty from Hollywood marrying into Monaco when I wrote that.[9] It was long before that. "If need be occupy a throne / Where nobody can call you crone" They'll never call her [Grace Kelly] a crone, will they? She looks safe. She's in out of the cold. [*Reads "Desert Places"*]

There's one that I shan't read you that's called "On the Heart's Beginning to Cloud the Mind." One line in it is taken out to be the title. [*Repeats title*] A little bit of psychology. And [I] like to look into something that I haven't read before. Here's one.[*Turning pages*] No! I'm fussy. [*Reads "Acquainted with the Night"*] All for the tune. Tune is everything. Wait, I saw one here. [*Turning pages*] This is a harder one. I may want to say this twice to you. It's short. [*Reads "Design"*] See, that hasn't any tune at all. That's the new way to write. That's getting all the resonance out of it that you can get out of it. There's plenty of tune to that "Provide, Provide," you see. And I guess I'll read you one that I've read so many times; but you'll let me read it again. It's called "The Witch of Coös" (if I can find it). [*Starts to read it; gives up after three or four lines. Pats his coat pocket to see if he'd brought along his glasses*] No, I can't read that. I'm not sure enough of it. I came without something [his glasses]. [*Reads "The Runaway"*]

This is called "One More Brevity." I've got a poem somewhere about couplets and how couplets symbolize metaphor. There's a pairing that deeper down in is the pairing of thought that is the metaphor. And if you watch me you can see in particular places how much I enjoy a pair of rhymes. I'm getting the couplet right in the long poem. The couplet is my game just the same as the metaphor is my game. The couplet is the symbol of the metaphor. I just found that out—same as I found out about Emerson. It's funny how long you live with a thing before it dawns on you what it all is. Cherub scorn! [*Says "One More Brevity"*]

Contemplating the lump of iron ore, Frost made a couplet in which he played with the idea that nature contains symbolically and materially the source of *both* peaceful tools and military weapons.

9. This is a reference to Grace Kelly, who married Prince Rainier of Monaco on April 19, 1956.

And that puzzles so many teachers and so many students they don't know what to say. They're seeking something more. People will say to me right out, "I know what you mean—just what's eating you?" So I put that in verse way, way back. I saw it quoted yesterday. It's called "Revelation."[10] This brings God into it again. "We make ourselves a place apart / Behind light words that tease and flout." You can say that about any poem you write. We still want to be found. Does seem a pity, doesn't it, that they don't get it: How far do you have to go with them? How far will you go with them? That's a long, long time ago, fifty, seventy years ago I wrote that—sixty years ago—nearly seventy. [*Continues reading "Revelation"*]"To inspire / The understanding of a friend": we have to be so damned literal about it. This is the same question [in the poem] of why God came to send us a son down in this neighborhood. Try to come from behind. And then, oftentimes when you come from behind and try to tell about it you haven't made it any better. Let's go back to this one—a young one that I love. [*Reads "Reluctance"*] That's one of the early ones, too. Now, shall I read an old-timer like "Mending Wall," and maybe one easy one to end it? [*Says "Mending Wall"*] See me try to make believe I'm reading it. You know, I've read that so often I've sort of lost the right way to say, "Good fences make good neighbors." See. There's a special way to say [it] I used to have in my imagination, and it seems to have gone down. You say it in two different ways there. All right, then. This is "Departmental."

ENCORES

[*Says "Take Something Like a Star"*] I might linger at that just a moment. It's just the same—"Some mystery becomes the proud." See. What is it that makes us hide to be sought out? It's kind of pride, I suppose, but it's a long story, isn't it? "Some mystery becomes the proud." And do you know I wrote that line in thinking of one of my fellow poets years ago?[11] I had him in mind, that his pride shut me out with his mystery, but I thought it became him.

And by star—I've just used that as though it might be some poet of a thousand years ago—two thousand years—something way out of all of this. [*Repeats in singsong fashion*] "When at times the mob is

10. "Revelation," in *A Boy's Will* (London: David Nutt, 1913), is not to be confused with "All Revelation" in *A Witness Tree* (New York: Henry Holt, 1942).

11. Frost is referring to an assumed rival, T. S. Eliot.

swayed / To carry praise or blame too far." When you say "the people, yes," you know, you mean the people yes *and* no, don't you? See. One more little one—see if I can think of something. "In a Disused Graveyard"—never read this before so I'll have to grope my way through it. Remember there's one right down the road here —disused graveyard.[12] [*Reads "In a Disused Graveyard"*] One of the odd things is to hear some of my friends say that "Stopping by Woods" is a death poem. Of course it ain't; 'tain't tainted. This is a death poem that Doc [Cook] wants me to say. [*Says "Away!"*] All right. Good night. That's all.

I feel like asking you just now, but you can't tell me, what are you here for: to hear me read poems or to see me read poems? Or to hear if I have anything naughty to say—something wicked about education or something? And I'm the greatest living authority on education. That's why I keep founding new colleges. But it isn't interesting to me. I've heard it said that everybody knows what I'm going to say. See. You knew I was going to say all that about this new college. You know I did. Probably they mean by that that they always know what my bias will be—see—what my politics will be, or something like that. You can tell whom I'm going to vote for next, probably. Probably you can, probably you can't. You could probably find out it you listened long enough that my second greatest admiration is Madison.[13] Madison, you see. You've heard that before, probably. I'm always wondering if you know what I'm going to say next.

Isn't it beautiful, you know, to think that "May be true what I had heard / Earth's a howling wilderness, / Truculent with force and fraud"?[14] See. I never got away from that in my life—that earth is truculent with force and fraud. The force is the first and the mouth is the fraud. See. And when the lawyers have stopped talking with fraud and you get sick of hearing the mouth going, the fraud going, why then, you go to war with the fist. That's what Emerson meant by that. He was no pacifist. "Truculent with force and fraud." But he thinks he got out of it by picking blackberries. Still it may be my turn to try to find out from you whether you know what I'm going to say, so there's no use in my saying that I'd better get to read so you can see me read. All right. Good night. I'll never know.

12. On Route 125, now Robert Frost Memorial Highway, about a half mile west of the Middlebury College campus at Bread Loaf, is the "disused graveyard" to which he refers.

13. James Madison was one of Frost's favorite American political figures.

14. "Berrying," in Ralph Waldo Emerson's *Poems* (Boston: Houghton Mifflin Co., 1918), p. 41.

CHAPTER 13
Attitudes toward Poetry
July 4, 1960

In the early part of this talk and reading Frost was playing for laughs, as they say in the theater. The city taxi drivers in New York and Boston were his straight men. After he had warmed up his audience for the evening, he settled down playfully to serious matters, using the illustration of the taxi drivers to lead directly into a personal pursuit of poetry. Characteristically, he asked rhetorical questions like "I wonder what people want to know," which he answered freshly, teasingly.

After speaking about the pursuit, he elaborated on his relationship to professors and their reading of his poetry. And, quite typically, he wandered into the reading and saying of the poems. Once launched on the poems, he lingered over some, for example, "The Star-Splitter." Then he spoke about commitment in metrical form, a discussion he had previously elaborated on significantly in "The Constant Symbol." (See the Modern Library edition of his poems [1964].) This discussion drew him into illustrative quotations from Christopher Smart and Robert Herrick and a reaction to the ultimates.

Reluctant not to be generous in his evening reading, Frost stopped twice and returned to give his views on politics, current and Roman.

Too many.[1] That's the complaint everywhere. Too many at all the universities. Just see those crowds who wanted to get educated. Can't get into Harvard so they came here. [*Laughter*] We want to do the best we can. I get my education from taxi men, in New York partly—you know, they're famous for everything down there—but I got a little in Boston too. I pursue it, I say. I began like this in New York with one

---

1. Over four hundred crowded into the Bread Loaf Little Theatre auditorium to hear Frost.

138

[taxi man]. I said, "Who tips you better, men or women?" He said, "Men, of course. The money's there. The women have to be careful how they spend any they get." Then I say, "Drunk or sober?" He said a drunk might give you all he has, and it might be nothing he has. Then he said, "But you and I aren't thinking of money all the time. See! I just put a man out of this car without taking any fare from him for taking the Lord's name in vain three times. I wouldn't listen to him." I said, "Holy Name Society?" He said, "Yes, sir." [*Laughter*] Then we came to my publisher's big building on Madison Avenue.[2] Then he got out, took my bag out, and took me clear to my elevator and shook hands with me and said, "Good-bye." See. Nice fellow, Italian, you see.

Now in Boston [*laughter*] I said to a fellow who was driving me: "You in college?" He looked about like that—looked as if he was crowding in for education. He said, "Yes." I said, "What you going to do?" He said, "There's a question whether there's anything to do in a time like this." I said, "Oh-ah"—sounds like Boston, you know. He said, "But Emerson says that no man should leave the world unless it's the better for his having been in it." He said, "But on the other hand, Voltaire says [*laughter*]: Mind your own garden. Mind your own business." I said, "That leaves you hung up somewhere." And he said, "Yes." Then I said, "Of course. Never give a child a choice." That was my wisdom to him. He said, "There's something to that."

Well, you can't write poetry and talk poetry and be around where it is without being pursued the way I pursue the taxi man. People pursue me that way. I sometimes wonder what they want to know. They want to know—I think the ultimate thing must be they want to know what my attitude is toward what you can't know—what my attitude toward it is. Do I deny there is such a thing? Do I mock at it? Do I play with the idea, or do I accept it? Am I an atheist? Am I an agnostic? How deep do I go? And the question is one of depth all the time, I suppose. It sounds that way, the way people talk about it. Seems as if I'm interested in just a simple question of why I made a mistake in that meter in the first line of "The Death of the Hired Man." It's wrong, you know. It was just a mistake. I didn't do it on purpose. There are six feet in it instead of five. Well, that's a simple question.

I was saying the other day about all this thing that you're studying, these ideas in their depth and their shallowness, that make us what we are and [make] our western civilization, that you're all busy with

2. Holt, Rinehart and Winston at 383 Madison Avenue, New York City.

this summer. I hear about it—echoes of it come down my way.[3] But I get a little tired of all that at my age. It seems as if it was the same words all the time. It's the same pieces. Just like chess, you know. There's a king and a queen, and there's immortality, and there's all this sort of thing. And they just push them around, and they push them around too seriously. I can push them for the hell of it, for the fun of it, and make mischief out of it. I like to do that. But you get no further—Freudian ideas and all that. Look, I've written a whole book without the word *sex* in it. Just think of that. [*Applause*] And that doesn't mean I've left everything out. [*Laughter*]

This question comes up all the time. Do you want any meaning got out of what you write that you didn't put in? They think that's funny—and that it's a joke on the professors and that I'm taking sides against the professors. And of course that's terrible nonsense because I'm one of them. Look! I'm always hinting, intimating, and always on the verge of something I don't quite like to say out of sheer delicacy. And the only thing I have against my friends, the teachers, is some of them are indelicate. They won't leave it where I left it. They want to go on with it. They want to take both my hands and pull me across the line of delicacy. I don't complain. I have complained of translating what I write into other and worse English. And I've complained of people who've sat side of me when I've cracked a joke and said, "He means . . . " [*Laughter*] That's in bad taste, isn't it? This is a matter of taste—just how far you'll go when you tell about something. If you mention an apple, I'm annoyed if everybody is carried away by the apple to the Garden of Eden. There are so many apples, why go to the Garden of Eden? There are a lot of McIntosh apples down here in the valley. And there are all sorts of mythological ones—four or five of them I can think of, famous ones—and always I find if I mention an apple everybody is in the Garden of Eden at once. And everybody's falling—falling for it. There is something goes wrong there.

But all the same, you're always doubling your meaning—always on the verge of something you don't want to say, quite. You're often annoyed that someone wants to go a little further with it. That's a personal matter. I can't be too annoyed at that unless it's made ridiculous and made ugly. Now I said to somebody today, that visited me from out West, that I've grown to hate the word *symbol*. And yet I ought not to. Symbol is always in everything that way. The thing I'm saying has got another behind it—all sorts of analogies. It's a symbol of many things. I said I wish we could change the subject a little and

3. He lived in his cabin on the Homer Noble farm, about a mile from the Bread Loaf campus of Middlebury College as the crow flies.

say *typifies*—*typification*—or something like that. When I describe a character as an oddity, an interesting person, he wouldn't be interesting to anybody else unless he were rather typical—the Dickinsonian way, they're exaggerated a little.[4] You enjoy the excess of it.

Now, I have a poem that I'll read you about a typical idealist; he's unscrupulous. Some people don't get that. I don't want to carry that too far. Let me tell you two stories of it. One of them is about myself. I had a clipping sent to me from a magazine that we won't name in which my name was used as having sent a box of apples—sprayed apples, sprayed with chemicals—and they were rotten when they got to my friend, and so my friend threw them onto a compost heap and it ruined the compost heap that year—the chemicals in it. See, it was an organic [farming] magazine. There were three lies in that. I never sprayed an apple in my life. I never boxed an apple in my life. And I never gave any apples to anybody. Three lies in one. That was all just in the interest of organic farming. Three lies. That's what I call unscrupulous. It's idealistic, though, you see, wanting to do that.

Now I'm going to read you one. When I was very young, one of the first books—one of the serious books outside of fiction—I read [was] *Our Place among Infinities*. It was by an astronomer—an English astronomer, Proctor—[of] the last century, one of the great astronomers.[5] And in this poem I'm going to read you I have a farmer who got to wondering about our place among the infinities. I didn't know about this book. I stole this expression. I use it in the poem. He wanted to know about our place among the infinities, and he thought everybody ought to want to know. And he couldn't afford a telescope, and he thought the best way to get some money was to burn his farm down in such a way that the insurance company would be deceived, and get the money for that and buy a telescope and go into the ideal business—unscrupulous idealist, see. Typical. Now that's all I want to say. I might as well use that as a take-off —read to you some. You see, these ultimate people wonder how you play with, how much you deal in [ultimates]. You see I play with them more than I deal with them. And I don't like to be asked by anybody to tell what mine are—how far I dare go, how deep I am.

I talked here on the subject, once, how deep is deep. What do you call deep? And when are you the wickedest, and when are you the most ideally wicked, and so on? A lot to it. I can see why people think that Longfellow isn't deep. You'd probably have to hunt rather far to see that he was deeply into things. I feel wonder at not thinking

4. Dickinsonian is a slip for Dickensian, I am sure.

5. Richard Anthony Proctor (1837–88) published *Our Place among the Infinities* (1876).

141

Tennyson went very deep in a thing like, say, "And freedom broadens slowly down from precedent of precedent."[6] Now that's a very deep, subtle thing—the change from precedent to precedent, always talking precedents, but always slipping in a punctuation mark, you know, or something on freedom, getting farther and farther down. That's the very name of Cardozo's book almost, you know, on the growth of the law—how freedom broadens slowly down from precedent to precedent.[7] Always talking precedent, sticking to the precedent but slipping a cog, you know. The world to freedom carrying it, and a thing [like]: "Lest one good custom should corrupt the world"[8] A thing like that. Those are deep things. Some of the [Tennyson] poems seem very shallow. "Let Darkness keep her raven gloss." That's a great line. That's in "In Memoriam." Nothing darker than that—a "raven gloss."[9]

And then Browning—they quote him in a sort of shallow, cheerio kind of way when he says: "Grow old along with me! / The best is yet to be"[10] That may be so; maybe it ain't. But he says that, you know, and it's used constantly; and "God's in his heaven— / All's right with the world!"[11] That's just one side of Browning. And there's this Browning in "Love among the Ruins." He speaks first, leading up to what's not in the world—not love in the sense Archie MacLeish means but in the sense Freud means, the other kind of love. He says, "Love is best," and forget it all; forget fame; forget glory; forget everything. "Love is best." A very pretty thing, but in it he had this description of life: "Lust of glory pricked their hearts up, dread of shame / Struck them tame, / And that glory and that shame alike, the gold / Bought and sold."[12] Glory and shame for sale. That's all he says life is. Different from the other cheerio [view]. And then he says, "Forget that love is best." You better say that, you know. The chief thing in favor of love is its own best chance to keep staying on in the world. It's very practical. That's the sense he doesn't mean in it. He means it in a romantic sense, not a Freudian sense.

All right. I still [can] go on with my subject. Let's begin with this criminal from Vermont. I had it marked and I've gone and lost it

6. Tennyson, "You ask me why," line 12. The line should read, "Where Freedom slowly broadens down / From precedent to precedent."
7. Benjamin Cardozo (1870–1938). Probably Frost had in mind *The Growth of the Law.*
8. Tennyson, "Morte d'Arthur," *The Idylls of the King,* line 242.
9. Tennyson, "In Memoriam" line 10.
10. Browning, "Rabbi ben Ezra," stanza 1.
11. Browning, *Pippa Passes.*
12. Browning, "Love among the Ruins."

—talking too much. [*Reads "The Star-Splitter"*] That covers a lot. That's the way we'll think of the election that's ahead of us.[13] "For to be social is to be forgiving." You've got to forgive the other side. Now if you had to tell children in class what that meant, it would be too bad, wouldn't it? A good deal is just leaving it where the writer wants it to stay, just short of flatness, flattening it out.

I ought to say one more case like that, you know. There was a fellow by the name of Bob Ingersoll.[14] And he was long traduced in the pulpits of America as a man who brought a son up in atheism and the son had gone bad and had ended up in prison and in the insane asylum, I believe, down in Saint Elizabeth [Washington, D.C.] or something like that. And Robert Ingersoll took no notice of it for years, and finally he did one day in a public speech. He says: "The trouble with that is I never had a son go crazy or go bad. In fact, I never had a son. That's all the matter with that story." All for the good cause. They had to tell it that way. Save the Church.

I ought to say a nice thing about the Church to offset that. You know one of the worst things in the world is people who belittle glory.[15] There's been a tendency lately to say that. There's no glory in our recent wars—that's an old-fashioned thing—military glory's all vainglory. But just the word *glory*. Sometimes I think there's nothing but glory. Nothing but glory. Let's see if I can say some of that thing. Let's see.

> Glorious the northern lights astream;
> Glorious the song, when God's the theme;
>   Glorious the thunder's roar:
> Glorious hosanna from the den;
> Glorious the catholic amen;
>   Glorious the martyr's gore.
>
> Glorious—more glorious is the crown
> Of Him that brought salvation down
>   By meekness, call'd thy Son.
> Thou that stupendous truth believ'd,
> And now the matchless deed's achiev'd,
>   Determined, dared, and done.[16]

13. Frost is referring to the presidential election of 1960 between the Protestant Richard M. Nixon and the Catholic John F. Kennedy.

14. Robert G. Ingersoll (1833–99), lawyer and orator, known as "the great agnostic."

15. A reaction to the first chapter of Bruce Catton's *A Stillness at Appomattox* (1953), which won the Pulitzer Prize in history in 1954.

16. Christopher Smart, "Song to David" (1763), written in an asylum.

All glory, you see, great glory, glory, glory. And those last three lines are the kind of things you wish on the world all the time. You wish for it now—now "that stupendous truth believ'd." See that stupendous truth believer. Nothing like that line anywhere. Now "that stupendous truth believ'd." Now that matchless deed achieved. Matchless, "determined, dared, and done." Those are the three parts of a deed: "Determined, dared, and done." It's the kind of thing that carries you far away from Robert Ingersoll's skepticism. That's a great poem; you know it, I suppose.

Thinking of Tennyson again—he helped to make the most of a gem of a little book of poetry the world's ever seen—lyric poetry—Palgrave's *Golden Treasury*.[17] It was his choices, a good part of it. It's beautiful—it's the top of the far of English literature, isn't it? There is another thing to think about in Tennyson: that he had a hand in the making of that beautiful book. But one thing again —everything has its lack. It hasn't any mention of that great poem.[18] Not even part of it. That great poem I quoted from has been included more and more in every anthology. Some [anthologist] began by putting in a few stanzas and somebody put in a few more and finally they got the whole business in. Christopher Smart. Funny Tennyson didn't think of that. Funny how he could have missed it.

Now I look this book over and sometimes I feel as if I always have another book before I get through reading anywhere. Somebody —this visitor—said today, "I understand you were many years deciding how to end 'The Death of the Hired Man.' " She said that's in a book. You know how stories get corrupted. The story is this: there was a book I never read and a teacher I never had that did more for me than anybody else in the world. The book I never read was *Piers Plowman* and the teacher I never had was William James. And both of those acted on me. *Piers Plowman* acted on me this way. I always wanted to do something about the kind of American hired man, you know, that I'd lived with and worked with and been. And just how to get it! I didn't have any definite idea about it. It was just a lingering sense about it. I thought that might be what *Piers Plowman* was and so I better let that alone for fear it would take the wind out of my sails. And I let it alone until I'd written "The Death of the Hired Man." And then I read it and I needn't have worried. It's another thing entirely—satire and all that.

Shall I just be old-fashioned and read "The Death of the Hired Man"? Or something else? I don't want to say "Birches" tonight. Will

17. Francis Palgrave, with an assist from Tennyson, his friend, to whom it is dedicated, published *The Golden Treasury* in 1861.
18. Smart's "Song to David."

you excuse that? Now I've just come from seeing a birch tree. [*Looks up "A Young Birch"*] I've got a young birch standing beside my house.[19] Now the thing about the young birch right by my door—the very young birch—is it's not quite up to what this poem is about. [*Reads "A Young Birch"*] Just a glimmer of white coming [in the birch by his cabin]. [*Rereads*] So that's another kind of poem. Let's skip around a little bit.

Driven to this question of how far down into the terribleness of things you go, I've been aware of it lately. I've made some couplets in my defense. This is my religious one: "Forgive, O Lord, my little jokes on Thee / And I'll forgive Thy great big one on me." [*Laughter*] And then the question of good and evil: "It is from having stood contrasted / That good and bad so long have lasted." That's ultimate too. That comes from thinking about Emerson a good deal. Emerson thought they [good and evil] weren't equal members of the thing. They stand up and support each other just the same as two playing cards do, you know, when you stand them up just right. They're very delicately stood there. I'm afraid they'll both fall down. Good and evil. Lose them both. And then the same sort of doubleness comes into this older one of mine. This is a couplet that isn't a couplet. It's a free-verse couplet. "I never dared be radical when young / For fear it would make me conservative when old." And then: "Nature within her inmost self divides / To trouble man with having to take sides." That's on a lump of iron—of purest iron—the purest iron in the world—iron ore—and this was about that, and pure as it looks, it's a double thing, good and evil; it's tools and weapons.[20] And then here's something that isn't often quoted. But you know who Divés was. This is his dive. Never had to say this out loud before. [*Reads "In Divés' Dive"*] That's all I know about cards. My whole card-life.

And then—I think I ought to dare to read—[*starts "The Onset"*] No, I don't want that one. That's my trouble, to get something I haven't read at all before. Here's one: this is way back, in the thickness of the book if you look at it—early—this is one that went to the *Atlantic Monthly* years ago and came back with a stamp right on the middle of it saying the date when it came in, stamped, and the stamp I'd sent for returning it pinned right into the form. I ought to have

19. By his cabin on the Homer Noble farm at Ripton.
20. Reference is to the lump of iron in the Meditation Room at the United Nations building.

kept that as a trophy.[21] I think I'm not seeing very well. Where's my glasses? I forget that I've got glasses. "Thought has a pair of dauntless wings." This is all about science. [*Reads "Bond and Free"*] See, that's all the difference is. That's the science of it.

[*Reads "The Oven Bird"*] A little poem that might go with that [is] "Nothing Gold Can Stay." I won't read that. [*Fumbles among the pages*] I'm going to read this one to you. I haven't read this since it was new. I read this thirty years ago some. I haven't read it since. "A Hundred Collars." It's called "A Hundred Collars." [*Reads "A Hundred Collars"*] That's an old-timer. Now I'm going to do some of the short ones. [*Says "The Night Light"*] I'm going to say that twice to you. [*Says "Dust of Snow"*; *"Away!"*]

You see, sometimes—I'm talking a good deal tonight. I feel like it to get away from some of the poems—you know, these pieces we push around about the soul and the body, spirit and matter, and immortality and transmigration and all those damn old tiresome things, and too much God and God's name taken too many times in vain, that you wonder how you escape it all.

Sometimes I'm always trying harder to tell what I mean. The little first stanza that you make, see, is a commitment and it's always very strict, you know.[22] You can only have a certain meter. We're very limited in meter. I haven't had any meter except strict and loose iambic. That is, I've never had more than two short syllables between the long ones. I've never had three between the long ones. Never in my life. And most people haven't. There are only a few cases of more than two anywhere in poetry—shorts on long—so there you are; very seldom more than five beats in a line. You have two, three, four, five, once in a great while six, but very rarely. That's all very settled. So that's as rigid as a tennis court, and as rigid as a kind of place you put on the pavement for hopscotch. You know how to play hopscotch. It's laid out for you or you lay it out, and you come onto it, you step onto it, and step a figure in it. In the rigid figure that you put on the floor, you step off a freer figure, but you still got to keep in a rigid figure. But the freer figure within the rigid figure—that's all it is.

And you see, somebody—a boy began like this long ago—he stole it, I guess, from Horace, didn't he? A boy he was—fifteen years old,

21. This is Frost's reaction to the rejection of "Bond and Free" by the *Atlantic Monthly*. It was written, according to a note in Thompson's *Robert Frost: The Years of Triumph*, p. 541, sometime between 1896 and 1900.

22. Frost's exposition on the commitment to meter in poetry was one of his fondest and most familiar. He liked to do this and usually added something important in the talking. This evening what he added was the homely analogy of playing hopscotch.

not much more than that, he was, wasn't he? Not much more than that. [He said:]

> Happy the man whose wish and care
>   A few paternal acres bound
> Content to breathe his native air,
>   In his own ground.
> Whose herds with milk,
> Whose fields with bread,
> Whose flocks supply him with attire,
> Whose trees in summer yield him shade,
> In winter, fire.[23]

Now he's kept that pretty stanza again, and sometimes you wonder how a fellow gets committed to a little stanza, free and happy. And he sketches on the ground for himself that way, the court that he makes like hopscotch. Now he's got to step into that again and again and make pretty figures out of his sentences. Now that's what I like people I'm interested in [to do]. I'd like them to see how pretty I can lay a sentence. The first stanza's a risky thing. I can make that always. I'm very free. Not so free as you might be, but I can make it myself.

Look at a stanza like this somebody else makes for you, like Christopher Smart's in "Song to David." That stanza's kept through fifty stanzas, I guess. Just that one. One of the stanzas goes like this:

> Strong is the lion—like a coal
> His eye-ball—like a bastion's mole
>   His chest against the foes:
> Strong, the gier-eagle on his sail,
> Strong against tide th' enormous whale
>   Emerges as he goes.

See how that goes with the stanza I quoted to you before—but kept all the way through it, once you've made a good one. And sometimes it seems the best stanza anybody ever writes is the first [stanza] because there's something about his [stanza that isn't tight]. He isn't as tight [as he will be in the others]—it's going to be tighter trying to keep that. Look back and see. "Fair Daffodils, we weep to see / You haste away so soon."[24] There's ten lines in that, and some of them

23. Alexander Pope, "Ode on Solitude."
24. Robert Herrick, "Daffodils," which appears in Palgrave's *The Golden Treasury*.

only have one beat in them—I guess you'd call it one beat—and others three and four. But ten lines in that stanza. He has to keep that ten lines in the next stanza. And I often look back to see if I think he didn't think he had a hard time doing that—had to count lines and work at it, you know.

[*Reads "The Peaceful Shepherd"*] Now, you see, what I'm interested in there is the three stanzas, to see if the sentences fall different ways in them. And I wonder if I get credit for that: to see if I can put a pretty sentence—a different sentence—lay them in their little stanzas. That one I said of Pope's I could have said it off four or five stanzas. Wonderful the way the sentences are laid in them. He had that sense of form.

[*Reads "A Record Stride"*] Then shall I say the dog one to you ["One More Brevity"]? I've lectured a good deal tonight about it all. I think I'm trying to escape from reading too many poems to you. Had so much of it this year. I ought to read you one new thing.

I think this will be one of these ultimate things we talk about. I suppose the most ultimate thing I think of is the fear I have of losing my meaning in the material, in the rhyme or the meter, or the grammar, or the vocabulary, or the shape of the little poem—that I don't carry out my meaning; but this, in a long poem, "Kitty Hawk," I have a passage like this. [*Reads from "Kitty Hawk"*]

> But God's own descent
> Into flesh was meant
> As a demonstration
> That the supreme merit
> Lay in risking spirit
> In substantiation.

See, we've got to risk spirit in substantiation and we mostly fail. And somebody said to me: "How can you say He had any risk?" I said it looks as if He had.

> Westerners inherit
> A design of living
> Deeper into matter
> (Not without some patter
> Of the soul's misgiving).

That is, the misgiving that we won't keep the spirit through.

> All the science zest
> To materialize
> By on-penetration

Into earth and skies
(Don't forget the latter
Is but further matter).

I'll say that again to you so you can see what the thought is. [*Quotes the lines again, stressing "Lay in risking spirit / In substantiation"*] That's when you write a doctor's thesis, you see. Nearly all doctor's theses are lost in substantiation. They have to substantiate but the spirit isn't strong enough to come through.

"Has been West-Northwest"—that goes on, but that's all there is of it there [i.e., on his sheet]. But that's a rather interesting idea—that the Bible, the alphabet, what we call philosophy, and science, and all of it started at the far end of the Mediterranean Sea and along there—the alphabet, too. Just think of that, and the whole business, the whole civilization, all that counts in the world, has been northwest from there—began there right near Moab, somewhere right in there.[25] Strange that the whole business—Asia you might as well forget. Northwest! All that. Isn't it funny! That's what I'm saying then, anyway. The plunge into the material, the spiritual plunge into the material, has been west northwest. Terrible risky thing to say, I think; I say [it] just the same. Let's call that all.

[*After applause, returns for encore*] I'll say just one or two in another mood. Just for the fun of it. [*Says "The Objection to Being Stepped On"; laughter and applause*]

There, let's see what else there is like that. Some of them I'm scared of saying, I've said them so many times. I'll say this one. Say, want to hear an ugly one? Not a funny one, say an ugly one too. Some of my friends say I shouldn't have written this [one], you know. They've got me into a sort of self-conscious state about all these things. I don't read any reviews but I get word of them and it's spoiling me. You see me all bothered up about it. This is a terrible one. One time the ruler of the United States said to Tobin, told him not to worry any more, they'd be taken care of from Washington, in unmarked envelopes, and that kind of thing.[26] I know that's coming —two worlds [capitalism and socialism]. I'm resigned. That's what I wrote on my income tax. Not retired; I write, resigned to everything.

25. Frost was impressed by the ancient nation of the Moabites in the hilly region east of the Dead Sea. Traditionally descended from Lot, the Moabites fought intermittently with the Hebrews. The Moabite Stone, erected by Mesha of Moab, with an inscription (850 B.C.) commemorated a victory in his revolt against Israel. It was discovered at Dibon in 1868. The language on the Moabite Stone is similar to biblical Hebrew.

26. A reference to Dan Tobin, leader of the Teamsters' Union.

[*Laughter*] I'm not going to contend against it, election by election. Every election I expect to be submerged, go under. I said after that, that speech, I named the speech, I named it to a president of a college who sided with the speech. But I liked to have the naming of that speech. I'd like to tell the president what to call it. I'd said I'd call it: "Every man's home his own poor house." He said, "You have a very biting tongue." This is about all that. Be prepared. See, I'm giving in. Don't worry about that; the hell I am. I'll go down joking, anyway. I'm going to say this horrible one. [*Reads "Provide, Provide."*] I wrote this long before the Monaco episode.[27]

I never had any life insurance in my life until I was compelled by law to get a little. I better shut up. [*Stops, then returns again*]

I might as well make it that kind of an evening—being very personal about it, sort of preaching to you. I had occasion to look up Catiline lately. I began in Latin. I had a lot of Latin, and I began, I was under the deception that went on, that all came from Sallust and Cicero. I mean Cicero. They made Catiline out an altogether bad man. Very prejudiced. And I began to suspect there was something wrong about that when I was young, when I was still reading Cicero. I thought it was crooked. Then I wondered why Caesar had Cicero killed—this lawyer with the great gift of the gab—and I began to look into that, always reading a little more about it.[28]

And I read some more the other night in the encyclopedia, that we must remember that this is all told by Sallust and Cicero, so it's prejudiced. You know, I didn't know I'd find that in an encyclopedia and, you know, Caesar took sides with the bad democrats. It was a great democratic movement. See, I'm talking against the democrats now. The great democratic movement was led by Catiline and Caesar. There were whole crowds of people that were outside, and those two people [Catiline and Caesar] realized they'd got to be brought in at any cost. It took a kind of Mussolini to do it named Julius Caesar. He succeeded. And he made a great democracy. You get more freedom that way in a tyranny. They don't know that. Very fascinating, it is. And Caesar—in the rebellion that Caesar encouraged secretly, that Catiline led, Catiline got the worst of it. He was killed in the battle and some of his followers were executed, and Caesar never forgave the people that executed his followers. And it

27. "The Monaco episode" is a reference to Grace Kelly's marriage to Prince Rainier.

28. Cicero, who prosecuted Catiline, as a republican, opposed Augustus Caesar and was put to death in 43 B.C. He had been banished for his action in killing members of Catiline's group.

was in their name that he had Cicero kill himself.[29] Funny thing. It's been all covered up in history. But that's coming, you know. I know that's on the way again. You've got to do something for these millions. They've all got to go to college. And you've got to have a socialist form of government to do it. And that's all. I might as well take a back seat. I'm not on Catiline's side. Good night.

29. Cicero did not kill himself; he was assassinated. In 66 B.C. Catiline was barred from candidacy for the consulship because he was accused falsely of misconduct. In his disgruntlement Catiline worked up an abortive plot to murder the consuls, but he and his confederates were acquitted. In 63 B.C. Cicero defeated him and exposed his conspiracy to gain power. Catiline, refusing to surrender, was killed in battle in 62 B.C. The question of Catiline's character and guilt is still open, since the only sources—Cicero and Sallust—were his enemies.

CHAPTER 14
On Reveling in Technique
July 27, 1960

On this particular evening Frost appeared in the Bread Loaf Barn unusually ready for the student questions. A list had been earlier prepared and reached him a few days before his appearance. Apparently he had thought considerably about these questions. Consequently, he said many important things about an ars poetica. He related good anecdotes, used effective illustrations; his wisecracks were sly and clever, and his insights into and judgments on literary subjects were certainly remarkable. This talk illustrates arrestingly the content of Frost's thought as well as his inimitable style.

Frost started talking at nine o'clock and kept right on until eleven o'clock. This talk is, I think, one of his stronger performances. The interlocutors were William Meredith, professor of English at Connecticut College and a member of the Bread Loaf faculty, and myself. In this transcript, because of the method of handling the Frost questioning, I. stands for interlocutor, and the poet is identified by F.

F. Are there any questions or anything that you want to talk about? I'll look at this paper with the questions on it to start the ball rolling. [1] There are some questions I won't answer because I can't and some because I don't want to and some because I'm scared to.

I. I know one you're really scared about: "From a mile or so down the road, how does the Bread Loaf brand of education seem to be going?" Doesn't that one scare you? It scares me.

F. It insults me. I won't answer that. I say: going to hell. [*Laughter*] What kind of question *is* that? [*Bends over to read the questions*] Have I got light enough? I guess so.

1. Three pages of typewritten questions, prepared by the Bread Loaf students, had been given to Frost several days earlier.

I. They [the students] want to catch you off guard.

F. Yeh, yeh! John Ciardi says I revel in technique. I revel in ideas, too, I hope. That's all right enough. This technique question comes up in another place. [2]

Let's talk about it right there. Speaking of technique, I said sometime that there are never more than two unaccented syllables between the accented [syllables]. Never. See. I know one in George Meredith and I know one or two in de la Mare. And I don't know any others. Someone confronts me with a Shakespearian sonnet: "Let me not to the marriage of true minds / Admit impediments." They say, "Well, what do you make of that, then?" How many accents are there in it? Three in a line of ten. So there must be more than two between the accents for some reason or other.

Now let me tell you something, an amusing thing. I've lived with this for a long time. [3] There are all sorts of metricists kicking around. One of the most noted of them in the old days was a man named Charles Cobb. Charley Cobb. He was also an authority on Persian rugs and the song of the lark. The lark sometimes went off note and he knew when it did; he kept a record of it. I know him very well. He went around the country on this subject—not where I went, but to some of the colleges, but I don't know which.

Now I knew another great authority on it. His name was Robert Bridges.[4] And I had adventures with both these people. Charles

2. Frost was referring to a question that read: "Last year you gave us Frost's law of metrics: never more than two unaccented syllables between accents. How, then, do you scan lines such as Shakespeare's 'Let me not to the marriage of true minds,' or 'Or bends with the remover to remove?'"

3. In 1959, Frost recorded with Cleanth Brooks and Robert Penn Warren a discussion that focused on the technical aspects of verse. It was entitled "Conversations on the Craft of Poetry" and was included in the third edition of Brooks's and Warren's *Understanding Poetry* (New York: Holt, Rinehart and Winston, 1961). Frost, at Bread Loaf, elaborates on some of his ideas about metrics.

4. Robert Bridges (1844–1930), deeply interested in prosody, wrote on the prosody of John Milton (1893, rev. ed. 1921) and John Keats (1895). His poetry reflects unusual experiments in English versification. Robert Hillyer, who closely analyzed Bridges's *The Testament of Beauty* (1929), noted that Bridges's main impulse came from classical prosody, "and in the 'loose Alexandrines' of *The Testament of Beauty*," showed that "he combined with this strong quantitative influence an element wholly derived from our own ancient verse; that is, great liberty in the number of syllables within the single line." Louis Untermeyer, *Modern British Poetry* (New York: Harcourt, Brace and Co., 1950), pp. 47, 48.

Cobb said to me one day on the street—let me see—we'd been talking about these lines of pentameter—it's called that isn't it? Five-foot lines. It's always known as the five-foot line. All those sonnets of Shakespeare are five-foot lines—five-foot, get that into your head—and that's been the way for ages—in Latin, in English. He said, "Let's hear you say the first line of 'Endymion.'" And I knew what he was after. And we stood on a street corner defying each other, old friends, you know, the insulting kind, we bothered each other. I said, "A thing of beauty is a joy for ever." He said, "Four beats." I said, "Five beats." He said, "You have no ear." I said, "You have no ear." We didn't speak to each other for two or three weeks after that. We parted on that. No ear! It's silly. Look! There are five beats. It's a pentameter line, that's all. That means five by the metronome—five by the measure—five by the number—by counting them.

Now you've got to learn to talk about two things in it—rather loose-minded talkers who have not gone into it far enough to see that there is a rhythm beat and a metric beat—"Let me not to the marriage of true minds." If you stop there with no sense of the meter at all in your early nature—it ought to be in your nature, it ought to be planted before you came to the school, in *Mother Goose* and all that—and if it isn't in your nature, if you are not aware about that beat, and under it all the metronome going, you've nothing to gain.

Now old Bridges was another adventure of mine. He was a good deal like Sidney Lanier. I never knew him [Lanier] but that was another adventure. I ran into him [Lanier] through great admirers of him. He said that you couldn't think about poetry at all unless you had a thorough education in music. Then, you know that kind of book of his, all on the side of theory, that you do it by music; the music of poetry, if you want to use it, is difficult.[5] The music of poetry is not like the music of music. And there's a conflict always. There's always a conflict with anything set to music. You are honored by having things set to music. I feel flattered a little but I'm always uncomfortable. The whole thing spoils my fun. It spoils the double thing that is in the poem—it fits the meter but the rhythm is a different thing. The music can't do the double thing in the poem.

Now the *tune* is the third thing. You don't notice me talking, but some of the time when I'm reciting I'm keeping the metronome going with my toe, or my finger. [6] Sometimes I favor the meter a lit-

5. Sidney Lanier, *The Science of English Verse* (1880).
6. See Elizabeth Shepley Sergeant, *Robert Frost: The Trial by Existence* (1960), p. 411.

tle, more than I should maybe; sometimes I don't, I favor the rhythm.

Robert Bridges went into the pentameters of Milton and worried hell with them before he got the habit and it's awful. And you can do things with prosody. A young poet coming along, [who] followed Robert Bridges in his theories about Milton and all that, could get his attention by putting some false accents on the words in his first book. Have be / gin instead of begin—put an accent on it; that type of oddity attracts attention, but it must be a great poet who understands the theory. Now there. Now you talk about tension a lot. That's part of that jargon, that cant of literary criticism. Everything's tension, tension, tension. That kind of jargon makes me sick anyway. But if you want to talk about tension, here's tension right away between the meter and the rhythm; and if the tension breaks it's love that makes the song, it's got to be a tension that holds—sometimes a very big strain, in that one, "Let me not to the marriage of true minds."

"Let me not to the marriage of true minds." [*Accenting it clearly*] And all that in the scansion. But if you haven't been brought up to scansion, to some scansion, you know, and interest in that, you'll always be interested in the rhythm. But if you're talking with somebody that decides to throw that all away—now why should he throw all the scansion away? If Shakespeare wanted to have three beats in a line, why didn't he have three feet in the line? Why didn't he get a line with six syllables? Always, in every single one of the sonnets, he has ten syllables to the line. And sometimes to make it there's something—a breath, or call it license or something. There'll be this—the "-ed" would be spoken—"Unmovèd . . . and to temptation slow"—"Unmovèd!" And "unmoved." It's the way he [Shakespeare] said, the way he heard, the way people talk—they say "unmoved." Why not? For Shakespeare wrote "unmovèd"—to get the feet all right; the feet are always there, always all right. And that's so all through the plays. A certain amount of carelessness you'll find. One of the most careless people that ever lived in the way his plays were issued, you know, and got into print, was Shakespeare. Only the scholars who come after him have tried to set him right. He didn't seem to give much thought to it. I don't know how it got out of his hands so much. He was a theater man and wasn't [as] much interested as the people who have come after him. All through his plays there are lines that are broken, of course, lines that you are doubtful about, corrupt lines that I've been speaking about that must be wrong. Take a sonnet like "They that have power to hurt and will do none." See. That begins that way. "They that have power to hurt and will do none." See, there is that rhythm. Three and a half, the rhythm is, if you want to call it. It [the rhythm] is not fighting it—it's straining it, though, straining the meter; or the meter is straining the rhythm.

I brought around this little book in case anything came up [it didn't]; that little book that I spoke of is such a poem in itself. Palgrave. [7] Curious thing I noticed while looking at some of the sonnets, and that sonnet I've just recited—"They that have power to hurt and will do none"—always has had my great admiration. But lately someone told me that it is considered one of the great puzzles. And I know that Strachey, the historian, writing about the Victorians, said that it was evidently about someone that Shakespeare disliked. And I always thought it was the opposite—about someone he admired because he was like George Washington. "They that have power to hurt and will do none, / That do not do the thing they most do show." That's the next line, and so on. It's in deep and deep, deep, in deep. You're dealing in the corruption that comes in doing something. It doesn't matter. Evidently these sonnets weren't given a name by Shakespeare, but in the Palgrave some of them are given a name. That one was given the name "Life without Passion." That's my idea of it. But it's supposed to be controversial.

But now—a long, long time, it began when I first fell in with Robert Bridges—I knew him pretty well, he was really a fine old bully, he sounded as bully as I'm sounding tonight. But, ah, goodness me, why did Shakespeare, why did Marlowe, why does everybody talk about pentameter? Is that just for the eye? The syllables—ten or eleven syllables—for a feminine ending? Why? There's no regard for the accent at all. When Keats calls for Prince, he says "prince of organic numbers"—see that—numbers; [8] somebody [Pope] lisped in numbers—numbers. Numbers is one name for poetry. Numbers, numbers. Count. Metronome. Figures. Measure. That's verse.

As I said: I'm not saying that's poetry necessarily; I'm not using the word *poetry* about it all. I'm reveling in technique. You come to poetry another way, you know. I said the other night—I think I said—that there's probably more love outside of marriage than in, more religion outside of church than in, more poetry outside of verse than in. See. I take verse the same way I take the others—that is, in those institutions. Verse is an institution of metrics. And if you

7. One of Frost's much favored books, Francis Palgrave's *The Golden Treasury*. The Shakespearian sonnet (94) in question was entitled "The Life without Passion" by Palgrave.

8. In "Lines on Seeing a Lock of Milton's Hair," John Keats writes "Chief of organic numbers."

want to get outside of it, write free verse, you may be more poetical than the people inside. See. But you're not a high priest of verse. The whole thing seems to me—you have to take it—that there are two words there: one is the meter, and another is the rhythm. The meter is iambic and if you want to change that you can turn it into trochees, you know, by just dropping it—having it long, short one, long short, long short, long short, instead of short long, short long, short long. You can do it that way. That's practically the same, and that better be kept the same way. All right, that's that question.

I. Where does Gerard Manley Hopkins come in here with his sprung rhythm?

F. That doesn't matter at all, that's got nothing to do with it, except you can leave out if you want, you can jump, crowd out a syllable, but that's not getting two in. I can remember when I was young, one of my first friends in this thing was a poet, an editor and all that; he would be Dick Wilbur's grandfather-in-law—he's in the anthologies of that time, the Stedman anthology—an old fellow named William Hayes Ward.[9] And I wrote without any thought of the sprung rhythm. It's been done many times. He made a business of it. You know what he did. "They that have power to hurt and will do none" rhymes with—let's see, "Unmovèd, cold"—"stone." "Stone" and "none" rhyme. In Shakespeare "Come hither" and "weather" rhyme. Now that is a slight flaw that you get all through poetry. And you get this same flaw occasionally in the sprung rhythm. But the only thing about it was that certain poets that I know now flaw all their rhymes. When I see a person doing that as a matter of business, I don't read the poem. Sprung rhythm—all right, you know. I like it as a flaw. Every rhyme is sprung to make an interesting word. And the off-rhyme, I don't know what I'd call that—just "off-rhyme," I guess, "near rhyme." I've forgotten the name of the fellow who it was that first did this steadily—all the rhymes there are—but it was someone in England, a friend of Edward Davison.

I. Wilfred Owen?

F. No, I don't know whether he did or not. Somebody. I don't think he ever announced it. Somebody declared it as a program —somebody who was coming over here lecturing.

9. Edmund C. Stedman (1833–1908) edited *A Victorian Anthology* (1895) and *An American Anthology* (1900); Richard Wilbur (1921–) is a contemporary poet of distinction; William Hayes Ward (1835–1916) became editor of the New York *Independent* in 1870. He was also a noted archaeologist. His sister, Susan Hayes Ward, was poetry editor of the *Independent* and accepted some of Frost's early poetry.

Well, that's two things: there's sprung rhythm and there's scansion.

> Let me not to the marriage of true minds
> Admit impediments. Love is not love
> Which alters when it alteration finds,
> Or bends with the remover to remove:

I'm hearing the metronome all the time. I couldn't read it without the sense of it.

I heard Pound say once how hard it is for people brought up in the meter, in metronome, ever to learn to write free verse, to shake off the iambic. Whitman didn't, he said. And Masters was terrible. He just couldn't shake it off, he says, it was all the time bothering him. It's in their dithyrambic. They've got a kind of another strict iambic.

When I say there can be two short lines between the longs, then that lets in dithyrambic—that's a good word for the others—two shorts and a long. And what I call borrowed verse has sometimes two shorts between the longs and sometimes one, just as it happens in the spring of the verse. But never three shorts and a long. That's in meter.

I told Charley Cobb once I bet I could write a line with only one beat in it in ten feet. I bet I could. [*Questioningly*] I did it with two anyway. It would be hard to get down to one. That will be in the rhythm. Well, let's see what else there is.

I. This might lead into the question here: "In the training of a poet, which should come first—prosody, figurative speech, content?"

F. What's that second one?

I. Figurative speech—metaphor—content.

F. Well, that's [figurative speech] content. Somebody mixed things up there.

I. Could you develop that, Mr. Frost—your idea about thinking as metaphor?

F. Well, thinking is always association, isn't it? Thought is association—more or less metaphor. And that's thought and thought is association. Being reminded of something you hardly knew you knew—by something that's in front of you, something that's happening to you, or the past emerging out of the very levels of your knowledge. Books and life and all that—that's the material. Then the prosody is another thing. That's what we've been talking about.

Here's this little book, Palgrave's *Golden Treasury*, which I admire—that little book—so much. I have one of the earliest editions of it; that fell into my lap. It was a very fancy little copy that didn't have any hard covers on it. It was meant for a gentleman's library, to put his own covers on. See. I've never got any covers on it. And it's wrapped up now and put away somewhere—I don't know just where—but I've got it somewhere. And I wouldn't have that book violated any more than I'd have one of Shakespeare's sonnets violated. And it gets violated all the time. People are always putting in more poems, calling it Palgrave's. It's a little book that's very beautiful in its thought, and left out some things of course. It's a pretty little sonnet of a book. And Tennyson was in it. And it's like throwing away Tennyson. It's the legacy of Tennyson. You'd be surprised to know how I've just had a letter from England asking me to do something about a society to keep us from forgetting Tennyson. Asked me to do that. I shall, gladly. Some of my friends belong to it but mostly lords belong. A very noted man—funny that he's taken that interest. It's as if Eisenhower should want to defend Longfellow.

I. Tennyson also revels in metaphor, doesn't he? Remember the poem about the eagle that has a beautiful image?

F. It's all metaphor and ideas. And again I don't want to be pitching too hard. What do you call it? How can you tell when you're thinking? I lectured on that once at Smith College. How can you tell when you're thinking? The way you can tell is that anything prevented your mind from recalling your thought—science and all that. Thoughts of science. Socialism. And metaphor is a subsidiary thing—that's a part of it—call it metaphor if you want to. I might call it synecdoche. I used to call myself a synecdochist just for the hell of it. And one time a friend lived in Schenectady, and I sent him a card once with his address as Synecdoche and he never got it. The post office refused to deal in that word. Synecdoche. A part for the whole, a hem of the garment, and all that. It's just another that comes under the head of association. Now what else?

I. There seem to be many people here who are interested in this matter of teaching poetry. Teaching poetry in the classroom —probably the high school classroom. [*Laughter*]

F. That's a fair question. What you ought to ask is what authority have I in that matter? Did I ever do it? No more than all the time. I had Latin, philosophy, mathematics. A nice man I saw the other day, just retiring from having taught mathematics all his life, and he and I had quite a talk about this word *numbers* in poetry. He said he never knew we used it for poetry. Numbers. That's the connection with mathematics. And that's very deep.

The teaching of it [poetry] is just like this with me. It's best when you can teach it without their knowing what you're up to. How can you do it? You can do it in the way you'd do it at home. If the children say papa's preaching poetry you've lost your hold on the children. Look out for papa. You've got to do it as if you weren't doing it. Now I think it's rather dreadful to memorize on purpose. But you can do a little of that—you can stand a little. Too bad that a person doesn't care enough for poetry so a lot of it clings to him. Someone later [in the questions] asked me what the connection is with natural things and spiritual things. What is that question? And in poetry it says somewhere: "How to rule the harsh divorce that parts things natural from divine."[10]

What is the harsh divorce that parts things natural from divine? What does it mean in the Bible when it says, "He is more to me than my necessary food?"[11] Can anything be more to you than what is necessary to you? God! "He is more to me than my necessary food." That's a good one, too. "How to rule the harsh divorce." That's all we're about in the poetry. Reading the harsh divorce—harsh it is, I guess—the harsh things, natural [separated] from the divine.

> It is from having stood contrasted
> That good and bad so long have lasted.

I'm making them of equal value. See. Don't I? And that might demoralize some people. They think they're just as valuable when they're bad as when they're being good. Maybe they are. That's why they executed Socrates. That was thought that way. That was thought to be demoralizing. They gave him a chance to leave town but he wouldn't. Big jury—about five hundred or six hundred, wasn't it?—condemned him. Not a small jury like ours. And it's all —this talking about—what your mind runs on, and how much work comes in. A teacher who is teaching poetry ought to be so full of it that he comes into some of his association.

I had a funny thing turn up the other day—a little booklet that I let a fellow print in college containing only one poem of mine, and that was in the days when I didn't know how valuable those things were going to get to be. And at Amherst. And this is the way that occurred. One day—on this question, how to teach poetry—I wrote on the blackboard everything anyone would tell me to write that you could do with a poem. I must have written ten things. And then I added, what can be done with a poem? What can you do with a poem? One is

10. The reference appears in Lawrance Thompson's *Robert Frost: The Early Years*, p. 427.
11. I have not been able to locate this verse in the Bible.

you can read it. Another is remember it. Another is print it. Another is analyze it. Another is glorify it, praise it, and so on. Then I wrote: What can you do with a poem—then I said—without outrage to the Muse? Then we crossed off all but the first three, I think: reading, memorizing, and print. Anyway, they [the students] crossed them off the board. Handy to have the others. Amherst, this was. And two of the boys in that class became printers. [*Laughter*] One of them is quite a noted one. Do you know this magazine—the Vermont magazine that you see on the stands?

    I. *Vermont Life.*

    F. [*Continuing*] He made that. And then he's had a lot to do with Sturbridge—down there and things they do there.[12] He's quite a favorite about antiquities and things like that and printing. He printed that poem of mine; it's called "The Gold Hesperidee."[13] And he made a mistake in it. And I was mad at him. I scolded him, and he said, "Let me do it again." So there are two printings of that poem that are worth quite a lot of money. Some of them turned up for me to autograph the other day. That's thirty years ago. He came out of that crowd and that very question of what you do with a poem without outraging the Muse—without outraging decency and everything else.

    You better go easy. Better go softly. I've thought—many many things I thought of doing. I spent an hour on that. You see that's one way of getting rid of an hour. I was always thinking of things like that. [*Laughter*] How was I going to spend three hours a week on others, you know? What kind of spirit could you put into it? You couldn't be reading all the time. That's horrible. I can remember reading certain things. I think we read with pleasure Milton's *Comus*. Real pleasure. Had a good crowd. That's a very lively poem. That's better than the big ones. Just big enough. Just the right size, and wonderful.

    I couldn't insist too much on praise or blame and finding fault. And I thought I'd confess sometimes that if you hear me liking a poem very much I'll never say anything against it.[14] I never do any

12. Earle Newton (1917–), who graduated from Amherst in 1938, was at Old Sturbridge Village (Mass.) from 1950 to 1954. He was founder and editor of *Vermont Life* (1946–50) and of *American Heritage* (1949–54).

13. "The Gold Hesperidee" was first printed in September 1921 in *Farm and Fireside*, is included in *A Further Range* (1936), and was republished by the Bibliophile Press, Cortland, N.Y., with no date given.

14. I saw this demonstrated once at the English School when Coventry Patmore's *Magna est veritas*, a poem Frost often quoted, was disparaged, or so he thought. On this particular occasion, he was quick to show displeasure.

"other handing." I'll cheat about a poem. Watch me, I said. I'll cheat for a poem I care about. I didn't [do] too much of it. Not with literary criticism at all. The poems were something else. One of my favorite books in that class was *The Voyage of the "Beagle."* I can remember. That wonderful book. And Thoreau.

That brings me to another memory here. My friend Conrad Aiken says that Emily Dickinson is a better naturalist. Is that what it says? Quote that, will you?

I. "Conrad Aiken, in introducing the Modern Library edition of Emily Dickinson's poems, says: 'In her mode of life she carried the doctrine of self-sufficient individualism farther than Thoreau carried it, or the naive zealots of Brook Farm. In her poetry she carried it, with the complement of passionate mysticism, farther than Emerson: which is to say that as a poet she had more genius than he.' "

F. Hah! Hah! Hah! I'll forgive him that. He's a friend of mine.

I. I think your laugh is the answer.

F. It's a great joke. That's the way it goes. She's the greatest lady poet who ever lived. Another extravagant statement. She was, I think. That's true. That's nonsense [Aiken's statement].

You know I had a funny adventure with her in England. I used to say to boys, when they had any book to write about for me, [to] tell me something that happened to them in connection with the book or poem. See. That's the kind of thing I like. Tell me something that happened to you. I'll tell you about Emily Dickinson's first edition with me. Somebody was so kind to me in England—an important lady—that I gave her my first edition of Emily Dickinson. And the next time I was at their house I wandered into a hall and there was a little bookcase with discarded children's books. And that [the first edition of Emily Dickinson's poems] was among them. That was before Conrad Aiken did what he did for Emily Dickinson in England. He had a lot to do with waking [them] up to who she was. I suppose he would temper that somewhat now, but he did that [the introduction] for the Modern Library, didn't he? This [the Palgrave *Golden Treasury*] is a Modern Library Palgrave that I have. All right. Anything else?

I. Several of the questions about education seem to want to know how bad a thing amateur poetry is and whether it should be encouraged in the classroom.

F. Well, you know, that's one of those big problems that I never solve. I read a good deal, quite a little, of aspiring poetry, you know. That's what you mean, don't you? I remember my daughter down at Barnard and another girl took a course in writing a sonnet a week that was under quite a noted teacher of English down there. And I don't think much of that. [*Laughter*] That is, I wouldn't do that to anybody. Neither of them are now writing sonnets. [*Laughter*]

Edward Davison, who used to come here and who is now connected with education at Hunter College and all that, and calls himself president of the Poetry Society recently—in the last two or three years—once ran a department in the *Saturday Review* that was nothing but this.[15] He gave the people a set of rhymes right down the side of a sonnet. They filled in the meaning. That was a sort of a practice. And he asked me to do that and I said I couldn't. He said, there are better men than you have. Education. I couldn't do that. I can't play a parlor game with anything like that. I care too much about it. Sometimes clever things get done that way, I have no doubt. But that's not my interest in it. I might rather revel in technique. The word *revel* is a queer word. Dr. Arnold called it reveling when you did anything at night that hurt you for the next day. [*Laughter*] I don't revel. The freedom of the words. The beauty of the freedom of the words, you know.

One of my great friends is Ivor Richards. He put all his discipline in the eight hundred basic words, and by gracious, that's a very useful thing in China in place of pidgin English.[16] That's all I know about it, breaking natives in somewhere in short order. I understand that they do that in the army. They have a scheme for learning any language very fast. They do it on somewhat the same principle. They take eight hundred basic words that you can do almost anything with—almost anything. [*Laughter*] We were talking about that—Phil Wylie and I were talking about it lately.[17] He knows Ivor Richards. Richards has a great influence; he's one of the great powers in Harvard, you know, and teaches teachers. And that thing simply devastated all the high-school teaching. They thought that the children who grew up in the language needed to be thrown back on eight hundred basic words, you know. Nonsense. But he's got over that. I said: "Did you once think that we're going that way to make English a universal language?" I put it right to him once. And he very, very modestly and very flatly said, "I did once." I got that

15. Edward Davison first met Frost at Bread Loaf in 1926. See Thompson, *Robert Frost: The Years of Triumph*, pp. 317, 320, 327.

16. Ivor A. Richards (1893–), who published *The "Republic" of Plato* (1942) in Basic English, had an important influence on literary criticism, changing the impressionistic tendency into a systematic and exact scientific approach. He was university lecturer at Harvard (1939–44).

17. Frost met Philip Wylie (1902–1971), a writer of popular fiction, known for his sharply satirical *A Generation of Vipers* (1944), while in Florida. Frost lived in Coral Gables and Wylie in South Miami.

right. Phil Wylie said to me once, "There's only one word for *talk* in there, I think, in the eight hundred." I said, "I know a lot of people who say *prate*." And he said: "I need to rant." [*Laughter*] *Prate* isn't enough. I want the word *rant*, and I want the word *prate* for certain kinds of people. I'm prating tonight, maybe.

But, you see, there's no teaching any more than there is preaching without some misgiving. You're no teacher if you aren't afraid of the job; of how you are going to touch these great thoughts, these great things that we care about. The beauty of poetry is that it admits of intimacy that you can't have any other way. You can be more personal that way with things. You can go further in good taste. Some of my objection to what they do with a poem is just that it grates on my sense of decency and I can't bear it for the poem. It's in bad taste. I can't bear it. It's so with philosophy. Some philosophical cant I can't take. Jargon. Why don't you say it in basic English? Get that down. That's what I mean by teaching: tread softly and speak low. And remember that delicacy about it. Some of the things you hear are indelicate. I can't stand if it's indelicate. I can't listen to it. That's all how you know about that, how you get some people to dare to say certain things. This isn't making mistakes but it's going too far with it. Further than I can go in a poem. I stop. The poem stops me in a certain place; I don't want somebody going on with it. I can't bear it. And that's so about some other people's poetry: that I wouldn't have them carried any further. Just as if some people—nice people they are—they take you by both hands and say: "I see what you mean but I wonder what's eating you." [*Laughter*] They try to pull you across the line and make you say more about how that happened to you. You've said as much of it as you've wanted to. That's what's happened to you. That's the experience the poem is. But I don't want to go any further with it.

I'm only saying that because—sometimes I say it perhaps too extremely, just as I said lately, around two or three places, that anybody who never encountered poetry until he reached it as a study is lost. I've actually known some who have never encountered poetry until they got to high school or somewhere. For that reason he [the student] ought to be led into it very gently. He ought not to be made too studious of it. That's the teacher's place—to ease it [the poem] to him. Temper it to him. Show him around. He ought to learn something for the ear and the play and the beat of it and the swing of it. Don't, don't, don't, don't let him study [it] until he's ready—until he's got some of that. The approach to it ought to be through *Mother Goose*. It ought to begin there. The best time's gone by the time they come to high school. They're lucky if they began with *Mother Goose*.

And lucky if they didn't have some of this made verse in the teachers' magazines—stuff that is made by people who have no business to write it. There have been only two or three people who have written children's poetry that's fit to read. There is nothing good for a child to read that isn't good for his parents. The reverse isn't true. *Paradise Lost* is good for the parents; that isn't good for the child. You hear people saying that around about. I hear parents say, "My infant never goes to sleep without my reading some of *Paradise Lost* to him." [*Laughter*] Well now, you haven't had any chance to retaliate about all of this.

I ought not to say that—it's frightening to say—if your first encounter with poetry is as a study you're lost. You're not. But it's very dangerous to come on poetry without having had it as a pleasure first. Pleasure first; study it later. I hate to hear anyone say his pleasure is increased by the study. I don't know. I don't belong with that class of society at all. I have to be tolerant. But I wonder. I don't know. Here I've got you in front of me and having a good time with you and I'm enjoying that, but I've never seen anybody operated on yet. I've never been to the operating table. And I don't like you any the better for not having seen you operated on. [*Laughter*]

I. Just before we leave this, Mr. Frost, the other evening we were talking about words, and I thought you said something that was very interesting to me. You think there's something before the word.

F. Well, you heard how I said that, you and Mr. Hadas and Mr. Hadley, wasn't it? [18] We were wondering if there was such a thing as a thought without words. And you hardly think there is. And yet there is always when a thing is going on, when you are coming into a piece of writing in a poem and finding the words to come along, you know, it seems to come out something else inside you, just before the words. You can just feel it.

I. That was rather nice about the exchange you had with Julian Huxley. It was Julian, wasn't it? [19]

F. Well, you know, you hardly ever make a new word. You never do almost. So it's as though you caught the old counters, the old pieces, you know, the old words.

18. Frost had been talking freely to Moses Hadas, Jay Professor of Greek at Columbia University, and Egbert Hadley, chairman of the Board of Trustees at Middlebury College, at Mr. Hadley's home during the evening of July 23, 1960.
19. The occasion was the symposium on "The Future of Man" in New York City on September 29, 1959. In addition to Frost, the panelists included Julian Huxley, Devereux C. Josephs, Ashley Montague, Herman J. Muller, and Bertrand Russell.

I. And made one. Thorosian. That's yours.

F. Yeh! That's a little quiet. And once in awhile you do something like that. But this very word comes to you. It seems to come on something that's rising in you. Something. There's a new word that comes. I don't know. Nobody who has taught psychology would admit that you had any thoughts without words.

I think I have this all the time. I'm in a place—that's where a poem comes from—all of a sudden I'm transported—I'm in a place. And just as I said that, I was suddenly beside a bare cliff with some cliff brake in it. Ferns. Just that came to me like that. But I'm in a place and I can pick words off that place and I can pick something off that place and sentences and phrases and things like that, and that's certainly before any words. It comes to me very much in that way if I'm very much in the place. See. It's a poem. That's what I write a poem from. I'm with somebody or in a situation and the rest follows. And I can see right away that all sorts of things come tumbling to it, all the details all around it. But when they ask where a poem comes from, that's as near as I can get to it. I think it's nearly always that way. I'm with somebody in a place—way off, unaccountably, in a kind of reverie, and all of a sudden something becomes prominent in the reverie. And I can pick the poem off it.

And it's so—I can carry this down to this. I use this analogy. Coming down the street towards somebody you know coming the other way, somebody I always pass the time of day with, as we met in going by each other and often in teaching, in an insulting way, you know, for the hell of it, you cock your head at each other. You approach each other. Sometimes you say something pretty good and sometimes you don't. [*Laughter*] But it's like that. Something in him does that to you, rises up, you know. Sometimes you get a nickname for somebody that way, you know. It comes over you what to call him. That's where these nicknames come from, I suppose. Somebody just thinks it that way over again—unexpectedly, you know—hunting for it and sees it in the newspaper next day.

That question of the origin of it all. Another question somebody asked me was: Do I write under pressure? I think that means, do you write a Phi Beta Kappa poem and things like that when you have to? And I never did. There are three or four of my books that have poems I read as Phi Beta Kappa poems. They knew I wouldn't write one so they said, "Bring us anything you have." That's always that way. Once I tried one to bring their name into it. I changed [one] to bring in Columbia once. I was reading at Columbia and I got that in as a tribute to them. But under pressure—what do you mean by pressure? Money? Goodness, if I thought that this little poem would be worth ten dollars to the family—couldn't write it. That occurred to me. I wouldn't know what that meant. The only pressure I know of is this other thing that comes over me—something special, specialness in the place where I am, or the situation I'm in, a place, has to be something special, you know. It's just like a joke coming. Where do you reach a point where you say that sort of thing? After years and years of this question of good and evil, I make what is a sort of little joke about it, a joke to myself. "It is from having stood contrasted / That good and bad so long have lasted." After years, pop goes the weasel. [*Laughter*] And then—the other one about science, you know—"We dance round in a ring and suppose,/But the Secret sits in the middle and knows." We suppose, and the secret itself knows. Somebody said to me, "I don't like that poem." And I said: "What's the matter with it?" And that's [the poem] in the book. That's an old one. And I said: "Sits!" It was a lady. And she said: "I don't like sits—everything's in motion; the world is going forward. [*Laughter*] Secrets can't sit still." Sitting must be on a hot stove. [*Ironically*]

Now that's an interesting question that I never answered. Again I try and try at it but—when I think of the long time somebody's been bothering you about—a long time—and the world's been bothering you, the world is full of the difficulties about war and peace. Now I was reading—what was I reading?—somebody (I guess it was Henry VIII) talking about the one thing a king ought to give the world. It's just what Eisenhower wants to give the world. Peace. Peace. He was campaigning for Peace. Talking Peace with a capital *P*. And they were arming for peace, I believe. [*Laughter*] Ain't it a joke? And if the UN will do anything about peace it will have to have an army of its own—it's getting one—it's a great joke. They can't do it by lying down in the road like Gandhi to get what he wanted. And he did it.

Then I said to Julian Huxley—we'd been talking about this great going forward and all this and peace coming. He believes in peace, no God and plenty of peace. He's an atheist, a frank atheist. And I'd been saying that it didn't seem to make much difference to me that I was descended from a monkey. I tried to live up to my ancestors. [*Dryly*] I do them justice and credit. But I hadn't been able to find out just what I ought to do to be descended from a monkey. But I said: "We've come up?" He said: "Yes, up! up!" He thought "up." He thought we'd come *up*, not down. I just wanted to know. And I said: "What do you suppose steered us up?" He was very vague about that. Then, in that kind of a corner, just sort of out of indignation, patient indignation, I just said: "Wouldn't it be possible to say that it was passionate preference—preference—passionate preference?" That didn't make a hit with him particularly. He seemed to think it was some sort of an upward uplifting, I guess, that was accidentally upward. No God in it at all. Nothing but spirit. I would think it would be something like that—that everything shows a tendency to prefer—even teachers. That's one of the things we've tried to throw away in teaching and give teachers. That's one of the things we've tried to throw away in teaching and give everybody the same mark. But we've decided we've got to do something about it.

My anger at that made me say that we were going to so homogenize society that the cream would never rise again. And that's the way some people are talking about education—so homogenized it that now they're looking for cream again. Beat the Russians. They're creaming, why shouldn't we cream? That's where a good deal comes from—that kind of pressure that you're cornered and you're bothered. There's a certain debate in your life that you don't ever feel you've got the best of, that there's still something unsettled. If He's a God of mercy, is He also a God of justice? Naturally there's a constant, natural conflict between justice and mercy. The big joke is that somebody on earth ought to balance them up. Probably God does. It could be assumed. That is the most Godlike thing: to balance them—mercy for justice or a just mercy. But there's something there that's almost too hard for a mortal man to get.

The Democratic party and the Republican party are having quite a time about it right now. They both want to sound merciful enough, and they both want to sound just enough. They're going to outdo each other in getting that right. The nice way is to choose the Democrats for being too merciful. Somebody calculated that the mercies that they promised the world were going to cost us about fifty billion dollars a year—if they did all that they had in their program. The Republicans have got to sort of match that somewhere if they don't get broke. You buy both, you better buy mercy than buy justice. All right now, come on now, some questions.

I. Let's have some questions coming from the group here. There are probably lots of them.

F. This is a good start. Those are good questions.

I. We've got some more in case they don't ask us any.

F. Go ahead, somebody.

I. "How would you define a tragedy? What is your conception of a tragedy?"

F. There are so many things you can say about tragedy. One of the interesting things to me is I think it best to have a tragedy with no villain. But Shakespeare differed. He always had to have a villain. There again I am wrong and Shakespeare must be right. [*Laughter*] It has always been a pride with me that I can [put] people into tragic situations with nobody to blame. That's in my feelings about it. And—see—I like to tell you about people I know. I knew Amy Lowell very well, and she said one night to me in her great house in Brookline, she said: "After all, what's the difference between your stories about New England and mine?" I said: "Amy, you're more like Shakespeare. You can't have a tragedy without a villain and I do it without a villain." She said: "You don't like mine?" And I said, "Yes, Amy, you're more like Shakespeare." [*Great laughter*]

That has been a kind of conflict, you know, between men and women where nobody's to blame, between nation and nation when nobody's to blame. That is what makes them predict. They think they can get the blame all out of it all and there won't be any more tragedy or conflict. It's tragic—isn't it?—when you have conflicting claims; that's all.

I. Let's take the other side. What about comedy?

F. That—what makes comedy? That's the same, only you're laughing at it. [*Laughter*] You say: "That's one on me." That's what slapstick is and everything, and that's what clowning is, you know. A clown is somebody who can laugh at his own expense. There's that wonderful picture of Picasso's—the clown—isn't that Picasso? Woeful creature. You know, looks as if he'd been beaten by his own humor. Whipping himself. Tragic. Makes you happy and makes you sad, as the song goes, you know.

George Meredith has a sonnet about that, hasn't he? "Passions spin the plot," he says. "In tragic life, God wot, / No villain need be!" See, he agrees with me. "Passions spin the plot."[20] And then this play of this sonnet of Shakespeare's, and Tennyson's understanding of it and Palgrave's understanding of it is a great, great people live a passionate life. Who has "power to hurt and will do none." "None" rhymes with "stone." Sometimes you're deceived by that changing pronunciation. I've heard people say "none." [*To rhyme with "stone"*]

I'm not dodging that question. That's really my answer: that tragedy is that kind of conflict without villainy. All we hear about is women and men, a woman and a man—and their natural conflicts. And that's in it, too. "Modern Love," isn't it—those sonnets of George Meredith? Love, love. Modern love is different than ancient love. Anything else?

---

20. George Meredith's "Modern Love," sonnet 43.

I. "What do you think of John Masefield's poetry? You knew John Masefield, didn't you?"

F. A little. You don't start me doing that. A friend of mine—you know, one way to get out of that is to say he [Masefield] has a following. [*Laughter*] There are some who like him. Some very fine things he did. He is not as much thought of right now. One of my ways out of that is to say I don't evaluate people at all but I can tell you about how they are rated on the stock exchange. I said that to a storekeeper—a young man selling me fruit—he asked me what I thought of Robert Service, and I didn't want to high-hat him. I said: "That's all right, you know," just like that. And then he said: "I suppose you wouldn't rank him around here with a fellow named Frost." I didn't know he knew my name. And poor Amy Lowell isn't quoted on the curb any more. [*Laughter*] This was a fruit store in Cambridge. Fruit store. See. There are people who would be very angry at me for saying that. But that's the state of the stock exchange.

I. You once said something about reputation that I think you were saying to be polite when you were getting a medal. And you said that the truth might lay somewhere between your own approval and the approval of the public.

F. Oh—ho!

I. You don't think that, do you?

F. Not quite.

I. It's very dangerous to say a thing [like that].

F. Somebody asked about this that I have in mind, that's in a question about any public, any person, you know. [21] No, how much communication is there to it? Some things I'm aware of—kinds of people I'm talking to, brought up with. I'm not thinking of them. No particular case in my mind or anybody's particular mind.

They used to tell me on the rejection slips, you know, to study our magazine for its needs. [*Laughter*] They really did. No, nothing like that. You're naturally talking to the human race as you know it. A cloud of witnesses, so to speak, you know, and people you're used to. I wouldn't talk Sanskrit because I wouldn't know anybody that knows it. I wouldn't put a word of Sanskrit in. [22] All right. And I

21. The question was: "Do you have an audience in mind during the writing of a poem, before, or after? If so, what immediate influence, if any, does this audience-consciousness have on a specific poem or on your poetry in general? If a poem is to communicate, with whom? Does the poet communicate with himself? his intellectual peers? the generality of men? an unrecognizable audience?"

22. Frost is sniping at T.S. Eliot's use of Sanskrit at the close of *The Waste Land*.

don't believe in putting in much Latin any more. I never did. [*Laughter*] One of the things you're commonly afraid of [is] highhatting anybody. It's fun to quote something—somebody—to make everybody wonder where you got that. I wouldn't tell you. I know one I said tonight that I bet none of you know. "The harsh divorce that parts the natural from the divine.". That one figure. [*Laughter*] It's fun to see people try from the kind of thing and places that you take it. All right. I don't believe in taking the blame for everything. Some things float around like that.

Something you can do. Make a basket. Make a dress. Make an order of an hour in a class, you know; shape it. It's a momentary stay against confusion. What do you think I mean by that? Is that all there is to it, is momentary? You know that kind of insults me. Do you know what the humanities are—what they call the humanities? They are the accumulation of those momentary stays that have survived. That's what the humanities are. They weren't momentary, they were good because they went on. They were so good they went on. You're gathered into the body of the humanities.

Did you ever think this about this question of the inductive or deductive, of whether what we know comes down from above or whether it comes up? Most scientists would tell you that nothing, no generation that has come up—once it gets up there you can deduce from it, you can bring down. There's nothing comes down from God. You created the gods and then you work down from [them].

I'm not traducing Julian Huxley. I like him. I had a good time with him, but I noticed that he talked like an atheist to me. When he was given an honorary degree at the celebration of Darwin out there in Chicago, he declared himself publicly an atheist. If I had to deal with him, if I saw more of him, in spite of everything, you know—"I believe there is no God, in spite of all the accumulation of the ages, I believe there is no God"—a great believer I say you are. They can't call that negative. You're a great believer. Not an unbeliever. That's a believer. It's a cant word to call a person an unbeliever just because he's an atheist. You have to believe strong. He's a good man—a good honest man. Had a great deal of difficulty same as the rest of us.

My greatest prejudice is against an agnostic. He doesn't believe either way. He's just afraid to believe—afraid to disbelieve and afraid to believe. Just agnostic. I saw somebody whose book ended with an agnostic prayer. It's nauseating.

But you know Masefield, speaking of something like that, of somebody—it comes over me of something he did well, you know. I can't quote the one about the tribe that had been hunted but tomorrow we'll be at it again, you know—hunted and tomorrow, a little

171

tribe, you know. Then: "Pious folk and other kinds of folk / That think it's a sin to troll the merry bowl around / And make the dollars spin / But I'm for toleration and for drinking at the inn / Said the old bold mate of Henry Morgan." That's great stuff. Henry Morgan—that's a great pirate.

I. "Reynard the Fox" is good too. I heard him read that.

F. That's a long thing. Do you know a lot of it?

I. I know none of it. I heard him read it. It seemed good. Are there any more questions [to pose]? You're having a workout.

F. That's what I'm here for.

I. "Do you think the new president—either Mr. Nixon or Mr. Kennedy—should appoint a cabinet member to take care of the arts?"

F. Yeh! That's one of my little fancies. Then I made a mistake down there in Washington when I had the Senate to talk to. And I was doing it for somebody else—doing it for Senator Case from the Black Hills, not for Senator Case from New Jersey.[23] He had a bill for a new cabinet of the arts. And he's a nice man and I hadn't been prepared for this. I knew what he was. But, really, I shouldn't have advocated the bill. I should have used the opportunity to say, why not go the whole length, and say, why not have a secretary of the arts? And that would obviate one thing—the danger of having one more member of the cabinet. You've got a big cabinet already. And that just rather stuck in his way. They've got a stranglehold on it, the gang does. You can't do anything with it, but if you had a secretary he'd be changing with every administration and that would be better. He wouldn't do wonders any more than Mitchell does for labor.[24] It's like that. You can show an interest. You can make other members of the cabinet pay attention to the arts. And it would show the world that we thought of the arts, and so on. I would like to have talked about that but I didn't.

I. Would you have anyone in mind? That's the other part of the question.

F. No! No, that could be up to—it ought to be some young fellow. He wouldn't matter too much, you know, but he'd have that concern for the arts, you know. They're going to have some kind of a department—that was in the air—Senator Clark asked me this time

23. The senator from South Dakota was Francis Case and, from New Jersey, Clifford P. Case. Frost had appeared on May 5, 1960, before the United States Senate subcommittee in Washington to favor legislation for the establishment of a National Academy of Culture.

24. James P. Mitchell was appointed secretary of labor in President Dwight Eisenhower's cabinet in 1953.

if this—Case's—would interfere with the larger plan—the big art department—I don't know what that's to be. That's going on —unusual to hear it. I've never meddled in affairs like that before. I just got down there by accident. Had a very good time. I liked particularly Senator Clark of Pennsylvania.[25] I had never heard of him before—except in the newspaper. He's a fine man and somebody I could talk to—Democratic, I believe, and that has nothing to do with it all. Fine man to talk to. Got a head on him. I liked to talk with him about these things. See if he could ask for something.

I. France does it with Malraux.[26]

F. Yes, what's he called?

I. I don't remember.

F. I don't think he has that kind of a station next to the president.

I. He's pretty high up and I don't think it's called that [a cabinet post].

F. I don't know. England does a lot for the arts. It has a civil list and gives money that you don't hear much about. I remember hearing—you hear of it accidentally now and then [when] some writer gets five dollars a week. I heard, I think, once of someone who got quite a big thing—maybe $700, I don't know. They notice the arts and that goes on. Trouble with all that is the senator [Clark] said: "There'd be a lot of corruption." I said: "Yeh!" [*Laughter*] And I said to Clark: "That's all the Senate does is punish corruption anyway." I did say that loud. [*Laughter*] All the committees for hunting corruption. Solemn, eh?

You get so sick of hearing about the Guggenheims my friends seek, [from] whom I hear about it for years. Everybody knows I'm no help to anybody. I lost interest in it long ago. About your own work and how you ought to have one. The best thing I've heard this year was that three or four of my friends were given quite a lot of money without asking for it. We won't go into that—the Ford Foundation did that. Who moved in the matter behind the scenes? Nobody, so far as I know. All without seeking. You couldn't do that long, you know. Just as soon as they find out that once, there'd be someone after him to do it again. Good habit. And you don't expect to get rid of that entirely. You just like to minimize that—keep it down. It would be good for the other members of the cabinet: to follow around a lot like that with the arts. Different kind of person from

25. The reference is to Senator Joseph Clark, Jr., a Democrat from Pennsylvania.

26. From 1958 to 1969, André Malraux was minister of culture in President de Gaulle's cabinet.

one time to another. Somebody that could give a little fresh feeling about [the arts].

I said down there, everybody down there is getting to be declared equal. All I ask is that poetry get declared equal to business, science, and scholarship. And the arts. I said: "If you don't declare it equal it will act superior and that's very bad for it." [*Laughter*] Too many of my friends think they're too good to be read. That's a disease. All right. Any more?

Some of this—you don't have to swallow it all, you know. Are you hearing me well?

I. Yes. Here's a question to end all questions: "Does 'Kitty Hawk' suggest that you have less need now of a crevice and burrow of the 'Drumlin Woodchuck'?"

F. [*Laughs*] That's a good one. All right. Tell you a story. When I first came out in America, my publishers emphasized the New England of it. I never did. But the third book is *Mountain Interval,* and I told them, please put on the jacket—I've never interfered at all but that once—I said, if they'd please put on it that I talk of universals in terms of New England. I think they did—something like that. But I talk about the whole world in terms of New England. But that's just because that's all I have around me. I could do a little better now. I've wandered around a good deal more. I know the Middle West. I knew a man said of the Middle West, quoting Kipling, "East is East, and West is West, and the Middle West is terrible." [*Laughter*] He was a great joker. I've lived out there; I've been out there. Quite a lot of my poems are outside New England; people don't know that. Very little outside of America. And the general admiration is about people and everything. I'd be sorry to think otherwise.

I. That's the implication in *A Further Range,* isn't it? In the title— *further* range?

F. Yes, that's right. That's what I did that for—call it adventures. That's about—it's got [the] Himalayas in it.

I. And the Madeiras are in there, too, aren't they?

F. Yeh! from Hakluyt's *Lives.* The Madeiras. "The Discovery of the Madeiras."

CHAPTER 15
An Interest in Science
July 3, 1961

Although this talk opens without any special flare, gradually, as Frost warms up to his subject, it grows more and more revealing. It is a highly personal talk, not because of anything Frost is telling us about his intimate life but because he is telling us a lot about the ideas that interest him, especially in science. Usually he talked about form. Here he talks about the influence of a world of science upon our time. He led typically in his "straight crookedness" directly from the Scopes trial to the youthful encounter with dynamos and suggested the source of his concepts in such marvelous scientific insights as Foucault's pendulum, which later produced our gyroscope.

The early part of his talk could be called his defense of science by finding out how much fun there is in it. And his comments take the curse off early statements which appeared so exasperatingly flippant, even as arrogantly obfuscating the patient and brilliant concepts of theoretical science. To paraphrase Frost in other connections: "Antiscientist—never!" Later, he read some of the earlier poems, and then hopped, skipped, and jumped around in Complete Poems.

The temper of the talk was exploratory; its tone was not satirical. Another interesting aspect of this talk was the frequent change of mood. Starting to read "The Black Cottage," he rejected it. "Naw!" he interjected. Determined to read a "prettier" poem than "The Witch of Coös," he turned abruptly to find "a harsh one," changed his mind and read "Neither Out Far nor In Deep," specifically identifying it with science. He began to read "The Oven Bird" and turned again abruptly from it to "An Old Man's Winter Night." His mutability of mood was startling this evening.

I don't know where to begin. There are the various premeditations I have a week or so before the thing that happens, and then I give them all up. Shall I say a speech to you I said at somebody's birthday the other day? I made that up the last minute. I changed it. I had another speech in mind, and just as I went I thought, "No, I won't do it. I've got another one." I said: my favorite forms of literature are English couplets in our language, couplets and Irish triads. And I didn't give them an example of couplets. I write some myself. But I said—for instance—an Irish triad by poet whose name I've forgotten. I'll have it. Three times whence speech is better than silence: First time it's when the king needs urging to war; second time it's when there's a good line of poetry to order—that speech is better than silence. And I gave them an example of that. I said: *At tuba terribili sonitu tarantantara dixit* (But the horns with terrible sound say tarantantara).[1] So I sound horrid. [*Laughter*] [*Repeats the Latin sentence from Ennius*] See, it's a good one. Sounds like it, doesn't it? You can all understand that. That's an easy one. And then, I said, the third time is when praise is due. And I said, "The man whose birthday we're celebrating has been saying some awfully nice things lately and he deserves some praise for them." And then I said, "And Harvard deserves some praise for producing him at Harvard, deserves some praise for having produced five presidents—two more than any other college." And the last thing I said was, you know them all. Two terrible Yanks, two Dutchmen, and a mick.[2] That was my speech. I remember those things for a little while after I say them.

Then I was thinking today about something I'm going to write. Maybe I'll take you into my confidence. I'm going to write a play —not called "The Scopes Trial" but called "The Telescope's Trial." I've always been interested in astronomy. And it'll be a little like the Scopes trial, if you know that.[3] Maybe you've seen the play made out of it—a great misrepresentation of everybody concerned. But I make it all right. And in the play I have it come out that we had more left to guide our lives, how to live, from science than we do from mythology. Mythology is the Bible or any other mythology you want. See. That is the way the play will come out. For instance, I'll say I'll offer it the first thing. I was brought up in San Francisco, and from the Chinese there I learned ancestor-worship. I became a worshiper of my ancestors. So every morning since then when I got up I thought: "What must I do today to be worthy of my monkey ancestors?" [*Laughter*] And you see where that comes out. Pick fleas off

1. Ennius, *Annales* 2. 18. 140 (freely translated).

2. The two terrible Yanks are John Adams and John Quincy Adams; the two Dutchmen are Theodore Roosevelt and Franklin D. Roosevelt; and the mick is John F. Kennedy.

3. Frost was referring to the play, *Inherit the Wind*, by Jerome Lawrence and Robert E. Lee.

each other, or what do you do? I believe they eat the fleas; they're tasty. And then the story of the Garden of Eden and the fruit of the Tree of Knowledge, you see—that's some mythology, isn't it, from our point of view? But it's about all the boys that I've ever taught. At the age I get them they just come out of the Garden of Eden. They're just having a go at the apple, you know. And,it's a thing I have had to deal with all the time—they've had to deal with all the times. And we have to deal with it decently without talking too much psychology or psychiatry or going to anybody at all about it—but it's the whole thing, you see. All the books we're reading, all the things we're thinking, have to do with that knowledge.[4] Now I'm not going to talk long, but that's just something else I thought of.

Another one you want to hear that I might have talked about —these things are always passing through my mind. When I was a young Greek in the high school in Lawrence, Massachusetts, I encountered the word *electron*.[5] I knew that we Greeks got it by rubbing amber—made sparks come. That's all I knew about it. And a very slight thing, you see, that's come to make the modern world: rubbing amber to get a few sparks that they gave the name to. That has something to do with sun-brightness—brightness of the sun.[6]

And then, not many years afterwards in a change of fortunes, I was working in the mills—in the dynamo room.[7] And I was handling magnets and electricity in various forms. I worked on the dynamos. And the dynamo is whirling magnets, you know. I saw them. There's a brush on the whirling magnets to pick up the sparks [i.e., electric charges]. And I didn't go too deeply in it because that wasn't my future. But it was very fascinating. I knew that from my Greek days, that the magnets came from Magnesia where the early magnets were found. And that little slight thing, you see, a little bit of metal from Magnesia, a little spark that you get from rubbing amber and that

4. Frost's notion of a play to be called "The Telescope Trial" is an interesting illustration of his tough whimsy. All in his head, what he said sounded like a plague on the houses of both religion and science.

5. Frost attended Lawrence (Mass.) High School from 1888 to 1892, sharing valedictory honors with Elinor White. He pronounced *electron* "el-ec-tron" with a pronounced accent on the first syllable.

6. *Elector* in Greek refers to beaming sun, just as *electrum* in Latin refers to amber.

7. During the summer of 1893 Frost worked as a light fixer in the dynamo room of the Arlington (textile) Mill, located between Methuen and Lawrence, Mass. He was responsible for replacing the carbon as soon as it was used up in the arc lights. In the slack periods, as noted earlier, he climbed into a hideout under the belts and read Shakespeare.

looked like just a plaything for children—look at what it's become!

And I was thinking—I know another slight thing that has stayed unused all these years. I remember seeing under a tall dome a pendulum swinging back and forward—north and south, see, so long and tall, and so sort of almost detached from the earth that it fell behind the movement of the earth.[8] Just a little bit, just enough to be something in the next five hundred years. You know what they're going to do in the end? They're going to find some way of leaving something behind while the world whirls under it, to get more force in the world than they've had before. The world's going to go whirling under something. They'll probably fasten it onto the moon. I'm going to leave that there.

Out of little things like that, you know, the future comes. It's coming out of that, I'm sure; I don't say how. But out of that . . . something that is left behind by the world and where that mighty world whirling at that terrible rate is a perpetual motion for others and you can go on multiplying; you know, as they say, there's only standing room.

All right! I'll just read because I read with no connection.[9] I joke about science. I'm not joking about what I'm saying at all. I've said a lot of half-fooling things. People misunderstand me sometimes; they think I'm antiscientist.[10] Isn't it interesting that in an editorial I read today about Hemingway's death they made a kind of dispute about him, whether he was or wasn't great or important? But one of the ideas was that he was antiintellectual. Uh-ha! Whatever that means. One way to be intellectual is to be awful—just the way he [Hemingway] was. I thought, go for things, you know, unsparing[ly]. But it seems they think it's a little unintellectual to be rough-spoken or something. He was—what is intellectual? [11]

8. In 1851, Jean B. L. Foucault demonstrated the rotation of the earth by means of a graduated disk which was seen to turn while a pendulum, freely suspended, maintained its plane of vacillation. Foucault showed that the direction in which the pendulum swings remains fixed in space, and this principle led to the invention of the gyroscope in 1852. Note Frost's avid curiosity and apparent interest in making a metaphor from this concept applicable to an idea.

9. Many times this was true, but not always. Frost was at times, even in these rambling talks, designing. Note in this one particularly the emphasis he is giving to science.

10. A very firm statement that ought to quench those critics who think he was hostile toward science because of the tart twitting of science in some of the poems in *Steeple Bush* (New York: Henry Holt, 1947).

11. Frost's reaction to Ernest Hemingway's critics has a solid base. He referred approvingly to Hemingway's short fiction, notably "The Killers."

How shall I get, just for the fun of it, a science one? [*Says "Why Wait for Science"*] I wrote that years ago, and the curious thing in that is that there's quite a theory going around now about how life began here by meteoric impregnation. You know, that's one of the flourishing ones. And that's quite an idea, and you know what's going on two or three times a year? We get an awful dose of meteorites trying, you know, to impregnate the earth [*laughter*] with something better than we are. Don't you see that? See how much fun there is in science? And how much fun there is in everything else? All right.

I'll settle down and be serious in a few minutes. A theory—like these I'm saying—if you hold it hard enough and long enough gets rated as a creed. [*Reads "Etherealizing"*] [*Laughter; applause*]

Then let me just run away from all that and get back to—I'm going to say a little poem I must have written back in *A Boy's Will* days when I was very young and I haven't got it quite in my mind and I haven't it with me. It's only seven or eight lines long but it so unmistakably sounds with the sound of that book, you know. You can tell if you've got an ear, you know. And the attitude toward life is so concentrated in that little thing; how it ever escaped me, kicking around on an old sheet of paper worth $1,000. [*Laughter*] You know, that's one of the funny facts of existence: that a little poem like that of mine that I gave to a friend—he sold it at an auction at a fair they had out in Chicago for *Poetry: A Magazine of Verse*, and it sold for about $600—a little sheet.[12] It wasn't as good as this one. Some old thing I left around. And then the person that bought it put it up the next year and it sold for $1,000. See, I know what the prices are. And that was all [a] church affair where people pay more than they ought to on purpose.

Well, let me just begin, read two or three little ones back there, put us way back where we belong and not all this fresh business. This [poem] is [about] autumn time. [*Reads "Reluctance"*] That's one of the early ones.

Then here's one about farming. This is called "The Tuft of Flowers." Now let me just say to those that don't know me: that was my job when I was young, to turn the grass after the mower. We called it "just turning it." It scattered it a little in the sun. He [the mower]

12. Frost did not "say" the seven or eight lines. But his comment on the auctioning of it, despite his lightness, shows unmistakable pride in the monetary value attached to his work. Unlike Thoreau's Indian basketmaker [in *Walden*], he had succeeded in making people appreciate with the clink of coin the handiwork of his special craft.

mowed it in the dew and I scattered it to be dried. [*Reads "The Tuft of Flowers"*]

And you see, the part of that that has something to do with everything I ever wrote, [I] put in there: [*Says*]

> The mower in the dew had loved them thus,
> By leaving them to flourish, not for us.
>
> Nor yet to draw one thought of ours to him,
> But from sheer morning gladness at the brim.

Just because he liked them. And that's the whole of the story.

Here's an odd little one back in those [*A Boy's Will*] days. [*Reads "Revelation"*] And you see that's why I'm here, to tell you what the poems mean. That's what that's saying, really. Back in those lonely days.

Then—no, I'm not going to stay in that book [*A Boy's Will*], I'm going to the next book—the end of the next book. I think I'm not seeing those quite clear enough. See if these help a little. [*Takes steel-rimmed glasses out of his jacket pocket, puts them on, and starts to read from "The Wood-Pile"*] "Out walking in the frozen swamp one grey day." No, I don't like that. [*Says "One More Brevity"*]

Then some little ones for the children. I've got some great-grandchildren down here of my own.[13] I'd get in trouble if I didn't say some of the little poems. [*Says "Stopping by Woods"*]

You know—just to ramble around a little more—how easy it is to get poems wrong. We've just been saying down at my house an old thing I've said a good many times about an old-timer—a hundred years ago—and just see what you make of it. [*Quotes from memory the following stanzas*]

> I know my soul hath power to know all things,
> Yet she is blind and ignorant in all;
> I know I'm one of Nature's little kings,
> Yet to the least and vilest things am thrall.
>
> I know my life's a pain and but a span;
> I know my sense is mock'd in everything;
> And, to conclude, I know myself a Man—
> Which is a proud and yet a wretched thing.[14]

13. A reference to the three children of his grandson, Prescott Frost, who were in attendance.

14. From Sir John Davies's "Man."

Now what might you think from that, take it all first—what is that? Is that agnosticism? That he doesn't know "nawthing," does he? [*Laughter*] But you couldn't make a greater mistake than [to] think that. You probably need to read some more of the poem—those two little stanzas are taken out [of context] and made of all over the world, but the rest of the poem would show you that it's very religious. What fills up the knowing is believing. It's a most intensely religious poem, least agnostic you ever heard; yet it sounds awful, doesn't it, that way? It's meant to. I like it that way. [*Repeats the two stanzas*] You know, the one word that lifts that into the rest of it is the word *proud*. Pride is faith. Almost the most religious time in the world. Davies, his name is. Any poem out of context with the part taken out might be like that—might be taken out of context of a man's life, you know. Other things you've said—many, many things, many moods, many times seeming inconsistent. This is like that.

Now I mustn't keep you too long. I must get around here. Here are two. See how these go together. [*Reads "A Soldier"*] Now that's one kind of way of taking life about war or peace. Here's one I don't know as well. [*Reads "Design"*] Do you want to hear that twice, to see how bad it is?[15]

Just at random: this "Triple Bronze" is sort of a political one. [*Reads "Triple Bronze"*] Some people don't think countries exist any more.

Then, shall I take time to read one longish one? I'll read "The Black Cottage." Naw! I want to get this light right. [*Reads "The Witch of Coös"*]

Let me finish off with a prettier thing than that. No. I'm going to say a harsh one, if I can find it. No, I'll change my mind there. [*Reads "Neither Out Far nor In Deep"*] That applies, you see, to astronomy too. "When was that ever a bar / To any watch they keep? / They cannot look in deep / They cannot look out far." That's about the telescope and the microscope. You didn't know till I told you, did you? [*Ironically*]

Then I want to say one more. "There is a singer everyone has heard" ["The Oven Bird"]. [*Turns from poem after reading first sentence*]. Let's put this one in. [*Reads "An Old Man's Winter Night"*]

I'd like a little farewell singing one. [*Says "Tree at My Window"*] Two or three little ones like that, and then I'll stop. [*Reads "Happiness Makes Up in Height"; reads "The Most of It"*]

That's all. [*Vigorous applause*] [*Returns to lectern*] I'll just tell you one

15. Obviously, he meant bad, *not* in form but in the implications of its content.

or two more recent ones—offhand ones. Let's see, this one. [*Says "The Objection to Being Stepped On"*] And then, let's see. This terrible one. This I'd never print but I'd say it confidentially.[16]

> Them two panacea guys
> Getting economics wise
> Bid mankind homogenize
> So the cream could no more rise.
>
> Am I simply telling lies?
> No, they did it in a dream
> Of which Stalin rose supreme.
> And who said he wasn't cream?

There could be more to that. And then [these] little couplets that are kicking around.

> It is from having stood contrasted
> That good and bad so long have lasted.

You all know how to settle this yourself. The introduction of evil is quite a different question.

> We dance round in a ring and suppose,
> But the Secret sits in the middle and knows.

Blind and ignorant.

You must be quiet if I say this one to you. Don't say a word. Use your self-control. There's something about it that releases something in wicked people. Gives them away. It's a prayer in a couplet. Promise me now. Not a murmur. Not a one.[17]

> Forgive, O Lord, my little jokes on thee
> And I'll forgive Thy great big one on me.

---

16. So far as I know, this is the only time Frost said the two-stanza doggerel in public. If this is true, "this terrible one" received its unique performance during an evening of varying moods. It shows Frost at his game: rough but not coarse ridicule his implement, his tone blunt and mocking.

17. Was Frost leveling with his audience or, in the play of contradictory moods, throwing the dust of levity in their eyes? I think he was, in reality,

Thank you. [*Stops, and then returns*]

This is another prayer. Like a prayer too—only this is as if I spoke to a star up there at the other end of the room. [*Says "Choose Something Like a Star"*]

That's to myself as much as to anybody. That's the one [in which] I hate myself for being too much one way and then too much another through fifty years of politics.[18] We may take something like a star to stay our minds on and be staid. You can get something far enough away like a star, you know, or like a poet—like some ancient poet —and think about it and take your mind off voting.[19]

I go over every year to finish up the Great Issues course at Dartmouth where they're all studying all year—every one in the senior class—how to get ready to vote once in four years. They tangle themselves all up, just the way I have. The everyday sways me this way and that, you know. When a new president comes in like this, every appointment that he makes is as if he hit me first on one side of the head and then on the other side of the head. I know so much about them [the appointees] all. But far away it's Catullus.

All right. Anybody want to talk about anything? Want to ask me something more, a poem? Never fair. Never do that here. One more little one—a familiar one like this. [*Says "The Road Not Taken"*]

Do you want to hear another dark one not by me—a religious one? You see, I just said this. I may start out sometime and do a whole evening of poems I remember of other people. Someday I'd like to recite all of (I know it by heart—I found it out the other night), all of Browning's "Protus." You know, go look at it and see what I carry. And I'll say it to you. Not tonight. But here's the dark one for you.

> In either mood, to bless or curse
>   God bringeth forth the breath of man.
> No angel sire, no mother nurse
>   Shall change the work that God began.
>
> One spirit shall be like a star,
>   He so delights to honour one:

---

trying to cover up for his apparent irreverence. At any rate, his words only stress the more the ambiguity in how a poet should be taken.

18. Quite an admission of his political fence-straddling and mercurial voting record.

19. The ancient poet is Horace as much as it is Catullus.

> Another spirit he shall mar:
> None shall undo what God hath done.[20]

I didn't write that. That's fatalism, isn't it? Just right out-and-out. You don't believe it, do you? You think that you can do it. Psychiatrists can do something about it. All right. Good night.

20. A. W. O'Shaughnessy, "Doom."

CHAPTER 16
Telling Stories
July 2, 1962

This evening Frost, at eighty-eight, was inclined to tell stories, not because he was an old man but because he was tired of reading poems. He had in hand his new book—In the Clearing—with fresh poems, and this rallied his spirit. It is worth noting that he returned to several of his favorite stories, including the one about the young American boy and the Russian czar, and also returned to themes like glory and Promethean defiance and the Thorosian one-worldishness. When he read from his poems, he was finicky about getting into the right mood.

Although repetitive, he kept bringing out interesting points, especially about maps and boundaries and the American past. His strong nationalism showed in the exaltation of Enoch Lincoln, and, once again, he showed a penchant for mentioning some obscure but worthy person not as commonly known as he deserved to be.

Frost's eyes were giving him difficulty. This led to interruptions in the reading of the poems but also accounted for his talking a good deal more than he sometimes did.

This evening Frost quoted from his own poetry rather freely. When he said "Take Something Like a Star," his version reads as follows:

> It asks something *of us here.*
> It asks *of us a certain height,*
> So that when at last *the mob is swayed*
> To carry *praise or blame too far,*
> You *may choose something like a star.*

I have emphasized the words which differ from the version of the poem as it appears in The Poetry of Robert Frost *(ed. Edward Connery Lathem).*

Suppose I just decided not to read any poetry at all but just tell you stories. That would be new, wouldn't it?[1] I might spend the evening just reading out of my new book, but I don't want to wear that out in a hurry.[2] Suppose I told a story or two.

Someone said to me—a young Italian friend—that he didn't think we Americans realized what we have achieved. We're too used to it. And I suppose that's more or less so. We have to stir ourselves up and shout a little and talk about it to remember it.

I heard of a boy back in the 1830s who must have been full of what America was. That must have been a great time—the time John L. Stevens was opening up Yucatan in the thirties and when Emerson was going strong writing poetry. I saw a government statement yesterday that Emerson was a literary man; he wrote essays. That came from Washington. [*Amused laughter*] Just think of that! Just think of that! Well, about that time, I think, Emerson was having his first little book of poetry printed in England.[3] He had his first book of poetry in England. He was a poet. In prose or verse, he was a poet.[4] And I had another message from Washington about how we had been too hard worked as pioneers ever to be literary at all, and way back then we had Emerson who will be remembered longer than this republic. You'd think literature had just come over us, that we'd just found time for it. That's Washington! [*Laughter*] Awful, isn't it? Emerson—one of the greatest of the great.

Well, in the thirties there was a boy from upstate New York, middle state, somewhat like the boy in *Redburn* about the same time, I guess.[5] He had sailed before the mast. And in Saint Petersburg when the ship got there, he said to his captain: "I wish I could see the czar." And the captain said: "I'm afraid that would be difficult." "Well, I

1. This is the last formal evening lecture-reading Frost gave at the Bread Loaf School of English before his death on January 29, 1963, after undergoing surgery at the Peter Bent Brigham Hospital in Boston and after suffering a subsequent heart attack. His self-consciousness about reading once again from his poems was very much on his mind.

2. *In the Clearing.*

3. Ralph L. Rusk in *The Life of Ralph Waldo Emerson* (New York: Charles Scribner's Sons, 1949) indicates that Emerson's *Poems* were published by James Munroe and Co. of Boston and issued on December 26, 1846, "though the date of the imprint was 1847" (p. 312). John Chapman, in London, published the English edition in 1847.

4. The sum and substance of Frost's thinking on Emerson were compressed in the address he gave at the American Academy of Arts and Sciences, on the occasion of the award of the Emerson-Thoreau Medal on October 8, 1958. He revised the address and it was published in *Daedalus* in the fall of 1959 as "On Emerson."

5. Unidentified.

want to see him." The captain spoke to the consul in Saint Petersburg, and the consul said the same thing: "That would be very difficult. I don't suppose that would be possible." And a message came from the czar presently for the boy to come see him. And he came before the czar—the American of these days. I can just feel him, the kind of boy—with his hand out like this. [*Doubles his hand into a fist as though he had a bomb or something in it*] And he said: "I have a present for you. It's an acorn that fell from a tree that grows beside the house of George Washington. He was a great ruler and you're a great ruler. I thought you might like to plant this by your palace." They planted it. I wonder if it's there. The czar sent for a shovel and they went out together and planted it. And then the czar said to him, in a splendid way, too: "Anything I can do for you? That's a great thing you've done for me." And he [the boy] said: "I always wanted to see Moscow." So he [the czar] gave him a cavalcade of horses and sent him up to Moscow. And his ship sailed without him. I don't know how he got home. That is what America was in those days.

And then, you know, there was the same thing, you know, that began this doubt about it, that must have had its beginning in the same way with pessimism, [like] the *Redburn* story [in Liverpool] that I mentioned. It's a terrible story—a sort of dismal boy abroad. But we had Americans and we've got them still, I suppose.

Now, I was thinking about glorifying America. What does that word mean? This comes from Washington, too. Somebody wants me to do something to glorify the space age and our part in it. [*Laughter*] That's prophesying, and I charge more for prophecy. [*Vigorous laughter*] That's prophesying a little to you. The first thing you think of to begin it is—without being ironic—you can't be gloriously ironical, can you? That's something you've got to think of; that always takes the wind out of the sails, irony does.

But trying to be glorious—first, you think of the space age of great Elizabeth. I don't know whose sentence it is that's in my mind—"the spacious age of great Elizabeth"—a space age that was, too.[6] And people radiated as much from her in the spirit as from anybody you know. It was, of course, the explorers going every way. Drake went all the way and left a marker—didn't he?—on the west coast of America. Her Drake. They went everywhere and the thoughts went everywhere. And this is the assumption: that everybody knew that they could have prophesied what a glorious space age it was, and nobody at all wanted to stake Columbus to a voyage. Everybody had

6. Frost was apparently referring to Tennyson's line (in "A Dream of Fair Women," line 7): "The spacious times of great Elizabeth."

their doubts about it. One minor queen got interested in him. [*Chuckles to himself*] And it couldn't have been very glorious. The glory is something you see behind you there—where they went and all they did and all they lost and all the wrong they did.[7]

But let's suppose we're going to Mars right away. I can leave it to you. You can glory in it. Maybe I don't do it right. I hesitate about it. If I were sure we were going to Mars and I wanted to glory in it, the way I would have gloried in Columbus's voyage if I had been any good—I wouldn't have been up to it; I know that. [*Laughter*] You know what I'd like to do? I'd like to go to Mars and warn them about how many mistakes we made with the people that lived in the country we came to. [I'd] tell them about what we did to the Indians. And they'd better be careful [about] our landing in Mars. Shoot me and shoot any more that came. I can't make any prophecy very glorious.

I suppose the glory of it is this—let's wind it up somewhere. Suppose you think now of your glory in it. I think the glory of it would be that we're making these passes of Promethean defiance against the unknowable space. Every plane, every motion we make through space—round and round the world and toward the moon and all that—is a sort of Promethean defiance of the unknowable. That's glory. That's all it is. And that's as far as I go. And I don't believe that's what they mean. [*Laughter*] I think they probably don't go any further than better communications between the stock exchanges of the different parts of the world. And that's going to be very valuable. Val-u-able! We're still at it; that's the splendid thing about science and about man. One of the most splendid things is his defiance of the unknowable—further into it—further into it—further into it—and always there it is—Promethean. Suppose I leave that for my prophecy. That will go on. I'm quoting a poet when I say, "It will go on!" Do you know the poet I'm quoting?[8] Never mind. [*Laughter*]

Something else I was thinking of not connected with glory. I'm speaking to all of you, and you're teachers that want to be taught. And that's a funny thing, isn't it? Funny kind of submission. It's nice—it's very nice. And what do you want to be taught in this same prophetic way—that the further we go in space the less we'll own anything or live any particular where? And I heard of a school the

---

7. On another occasion at Bread Loaf—July 4, 1960—Frost spoke feelingly in favor of the effulgent noun *glory,* and he quoted one of his favorite poems, Christopher Smart's "Song to David," which celebrates glory. "You know," Frost said, "one of the worst things in the world is people who belittle glory."

8. Unidentified.

other day—a kindergarten—where they put [on the board] for the children this couplet to correct.

> Buttercups and daisies, Oh, the pretty flowers—
> Are they any less so for not being ours?

See, that's Thorosian and one-worldish. Universal. Now, it was put this way for them to correct.

> Buttercups and daisies, Oh, the pretty flowers—
> Are they any better for their being ours?

You were supposed to make it: "Are they any less so for not being ours?" That's the same question of where we are, and whether Vermont is anything to us, or any property is anything. That's very Thorosian. Thoreau's all loose in the world on account of that. He talked that stuff all the time. No property. He could enjoy everything that belonged to other people.[9] He could eat their meals, too. [*Amused laughter*]

Now I'll read you a little. I'm going to begin with some of the little ones that I have in my head; old ones, too. Suppose I just go back to one or two of the old ones first. I'm groping for what I want. I want to get the mood. [*Reads "Mowing"*] That was one of my earliest ones. That is one of my earliest convictions about poetry: that fact is the sweetest dream that labor knows, that poetry is gloating on facts. I found that for myself when I said that.

And then another one that has a definition of poetry in it, that the fact is the sweetest dream that labor knows: this is called "The Tuft of Flowers"—another early one. [*Reads "The Tuft of Flowers"*] Of course the heart of it lies right in those lines in the middle: "The mower in the dew had loved them thus." That's the poem you write. To leave them to flourish but not for us, "Nor yet to draw one thought of ours to him, / But from sheer morning gladness at the brim." That's the first part of it. And the social part of it is secondary. Each one of the poems was me getting on with my own thoughts about life and what it was, step by step.

I guess this one isn't so much like that. The very first one in my book [*Complete Poems*] has something to do with it all. This is about wilderness—the desire for the wilderness. [*Reads "Into My Own"; reads the last two lines as follows:*] "They would not find me changed

---

9. "I have frequently seen a poet withdraw," wrote Thoreau in *Walden*, "having enjoyed the most valuable part of a farm, while the crusty farmer supposed that he had got a few wild apples only" ("Where I lived, and what I lived for").

from *what* they knew / Only more sure of *what* I thought was true."
[Italics added to distinguish from version in *The Poetry of Robert Frost*.]

That, again, is a certainty. The Emersonian idea of being pleased with your own inconsistency I never had. I always hoped that the thing would tie together some way. If I couldn't make it, that was up to God.

Suppose I skip from there to some of the later ones in the little book [*In the Clearing*]. A few short ones, and then I'm going to read part of a long one. I'm not going to burden you with a very long one. This little one's called "Away!" [*Says "Away!"*]

I put those together like those first ones that I read. These later ones "would not find me changed from him they knew." You know, I was thinking in a scientific way a lot lately, and the latest thought I've had about that is that some day the scientists are going to find out that the thing they've been looking for as created by the right elements put together is the thing that brings the right elements together. And it's another element itself called life. And they're [the scientists] going to say that some day before long. They're still looking for and putting things together. It's not a resultant, it's the cause. It's in everything—the attraction of one element with another. Valence and all that sort of thing they talk about.

Here's the last one I had before that [thought]. It's called "Accidentally on Purpose." That's a piece of my sarcasm. Now this has in it the next thought I had—that just as oxygen and hydrogen and iron and tin and silver and gold are elements, life is an element, so subtle that they haven't put their finger on it. They hope to get along without finding it. They think they can make it, by putting the right things together; for instance, they try marrying everything. Oxygen doesn't marry very well with gold, it marries better with silver, and so on. They're interested and working at that sort of thing all the time, and so am I. [*Teasingly; laughter*] Accidently on purpose! I was brought up on that expression. When I did anything I shouldn't, I said I did it "accidently on purpose." [*Reads "Accidentally on Purpose"*]

That's that. These [poems] are doctrinal, too. [*Laughter*] Then another little singsongy one. [*Reads "Peril of Hope"*] Note the last stanza changes. "For there's not a clime / But for all the cost / Will seize that time / For a night of frost."

A longer one: this is about us—the thing I talked about at first—about knowing ourselves. [*Reads "A Cabin in the Clearing"*]

A little bit of a longer one; it's long enough so I can find it. Now this one I'm only going to read you part of. The title is "How Hard It Is to Keep from Being King When It's in You and in the Situation."

190

And this has ironies in it, but it's partly out of the fun of an old story in the *Arabian Nights* that you probably never read unless you've gone a long way in the *Arabian Nights*. [10] I found it somewhere near the tail end of Burton. It's stayed with me. I thought of another one the other day I could make a story-poem out of. I haven't written many story-poems. Now I'll read this very carefully. [*Reads "How Hard It Is to Keep from Being King When It's in You and in the Situation"*] I'm not going to read any more [of it]. [*After breaking off in the middle*] There's a lot more of my ideas about things. I'm not seeing too well. I seem to be having trouble with my glasses.

[*Says "One More Brevity"*] Let me say something without reading. [*Says "Take Something Like a Star"*] That's preaching to myself, not you. You might not notice: I say in one place "Some mystery becomes the proud." You don't know what that line cost me in the way of living. It took me a long time to accept obscure poetry, but I decided it was a lofty spirit made them obscure. Many a line is like that; wrung from you. You don't get credit for all you've suffered to get it. They ask if it takes you long to write things. No, it takes you long to live 'em. [*Chuckle*] You write them quick. That poem is full of things about myself that way—just like the fact is the sweetest thing. Just unconsciously I've lived by that. Gloating and doting is the whole business, you know. Dwelling on things! Dwelling on things! Dwelling on the fact! If it's beautiful statistics—you know, there are some very beautiful statistics to gloat on, too. That's what it all is—dwelling on something that vibrates and stays in your mind and keeps coming back, and the last of that I've often called attention to. I don't think I've called attention to that before. I was thinking of a particular person when I said "Some mystery becomes the proud." [11] Never mind him. I won't tell you who he is. I am giving him credit for loftiness. More than he deserved. [He's] still hard to take.

And the last part: "It asks a little of us here. / It asks of us a certain height, / So when at times the mob is swayed / To carry praise or blame too far / We may take something like a star." And I often think it's Catullus. I get out Catullus when I'm too bothered about my having been wrong in politics. When I voted wrong—and voted wrong with the mob and everything—[I] read Catullus, and astronomy is like that to me and so is hoeing and so on. Take something like a star to stay your mind on and be staid! You want to be more or less a staid person.

This book [*In the Clearing*] has mistakes in it. It's got to have some corrections. Here's one I'm going to put a stanza back into. I don't

10. Unlocated in the Richard Burton edition of the *Arabian Nights*.
11. Apparently Frost had Ezra Pound in mind.

191

often monkey with poems, but this I publicly monkeyed with. I'll say it and partly read it. It's called "Closed for Good." [*Reads "Closed for Good"; starts by quoting the first stanza of the poem as it appears in* Complete Poems, *p. 576; then reads the remainder as it appears in* In the Clearing, *p. 19*] See that stanza [the first] I threw out and it ought to be back in. [*Repeats the stanza*] That's the way that's going to be. That's taking you into my confidence when I talk about these things. The book has a whole lot in it of my thinking about science and all that—a great deal I don't want to go into tonight.

Here's a little one I have here I want you to have. Aw gee, where is everything? This kind of thing that I don't know whether it's meant to recite, it's such a quiet sort of thing. [*Reads "Questioning Faces"*] This is difficult to read. I could almost wish you could remember that for me, I say it so carefully. [*Repeats the poem*]

And then before the book went out after my being badgered and bothered, I finally sent it [the manuscript] out, and I wrote this ["In Winter in the Woods"] while it was going [to press]. [*Amused laughter*] It's the same thing when you say, "They would not find me changed from him they knew / Only more sure of all I knew was true." What changes all the time is your thoughts about science. Take a revision of life every little while and all that, but it comes out about the same.[12] [*Reads "In Winter in the Woods"*]

That's a threat to write another book. I didn't write it for that, but that's what it comes to. That's my interpretation of it. You see, it's got the same rhyme all the way through. Just wrote it right off the reel. [*Rereads the poem*]

I guess you've had enough of me. [*Applause*]

●

[*Says "Stopping by Woods" and "Reluctance" without comment; turns to one of the poems in* In the Clearing, *entitled "Lines Written in Dejection on the Eve of Great Success"*] I'm going to read eight of them [lines] and leave the rest out. The next book is just going to say "Eight Lines Written in Dejection on the Eve of Great Success." See, it's stealing from Shelley and all that.[13] But I put in eight this time. It isn't in the book. The rest of it I'll forget. [*Reads "Lines Written in Dejection on the Eve of Great Success"; laughter*]

12. He was insisting on the fact that the last poem he was to publish in his lifetime ("In Winter in the Woods") was not closely related to the first one to appear in *A Boy's Will* ("Into My Own").
13. Frost is undoubtedly referring to Shelley's "Stanzas Written in Dejection, near Naples" (1818).

You feel the same way I do about it, but you see how cautious I am, saying "Lines Written in Dejection," see, "on the Eve of Great Success." They may be at the moon tonight.[14] I don't know. Where is the moon, anyway? I haven't thought of it. I may be refuted in any day, any minute, but I fixed it so I'm all right. Dejection!

And then some other half-absurdity—you must remember that little couplet that you got to fix:

> Buttercups and daisies, Oh, the pretty flowers—
> Are they any less so for not being ours?

That involves the whole question of Thoreau and property and, you know, the future. You don't know where I got it. I won't tell on anybody. [*The audience asks for "The Gift Outright" and "The Road Not Taken"*] All right, suppose we finish on these. [*Says "The Road Not Taken."*]

And then the other ["The Gift Outright"] that others chose for me—I didn't choose it—for the president. I gave it to him for his inauguration, and it's just a history of—a little piece of history—about the Revolutionary War. Isn't it funny about how politics comes into poetry somewhat, you know? The Revolutionary War! I often say that most tragedy is like that great tragedy—a conflict of good and good.[15] Colonialism is good. Something else has come to the world now; we don't know how good and bad it is. Colonialism is gone; it's out. Today's papers [have] some more of it. We [U.S.A.] led off in that way [colonialism], and for very slight reasons.

You know one of the reasons we were out of sorts was [that] the big pine trees on our farmers' lands—the great big pines—were good for ships' masts, and the king marked them for his and we couldn't have them for ours.[16] Right on our own lands—irritations like that, little things, you know. We decided we had to go alone, and right away we were George Washington and Thomas Jefferson and Madison and John Adams and the great poet like Emerson and all that. Right away, now, it set us going—enterprise—having a country. It worked well with us. I hope it works well for everybody. But this

14. On July 22, 1962, the United States launched Mariner I—a Venus probe—which was intentionally destroyed after a launching rocket had deviated from course. Frost's lines are satirically pointed at the apparent failure of our scientists to beat the Russian scientists in the moon race.

15. See "To a Young Wretch" in *A Witness Tree.*

16. The tallest straight-grained pines in the northern New England forests were designated as the king's pines and chosen for man-of-war masts in the Royal Navy.

poem ["The Gift Outright"] is about that. "The land was ours before we were the land's." That's all. See, we didn't belong enough to where we lived. This is more of the doctrine of belonging [to] the ground, you know. I can't get it out of my system. [*Says "The Gift Outright"*]

> Possessing what we still were unpossessed by,
> Possessed by what we now no more possessed.

We were possessed by Parliament and all that, you know.

> And forthwith found salvation in surrender.

To the land, you see.

> Such as she was, . . .

It comes out pretty good, you see.

I didn't say both times. I was careful not to say too much for the land or for us. "Such as we were we gave ourselves outright / (The deed of gift was many deeds of war)." And we had an amusing time for the imagination about whether we would make that into something else—such as she will become, under this administration. [*Laughter*] I often said, "Such as she was, such as she *might* become." I changed that word in there several times myself. But I've kept it, finally, "Such as she was, such as she would become." However, I'm preaching to you now, talking about politics again.

There's nothing like a good map. [*Emphatically*] And the evidence of that is that we've got a good map—from the Atlantic to the Pacific—laid out as neat, however we got it, by hook or by crook, I don't say; it's a great map. And Berlin is the worst map the world ever saw. See, bad maps make bad troubles. Maps do it—that's all—maps do it. Good night. [*Applause*]

I just couldn't read with glasses tonight. [*Apologetically*] I did better without them. I have had forty doctors look at them [his eyes]. Something the matter. They say I'm a mental case. [*Laughter*] Let's see—that's the great sentiment of the evening: there's nothing like a good map, having a good map, these boundaries.

I know a minor poet who, when he was rather sickly, a young man in Maine, came to teach in Fryeburg, Maine, a little town, way back more than a hundred fifty years ago, and he became the governor of the state of Maine. And he fought for the boundary line in northern Maine. Strangely enough, I've heard about that boundary [while] sitting at the president's table beside a Canadian minister's wife. Not the minister now—the liberal minister, I might call him. And she talked about that boundary and how we got it, and I knew more about it than she did; she didn't know it was this little man. He is a small man—he was—buried in a tomb in all his glory in Augusta, Maine, and his name was Enoch—you know, a fine biblical name, Enoch Lincoln. And I know a lot about him.[17] Lincoln, Nebraska, is named after him—the capital of Nebraska—and I told her that. [*Laughter*] It wasn't Abraham Lincoln. This was Lincoln. He wrote a little book of poetry called *The Village,* and it's exhibited in the library in Lincoln, Nebraska. It's in a glass case there, and I have a copy of it. Since I've been bragging about him some people have sent me copies of it. It was in those great days back there that I've been talking about when Americans were all alive to being Americans. And it's quite a book—it's what you'd call a progressive book. It was fine about women and about Indians. Isn't it wonderful history got that way? I've always wanted to go and live in Fryeburg a little while in his honor. He's just there. He wrote the little book about Fryeburg —right through the mountains there in Fryeburg, at the edge of the mountains, near where I've lived. Enoch Lincoln. I take pleasure in glorifying him, you know, not the space age. All right. Good night. [*Applause*]

17. Enoch Lincoln (1788–1829), a lawyer and Maine politician, served as governor of Maine from 1827 to 1829 and was highly regarded as an efficient executive. Significantly, Frost's humanism asserted itself when he said: "I take pleasure in glorifying him, you know, not the space age." *The Village* was published in 1816.

PART THREE
Surmisings

CHAPTER 17
The Masking of a Poet

I'm naturally a teacher.
Bread Loaf School of English, June 28, 1951

"Genius," Schiller wrote, "is ever a secret to itself." Undoubtedly this is true. Frost could hardly have explained his genius. "Beautifully simple himself," wrote Gorky of Chekhov, "he loved everything simple, genuine, sincere, and he had a peculiar way of making other people simple." Superficially Gorky's statement seems to fit Frost. If by simple we mean natural, he was his own man, attracting both believer and innocent, approached often humorlessly by the former as though he were a secular saint and more thoughtfully by the latter as a wise counselor.

On a deeper level, Frost had little of the unsophisticated simplicity of a countryman like the Ayrshire Burns. Early and late, he more nearly resembled in the Emersonian sense a Poet Farming, whether in Derry and Franconia, New Hampshire, or in South Shaftsbury and Ripton, Vermont. Shrewd, empirical, and speculative, he was hardly rustic. Paradoxically, his simplicity consisted in a containment of opposites in uneasy equilibrium: proud independence, sometimes mistaken for egotistic arrogance, offsetting friendly amenability; a kindly consideration muting tart, acerbic thrusts; shyness counterpointing candor in views; a teasing social conscience counterbalanced by passionate vocational aspiration; insistence on clarity and order in poetic form juxtaposed with a disarmingly relaxed conversational habit; and awareness of exigent change countered by belief in the continuity of tradition.

Seriously committed to the vocation of poetry, Frost's sensibility was as acute as that of one of his favorite poets, John Keats. A passion for poetry burned in him like a core of fire. Equally put out by Plato's diminishment of the poet's status in the *Republic* and by Bacon's mistrust of poetry, his self-elected vocation was simply to write well.

199

This searching sense of responsibility underlay an otherwise playful manner, a hovering wit protecting him as if he were a Homeric hero watched over by a galeated Athena.

Guarded and reserved and reticent Frost certainly was, and gregarious too. Like Mark Twain, he courted popular response. Early in his career, before he received a deserved recognition, he wrote revealingly to his friend John Bartlett, "There is a kind of success called 'of esteem' and it butters no parsnips." He explained: "It means a success with the critical few who are supposed to know. But really to arrive where I can stand on my legs as a poet and nothing else I must get outside that circle to the general reader who buys books in their thousands. I may not be able to do that. I believe in doing it—don't you doubt me there." And in a remark to his California friend Louis Mertins, I detect Frost's inclination toward reticence, otherwise interpreted as a natural tendency toward evasiveness. "Maybe," he told Mertins, "I'm one who never makes up his mind." It is, I think, a statement to be taken as self-justification, not self-reproach.

Frost also exhibited a curiosity to know and talk about things. An inquisitor-general, he resembled Noah, whose interest in the creatures of the ark was wide and proprietary. Things talked about had a way of casual breeding in Frost's presence, one thing leading to many others in a rabbity way. An imaginative conservative, for instance, it was his capability in politics, as in nearly everything else, to feint left *and* right. He could be partisan—note his nationalistic bent. He could be detached—note his advocacy of magnanimity among people and nations in the celebrated interview with Khrushchev in 1962. But it would be a mistake to take him, say, from left to right as though he held a rigid reactionary position. In 1935, under the Federal Emergency Reconstruction Act, war veterans were set to work building causeways along the Florida Keys and two hundred were drowned during a September hurricane that destroyed the railroad between Florida City and Key West. The disaster, aggravated by bureaucratic negligence, rankled in Frost and influenced his biting denunciation of F.D.R.'s do-good New Deal. But he could and did sharply attack partisan politics of an opposite persuasion. He never ignored what happened to conservatives and radicals. "I never dared be radical when young," he asserted in "Precaution," one of his "Ten Mills" in *A Further Range*, "For fear it would make me conservative when old." Even more revealingly, he once indicated that "Take Something Like a Star" was really self-addressed. "That's to myself as much as to anybody," he once said. "That's the one in which I hate myself for being too much one way and then too much another through fifty years of politics. We may take something like a star to stay our minds on and be staid. You can get something far enough away like a star, you know, or like a poet—like some ancient poet [i.e., Horace]—and think about it and take your mind off voting."

Indeed, at once reticent about his private affairs and unreserved in his opinions, Frost both purred and scratched. He purred in admiration of the Constitution as a document and the Supreme Court as a balancing force; ranked James Madison next to George Washington—"my second greatest admiration is Madison"; exulted in *The Voyage of the "Beagle"*—"that wonderful book"; praised Palgrave's *Golden Treasury*—"that pretty little sonnet of a book"; described Thoreau as "the most noticing man that ever lived, maybe"; and exalted Emerson as "one of the greatest of the great." But, as we have seen, he scratched at the lapses and vagaries of the welfare state, the "cant of literary criticism," footnoting poems, notional free verse, poetic rivals like Ezra Pound and T. S. Eliot, Marxism, and Freudian psychology. Scratching in doggerel, he wrote:

> Them two panacea guys
> Getting economics wise
> Bid mankind homogenize
> So the cream could no more rise.
>
> Am I simply telling lies?
> No, they did it in a dream
> Of which Stalin rose supreme.
> And who said he wasn't cream?

And when a lady remonstrated over his use of "sits" in "The Secret Sits," saying emphatically, "I don't like sits—everything's in motion; the world is going forward; secrets can't sit still," Frost said dryly, "Sitting must be on a hot stove."

Whether "barding around" at the lectern or in his Ripton cabin, Frost's infectious humor ranged puckishly from dry jest to wry and rueful taunts. Out of mood he could be sour and peckish, perverse and mocking, gruff and testy. But in form, when amused he was amusing. He played seriously, like one who made his vocation a high profession and not time's holiday. Play of mind shows in his serious jokes, in his funny gravities. To borrow a phrase from Santayana's *Dialogues in Limbo,* he "laughed at the world without ceasing to love it." Life's little ironies bemused him as frequently as contretemps in the chivying of human behavior, and from their confrontation, he pointed an anecdote, sharpened an epigram, extracted a biting phrase, rallied a snappish sally. "I'm not confused," he would explain. "I'm only well mixed." Or, "I might look like a convertible, but I was a hardtop." When honorary degrees were conferred on him at British universities in 1957, he remained uncompromisingly reserved toward the rewards of higher education. "I told them over in England," he made clear to an American audience, "I'd rather get a degree from a university than an education any day."

Now that we have had a plethora of critical studies, biographies, and reminiscing, are we to believe those who contend Frost *consciously* assumed a mask? Or is the validity of the assumption greatly open to question? The attempt to understand any complicated man is difficult, to say the least. How much more difficult it is when we confront Frost's complexity both as a public figure and as a private person. As a poet, the intimate psychic sources of his art remain inward as an ultimate mystery in poetry, not to be explained away. Any attempt at resolving the problem of a conscious *or* unconscious projection of an image is complicated by the double vision—the biographical details and the writings—in the approach of New Criticism. The latter view, influenced by T. S. Eliot's doctrine that "the emotion of art is impersonal," dissociates the biographical details of a man's life from the poems he writes. It would concede Frost his humanity while remaining reluctant to relate the poems to the context of his life. Finally, as Freud contended in his study of Leonardo, "we have to admit that the nature of the artistic attainment is psychologically inaccessible to us." And, as Freud again stated in his study of Dostoevsky, "Unfortunately, before the problem of the creative artist, analysis must lay down its arms."

I do not myself think Frost was in any way, shape, or fashion a fantasist who *consciously* projected an imaginary idea of himself. Assuredly, though, he did appear differently to different people. But I never sensed that in his life there existed, as in Walt Whitman's life, such an unsettling identity crisis as "an American, one of the roughs, a kosmos" implies. Some of his critical interpreters seem to think there was a considerable gap between the Yankee sage who faced them at the lectern in New Lecture Hall at Harvard or in the Memorial Building at the University of Detroit and the cunning craftsman whom they encountered in the poetry. The only differences I could see between the public figure with his dry nipping wit and the roguish private man, reticently occupied with writing poetry, were those changes that occur naturally with the times and those peculiar emphases the traits of temperament make in one's life like the scorings of the Ice Age on glacial boulders. In the sense that by self-ascription he reveled in a springtime passion for the earth or had been traumatically acquainted with the night, had been a more or less steady watcher of the void or an involuntary defiant lone-striker and an assertive one-man revolutionist, had quarreled with the world as a lover or moved deliberately about like an Old Slow Coach, Frost was indeed protean, and, so to speak, "a man of masks." But the metaphor strikes me as inexact. The double consciousness of public and private was integral, not divisive. It betrayed no confusion on his part as to who he was or what he should be doing, any more than Jefferson was confused by being a Virginian, a political philosopher, and a democrat. The continuity in his life was incremental and hardly produced an identity crisis. Yet it is important not to mistake the poet *in* the man for the man detached from the poet.

The problem of how to take Frost is related to criticism as much as it is to biography. How do the critics see Frost? They see him variously, of course, which reminds us of the tendency of critics time out of mind to fail in agreement upon a common judgment. Take, for example, the critics of Mark Twain. Van Wyck Brooks thought Twain was a wounded genius who had been deprived of success by an environment which lacked cultural opportunities on the western frontier and in the East tended to corrupt him by its acquisitive goals, its polite decorum of the lingering genteel tradition, and by the domination of friends, family, and editors. De Voto did not agree with Brooks's theory. Twain, he thought, exemplified the freedom and humor of western culture and exercised a craft which transformed a wild and reckless environment into an entertaining and nourishing art. V. F. Calverton thought Twain in his eastern association was eager to be a Hamlet and forced to remain a Falstaff; and others, like De Lancey Ferguson, regarded Twain as "a highly skilled man of letters." The result is often just as unsatisfactory when we turn to the writer himself. When Sinclair Lewis was asked to write a self-portrait, he considered himself not as a satirist but as a storyteller (and from his description, a very important one), "just as naive, excited, unself-conscious as the Arab story-tellers beside the caravan fires seven hundred years ago, or as O. Henry in a hotel room on Twenty-third Street furiously turning out tales for dinner and red-ink money."

Frost was angular, and his angles appealed to interpreters variously. The expatriate Ezra Pound found him "vurr'y Amur'k'n." G. R. Elliott, an early Amherst acquaintance, discovered in him a glorified Neighbor, and Sidney Cox found him "an original ordinary man." Gorham Munson, one of his earliest biographers, identified him as a classicist and humanist and did not change his view in this respect late in life. Louis Untermeyer, aware of Frost's tendency to think independently, described him as "a revisionist." Yvor Winters called him pejoratively both "a spiritual drifter" and "an Emersonian Romantic." Amy Lowell, early on the scene, referred to him as "a bucolic realist and localist." Other views by other interpreters are encompassing. They include Frost as an agrarian regionalist, homespun sage, bard, seer, and diversionist. He preferred to call himself "a synecdochist," realizing like the imaginative poet he was the importance of the part to suggest the whole and what to make of a diminished thing.

What a difference there is, though, between a man of angles and Lawrance Thompson's connotative "masked man." Where, in Frost, is there an appearance of dramatized ego as in Ezra Pound's assumed personae of Sigismondo Malatesta, Odysseus, Confucius, and John Adams as well as "old Ez," and "a lone ant from a broken anthill" which dominate his Cantos, or of Byron's Harold in *Childe Harold,* Proust's Marcel in *Remembrance of Things Past,* or of Stephen Dedalus in Joyce's *A Portrait of the Artist as a Young Man?* The mask is in Frost's poetry only in the sense that it is in any man. I think what Frost wanted most as a serious practitioner of his vocation was *"how* to have something to say" and a way of saying it. The responsibility of his art consisted therefore not in self-explication but in *self*-discovery. The little voyage he took on a quest of discovery validated the self in his self-expression.

However, such a quest does not belie the appearance of an image in the poems. Frost is both a self-improving and a self-trained Yankee schoolmaster. With consummate skill he is careful not to load his anxious wards with factual impedimenta. What he told the students at Wesleyan University in 1926 was his touchstone in both writing and teaching. He wanted students to have the freedom of their material; a freedom to put two and two together, and the two might be anywhere "out of space and time, and brought together" in metaphor as analogy. Moreover, using "The Celebrated Jumping Frog of Calaveras County" as his parable, his method was not to load the students with information but to stir their imaginations. "Flies, Dan'l" was the triggering art. He stimulated their imagination by subtle hint and provocative suggestion in the contemplation of options in an open-ended universe.

There is not, to my knowledge, any prescriptive information by which the rearing of genius can be guaranteed. Evidence to the contrary is persuasive. Who doubts that self-tutored minds, like Keats and Rimbaud, Dostoevsky and Dickens, Melville and Twain, Faulkner and Frost can, without the benefit of higher formal education, invent fresh ways of expressing a vision of human experience? Frost was, by self-admission, sharply critical of the shortcomings in conventional education. "I'm a terrible critic of schools and school people," he said. However, he was a remarkable teacher-at-large *in partibus infidelium*, and he had this paradox in mind when he referred to "my curious career in teaching." As a teacher his major message was "all there is to know is how to express yourself and knowing how to have something to say—the wisdom and the fact." As a teacher, he commonly performed his role before packed audiences, especially in the Little Theatre at the Bread Loaf School of English where graduate school teachers were in residence from all over the country. Making his pitch accordingly, he used his poetry as an object lesson and his flexible voice and wit as the medium of communication.

His appearances served two immediate purposes and a third —very important—tangential one. First, he helped these teachers make poetry accessible in the classroom. Secondly, he offered enlightening glimpses into the sophisticated art of poetry. And thirdly, his shrewd and revealing statements on the poetic craft embodied a personal theory of poetry. Fragmentary and tentative as his introductory remarks often were, when organized they formed a pattern as firm and distinctive as Inca masonry. "They don't lead up to the poems, they are not prefaces," he once explained. "They are just my little preliminary indulgence. I want to have a little fun out of this. [I] don't want to keep repeating the same poems." Intended chiefly as an entertaining warm-up for his readings, these statements are not only clarifying and informative, they are self-defensive. Frost made a case for no one else's poetry except his own. And why not? Who else's poetry did he know as well?

Several times he insisted he might read an entire evening from someone else's book of poems. "I thought as I came in that I ought to bring someone else's poems," he once said. "I'll bring Shelley or Milton or somebody, you know. Forever me, you know, and it's just because people want to hear the way I say the poems." Had he done so I am sure he would have disappointed his audience. They considered the threat of a switch in presentation more as a denial of privilege than as an opportunity to see him extend his range in the great tradition of poetry. How revelatory it is that he read exclusively from *Complete Poems*. I do not except the fact that occasionally he quoted aptly from other poets, like James Shirley or Walter Savage Landor, Blake or Shelley, Keats or Francis Thompson, to illustrate a point. But how expertly he used his retrieving memory, like a casting net fetching in this stanza or that quatrain, a line, a couplet, even a short ballad like "Sir Patrick Spens" from the free flowing stream of his consciousness. It was as though, in the role of a teacher, he made of these appearances a means to impress upon his audience an acceptable approach to the craft of poetry by one best qualified to do it.

In his teacher's role it was generally impossible to distinguish a separation between the objectivity of wise counsel and a self-defensive egotism. Nearly everything he said was said as personal to himself, and this is equally true of the things which in reticence he repressed saying. Even as a teacher he was an acute self-protector in the art of public appearance. Seemingly, he was free and candid; in actuality, he was warily defensive. Yet when he counseled teachers to make their first aim the ability to generalize, he was suggesting what he always did himself. He advised them "not to be afraid to be an unscrupulous generalizer; that is, the one that doesn't stick at trifles, you know." It was important "to learn to be sweeping about history and art and everything you know and have things to say," a tactic he was adept at, drawing parallels from history, politics, education, science, and if he ever had a moment's lapse in having something to say, it is unrecorded.

But he was a challenger and his notional theories were just as provocative as his perceptive comments and aperçus. In spite of his relaxed manner and idiosyncratic use of "well" and "see" and "you know," which might annoy an attentive purist, Frost achieved what many teachers never do. He phrased memorable things distinctively. The following comments are representative of his views and style:

I've often said in teaching that the best kind of criticism I know is not in abstractions . . . it's in narrative.

It's education, the book of the worthies, what the worthies have done. It's the great book, you see.

The best thoughts you've ever had from anybody are just a challenge to you to have one, too.

I don't want less than an education from the thinking minds of America. I want more than an education. See. I want an achievement, and you can go on from there.

Thinking is always association . . . being reminded of something you hardly knew you knew by something that's in front of you, something that's happening to you, or the past emerging out of the very levels of your knowledge: books and life and all that—that's the material.

It's best when you teach poetry with the students knowing what you're up to. How can you do it? . . . You've got to do it as if you weren't doing it.

There's no teaching any more than there is preaching without some misgiving. You're no teacher if you aren't afraid of the job. How are you going to touch those great thoughts . . . that we care about. The beauty of poetry is that it admits of intimacy that you can't have any other way. . . . That's what I mean by teaching: tread softly and speak low.

Feeling is always ahead of thinking.

CHAPTER 18
The Sayer

Now we are getting on together–talking.
"A Hundred Collars"

1.

Frost was, as is now pretty well established, one of the great talkers of his time. So in possession was he of the necessary gifts of an easy conversationalist—ideas, words, manners, and the ability to keep the talk in circulation—he belongs in the company of other great talkers time out of mind, like Dr. Johnson and Coleridge, Carlyle and Wilde, Mallarmé and Baudelaire, Henry Adams at 1601 H Street, Washington, D.C., and Bernard Berenson at his villa I Tatti in Florence.

Frost's conversation, fluent, canny, and idiosyncratic, depended upon a free association of thought and was predictably often repetitive. He analogized and alluded, epigrammatized and quoted, told stories inimitably and commented pointedly on current events. The most idiosyncratic features of his conversation were the unselfconscious ease with which he got a purchase on any subject, the constant play of humor, and its monologue-like mode. A warm wave of friendliness invited the listener who, in detachment, must have visualized himself at times as an exaggerated ear and at other times as a sounding board for the continuous flow of talk from his low-pitched, drawly, unmistakably inflected and flexible voice, now gruff and mocking, now affable and beguiling.

Not only a one-way talker, Frost was an interested inquirer and a patient listener. He would ask what I thought of St. John Perse's *Seamarks*—I hadn't read it—or Arthur O. Lovejoy's *The Great Chain of Being*, which I had read. He wasn't short because I did not launch into a five-minute briefing on Lovejoy's seminal book. He would spin out a long sunlit summer afternoon in the cabin at the Homer Noble farm in Ripton at stretch with the door closed and the windows down, recalling familiar ideas, trying new ones, and ranging widely. Great at stories, he was adept at shifting speech rhythms, now quoting Robert Burns in Lowland Scotch, or imitating John Millington Synge in a run of Irish brogue, satirically parodying High Church English, or taking off some recent neighborhood event in Ripton rustic. He could be precise, but often the syntax would slouch, the phonetics would blur, and interjections punctuated the talk. "You *see*," he would insist; "You know," he would assume; "Yeh-h!" he would exclaim bitingly; "Sure," he would admit casually.

Most apparent was an inquisitor's pointing mind. "See," he would murmur. "See!" "Do you see?" "See!" And the alerting word, an all-duty enforcer, suggested its Latin root, *video*, a perceiving and a knowing. "Voir n'est-ce pas savoir?" inquires Balzac's emissary of Raphael in *La Peau de chagrin*. Where there is sight, such as Frost anticipated, there is insight. To see is to know. But the implication of the imperative *see* was more challenging than explanatory.

Thomas De Quincey, in *Biographic Sketches*, described the distinguishing principle of Coleridge's conversation as "the power of vast combination." Although Frost nimbly made associations and often, as did Coleridge, started with a lowly subject, his conversation did not ascend "like Jacob's ladder, by just gradations, into the Heaven of Heavens, and the thrones of the Trinity." Sir Walter Scott, after dining with "that extraordinary man Coleridge" on April 22, 1828, noted in his journal: "A most learned harangue by Coleridge on the Samothracian Mysteries," after which he "diverged to Homer." Fairly overwhelmed, Scott exclaimed: "Zounds! I was never so bethumped with words."

2.

The impression Frost's talks made upon his listeners was never so physical as Scott's reaction to Coleridge or so rarefied as De Quincey's description of Coleridge's afflatus. What one chiefly remembered from a talk was Frost's ability to sharpen a point. Describing the relational approach in thinking, he would say, "There are things you can't convey except in similitudes. Our whole thinking is that." He would clinch a view of the open-ended universe by asking rhetorically: "What's the finality in anything?" To score a point in approval of dramatic sentences, he epigrammatized: "Always dramatic; always alive." Good at summing up, he would assert: "There is nothing so entertaining as each other's attitudes. There is nothing so composing as composition." When he praised a favorite book like *Walden*, it was with an appropriate grace note. "It's one of the wonder books," he said charmingly. So the compelling moments in his conversation happened; they didn't seem to be invented.

Speculatively, he concocted sweeping historical theories, but not without provoking demurrers and reservations. One of his recurring notions, typical of his speculative tendency, deserves elaboration. He urged upon his listeners the view that the direction of Eurasian culture was specifically "west northwest." "Just think of that . . . all that counts in the world has been northwest from there . . . near Moab. . . . Isn't it funny! That's what I'm saying then, anyway," he told his audience. "The plunge into the material, the spiritual plunge into the material, has been west northwest. Terrible risky thing to say, I think; I say it just the same." Talking publicly as well as privately about this notion, he would state flatly that Africa had so far contributed little or nothing to history. The great impetus in intelligence, ingenuity, and enterprise had been initiated on the evidence. according to Frost, of known neolithic cultures in the fertile crescent on the Anatolian plain of southern Turkey. This relatively early culture, which Joseph Campbell, in *The Masks of God: Primitive Mythology,* dated circa 7500 B.C. and located in Asia Minor, was designated by the cultural anthropologist as "the basal neolithic."

Frost, deeply interested in archaeological matters, assumed in his "west northwest" notion that the land diffusion concomitant with a cultural diffusion had worked its way out of the Tigris-Euphrates region (probably ca. 4000 B.C.) and over the Caucasus to the northern shores of the Black Sea and from the Aegean into the Balkans. One thrust followed the valleys of the Danube and the Dneister into Central Europe. Another thrust followed the Dneiper and the Don into the Vistula and the Baltic. These thrusts seem to support Frost's intriguing theory. The reliable G. M. Trevelyan in his *History of England* wrote: "The Levant was the cradle of European civilization. The inhabitants of Mesopotamia, Egypt and Crete . . . evolved agriculture, metalcraft, shipbuilding and many other of the arts of life. Such Promethean secrets, starting on their journey from South and East, handed on from trader to trader and from tribe to tribe ever northward and westward across the forests of barbarous Europe . . . reached at last those half fabulous 'tin islands' in the mists and tides of the northern seas."

Some modern archaeologists, however, using the resources of modern science, find the application of such a theory open to question. Applying Willard Libby's Carbon 14 or "nuclear clock," they according to these archaeologists, a culture existed in Britain. And Leo Frobenius (ca. 1898) proposed in his "culture area theory"—*Kulturkreislehre*—an alternative cultural route. Extending from equatorial West Africa, Frobenius's route runs *eastward,* point out that Britain, the northern point of the theory, already had a culture which appears not to have originated in the thrust of cultural diffusion out of the Mesopotamia region. As early as 3000 B.C., through India and Indonesia, Melanesia and Polynesia, across the Pacific to equatorial America, eventually by diffusion reaching our northwest coast. Among many plants, like Asiatic cotton and amaranth, there early appeared the bottle gourd on the coast of Peru. A wild plant, it required human care for its preservation. Frobenius—and others—mindful of such evidence, suggest a direct cultural relationship between Polynesia and the New World. But although Frost's knowledge of Frobenius is problematic, he held tenaciously to his notion of "west northwest" and incorporated it in "Kitty Hawk," among his last poems.

3.

Another subject less theoretical than cultural diffusion and often mentioned was science, *the* dominant force of our time. Despite "Skeptic," "A Wish to Comply," "Why Wait for Science," and "Some Science Fiction," I think Frost was hardly a victim of divided loyalties in an assumed antithesis between science and poetry. Shrewdly enough, he recognized that each of these great areas in human experience is, as Elizabeth Sewell describes them in *The Orphic Voice*, "the pre-condition of the other's working." Moreover, he recognized a common meeting ground for science and poetry, not quite in Elizabeth Sewell's terms as "related activities of thought, instruments toward a particular end," but basically because both science and poetry dealt with numbers. Frost illustrated his contention by counting the fingers of his hand, saying, "It's like this, one, two, three, four, five. And then you play a tune on top of that, see?" Frost was in good company. Thomas Dekker added "to golden numbers, golden numbers." William Congreve hailed "magic numbers and persuasive sound." Pope lisped in numbers "for the numbers came." And both Wordsworth and Keats celebrated numbers in notable lines. "Numbers is one name for poetry," said Frost.

Frost believed poetry, no less than science, could handle words with rigorous precision. "Science cannot be scientific about poetry, but poetry can be poetical about science," he contended. "It's bigger, more inclusive." On the evidence, Frost was impressed both with science as a force and with Albert Einstein as one of its master exemplars. In a symposium on "The Future of Man," September 29, 1959, he admitted, "I'm lost in admiration for science." Clarifying the basis for his admiration, he said, "It's the plunge of the mind, the spirit, into the material universe," and added unstintingly, "It can't go too far or too deep for me." He praised I. Bernard Cohen's interview with Einstein, which appeared in the *Scientific American*. "Very beautiful thing," he said, "very moving thing. Very lofty person. Even his [Einstein's] uncertainty is very attractive." He described Einstein as "a great philosopher among great scientists."

Once at the Bread Loaf School of English [June 29, 1959] he quoted from Emerson's "Uriel" the brilliant phrase "cherub scorn," which he made the motif for his remarks on science. He called it the scorn "a really eager spirit" has for those—usually of the older generation—who are, in his phrasing, "lost in the difficulty of betterness." A variant of "betterness" was "newness." Frost was taking a new look and making a fresh revision in viewpoint. He too was about to unsettle something in the name of *betterness* and *newness*. This talk was to be the measure of his own "cherubic scorn," and "Kitty Hawk" was the direct evidence. "Kitty Hawk" was, as he said, "a good deal about flight." So the space venture in the science of flight—in effect, the NASA moon shots—was on his mind. He explained he had once thought science strictly "domestic science," and it took some time for him to outstrip this view. Then one day, to use a favorite word, it "dawned" on him that all science is "domestic" because its basic concern is with "our hold on the planet." The space program, he referred to dryly as "a kind of interplanetary tourism," as though, rather than go visiting our near or next-door neighbor, we were intent on visiting our far neighbors—the moon, Mars, or another distant planet. He said: "But it dawned on me at that point that all . . . the great enterprise of life, of the world, . . . of our race, is our penetration into matter, deeper and deeper; carrying the spirit deeper into matter. And though it looks like something different out into space, that's just deeper into matter. . . . Put it that way. And that is our destiny—that is why science is our greatness."

He extended the analogy to the Christian religion, which was concerned with "God's own descent into flesh," or "risking spirit in substantiation." For Frost, the accolade, "the supreme merit," was the *risking* of the spirit. Although art was a risking of the spirit in its material embodiment, he said: "But we've got to take the risk." And he admitted, "Sometimes in the by-product of science we lose the spirit entirely; but not in the act of scientific penetration—deeper, deeper,

deeper, further, further, further." And recalling lines from "Neither Out Far nor In Deep"—"We cannot look out far. / We cannot look in deep"—he gave them a positive contextual reading. "But—as far as we can and as deep as we can," he said, "still we penetrate into matter, further into matter."

I note, first, that while Frost is critical of the arrogant pretensions of science in "Why Wait for Science" the great thrust of science into space is his admiration. Second, he applied and extended the idea of on-penetration and showed it was central to "Neither Out Far nor In Deep," "Our Hold on the Planet," and "Kitty Hawk." Third, he answered his own rhetorical question—"And how do I get there?"; that is, how had he arrived at this view—by admitting: "Through reading a good many pages." Fourth, the idea was extensible and applied also to religion as well as science, to art as well as scholarship. Fifth, he showed a capacity to grow on the stretches of his thought through reviewing and revision of basic concepts. And sixth, he identified himself with the Emersonian tradition of cherubic scorn, as he interpreted it—cherubic scorn representing "the very heart of it all, and the heart of all of Emerson."

The talk characteristically displayed Frost's ability to communicate in public with the same naturalness he showed when extending the dimension of an idea in private conversation *ex tempore*. The force of his commentary on science came over like the irresistible force of the great ninth wave. "I just wanted to show you a little cherubic scorn of my own," he explained simply.

Agility in searching out the secrets of the universe in our time has produced fantasy heroes like Superman, Captain Marvel, and Batman, just as in early history Prometheus and Dedalus and Apollo held distinguished positions in the Greek pantheon. Who, in this epoch of motion, space, time , number, fixity, direction, and matter, is about to put down tangible wonders of space vehicles, nuclear power, new synthetic chemicals, and medical advances? But when man in his specialized interest tends to be preoccupied with programming charts and industrial indexes, computerized statistics and mathematical symbols, it is neither the subtleties of analytical methodology nor the brilliant instrumentalities of technological gadgetry that leave their mark upon Frost. The energy of spirited enterprise and the thrust of science in on-penetration of matter, symbolized by the Wright brothers at Kitty Hawk, were chiefly impressive to him. Frost, aware of two ways to look, acknowledged both "the plunge of the mind," reaching out into space to explore moonscapes, to split atoms, to discover antibiotics, *and* the inclusiveness of poetry in what he called "the wonderful description of us in the humanities." In some respects this is what Frost's poetry has been all about—finding a language in which to communicate thoughts and feelings of one man in his time, and part of his search has been an interest in what science has been trying to do.

4.

In lieu of an unusual combining power such, for example, as De Quincey ascribed to Coleridge, Frost had the great gift of a vigorous retrieving memory—apt recall—from a packed mind. When, for instance, he talked about poetry, he raided his memory and returned like a forager from a raid brandishing words, lines, stanzas, and whole poems as touchstones of excellence. He would summon the opening lines from Keats's "Hyperion," quote with vigor from one of his early favorites, Francis Thompson's "The Hound of Heaven," and even from John Masefield's rollicking "Captain Stratton's Fancy." He quoted *Mother Goose*, he quoted Chestertonian quatrains, he quoted from the *Oxford Book of English Verse* and Palgrave's *The Golden Treasury*, and always for a purpose, scoring a point or calling attention to the "pretty [a favorite word of high praise] trio" of words in Christopher Smart's "Song to David." "Thou that stupendous truth believ'd, / And now the matchless deed's achiev'd, / Determined, dared, and done." And even, *mirabile dictu*, quoting in its entirety Robert Browning's "Protus," slipping on only the phrasing in a line or two. Perhaps Frost remembered so well because he had depended so little upon a notebook. What interested him he carried in his head. But, of course, he did repeat himself and recounted frequently the small anecdote or the allusive story.

5.

Although Frost talked freely, he did not thereby talk loosely. However, in the latter years he seemed less unwilling to make personal disclosures. Upon returning from a visit to the World Congress of Writers at São Paulo, Brazil, in 1954 where he had been sent as a delegate by the United States Department of State, he told an audience engagingly: "I have in my pocket a little corncob about three thousand years old. I thought I'd bring it home to my farm." And during the relatively brief visit, the tales of explorers, the rounding of Cape Horn, Darwin's discoveries, Bolivar's statecraft, the Inca civilization, the Amazon and the Andes and the pampas seemed to fade into the background as he kept thinking so characteristically "whether," as he confessed, "the deer got into my garden" on the Homer Noble farm at Ripton. "I'm not a traveler" summed up his apologetics. The homely and familiar detail, like the "booming laughter" of Albert Einstein reported in the *Scientific American* article, impressed him; or a sudden wave of a lonely past in the early New Hampshire days swept over him as he prepared to "say" a poem at a reading. "Back in those lonely days" was a *cri de coeur*, as self-revealing as he ever permitted himself—he who did not, like Shelley, bleed on the page. But in our time when the great abstract verities are temporarily in eclipse, he would confess unashamedly: "Glory. Bravery. Honor. That I go with in all my heart, all my days." When lightly reproached after admitting he had taken a long time to get the point in the last lines in Emerson's "Brahma," his retort bore no asperity. "Let it happen to me in its slow way," he said simply in self-admonishment.

Quite as self-revealing were his offhand comments at a public reading. Of "Reluctance" in *A Boy's Will*, he said: "Let's go back to this one—a young one that I love." The self-admission was so quietly made I wondered if I had heard him correctly. For the first time in nearly forty years I had heard him express a preference among the poems. What apparently had previously been a tenaciously guarded secret was now an open one. In his later years he grew self-conscious about rereading familiar poems. Before reading "Mending Wall" he once confided: "See me try to make believe I'm reading it. You know, I've read that so often I've sort of lost the right way to say 'Good fences make good neighbors.' " A purist in the performance of his craft, Frost could be critical of other able practitioners like Robert Bridges and T. S. Eliot. Getting the meter right in a poem was important to him, but one summer night in 1960, he confessed an odd and interesting mistake in, of all poems, "The Death of the Hired Man." "Seems," he admitted, "as if I'm interested in just a simple question of why I made a mistake in that meter in the first line [i.e., "Mary sat musing on the lamp-flame at the table"] of 'The Death of the Hired Man.' It's wrong, you know. It was just a mistake. I didn't do it on purpose. There are six feet in it instead of five."

Emerson, he said, had triggered an unpublished couplet.

> It is from having stood contrasted
> That good and bad so long have lasted.

The couplet came from thinking about Emerson "a good deal." Apparently "Uriel" was his stimulus. He linked the Emerson-inspired couplet with "The Secret Sits" and stated the couplets were "about science, you know." They represented "a sort of little joke about science, a little joke to myself." He would refer to the pairing and grouping of his poems but nearly always without extended comment. "Nothing Gold Can Stay" and "The Oven Bird" made a pair. Of "A Soldier" and "Design," he said: "See how these go together"; a pairing in form but not in content.

Frost displayed a similar agility more amusingly in a bit of give-and-take with Amy Lowell when visiting her at Sevenels in Brookline, Massachusetts. "After all," Amy Lowell said to Frost, "what's the difference between your stories about New England [in *North of Boston* and *Mountain Interval*] and mine?" Frost had explained that while Shakespearian tragedy had its villains like Iago and Edmund, Antonio and Lady Macbeth, he had placed his people in tragic situations "with nobody to blame." In reply to Amy Lowell, he said: "Amy, you're more like Shakespeare. You can't have a tragedy without a villain and I do it without a villain." Amy Lowell, with her guard down, asked, "You don't like mine?" And Frost, on guard, replied, "Yes, Amy, you're more like Shakespeare."

How often those who listened closely to Frost detected, like the kneeler at the well-curb in "For Once, Then, Something," "beyond the picture, / Through the picture, a something white, uncertain, / Something more of the depths—." Frost closed this line, "—and then I lost it." Often I lost "something," either because Frost left his thought unfinished or because it was impossible to reproduce the exact phrasing, so essential to an understanding of his meaning. Take, for example, his oft-quoted statement about "a momentary stay against confusion" in "The Figure a Poem Makes," which served as a heavy-duty introduction to several editions of the collected poems. In remonstrance to those who emphasized the word *momentary* without quite grasping its relationship to the whole, he said: "What do you think I mean by that, is that all there is to it is momentary? That kind of insults me." But why was he insulted? "Do you know what the humanities are? They are the accumulation of those momentary stays that have survived. That's what the humanities are." Underscoring how he intended the word *momentary* to be taken, he added: "They—the humanities—weren't just momentary; they were good because they went on." "Momentary stay" was to be understood *precisely*, that is, not negatively as a faltering stopgap in a general decline but positively as an interruption in a continuum of the humanities.

That Frost coveted his little secrets, that his apparently simple statements were often deceptive, is one of the more openly shared secrets about him. "It's fun," he would say, "to quote something to make everybody wonder where you got that." Once he quoted a strong line: "How to rule the harsh divorce that parts the natural from the divine." And he said challengingly, "I bet none of you know its source." Nor did we. Only after returning to some of his poems previously taken for granted have I discovered subtleties in interpretation which had escaped me. A poem is, indeed, as Frost believed, "a thought-felt thing," and what is important in it is its psychological overtones and undertones. If Frost experienced self-surprise in the writing of poems, his readers have experienced similar surprise in a close reading of the poetry.

CHAPTER 19
The Craft of Making

Perhaps you have the art of what I mean.
"The Generations of Men"

1.

The details of Frost's life lived outside the poems have now been elaborately recounted by Lawrance Thompson in the first two volumes of the official biography—*The Early Years, 1874–1915* (1966) and *The Years of Triumph, 1915–1938* (1970). The importance to us of these details arises in part from the fact that Frost, unlike such contemporary poets as Theodore Roethke and Robert Lowell, John Berryman and Randall Jarrell, James Dickey and Anne Sexton, did not write straight-out autobiographical poems. An inveterate reticence made him shy away from the autobiographical practices of other poets, a tendency which did not necessarily make him evasive—only more detached. Nor did it keep him from openly reacting to time and place in ruminative monologues like "New Hampshire" or "Build Soil," but in a very real sense his life *is* in *Complete Poems.*

Even if the intimacies of his private life are more fascinating to a gossip-oriented generation, at least as important as confessional revelations is a poet's belief about his craft. The statements about a poet's craft are not only a warrant of how seriously he takes that craft, they make the poems more accessible to us. Frost's theory leads us directly into the poems. A remark by the urbane Lord Clark in *Civilization* illuminates such an impulse. "If I had to say which was telling the truth about society," wittily explains Lord Clark, "a speech by a Minister of Housing or the actual buildings put up in my time, I should believe the buildings." In the same way, if I were asked which was telling the truth about poetry, a theory of poetry or the poems, I would believe the poems. What can stand as Frost's theory is recoverable from numerous shared hints and direct statements,

218

which indicate *(a)* how conscious he was in his art, and *(b)* how closely he fulfilled his poetic objectives.

His correspondence—especially the letters to John Bartlett, Sidney Cox, and Louis Untermeyer in which he spelled out his aims repeatedly—shows how clearly in his poetic vocation theorizing complemented the writing of poems, a theorizing concerned chiefly if not exclusively with his own poetry. He compounded his theorizing on poetry in letters, prefatory essays, and in a host of conversational comments both public and private. Yet as conscious theorist and responsible craftsman, only occasionally—for example, in "The Figure a Poem Makes," which prefaces *Complete Poems* (1949); in the introductory essay, entitled "The Constant Symbol," in the Modern Library edition of his poems; and in his private notebooks—did Frost commit to paper his theory and insights on his craftsmanship. But to say that Frost theorized freely is different from contending that he wrote the poems to a fixed theory. His poems were not theorized into existence. In his dicta he was only explaining what interested him at some particular time in the practice of his vocation. Hence his views on the writing of poems represent a lifelong extensible theory in which the poem was generally antecedent to—or at least concomitant with—rather than subsequent to the theory. Obviously the poem, not the theory, is the important matter since it is the natural culmination of the creative process.

It might be strongly argued that when a poem is fully realized, theory is unnecessary. Or, if we want to discuss theory, then we can reconstruct it from its embodiment in the poem. But in a general way a poet's theory—for example, Sidney and Shelley, Ben Jonson and Wordsworth, Pound and Eliot, Hart Crane and Wallace Stevens—is important as an expression of his individuality. It provides a chance for the poet to explain alternative ways of using language and exploring human experience. So long as there are poets, there will be new and fresh ways of looking at life, and the theories of the poets not only defend but define the ways they have found to communicate these discoveries.

In Frost's case a constant preoccupation with the theoretic indicates an alliance between a constructive faculty and emotional impulses. It would be agreeable to say that he embodied his method, exemplifying it through the poems he wrote. Yet we have the direct report in the correspondence which shows that concern for what he was trying to do was certainly as strong as the ways he found to do it. In later years we see how early the special pains he took to make clear how he should be taken were an essential part of his poetic strategy, now given wider and fuller publicity and clarification.

I think he started by believing, as W. H. Auden does, that "we were put on earth to *make* things." And I think he also realized cannily that it is not enough in any society that poets produce poems and take pleasure in what they make and do. He saw clearly enough that in a utilitarian society of commerce and high finance the arts may be given short shrift. Like Thoreau's Indian basket-maker in *Walden,* the poet must also think whether he has made his product worth someone else's while to buy it, or study rather how to avoid the necessity of selling it. In effect, form in craftsmanship was insisted upon by Frost. Practitioners of loose and limp lines represented to him an invidious relaxation of the prescriptive rules of art, with a resultant vulgarization of material and an indiscipline in form. Free verse he dismissed in a witticism as playing tennis "with the net down." Although he deprecated "this looser writing," as he called free verse, he admitted grudgingly: "I speak lightly of it. But it's something else. That's all." It is art, not writing, that plays hard to get; a performance, by definition, in form.

The fact of form evokes the classical concept of art as imitation of archetypal forms. In what relationship did Frost stand to this concept?

He did not think of form in Plato's terms. The mimetic theory of mirroring the great abstractions of the Idea, the One, or the Form of Forms and the use of archetypal Ideas of reason and justice, virtue and beauty, in whose perfection the poet measures his own made as little appeal to him as the relegation of the poet in the *Republic* to a status inferior to that of the philosopher-statesman. The empirical Frost thought of form inductively, explaining its impulse as "just the desire to take whatever comes to hand—whatever is in front of you—and shape it." Here the emphasis is on form as making, not on form as imitative of an ideal or as the reproducing of an archetype. But what, one might ask, constitutes making? "Shape," he thought, "has something to do with the consistency of parts"; presumably the parts of the structural method of organization in the poem: metrical beat in line and stanza, rhyme, idiom, and tone (with its implied tempo, pitch, and accent). In making, Frost extended his view to include what he described as "the larger forms" around him, by which he meant those overtones of the national in the local, of the universal in the national.

"Whatever comes to hand"—not, then, mimesis or the imitation of Love, Freedom, Virtue, Reason, and Justice as canonized in Plato's pantheon of archetypal Ideas, but common subject matter and simple values discovered in the world of reality; hence, in his writing, the incidence of concrete materials that assert life—a south wind, flowers, birds, animals, snow, rain, trees. In a two-way movement of mind his reading, early and late, was well anchored in the great stabilizing traditions of the Greek (Homer) and Roman (Virgil and Catullus) classics and of the entire range in British poetry. He also read to some purpose in the native American tradition, especially in Emerson and Thoreau. Yet his subject matter was little dependent upon literary derivations. "You can see," he once told an audience, neither bragging nor apologetic, "how little I depend upon books for anything I do."

As he drew his subject matter directly out of the local landscape, no apparent dislocation existed between him and rural upland New England and its small white-steepled villages centered at the general store or its country folks on their rocky farms, sowing and harvesting crops, ditching meadows, haying, blackberrying, picking apples. He was as familiar with the people of this country as Robert Burns was with Highland crofter and Wordsworth was with Cumberland dalesman. In any case, Frost does not particularly remind us in *North of Boston* or *Mountain Interval* of the classic *rus* of the *Georgics*. Frost's country includes the fields and woods of Derry and the intervales of Franconia in New Hampshire, South Shaftsbury flanked by the Taconics, and the rugged mountain country of Ripton, Vermont, where the thrushes call from the deep woods at sundown and where on a summer day fireweed burns along the back roads and joe-pye weed stands tall in the upland bogs.

The genesis of the poem for Frost, unlike the venerable Bede who discovered it in inspirational dictation, "seems," as he said, "to come on something that's rising in you."

I think I have this all the time. I'm in a place—that's where a poem comes from—all of a sudden I'm transported—I'm in a place. And just as I said that, I was suddenly beside a bare cliff with some cliff brake in it. Ferns. Just that came to me like that. But I'm in a place and I can pick words off that place and I can pick something off that place and sentences and phrases and things like that, and that's certainly before any words. It comes to me very much in that way if I'm very much in the place. See. It's a poem. . . . I'm with somebody or in a situation and the rest follows. And I can see right away that all sorts of things come tumbling to it. . . . When they ask where a poem comes from, that's as near as I can get to it. I think it's nearly always that way. I'm with somebody in a place—way off, unaccountably, in a kind of reverie, and all of a sudden something becomes prominent in the reverie. And I can pick the poem off it.

221

The question is: how does the poet keep spontaneous the unself-conscious magic by which he casts his spell? Since poems originate in moods, and rhymes are unanticipated hits, Frost depends upon the times when he is in form, a euphemism partly explained by luck or what he refers to as "lucky snatches" from mood and place. Or, he will say, "I summon something I almost didn't know I had. I have a command," which is about as far as he would—or could—go in explanation.

But hits may be flukes, scores accidents, and, by extension, deliberations may produce only banalities. What is often assumed to be an unconscious activity may be intuitive knowledge, and a poet's secret simply a favorable functioning of the unconscious. Frost obviously took advantage of the moods for the inception of his poetry, but he is in the Horatian tradition, and consequently observation, mental agility, the recollected and contemplated, and the continual self-surprises he explained were the incremental rewards of skillful practice in a highly self-disciplined art.

Frost was usually skeptical about trying to explain the processes of poetry in terms of esoteric mysteries. If there are mysteries in the writing of poetry—and who doubts it?—they are to be found in the psychological aspects of the human condition. He thought a poet's relationship to his craft depended upon being in form, a psychological condition, not of inspired seizures like Bede's, but of a natural ebb and flow in energy and impulse. He used the metaphor of the athlete—notably the baseball pitcher who feels either in or out of form, as the case may be, on any given day. In his practice, we find the use of language gathers force from precision of expression and suggestiveness from variations in pitch and rhythm.

2.

Aristotle used "imitation" differently from Plato. M. H. Abrams, in *The Mirror and the Lamp,* makes clear that imitation is a term "specific to the arts." A poet in discovering the source of his subject matter and language in the external world would follow closely the meaning in the Aristotelian concept of *Mimesis.* When Wordsworth and Emerson identified their aim to use language commonly spoken by men, both tacitly subscribed to the Aristotelian position—at least in theory—as the following statements by Wordsworth in the preface to *Lyrical Ballads* and Emerson in *Nature* indicate. Wordsworth aimed "to choose incidents and situations from common life, and to relate or describe them—in a selection of language really used by men." Emerson asserted: "This immediate dependence of language upon nature . . . never loses its power to affect us. It is this which gives that piquancy to the conversation of a strong-natured farmer or backwoodsman, which all men relish."

When, on August 6, 1913, Frost wrote John Bartlett as follows from Beaconsfield, England, he was more nearly Aristotelian than Platonic. "I am," he said, "one of the few who have a theory of their own upon which all their work down to the least accent is done." Five years later—in January, 1918—he reiterated his conviction in a letter to Regis Michaud. "I am as sure that the colloquial is the root of every good poem," he told the French professor, "as I am that the national is the root of all thought and art." That Frost used the locutions of people as he heard them on the lips of countrymen north of Boston is now a commonplace. Voice tones were the base of both monologues and dialogues in *Complete Poems,* and voice tones as the source of the colloquial are in the great tradition of British poetry time out of mind, from "The Seafarer" through Yeats.

Once, in demonstration of the use of voice tones in the great tradition, Frost quoted from one of the speeches of the Lady in Milton's *Comus.* "'Shall I go on? / Or have I said enough?' See, that makes a line." Repeating it, he commented: "I like to think of it as two such lovely tones of inquiry." Repeating the Miltonic line, he said: "And that's what I think makes poetry, you know. That's a very high line of poetry." In speaking the Miltonic line, he gave each inquiry its special emphasis, just as he would give the words, the lines, the speeches in "Snow" and "The Witch of Coös," or "The Death of the Hired Man" and "Home Burial," their distinctive tonalities, not tonalities in orchestration, not instrumentally, but *human* tonalities, generally subdued and low key and ranging through the scale of human emotion, including tenderness, scorn, and blandishment. I hear commonly in Frost this difference in voice tone.

> Because I want their dollar? I don't want
> Anything they've not got.
> > ["A Hundred Collars"]

> *You*—oh, you think the talk is all. I must go—
> Somewhere out of this house. How can I make you—
> > ["Home Burial"]

> She has him then, though what she wants him for
> I *don't* see.
> > ["Snow"]

> . . . I think you see
> More than you like to own to out that window.
>
> ["In the Home Stretch"]

"To be a writer here," Igor Stravinsky's Dublin cabbie told him, "all you have to do is keep your ears open." What the Irish cabbie told Stravinsky about Dublin, Frost instinctively discovered to be true of upland New England, where the writer is, in the Jamesian sense, "one upon whom nothing is lost." In Chaucer's dialogue, Shakespeare's lean speaking lines, and, as we have noticed, in Milton, we hear the thrust and stress of voice tones. "Vocal images," Frost aptly called these tones of voice.

When he once defined poetry as a "renewal of words," the emphasis in his definition was historical as well as literary. He was emphasizing an accomplishment in time, not simply in linguistic innovation. His words are really those used by man; not, we note, because his diction is identifiable by correct usage but because it catches accurately the tones of voice of those who utter them. His interest is not feudal; he is not using language to set off one class from another. On the contrary, his interest is democratic.

"Renewal" meant for Frost the use of words so accurately and sensitively they evoked the ideas they stood for as signs. What makes his use of language poetic despite what seems antipoetic diction —the flat conversational idiom and often monotonous regularity of diction—is the enforcement through words not only of a freshly perceived idea but of a passionate feeling.

> I craved strong sweets, but those
> Seemed strong when I was young;
> The petal of the rose
> It was that stung.

This is a *felt* experience, both in the giving and in the receiving.

Early in his practice as a poet, Frost said emphatically that he wanted to write down certain brute throat noises. Are we to infer from this acknowledgment of intent that, unlike Emerson and Coleridge who believed in the word becoming one with the thing, Frost is leaning toward the Lockean theory of language which believed words are separable from all reality and are, in consequence, only noises, a growl, a scream, a howl? If this is true, it might help to explain other than psychologically his considered rejection of verbal sensationalism, white-hot intensity, the excesses of rhetoric, and incantation; and, in opposing these tendencies in the handling of language, it might explain why he chose to stick deliberately with the shock of fact and the rigors of common sense. He seems to have agreed with Hugh Blair who said: "Words . . . may be considered as symbols, not as imitations; as arbitrary, or instituted, not natural signs of ideas." His avoidance of literary language and formal diction and his preference for the idiomatic at least indicate the direction he took on his road—away from the symbolistic movement.

How shall Frost's preference for the plain idiomatic style be explained? Was it a shrewd compensation or cover-up for a constitutional inability to incant verbally? Or is his command of the idiomatic an achievement sought and won by assiduous attention to the rigors of art? Are his style and method indications of personal and literary limitation, or are they evidences of a natural grace?

What is true still may not be true enough. What is realistic may not be uncompromisingly realistic. In Frost's case, what he shares with other New England writers, like Thoreau and Sarah Orne Jewett, Lowell and Longfellow and Whittier, is the handling of the things common in experience *without* preciosity but with a sense of their essential reality. Yet as deeply rooted as his common sense is in the principle of reality in poetry, it is still through language that Frost creates his world.

Denis Donoghue, for example, praises in Yeats's "Nineteen Hundred and Nineteen" and Wallace Stevens's "Evening without Angels" an elevated eloquence. Frost, he thinks, lacks "an Art of Elevation," a distinction which might baffle a reader of Frost for two reasons: first, because it assumes only one kind of eloquence by which to measure the quality of a poet's gift, and secondly, because the important point should be not primarily how the poetry of Frost differs from that of Yeats and Stevens but how the poetry affects us.

Relative to the first reason, is it not true that when the language used is at one with the view expressed there is a sufficient elevation? In "The Lesson for Today," Frost says *elevatedly:* "Art and religion love the sombre chord / Earth's a hard place in which to save the soul." Something positive must be said for an eloquence that bears an unmistakable elevation and a convincing ring of truth. The grandeur of simplicity is quite as moving as rhetorical eloquence, no matter how sophisticated the latter is. In "All Revelation," "The Most of It," "Directive," and elsewhere, the reader of Frost does not hear any extravagance of expression aggrandizing as meaning, but he does find a suggestive language accurately releasing a veracious meaning.

On the second point, Yeats and Stevens and Frost certainly differ in view, content, and technique. The stuff of myth, which so largely comprises a whole segment of Yeats's early poetry, is a realm Frost wasn't familiar with, so close was he in ambience to the reality of time and place. Stevens is a dazzle and a resonance, while in Frost's diminished auditory and visual imagery there is a flicker of lantern light and the subdued interjectory murmur, as of voices in a farmhouse kitchen. But the important point is what each of these poets gives us that is unique and how accessible each is through the special art of his poetry. In this view Frost is surely as accessible as either the impassioned Yeats or the scintillant Stevens. What a Frost poem means may have multiple translations, but there is no withholding of meaning behind meaning. Seldom is a Frost poem esoteric, as the poems of Yeats and Stevens often prove to be.

Perhaps it is academic whether Frost anticipated the subtle changes from a metaphorical to an analytic use of language in a dominantly scientific epoch and thus chose to make his language more literal than figurative in statement. On the evidence of his correspondence, he seemed to be reacting independently as he moved away from Victorian exuberance. His language depended upon objects directly observed, and, as Ezra Pound said in "A Retrospect," "the natural object is always the *adequate* symbol." To find his adequate symbol in the natural object, whether tree or house, snow or wind, stars or stone walls, was Frost's habitual tendency. Pound's statement helps to explain Frost's empirical method and to identify his kind of language, which W. H. Auden has termed (after Prof. C. S. Lewis) "Good Drab." Yet the mistake a reader can make is to read this seemingly faded language only at a literal level, when so often it is speaking to us in the doubleness of parables. Consequently, there are usually more overtones in the ordinary language of the poetry than reach an inelastic imagination.

When, for example, Frost says, literally enough, "As I came to the edge of the woods" in "Come In," or "those dark trees" were "the merest mask of gloom" in "Into My Own," or when he says in "Stopping by Woods," "Whose woods these are I think I know," what a capacity his ordinary, nonrhetorical language has for making the reader feel the depth of the dark woods *from outside*. In his poetry, we are not commonly inside the dark woods, as in Grimm's *Fairy Tales* or Faulkner's "The Bear." How effective, though, the brooding presence of his landscape is, evoking, as it does, northern New England where solitary weather-boarded back-country houses stand in melancholy aloofness at the edge of the somber woods.

His early letters show that before he went to England in 1912 he knew what he wanted to with language in poetry. Even earlier he was experimenting with the possibilities in a more exact and literal use of language in his poems. On the evidence, therefore, I am inclined to think the source of his relation to language lies less in a reaction to the dominance of science than in the discovery he made in reading Shakespeare "from the hip pocket," while working as a light fixer in the dynamo room of the Arlington textile mill in Lawrence, Massachusetts. In *Julius Caesar* and *Hamlet* he heard dramatic tones of speech which brought him closer to a living language and stirred him to make their study his practice and innovation.

After the publication of the first three volumes of his poetry, he was ready to appear before the public as a practitioner of the Wordsworthian precept of language really used by man and as a renewer of the resources of this language in the up-country people north of Boston. While I hesitate to refer to him as an innovator in subject matter and idiom, since the local colorists and the dialect poets had already in the nineteenth century so widely explored the use of place and colloquial language, his contribution in freshening and renewing language is surely one about which he had a lot of self-assurance. "To be perfectly frank with you," he wrote John Bartlett unabashedly on July 4, 1913, "I am one of the most notable craftsmen of my time."

Frost's theory of voice tones contrasts sharply with Sidney Lanier's contention in "From Bach to Beethoven" that language is "a species of music." Concerned with the natural rhythm of speech—its tempo, pitch, and accent—he said, "the music of poetry is not like the music of music." Consequently his poetry calls for some care in reading. Through a treachery of the ear we can mistake the tone and be betrayed. When an interviewer (Richard Poirier) once inquired about an example of the poet's "feat of association," Frost turned to *A Masque of Reason.* When God says, "I was just showing off to the devil, Job. Do you mind?" the puzzled Job replies: "No, no." "That tone is everything," Frost said, "the way you say that 'no.' I noticed that—that's what made me write that."

Obviously, then, the most valid point of relationship between Frost and the Aristotelian concept of imitation is in the way language copies nature. Except for this concession, how apparent it is that it is not Aristotle who bent Frost to his purpose but Frost who used Aristotle's concept for his purposes. By no means does he derive from and make a formulation of the classical theory of imitation. In "The Aim Was Song," he shows us how directly he humanized the natural forces observed directly in experience by adapting them to his purposes through "making" or art. "By measure. It was word and note, / The wind the wind had meant to be." Not imitation but original response is the key to Frost.

227

In distinguishing between the scientist and the literary man in the use of language, Elizabeth Sewell is acute in *The Orphic Voice*. "One result," she writes, clarifying the appearance of language-as-science in our time, "has been the general tendency in modern poetry toward the dry, ironic, self-deprecating conversational tone, the deliberate essential abdication from that power which language-as-poetry wields, a tendency broken only by occasional despairing incursions of language-as-poetry into a world of magic." To illustrate the difference between the two languages, recall the difference between the Elizabethan Chapman and the Yankee Frost in the twentieth century. In *Bussy d'Ambois*, Chapman illuminates in eloquent metaphor the splendor of a dark saying: "Man is a torch borne in the wind: a dream / But of a shadow, summ'd with all his substance." Frost, on the other hand, to communicate the essential mystery of human experience wittily compresses his observation in nonrhetorical aphoristic couplet: "We dance around in a ring and suppose / But the secret sits in the middle and knows." There is never in Frost any tendency toward separation from his reader. In this respect he differed from Sir Philip Sidney who, in "A Defense of Poets," makes the poet exceptional or from Emerson who, in "The Poet," idealizes the poet as an archetypal "Sayer." Frost the sayer is always "a man talking to men."

The energy of language consists for the writer in the precise and vivid use of words. What a lot of energy is, for example, communicated in Michael Drayton's use of "stretch'd" in a stanza from "To the Virginian Voyage."

> Britons, you stay too long:
> Quickly aboard bestow you;
> And with a merry gale
> Swell your stretch'd sail
> With vows as strong
> As the winds that blow.

A lively word, it evokes a lively image. In Captain James Cook's *Voyages*, the *Resolution* and its crew is described on leaving Cape Kidnapper in Queen Charlotte's Sound in exactly the same way as Drayton describes the forward motion of a sailing vessel. "They now *stretched* to the southward . . . ," it reads in *Voyages*, and the kinesthetic word vigorously thrusts us forward. In "Bereft," when Frost writes: "Out in the porch's sagging floor, / Leaves got up in a coil and hissed," the image is certainly kinetic.

With equal adeptness, Frost could use colloquial words like *swale*—as in the line in "Mowing": "To the earnest love that laid the swale in rows." The word appears in its particular line as natural as a warped board in an old barn. In an art which Puttenham referred to gracefully as concerned with "the ministry and use of words," Frost was notable for the attention he gave the words he used.

Coleridge recognized but did not greatly use "the sort and order of words which the poet hears in the market, wake, high-road, or ploughfield." Long before Coleridge, the seventeenth-century Ben Jonson in *Timber, or Discoveries* (1640–41) took a stand that "words are the people's," whose source is the camp, the council-board, the shop, the sheep-cote, the pulpit, the bar—noting how each vocation had its own speech to be used "fitly." Take, for example, Gilbert White's *Journals*, where the humble but observant country curate-in-charge found and noted in the vicinity of "The Wakes" at Selborne, numerous locutions. Droughts are "dry fits"; foxhounds barking at sight or scent of the quarry run "hard open"; drizzling clouds are "flisky"; barley growing "in the suds" is in flooded lands; and larks frolicking in the air are caught in nets by means of a twinkling glass, a method called "daring" or "stupefying the birds." Similarly, Frost listened for and used the local locutions. He would "say" the first couplet in "The Tuft of Flowers":

> I went to turn the grass once after one
> Who mowed it in the dew before the sun.

Then he would explain: "And I might just say that in the old days we mowed by hand a great deal. More than we do now. There was always a boy or somebody around like me to toss the grass, open it up, let the sun at it. The mowing was apt to be done in the dew in the morning for better mowing, but it left the grass wet and had to be scattered. We called it—the word for it was *turning* the grass" (italics added). Like Gilbert White and with about the same degree of conscious attention, Frost used words and phrases he heard "really used by men"; country words like *leastways, daft, dite, tote road, windrows, shooks, swab, jag, water bars, stoneboat, hugger-mugger, beholden to,* and *to stint;* colloquialisms like *dunno* and *mebbe.*

Handling this speech "fitly" might be called one of Frost's major achievements in his verse. His tempo, pitch, accent, and rhythm of speech are "fitly" appropriate, and doubtless he would have nodded in agreement with Elizabeth Sewell in *The Orphic Voice* that a poem is "only the resource of language used to the full," since one of the resources was the language as heard on the lips of real people. "We *shan't* have the place to ourselves to enjoy," says the countryman in

"Blueberries." "So when he *paired off* with me in the hayfield," says the haymaker in "The Code," who also says, "I *built* the load and *topped it off.*" "But I got *wonted* to it," says the housekeeper in the poem of the same title. (Italics added.) "A good deal comes on me when all is said," Lafe tells Doctor Magoon in "A Hundred Collars"; and of her father's brother, the lonely, put-upon woman in "A Servant to Servants" says, "They soon saw he would do someone a mischief / If he wa'n't kept strict watch of." Similarly, in *The Rise of Silas Lapham,* William Dean Howells reflects a fidelity to experience in his use of idiomatic locutions. He writes: "I don't know but the mother and the daughter would have *let* you feel so a little, if they'd showed out all they thought." And again, "I don't want you should let things go too far." This is the authentic Yankee speech.

But is Frost as careful and exacting in nonidiomatic poems? After reading "The Most of It," which he described as a psychological poem, he explained: "See. Just look at it. I have one word in 'The Most of It' I shouldn't have used maybe." Then, reversing himself, he added, "No, I don't go by that. I use what I have. On a percentage basis the reader gets them." By them he referred to apt words which a poet is lucky enough to fit to his purposes. Although he didn't identify the word, my guess is he had in mind "crumpled" in the line, "Pushing the crumpled water up ahead." It would hardly have been the compound "counter-love," which is unexceptional. Upon rereading the poem, he added revealingly: "Do I have any desire to emphasize [the poem] any more than that? I'd rather you see it as I'm reading it, I think. I have a little desire to force it, impress it a little by reading it twice. But if I lingered over details in it to make you like it, I'd be ashamed of myself." Then he mused: "You might wonder why I wrote it—you know, what are the parts of it, what's the fascination of writing it?" After a pause he added, "Certain words. It would beat me to tell you what they are. Certain words. That's what a poem is —certain words." "You know," he confided, "as I went by a certain word [in "Birches"], having talked against explication as I have before I began, I came upon the word *crazed.* See! 'Cracks and crazes their enamel'! See. See. See. See. Too bad if you don't get it." After pausing, he said slyly, "And then you wouldn't know, you know, unless I wrote a masterpiece of explication to say the line that probably means most to me now is 'It's when I'm weary of considerations.' See."

Once he played, in his terms of the word, with *surmise* and *guesses*, and he cited a favorite poet to score a point on the use of the "deep" words, the strongly connotative and vigorously imaginative ones in which he found the height of poetry. In Keats's poetry, two words—"terribly deep to me"—illustrated what he meant. The first appeared in "Ode to a Nightingale"—"She stood in tears amid the *alien* corn" (italics added). "And this is such a high poetic use of that word *alien*," he commented, "that it just got to all the poets that wrote for a hundred years after." And secondly, "this 'wild surmise' in Keats's sonnet ['On First Looking into Chapman's Homer'] is another wonder. How deep that goes! I suppose I never said that word without something so beyond any symbolism or anything like that, or echoes, just as over some deep hollow in my nature."

Frost, who, in public, exercised a rigorist's eye for the special magic in the use of words by Chaucer or Shakespeare, Milton or Keats, took a special pleasure in phrasing in his own poetry. He mentioned his pleasure in this line from "The Tuft of Flowers"—"from sheer morning gladness at the brim." "I don't get enough credit for these things," he said of it and thought it had a lot to do with his vocation as a poet. He used it as a touchstone. "I didn't see it when I wrote it, but I've thought a good deal about it since. . . . That's where the poetry transcends sociology and reform and everything like that." How often, for example, intensely realized imagistic associations appear in his poems. "The beauties of association are always something you didn't know you were going to have," he says modestly. In "Waiting" there is the moving auditory image of the encircling nighthawks.

> I dream upon the nighthawks peopling heaven,
> Each circling each with vague unearthly cry.

Or, in "In the Home Stretch," the visual image of firelight from the wood-burning stove reflected on the ceiling is as sharply observed as a detail in a Flemish painting.

> The fire got out through crannies in the stove
> And danced in yellow wrigglers on the ceiling.

In "A Prayer in Spring," a hummingbird is "The meteor that thrusts in with needle bill, / And off a blossom in mid-air stands still." In "The Black Cottage," the little clapboard cottage is "Fresh painted by the shower a velvet black," and "The warping boards pull out their own old nails." In "Ghost House" the whippoorwill comes "to shout / And hush and cluck and flutter about," and in "The Self-Seeker," "You can hear the small buzz saws whine, the big saw / Caterwaul to the hills around the village / As they both bite the wood." So it is that his sharp eye and true ear enhance the use of details in a style of simplicity, economy, and precision.

True, few poets do get "the credit" for their "feats of association," but surely there is something more than sheer luck in Frost's hits. *A Boy's Will* is exemplary. Italicized in the following lines are what appear to be lucky hits in the subtle craft of making.

> The orchard tree has grown one copse
> Of new wood and old where the woodpecker *chops*.
>
> ["Ghost House"]

> That none should mow the grass there
>   While so *confused* with flowers.
>
> ["Rose Pogonias"]

> The crows above the forest call;
> To-morrow they may *form* and go.
>
> ["October"]

> And make us happy in the happy bees,
> The swarm *dilating* round the perfect trees.
>
> ["A Prayer in Spring"]

In spite of his deprecatory view of explication, Frost revealed a good deal about his art. When he disclosed his feelings about certain words in "Birches," he gave a searching insight into what makes a poet's use of descriptive words stand up. And how cavalierly he did it! He offered "this little note on 'Birches' before I begin to read it. See. The kind of explication I forbid," he said self-consciously. Then with disarming slyness, he said: "I never go down the shoreline [from Boston] to New York without watching the birches to see if they live up to what I say about them in the poem." Invariably the listener laughed, but on the double take he realized that Frost, the careful craftsman, was confirming his assertion that birches bend to left and right *by verification*. Getting details right was a telling responsibility. His birches, he insisted, were *not* the white mountain or paper birch of northern New England *(Betula papyrifera);* they were the gray birch *(Betula populifolia)*.

We can gauge his honesty by his self-admissions and accurate observation. In "The Thatch" reference is made to birds flushed out of their holes at night, and in "Come In" to one's shifting its nocturnal perch. Of "Come In," he admitted: "I've been told by a birdman, somebody who knows a lot about birds, that birds never shift their perch at night, and I've felt corrected somewhat." Recalling the lines, "Too dark in the woods for a bird / By sleight of wing / To better its perch for the night, / Though it still could sing," he explained: "I made a generalization out of having made birds shift and I've distressed myself about them." Of "The Thatch," whose source was an English experience, he said: "One of the amusing things was I used to walk in the night along a thatched roof—a very old thatched roof that came clear down from way up; came down to my shoulders —and I used to scare the birds out of that in the night if they lived in the thatch. . . . It bothered me a lot because I didn't know where they went when they roosted on the ground the rest of the night, and I was in distress myself, but I was sorrier to distress the birds. And that's always been with me—the notion of what becomes of a bird that is scared off its perch. Just that line, that little thing I don't get credit for." He was indeed a master of the single word or phrase, lacking which we get banality. In "Good Hours" the certain word is "profanation," and it carries a slyly humorous comment on life in a sleepy back-country village: "Over the snow my creaking feet / Disturbed the slumbering village street / Like profanation, by your leave, / At ten o'clock of a winter eve." And how retinally sharp is the image in "Blue-Butterfly Day"—"Where wheels have freshly sliced the April mire."

When critics gave little evidence of noting thrust of penetration, range of curiosity, suppleness in association, or skill in handling mnemotechnic devices like rhythm, assonance, and rhyme, the poet was justifiably reproachful. He pointed out in "The Peaceful Shepherd": "Now what I'm interested in there is the three stanzas, to see if the sentences fall different ways in there." Then he would add: "And I wonder if I get credit for that: to see if I can put a pretty sentence—different sentences—in their little stanzas." "Pretty," often used by the poet when referring to couplets, stanzas, and especially poetic sentences, was a favorite approbative word. He wanted to write these pretty sentences with spontaneous "self-surprise." As self-surprising strokes of luck, images of perceived beauty in a run of sentences were closer to conjury than self-conscious art only because of a disciplined imagination and a sense of form.

No matter what form his poems took—and he leaned strongly toward the parable in "Mending Wall," "The Grindstone," and "The Wood-Pile"—they are closest to his esthetic ideal when they embody a single-minded concern with art, rather than when they exhibit an overt formulation of social or political conceptions, as in "Build Soil" and "The Lesson for Today." This is not to say the poet excluded the social vision. Indeed he did not, as some of his most effective poems—"Directive," "The Death of the Hired Man," "The Most of It," and "Desert Places"—show us. Like the wonderful ashen staff of

Yggdrasil in the great myth, they are the pivots around which the poet's heaven spins. But they do not sacrifice ultimate things either to the programmatic or to *l'art pour l'art*. Single-mindedly, the poet sticks to his art. In a revealing moment he said, "I suppose the most ultimate thing I think of is the fear I have of losing my meaning in the material." It was a risk he had always to take.

Frost's metaphors are "feats of association" whose usual source is concrete natural objects. Secondly, they are more constitutive than illustrative. Thirdly, they are commonly restricted to ground level. Fourthly, in tone they are quiet; a respiration is a *cri de coeur*, a suspiration is elemental. Fifthly, they appear less as ornaments and artifices and more, in Elizabeth Sewell's words in *The Orphic Voice*, applied to poetic expression, as "a living instrument of a lively speech." For example, in "The Fear of Man," Frost metaphorizes: "But there are little street lights she should trust / So jewel steady in the wind and dust." And in "Directive": "But only a belilaced cellar hole, / Now slowly closing like a dent in dough." How sophisticated the former; how idiomatic and colloquial the latter.

Figurative though it is, Frost's poetry is hardly so in an exhibitionistic way. One of his greatest triumphs must certainly be the sustained one-sentence figure in the fourteen lines of "The Silken Tent." Natural and unresistant like the quiet tone of an unhurried voice, his metaphor exemplifies what Bacon described as "that commerce between the mind of man and the nature of things." Illustrative of the Baconian "commerce" between the poet's mind and the nature of things are the three following succinct, direct, and familiar similitudes: "Clematis / Had wound strings round and round it like a bundle" ("The Wood-Pile"); "The attic wasps went missing by like bullets" ("A Fountain, A Bottle, A Donkey's Ears and Some Books"); and the butterfly on the milkweed pod "hangs on upside down with talon feet / In an inquisitive position odd / As any Guatemalan parakeet" ("Pod of the Milkweed"). Extended figures reveal emotional involvement as in the following when Mary, in "The Death of the Hired Man,"

> . . . put out her hand
> Among the harp-like morning-glory strings,
> Taut with the dew from garden bed to eaves,
> As if she played unheard some tenderness
> That wrought on him beside her in the night.

And the developed figure, at once denotative and connotative in "The Ax-Helve," where the French-Canadian woodchopper

234

> . . . brushed the shavings from his knee
> And stood the ax there on its horse's hoof,
> Erect, but not without its waves, as when
> The snake stood up for evil in the Garden.

In general, Frost shows more of a speculative imagination than a figurative one. Just as he was good at what the Spanish would call *indirectas,* hints or insinuations, so he was good at the more generalizing metaphor. A validating example appears in the three poems on the defense motif: "Mending Wall," "A Drumlin Woodchuck," "Triple Bronze." When Frost uses the star image metaphorically, the result is not facile. "Those stars like some snow-white / Minerva's snow-white marble eyes / Without the gift of sight" is a simile that signifies an impersonal universe, not solely a visual act. Moreover, he is wryly ironic; the starlike eyes see *nothing.*

"Every poem, almost, that I write is figurative in two senses," Frost said. "It will have figures in it, of course; but it's also a figure in itself—a figure for something, and it's made so that you can get more than one figure out of it, I suppose." "One Step Backward Taken" illustrates his view. The basic metaphoric figure is of a deluge extending to a universal catastrophe. In its doubleness the poem has "a figure for our times in it," as he says, "if you want it"; a figure for "the universal crisis" of World War II. Readers might object to a poet's resolution of such a terrible time in a figure less than awful. The poet's figure implies detachment—"one step backward taken"—in order to save oneself. The weather changes, the flood subsides, the crisis passes—which reflects Frost's sanguinity. But the committed and involved person—Albert Camus's *l'homme engagé*—may find indefensible the passivity of Frost's facile resolution of such a mind-bending catastrophe. It might seem hardly becoming in gravity to carry the weight of a cosmic situation where the motives of men are unpredictable.

Frost also thought of metaphor in terms of poetic form, of how couplets symbolize metaphor. "The couplet," he once said, "is the symbol of the metaphor." What he meant was that the couplet was essentially metaphoric when it paired thought. And since he remarked upon this after reading "One More Brevity," a favorite reading poem, we might scrutinize the metaphors in the pairing of the couplets. "The couplet," he explained, "is my game just the same as the metaphor is my game." For example:

> He dumped himself like a bag of bones,
> He sighed himself a couple of groans,

And head to tail then firmly curled
Like swearing off on the traffic world.

4.

No one should insist on viewing Frost through the lens of the
Platonic mimetic theory or, say, the romantic theory of individual
expression. I find nothing in his poetry which reminds me of the cultural primitivism of the eighteenth century. On the contrary, I find
evidence against his being linked with the neoprimitive. He was not,
in the first place, an instinctive child of nature like, say, Stephen
Duck, the Thresher Poet, or Henry Jones, the Poetical Shoemaker;
he was a sophisticated poet. Secondly, he kept his eye on the subject
and a wide audience. As he said: "You're naturally talking to the
human race as you know it." Social communication quite as much as
self-expression directed his aim. And thirdly, although he never
denigrated spontaneity, his deliberate art emphasized self-criticism
and revision.

In the antithesis of nature and art, he did not set up a rigid
dichotomy between the two. Instead he paralleled the natural and
the artful, and by sticking to the conventions of traditional form
leaned a little more toward art than nature. If he had gone all the
way of nature, would he not, like Whitman or Henley, have allowed
the language of feeling to flow into uninhibited rhythms? His
adherence to traditional metrics did not thereby suppress natural
feelings; the conventions of art served the poems well when the
poet's craft harmonized the parts. Two caveats were observed: (1) he
avoided artifice by deliberately adapting conventional language to
feeling; and (2) he did not follow a questionable practice by bending
linguistic means to the achievement of poetic effects.

But certainly an intelligent way of approaching his poetry is *not* to
insist that it is only to be understood by remarking on theories applicable to poets of other times and other places. Well aware of the
power of poetry, he early identified it as "words that have become
deeds." To this end he activated his language, to give deeds with
pleasure, as in Horace, who thought the poet's aim was "either to
profit or to please, or to blend in one the delightful and the useful."
Late in life, Frost summed up his intent in a nuclear statement which
showed no inclination to deemphasize *delectare* (to delight) in favor
of either *prodesse* (to teach) or *movere* (to move). He declared: "*Our objective is to entertain you by making play with things you already*

know"(italics added). The statement includes five important aspects in an approach to his poetry: (1) the entertainment or *delectare* angle; (2) the *making* of the poem, which emphasizes the Greek *poiein,* or the poet as maker, rather than the Roman *vates,* or the poet as diviner; (3) the emphasis on "you," the knowledgeable audience; (4) the idiosyncratic play angle—"By making play! That's the height of it—the apex"; and, lastly, (5) the emphasis which is not inspirational dictation but deliberate craftsmanship, implied by the word *objective.*

When he generalizes that the object of the poet is to entertain by making play with the things he expects the reader already to know, like Anatole France's muse of history, Clio (in *Le petit Pierre*), he exhibits the capacity to interest, move and entertain us. In his case, it is a disarmingly sophisticated kind of entertaining, without the puzzle solving and decoding of meanings we grew accustomed to in Pound and Eliot. So far as I know, he never ventured any sanctions in support of poetry as legerdemain. If poetry is play, it is, as Frost insisted, a play with things already known. He made it clear that play was not frivolous. "I can't play a parlor game with anything like that," he said of writing in conventional forms. "I care too much about it." What he really liked was "the beauty of the freedom of the words." This was his kind of play—and also to play at the higher levels in ideas with such ultimates as soul and body, spirit and matter. "You see I play with them more than I deal with them," he said dryly. "And I don't like to be asked by anybody to tell what mine are, how far I dare go, how deep I am."

Slowly his poetry made an impact, but it was not until the last thirty years of his life that his eminence in the craft of making was generally acknowledged. Yet throughout a long career his poems do not seem to have been written either to defend a theory or to settle comfortably in a household tradition. His praxis gave us a poetry of passionate sincerity and natural style, deeply rooted in the reality of things. Neither more nor less than what they are, the poems move us at three levels of intensity: in their passionate belief in the vocation of poetry; in the concept of art and play with "ultimate things"; and in the renewal of language through voice tones.

CHAPTER 20
The Act of Taking

The voices give you what you wish to hear.
"The Generations of Men"

Poetry is a way of being taken by those who know how to take you.
Middlebury College, May 27, 1936

1.

Well, who riddles the riddler in the age of the put-on? I am not sure, but I would guess it is a mischievous impulse in Frost that produced the comic paradoxes and subtle ironies, the wisecracks and the cryptic quatrains, the facetiae of his jesting in "The Secret Sits" and "Forgive, O Lord." The quips enabled him to move lightly but warily among the orthodoxies, teasing and unattached. But, with his friends, he came and went unguardedly at the back door of the mind, the quiddities of his genius usually protected by tact and loyalty.

A literary partisan finds admirable the finished art and the traditional wisdom in a poet. The disciple prefers what is programmatic and unfinished and therefore stimulating to his talent and capabilities. Frost had the admirers; Pound and Eliot had the disciples. Frost's admirers were of several sorts. Among the first were those who regarded him as a popular household poet and thought all one needed to read him was good breathing. In the same group were those who sat expectantly in the lecture hall waiting to be excited as though he was a kind of magnified tourist attraction performing in the brighter element of poetry. He also appealed to some scholar-teachers who, like the keepers of the Eleusinian mysteries, guarded the meanings in the more cryptic poems. And there were many others, often high in public life, who were greatly drawn to both man and poet.

After a public evening his auditors usually carried away a vivid memory of voice and personality. Some saw in him a pastoral poet whose bucolic impulse celebrated the rites of the season and the old and wonted ways of rural occupations in a preindustrial epoch. Yet turning earth and marginal farm, grindstone and stoneboat, were at most tokens of a "strategic retreat," a vantage ground, an outpost, from which to launch a lifelong campaign in writing about people and their problems and in showing us what sense he had made of his place in the universe. The sign of dedication was the refinement of simplicity, and the sign of pride was the performance. Although we know he coveted the Nobel Prize, what could it have proved? Honors notwithstanding, the poems, whether read sympathetically by household admirers of poetry or searchingly by scholars, will continue to be read for a long time to come. Meanwhile, the best book on Frost remains in the poems.

But how did he want to be taken as a poet? What did he have to say to help the reader communicate with him? "When we really understand a poem," says Martin Buber in *Between Man and Man* (Boston: Beacon Press, 1955), "all we know of the poet is what we learn of him in the poem—no biographical wisdom is of value for the pure understanding of what is to be understood: the *I* which approaches us is the subject of this single poem. But when we read other poems by the poet in the same way their subjects combine in all their multiplicity, completing and confirming one another, to form the one polyphony of the person's existence." Buber's statement seems reasonably true. "Pure understanding" must mean a direct and objective concern with the poem. Few biographical details are necessary in a discussion of one of Frost's poems. In the poet's theory of circulation (in the preface to *Aforesaid*), when several poems are discussed they refract light on one another, and form, in Buber's words, "the one polyphony" of Frost's existence.

After nodding approvingly in Buber's direction, I want immediately to qualify acceptance of his theory by suggesting the helpfulness of a few biographical facts. I have in mind a statement of Frost's (in 1960) which is self-revealing.

There was a book I never read and a teacher I never had that did more for me than anybody else in the world. The book I never read was *Piers Plowman* and the teacher I never had was William James. And both of those acted on me. *Piers Plowman* acted on me this way. I always wanted to do something about the kind of American hired man, you know, that I'd lived with and worked with and been. And just how to get it! I didn't have any definite idea about it. It was just a lingering sense about it. I thought that might be what *Piers Plowman* was and so I better let that alone for fear it would take the wind out of my sails. And I let it alone until I'd written "The Death of the Hired Man." And then I read *Piers Plowman* and I needn't have worried. It's another thing entirely—satire and all that.

In 1936 Frost said: "I have written poetry ever since I was fifteen years of age, and there come to be quite a number of people who know how to take me in my wry, twisted way, with the words cocked a little like a cocked hat. The large strain of poetry is a little shifted from the straight-out, a little curved from the straight. Within the large thing itself are the lesser personal twists. One belongs to me; one belongs to someone else." He advised taking him "cavalierly"; certainly he didn't want a reader to press too hard for meaning. "Poems," he remonstrated, "can be pressed too hard for meaning." Yet, characteristically, as if to amplify this view, he said: "The poet is entitled to everything the reader can find in the poem." He didn't want the reader to try too hard; nor did he want him to think there was too little beneath the poem's surface. When directly questioned about meaning in his poems, he exercised a poet's prerogative for options leaving open the choice among possibilities, which could result in ambiguities. At the center the secret sits but not always as stationary as some impatient and aggressive scholiast might think. "I don't care how many meanings they take out of a poem," Frost would say, "as long as they leave me one in."

As a strategist of poetry, he did not try to enforce choice; he suggested alternatives, a flash or hint, and a continuous movement in which every part of the poem must be kept in mind. Like Autolycus in *The Winter's Tale*, the reader thought: "I am courted now with a double occasion." Invariably there were double occasions, and it sufficed if the poet left us at a crossroads where the signpost was properly marked. A poem was, in effect, a situation at the crossroads; it was exploratory and speculative. But, dismayed by overblown analyses and by critics probing for obscurity, Frost said to Louis Mertins, with a touch of impatience, "These people can't get it through their heads that the obvious meaning of a poem is the right one. That's too easy. . . . Most poets are clear and intend to be understood just as they write." Since books were Frost's resources but not commonly his dependence, a good reader often gets closer to the meanings in the poems by following his direct vision where it originated.

Believing the important thing was readiness to give a good answer, his poems are the seriocomic, confessional, grave, cavalier answers he made to the situations in which he found himself. An example of his habitual ability to give a good answer—it almost amounted to genius—occurred on "Meet the Press" (March 22, 1959) when he was interviewed by a group of reporters.

> *Mrs. Craig* [of the Portland (Maine) *Press Herald*]: Mr. Frost, did you hear what the president [Eisenhower] said in his message from the Atlas missile from outer space?
> *Mr. Frost:* From heaven, do you mean?
> *Mrs. Craig:* He said he was giving a message of peace on earth, good will to men, and, of course, the Atlas [went] around the world. That was a prose poem, don't you think?
> *Mr. Frost:* Yes, I didn't hear it. [As much as to say, I knew about it but I didn't listen.]
> *Mrs. Craig:* It was a prose poem. He said: "Peace on earth, good will to men."
> *Mr. Frost:* Do you think the word *peace* makes it a prose poem?
> *Mrs. Craig:* Yes, do you have much hope for a world that has its mind on military things?
> *Mr. Frost:* Yes.
> *Mrs. Craig:* How do you think we can save ourselves from destroying each other?
> *Mr. Frost:* We were sent here to destroy each other in honest competition.

First, ironically, Frost substituted "heaven" for "outer space." Secondly, he asked Mrs. Craig quizzically if the word *peace* made the president's message a prose poem. Thirdly, his reply to Mrs. Craig's conventional stance in opposition to the military was directly opposite to the expected answer. And, finally, he offered an unorthodox supporting statement for a well-considered position. If he hadn't considered this, at least he was ready for Mrs. Craig's questions. His statement was not frivolous but a judgment which contained the telling phrase "in honest competition." The interview, illustrating the typically shrewd rejoinder one grew to anticipate in Frost, goes to the heart of any discussion on how to take him. Despite Buber's view, to understand a poem the reader must first get the poet's tone right. Frost, above all else, was notably a poet of voice tones. Auden is probably right that a poem is "a contraption," but it is a contraption with "a guy inside."

An interviewer—Chester Morrison—noticed especially Frost's idiosyncratic style—how the speech was the man and how often it broke naturally into cadences. After listening closely, Morrison gave several of the poet's reactions a stanzaic form, and the style of his conversational speech was hardly to be differentiated in cadence from his familiar metrical verse.

241

This is a cabbage palm, native to these parts.
    They think it is a weed.
They're after me to cut it out and clear the space,
    But I will keep it here.
I like things wild.

Undeniably this short sequence of sentences has the Frostian ear-mark and rhythm. In the following passage from a letter to Wilfred E. Davison, the listening ear catches the same characteristic rhythm.

I want to try to tell you the number of times we changed our minds between going to your pond and not going to your pond. In the end the day of starting for home caught us determined to go to it; and we went. On the way we were charmed once on the rather terrible detour with a little farm house high up on a banking above the full swift stream of Joe's Brook. Henceforth that will always be one of the spots on earth where we may come to rest from our wanderings. And so might the pond be too if the population around it can be made to fall off a little. For we were charmed with the pond itself. And your cozy house. There's no prettier piece of water in the woods anywhere. I suppose it must be one of the highest set in New England if not the very highest. We had a beautiful still evening by it and a beautiful morning. And by way of extravagance to express my feelings I walked on up your road a piece and priced the Ewen farm with all the shore and woods thereunto appertaining.

And in "The Lovely Shall Be Choosers," we hear the unmistakable voice tone.

She fails from strangeness to a way of life
She came to from too high too late to learn.

In his unhurried and reflective deliberativeness these voice tones represent an important way of taking Frost.

2.

In discussing poetry—and he was not thinking narrowly only of his own—Frost would exhort an audience to adopt what he termed "the pre-graduate school" approach. Both college and high school should be kept as free as possible from applying the scholarly methods of the graduate school. "Most of the students that you have in the high school and college are not going to be scholars," he would say, "and why should you handle them as if they were going to be scholars?" First, he would encourage a liking for poetry; he was never "in favor of studying it very hard," a view not to be taken as a tacit rejection of scholarship. "Now the great scholarship," he said emphatically, "I venerate it." Yet it was not scholarship but "poesy pure"—unresearched, unfootnoted, untampered with—that was of first importance to him. "That's what I'm speaking for," he asserted. "My equals are those I don't have to write footnotes to. The footnotes, if I used them, would be a condescension to the people that can't keep up with me." Referring to Shakespeare's plays, he reminded, "They've all got a first quality of entertainment: making play of things we [the poets] can trust you largely to know. And if I have to say too much to prepare you for the poem, it is too bad. If I have to say anything to you while the poem is going on—it's worse. And if I have to say anything after it—well, I hope you will have gone home."

The basis of Frost's approach might be summed up in the word *natural*. "But the study of poetry isn't anything, you know. Goodness' sakes, the beauty of those poems at the top of everything [in the *Oxford Book of English Verse* or in Palgrave's *Golden Treasury*] is that some of them must be in your nature, you know, in your head. You can't hear them without their catching on to you without being studied." In illustration, he quoted one of Emily Dickinson's poems:

> My life closed twice before its close;
> It yet remains to see
> If immortality unveil
> A third event to me
>
> So huge, so hopeless to conceive
> As these that twice befell.
> Parting is all we know of heaven,
> And all we need of hell.

"Now when you stop to look at that, does anything more than the thing itself occur to you?" he inquired. "One can say always that some days nothing more than the thing itself occurs to you. It's huge [enough] just in itself. . . . Sometimes something extra occurs to you." He called attention to the lines "If immortality unveil / A third event to me," and remarked: "The beauty of that, it occurs to me, is that she said, 'My life closed twice before its close; / It yet remains to see.' Now she doesn't say 'death' in there. It's the way—it's the curious use, the brilliant use of, the high poetic use of the word *immortality*. I agree to that. That's very high. Then the last two lines . . . are wonderful epigrams. But did you ever notice as you said it that parting is all we know of heaven. What do you know of heaven? You only know that some people go there. She means *knows*. 'And all we *need* of hell.' That's another word, you see. She doesn't say 'know' of hell; she says 'need'. Wonderful that 'need' in there. Sometimes you get a thing like that in your head and it dawns on you. You don't want somebody to tell you about it." Remonstrating against footnoting, he said: "Any note is a hell of a note." And "taking the top of poetry . . . there isn't anything in any of [the poems] that needs a note when you get up to that height of poetry."

Training in scholarship belonged to graduate-school education, but in reading poetry "there must be no suspicion of training at all." He clarified: "It must be the spreading of this kind of general knowledge that makes you so you can handle the poetry of the world without straining yourself. The knowledge shouldn't be the strain; the strain is how you catch it." He emphasized: "All you have to show in reading is that you've had the experience of poetry, you've lived with poetry, and you're good at getting the ideas. You've seen others who have beat you at it, and it makes you so jealous you tried to catch up."

He quoted: "'Trembling at that where I had stood before.'" "Well," he said, "anybody who has climbed mountains , you know, at the top looks back at places where he was. . . . You might miss [it]. And if you do miss something and see it years later—all right! You're missing some, of course. Take Keats again:

> No stir of air was there,
> Not so much life as on a summer's day
> Robs not one light seed from the feather'd grass,
> But where the dead leaf fell, there did it rest.
> A stream went voiceless by, still deaden'd more
> By reason of his fallen divinity
> Spreading a shade: the Naiad 'mid her reeds
> Press'd her cold finger closer to her lips.

See, that's just taking a little observation out of a little spot in the opening of 'Hyperion.' Then [Keats] said, 'the chill.' He gives the chill in that one, you know. Fancy sitting there. Then he says, 'the Naiad 'mid her reeds / Press'd her cold finger closer to her lips.' . . . [Keats] is full of it."

When he turned to his own poetry Frost was just as adamant about the natural approach. He would say: "I suppose a poem is a kind of fooling." To make his point, he referred to a Unitarian friend who sent him a sermon which insisted on "the foolishness of God"; foolish, I gathered, in the sense of God's fooling. Then Frost referred to one of the quirky idiosyncratic things about Albert Einstein: that every few minutes while talking about something philosophical, about relativity, about Newton, there was a burst of laughter. "[Einstein] got," as Frost explained, "a great laugh over his little quarrel with Newton."

Of course, if the height of everything is fooling—God's foolishness—then poetry mounts somewhere into a kind of fooling. It's something hard to get. It's what you spend a good deal of education on—just getting it right. . . . It's [poetry's] so simple and so foolish that only little children can understand it. We try too hard—we strike too hard—that's the danger of it. Now take God's foolishness. . . . You've got to be in an awfully easy mental state [to take it right]. That's the thing you acquire through the years of poetry—from *Mother Goose* on—easy does it. . . . As I say: . . . you can take it a good deal your own way—that's for conversation. You don't have to contradict it. . . . But make it a rule, almost, never to contradict anybody. Just say: "Let them have their say and then take it your way."

Frost would say: "That comes to this question of who has a right to do what he pleases with my poetry." And virtually in the same breath he added:

The right kind of people that can take it their way. There's a good deal of sway in it. There's a certain deftness, definiteness, but it sways at its anchor. It swings at its anchor tow. And of course that's the fun of it . . . this matter of getting it right and wrong. That's what you grow up in, getting it right and wrong, in and out, trial and error with it. . . . And there's such a thing as throwing dust in the eye, you know—a person can write so that he's insulting. He is just throwing dust in the eyes. And that's again just going a little over the edge about this play, this fooling. To tease people is all right but to insult them is going too far. It's always one of my concerns.

Undoubtedly he made the overture Wordsworth did in "Intimations of Immortality" when the Lake poet wrote solicitously: "We in thought will join your throng / Ye that pipe and ye that play." Frost also is one of the pipers and one of the players.

One of his talks (in 1953) was entitled: "On Being Let in on Symbols." After the New Critics of the 1940s insisted on reading poetry closely, the word *symbolism* frequently cropped up. Frost admitted that in order to communicate everybody was supposed "to get the hang of everybody's symbolism." He said: "We're always trying to communicate with each other with double tongues. We say one thing to mean that and another beside." And he defined a parable simply as "a story that means what it says and something besides." He amplified revealingly of "Directive":

> And according to the New Testament the something besides is the more important of the two. It's *that* the nonelect are supposed to miss and so not go to heaven. Saint Mark says so and somebody else says so; it occurs twice in the New Testament. And these things are said so as to leave the wrong people out. I love that because it sounds so undemocratic. That's not because I'm smart either but I just love to be shocked, don't you? I like to come right up against something like that.

Frost's explicit caveat to an uninitiated trespasser in the realm of symbolism has its parallel if not its inspiration in Sidney's "Apology." "To beleeve with me," says Sidney, "that there are many misteries contained in Poetrie, which of purpose were written darkely, least by prophane wits, it should bee abused."

Confusion and misunderstanding, Frost felt, came from having been "let in on somebody's symbols," an initiation he thought was going on mainly in the colleges. "People are there to get let in on so-and-so's symbols. . . . That is something I hadn't thought about until I had grown up to the present age. I always supposed I was good at symbols without being let in on them."

Another thing about symbols was being initiated into them *in poetry*. He recalled the numerous references to the mysteries in the Bible, especially in Corinthians. "And the people of Corinth were all fooling with ancient mysteries, Eleusinian and things like that. All those cities were full of it, and the word keeps occurring so that you wonder if there isn't black magic alluded to—ancient rites and things you wouldn't be able to guess unless you were initiated —unless you've been to a graduate school. No matter," he thought, "how good you are at that sort of thing, how you fancy yourself as quick in taking it, you can't do much with mysteries—the real mysteries. And that's so with some people's poetry. They want it to be mysterious." Of these people, he said tartly: "And if they want it to be—if they've got some secrets, let them keep them."

He preferred being good at rather than being initiated into. Then, in one of those wonderful little Frostian bursts of eloquence, he said jubilantly of poetry: "It's a fair field, see, it's a fair field, that's what poetry is; for people . . . that have come up from *Mother Goose* . . . and its figurativeness into the general figurativeness of grown-up people. . . . And the poetry is the height of it, isn't it? That's why poetry is *the* liberal art." Plainly he thought his poetry should be read without strain. "The first surface meaning, the anecdote, the parable . . . have got to be good and got to be sufficient in itself. If you don't want any more you can leave it at that."

"Poetry," he believed, "is a way of being taken by those who know how to take you." In his public appearance he made central this explanatory introduction of how he wanted to be read. Sometimes he did it indirectly, as we have seen, by quoting a line from Keats or Browning, a stanza from Emily Dickinson or Christopher Smart, a quatrain from Walter Savage Landor, or a short poem of Tennyson. More often his introduction was direct and his own poems were the examples.

3.

Because he had appeared so often at the Bread Loaf School of English, he had grown self-conscious about reading again and again the poems which he thought everyone must have heard many times by now. He said: "Some of them I'm scared of saying, I've said them so many times." So he would launch into a kind of speculation, musing, turning this way and that in his thought. "I think," he would explain, "I'm trying to escape from reading too many poems to you." Nevertheless, he would get back to the poems and continue to interject his views about politics, religion, science, and education between saying the poems.

Invariably he emphasized something else than meaning. If anyone in his audience waited breathlessly to be let in on the secrets of the poet's meanings in particular poems, he was soon discouraged. Take "Design," for example. Did he really think of design in eighteenth-century terms? Any hints? He whetted expectation by stating it was a poem he was never quite sure of. But why was he not sure of it? Because he was, as he explained, "too observing." He had rather be psychologically observing—"seeing into people." And "this one is a very special piece of observation." No commitment as to meaning was made, but only a deeply self-conscious reservation about looking too searchingly into nature. Was he reacting like the youth who lifted the dread goddess's veil at Sais and was shocked into silence by what he saw? "And I always wanted to be very observing," Frost said in a deeply self-revelatory statement, "but I have always been afraid of my own observations." Truth, Melville said in *Moby Dick,* is "a thing for salamander giants only to encounter." Did Frost, thereby, withdraw from any Euripidean, Lucretian, or Melvillean vision of the nature of things?

In his diffidence about meaning it might be contended he was playing a little game with his readers, to keep them off-balance. Of "The Most of It," he would say dryly: "It's another one people have bothered around about—the meaning of—and I'm glad to have them get more out of it than I put in. That's all right. I do that myself. I get more out of them as the years go on." The longer his comments are contemplated, the more I, for one, am inclined to think he wanted the reader of poetry to see what a poet was really up to; *how* the poet functioned as a craftsman. Consequently, he interjected comments on the importance of the rhyme. "No matter what I think ["Tree at My Window"] means, I'm infatuated with the way the rhymes come off there," he said. In "A Case for Jefferson," he was less concerned with what the poem was saying than with how it was said. "Those things I've cared about," he said of the political connotations, "but not cared about the way I care about rhyme and meter." Of "Closed for Good," he said casually, "It's just about a road that's been abandoned," and immediately he alerted his audience to matters of technique. "Again, watch the rhymes for my sake—to please me"—or the tone of the last line of "Closed for Good" ("For having once been there") or the very first line of "The Most of It" ("He thought he kept the universe alone") that "strikes the note." Of the reverential sound in the first line of "October" ("O hushed October morning mild"), he said: "I was very much aware that I was giving it a prayer sound. . . . I wouldn't have put that 'mild' to that if I hadn't been prayerful." As for sound, after reading "Acquainted with the Night," he said: "All for the tune. Tune is everything." Distinguishing between "Design" and "Provide, Provide", he said of the former: "See, that hasn't any tune at all. . . . That's getting all the resonance out of it that you can get out of it. There's plenty of tune to that ["Provide, Provide"], you see."

If anyone doubts the seriousness of his interest in form he should have heard the deceptively simple and brilliantly searching comment he made during an evening reading. After referring with vehement indignation to "all those damn, old, tiresome things"—soul and body, spirit and matter, immortality and transmigration, and God—he said in another remarkably self-revelatory mood that his "great interest" was to be among these things and then to play with them. In his own words, he said: "My interest, I think, is to be among those things—you can get among them—and then you play with them like pieces."

In "The Peaceful Shepherd," he said what he had tried for was to see if he could put a pretty sentence—"a different sentence"—in its little stanzas. Then, with Robert Herrick's "To Daffodils" in mind he said: "Wonderful the way the sentences are laid in them. He had that sense of form." In praising Herrick, it was apparent not only how familiar he was with the British poets in a great tradition but also how he drew his standards of excellence from representative poems in that great tradition, to justify his encomium and emulation.

In his awareness of such a stress on form, he was not unmindful of the great danger of a poet's losing meaning in the closeness with which he pursued form; in this case, the rhyme, the meter, the grammar, the vocabulary, "the shape of the little poem." He used the passage in "Kitty Hawk" describing the risk of spirit in substantiation to dramatize the poet's risk of losing his meaning in the form. Always, he made it clear, the important thing was to take this risk and to hope the spirit would be strong enough to come through the substantiation. Indeed, this would demonstrate not only "the supreme merit" of the poem but the poet as craftsman.

It is this risky thrust of the spirit in poetry that so much concerned him, not only in attempts at couplets like "From Iron" and "Precaution" to make intimations double his meanings but in the annoyance he felt when readers showed a lack of taste and indelicately presumed to read into a poem what he had never intended. "This question [of reading for symbols] comes up all the time. Do you want any meaning got out of what you write that you didn't put in?" When he mentioned an apple in a poem he was annoyed, as he said, if everybody was carried away by the apple to the Garden of Eden. "There are a lot of McIntosh apples down here in the [Champlain] valley. And there are all sorts of mythological ones —four or five of them I can think of, famous ones—and always I find if I mention an apple everybody is in the Garden of Eden at once. And everybody's falling—falling for it. . . . Something goes wrong there."

Obviously something does go wrong, and just as obviously, to read a poet of Frost's deceptive accessibility should keep the reader on his toes. The assiduity of modern criticism has so overalerted the reader of modern poetry he is constrained to approach every poet as though he were laying siege to an interpretation of Pound's Cantos. Yet here is Frost telling an audience there is more in his poems than meets the casual eye or reluctant ear. "Look," he said, "I'm always hinting, intimating, and always on the verge of something I don't quite like to say out of sheer delicacy. And the only thing I have against my friends, the teachers, is some of them are indelicate. They won't leave it [the poem] where I left it. They want to go on with it. They want to take both my hands and pull me across the line of delicacy." Right here we have the measure of Frost's sensitivity. To read him as he preferred to be read—that is, in a responsive mood—one would have to share a comparable delicacy of taste, neither over- nor under-reading the poem. Because, as he made very clear, he was "always doubling [his] meaning"; "always on the verge of something you don't want to say, quite."

Doesn't his self-admission go to the heart of the poet's vocation? Isn't the poet, like the scientist, making a thrust of the spirit? But while the scientist does it with space capsules and rockets, electrons and viruses, galaxies and gravitational fields, natural selection and DNA, the poet does it with symbols, analogies, and the connotative power of words. Although Frost, as he admitted, had grown to hate the word *symbol*, he realized he ought not to. "Symbol is always in everything that way," he agreed. "The thing I'm saying has got another behind it—all sorts of analogies. It's a symbol of many things." So it was not really the word *symbol* he hated, it was the misuse of symbolism and a reader's tendency to press poems too far that annoyed him. He suggested that rather than using the word *symbol* one might use the word *typifies* or *typification*. "I said I wish we could change the subject a little and say *typifies—typification*—or something like that."

He dubbed overreaders of symbols as "these *ultimate* people," and although he acknowledged interest in "the ultimates," he remonstrated: "You see I play with them more than I deal with them. And I don't like to be asked by anybody to tell what mine are—how far I dare go, how deep I am." Rather than using his own poetry as illustrative of this play, he turned to the critics of Tennyson. "I feel wonder at not thinking Tennyson went very deep in a thing like, say, 'Where Freedom slowly broadens down / From precedent to precedent' [in 'You ask me, why']. Now that's a very deep, subtle thing —the change from precedent to precedent, always talking precedents, but always slipping in a punctuation mark, you know, or something on freedom, getting farther and farther down." When reading "The Star-Splitter," he once paused at the line, "That varied in their hue from red to green," and said he thought it would be too bad if one had to stop in the classroom to tell what it meant. "A good deal," he recommended, "is just leaving it where the writer wants it to stay, just short of flatness."

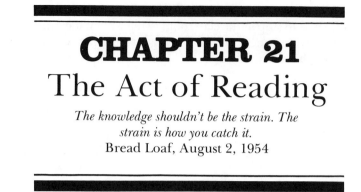

CHAPTER 21
The Act of Reading

*The knowledge shouldn't be the strain. The
strain is how you catch it.*
Bread Loaf, August 2, 1954

1.

A poet's dilemma is to avoid becoming everybody's idol for the
wrong reason or someone's proprietary hero for the right reason. If
only there could be a more general perceptiveness in reading poetry
and a greater prevalence of interest in poetry. Frost has not escaped
the sentimentalized reading that accompanies popular acknowledgment. A familiar household poet—Emerson, for example—just
barely escapes the quick passage from uncritical popularity to un-
read attachment, but the creeping paralysis of diffidence and a sudden shift in taste will push the Longfellows and Whittiers further
and further back into the recesses of our library alcoves.

If indifference is one hazard, another predictable one is the possibility of a failure in percipience on the part of the reader, and this
failure is compounded by several others—notably by a lack of
aesthetic sensibility and tact, which tends either to overread ex-
travagantly or to misread incompetently. A vanity in the human
condition leads some critics to assume an unjustified superiority to
the poem or the poet. The corrective for this tendency is an informed intelligence and a becoming humility. Yet do we have any
justification for criticizing an interpreter's *explication des textes* as long
as he does not ignore a poet's avowed counters of intention?

Obviously the general reader should be on guard against a critic's
misapplied inventive powers in the exuberance of his exegesis. All
readers should be on guard when the critic succumbs to the human
temptation to substitute *his* poem for the original one. Such vulgar
exhibitionism invariably subverts the true function of criticism,
which is to interpret to the general public the poem as it was written.
Yet the phenomenon appears not so extraordinary when it is under-

stood that a critic is often a thwarted poet. Not in a tone of petulance but certainly in a tone of civilized remonstrance, Frost explained his position: "Most poets are clear and intend to be understood just as they write. Critics have to do what readers expect of them. So they fog it all up." And one reason the critics fog it all up is, I suspect, because some of them have misapplied the New Criticism. So they have thought to pay Frost a favor by making it seem as though his poetry, like T. S. Eliot's and Wallace Stevens's, should be examined as though every show of simplicity was ingenious, every nuance a paradox. (I exclude from this mild demurrer Randall Jarrell's two brilliant essays—"The Other Frost" and "To the Laodicean"—in *Poetry and the Age.*)

The act of reading is more than an act of recognition, it is also an act of correspondence, "when," in Frost's figure, "you curl the filaments of your brain and wave them to correspond with me." To read any poet comprehendingly is no easy matter, and in Frost we need to curl the filaments in correspondence with voice tones, sleights of art, and dimensional views.

To be sure of vocal nuances and quirky shades of mood, I listened long to Frost's voice as I heard it in vis-à-vis meetings, in the lecture hall, on recordings, and on tapes. In a reading the poet depended intimately upon the expectancies of the audience, and at the top of his form in the later years, notably in the reading of the "The Witch of Coös, he played dramatically with the dialogue, now taking the part of the deluded mother, now of the bewitched son. His art rode on the sentences talking, not on rhetoric. During the high moments in his performances when he "said" his poems, what he didn't need to explain *was* the poem. Just as the learned Brahmans, according to Joseph Campbell, communicated the meaning in the verses of the Vedic hymns by the way they manipulated them, so too did Frost's art consist in varying vocal intonations. In pitch, tempo, and volume his voice played with the words in "The Witch of Coös," but not in the high foolery of the *Masques,* nor as though jigging around the maypole of some of his lighter verses. Now gruff and engaging, now ironic and mocking, the voice raised an anecdote of back-country New Hampshire to an echo-sounding of the self-induced spell that loneliness exacts of human credulity. Indeed, it was "a tale which," as Sir Philip Sidney once said in other times, "holdeth children from play, and old men from the chimney corner." The originality of Frost's viewpoint was sharpened by language rooted in common speech, a truth Hardy exemplified in his writings. Sounds, Hardy said in *The Return of the Native,* "intrinsically common become attractive in language," just as "shapes intrinsically simple become interesting in writing." Frost had here the common sounds and the simple intrinsic shapes.

Frost also delimited the old fadeaway New England region of small villages and marginal farms, upper pastures and woodland stands, granite outcrop and bared scarp, brook and flower stations, and made its intimate range his familiar. The intervales north of Boston were as identifying for him as the big river in Mark Twain, the high Nebraska plains in Willa Cather, the long valley in John Steinbeck. The poems coming out of place are, as Pound recommended all literature should be, "simply language charged with meaning to the utmost possible degree"—but how casually his sleights of art make profundity seem obvious. How independently he worked upon objective reality. Inwardly, he shaped the challenge of the outer world, and unlike T. S. Eliot who italicized what he had read, Frost, like Hardy, remembered chiefly what he had seen. For example, in his use of the dramatic monologue he is Browningesque, but how little of a Browning transplant he really was. The key to his technique—simple diction and syntax, verb-form contractions, envelope parentheses, colloquial locutions, mobile verbs, and preservation of normal order of words—is "the tradition of simple elevation," as Marie Borroff sets it off from "the tradition of ornate or learned elevation." With a surpassing beauty, he says: "Snow falling and night falling fast, oh, fast, / In a field I looked into going past," or "The shattered water made a misty din. / Great waves looked over others coming in," or "The sweep of easy wind and downy flake," or "Winds blow the open grassy places bleak." In addition there are the multiple sleights of art in imagery, use of symbols (or what he preferred to call typification), metaphor, and paradox.

To read him comprehendingly he must be read in and out of his time. Topical references to the welfare state are in "Build Soil" and to science in our technological age in several poems. However, when his poetry is read for what it shows of loneliness, grief, and fear, or show of courage and resolution in the human condition, we are closer to timelessness and his psychological emphasis on poetry as "thought-felt."

In spite of Frost's almost obsessive preoccupation with being read right, there are other ways to take the poems and these should not be precluded. In the act of reading one might well be alerted rather than authorized by his admonitions in order to review the poetry for its handling of comic and tragic modes, for image, metaphor, and symbolism, for ambiguities and paradoxes, for single meaning, double parabolic thrust, and an overarching design. All the examples selected stand well within the family, since genetically they are kin, begotten by the same poet, bearing an unmistakable family resemblance, and all in evidence of the genius of his handiwork.

2. Taken Singly: "A Winter Eden" (1927)

Once, when reproached for obscurity, it is reported that Dylan Thomas petulantly replied, "Read Frost." So! But are there no ambiguities to be found in Frost's poems—even in those thought to be taken "singly," as though uncomplicated by refractions? To resolve this inquiry satisfactorily is not easy. Not because Frost is obscure, but because the essence of poetry is suggestibleness. Consider, for example, "A Winter Eden," typically bucolic in setting and directly descriptive in method. In context it seems explicit enough to warrant only the slightest explication.

In "A Winter Eden" we glimpse sportive conies and loveless birds contentedly surviving winter, presumably in a New England alder swamp. Obviously it is intended that the reader be alerted by an implicit disclosure because of the ultimate word "Eden" in the title. To forestall any association with a fabulous vision such as we find in the Old Testament, this prelapsarian Eden is without seduction, greed, or guilt. It presents a natural condition of relaxed contentment, not in a temperate earthly paradise but in a chaste, subarctic alder swamp. The dominant metaphor is paradoxically a *winter* garden, not in any sense a vegetable garden, peopled by wild creatures whose sensual existence of playing, feeding, and sleeping defines them. Unlike Poor Richard, these creatures do not worry about keeping their shop; their shop will keep them. It is not thereby an Aesopian fable whose aim is to image the human condition. Frost was no fabulist of speaking creatures, whether pullets or crows, Morgan colts or bears, cows or deer, although the moralist can infer an ethical comment, a statement, an assertion.

If, however, we are decoders, eager to find subtleties in a deceptively simple form, then it must be in the last stanza and especially in the closing couplet that we detect a flicker of *extra*ordinary suggestion.

> An hour of winter day might seem too short
> To make it worth life's while to wake and sport.

This suggests that even in nature's economy there exists a lack of resiliency sufficient to counterpoise seasonal rigidity of routine. Amicable teasing points out a locked-in instinct operative in birds and animals who prefer sleep to activity. By extension, when *lifted* to a human plane, a reader might infer the poet is advocating homage to a play ethic as a replacement for the familiar Puritan work ethic. The romping conies, the ever-normal granary of red barberries "shining bright," the bark-girdling luxuriating beast, the choosy bud-inspecting birds exemplify an appetitive sensual indulgence. During the immobilization of sleep, no exacting decision, no exercise of option, no self-effecting action will be made. Untypical of the Puritan ethic, glorified ambivalently in the history of our captains of industry in a technological society, the emphasis is on contentment, not on achievement, on enjoyment rather than duty, on recreation, not good works, on the maypole at Merry-Mount, not on salvation by grace in King's Chapel. Since there is no direct reproach to light-hearted goings-on in the alder swamp, and only the mildest rebuke to inactivity, the poet might be asking: Is the world of nature after all so little given to kicking up its heels, so reduced to seasonal somnolence that animation suffers and every living thing—loveless birds, romping conies, and even activated feather-hammers (northern flicker)—should knock off early and succumb to sleep? So gentle is the low-keyed tone, so ruminative the note which characterizes a poet's open-ended universe in which there are always *at least* two roads to choose between.

Such a genial poem attracts by its familiar imagery of tree and snow, berries and creatures. Into this winter Eden, inviolate in the purity of its northern landscape, is introduced the disarmingly comic figure of "a gaunt luxuriating beast" whose presence faintly poses an objection to inanition as a way of life and ever so gently sides with exuberant sportiveness. Skillfully, the poem withholds commitment in its key word "might" in the penultimate line, a mighty *"might."* No apologetic statements are made, no evidences of divine justice appear, no social judgments are imposed. Instead of ambrosia, the Edenic meal is austerely and becomingly bark, buds, and berries.

So subtly is Frost's ulterior image of winter Eden handled, the poem becomes the more refractive when contemplated, advocating neither a way of life by festal delight nor yet one of "quiet desperation," but simply showing congenial adaptation within the conditions of one's environment. Claude Bernard, the French physiologist, for example, believed the stability of the interior environment had to be maintained before any measure of external freedom was attainable from the immediate surroundings. And in *Moby Dick*, Melville sang the praises of "interior spaciousness" in the whale's thick blubber, which enables it to move freely at the equator and the Pole. Is this not the "hint" which Frost once suggested his poem was making? In a winter Eden, the vivarial freedom results from stabilizing an interior environment with its immediate surroundings. The compelling image of the snugness of life at the center of a crystalline winter scene in the northern hemisphere *is* indeed Edenic. Moreover, in the context of Frost's poetry, "A Winter Eden" suggests that limited as we are by space and time we have it in us to stay snug in the limitless and to make as much as we can of transience. "A Drumlin Woodchuck," "Carpe Diem," and "I Could Give All to Time," among other poems, are variants of this central theme.

The pivot of "A Winter Eden" is antithesis: neither of pleasure nor duty but of daylight (sporting and romping) *or* night (sleep, perchance to dream). A spectrum of opposites is contained in this Edenic vivarium—not only atmospheric light *and* dark, but meteorological cold *and* heat, seasonal winter *and* memory of spring, biological sexual dormancy *and* seasonal mating, and even altitudinal snow depth raising the creatures heavenward in sharp contrast to the bare ground of summer. Indeed, the poem is less about a normal winter day than about the spectrum of possibilities in place. The poem has the unmistakable Frostian idiom—"As near a paradise as it can be / And not melt snow or start a dormant tree." It has beautiful run-on lines:

> It lifts a gaunt luxuriating beast
> Where he can stretch and hold his highest feast
> On some wild apple tree's young tender bark.

and effective end-stop lines:

> A feather-hammer gives a double knock.
> This Eden day is done at two o'clock.

An awkward interruption in rhythm in "Content with bud-inspecting" is compensated by activated verbs—"to *start* a tree" and "Here loveless birds now *flock*" (italics added).

Read in the Frost context, the poem parallels in the realm of nature the social view of "Good Hours," and an instinctual renunciation of activity is less to be recommended than awakeness and sportiveness. Avoiding whimsical triviality at one extreme, it also avoids platitudinousness at another. To read it as a parabolic expression of the inflexibility of instinct in the natural world is to bear down too hard. Rather, it is "a boundless moment" of the scene as observed, heightened by its biblical association; a prelapsarian winter Eden, where, in response to a deep instinctual impulse, sleep and inanition replace sportiveness and animation. Why not indulge oneself in the delight of fun, joy, rapture? the poem seems to say, riding as it does lightly but not unspeculatively on a spontaneous flash of humorous insight.

3. Taken Doubly: "The Objection to Being Stepped On" (1957) and "A Cabin in the Clearing" (1951)

"There are things you can't convey except in similitudes," Frost said. "That's the way we get from one thing to another—from one place in thought to another; by similitudes, of course." Another name for similitude was parable. By way of example, he referred to "Mending Wall," "The Wood-Pile," and "The Grindstone." There are many others, including "Mowing," "Hyla Brook," "The Vanishing Red," and, as Marie Borroff says, "the conclusion of 'Directive.'" In "Education by Poetry," he explained, referring to poetry as "one permissible way of saying one thing and meaning another," that "we like to talk in parables and in hints and in indirections—whether from diffidence or some other instinct."

Basically, a poetic parable is a figurative tale, told in an allusive language, signifying *something*, and Frost dealt in parables whose idiosyncratic quality was often an amusing instructiveness, not as in the customary tale sober-seeming but as with humor. The tone of the language suspended the moral in the telling, which is the art of a parable. A parable is always a means to an end whose art consists in implying that end. So it is in "The Investment" or "Out, Out—" and "The Oven Bird," but not so subtly accomplished in the parabolic "Two Tramps in Mud Time" or "The Tuft of Flowers."

"The Objection to Being Stepped On" illustrates Frost's continuing addiction to parable. A homely incident suggests a general idea in his irregularly rhyming eighteen-line parable. His often noted deceptive simplicity underscores what C. P. Snow, in another context, has called "the Alexandrian situation," in which the Alexandrian writings of Callimachus and Lycophron reflect a surface artificially complex but mindlessly conventional beneath. Yet Alexandrian science produced Archimedes, who represented in his experiments exactly the opposite—a superficial simplicity but a deceptive profundity. Frost's parable more nearly resembles Alexandrian science.

Easy rhyming and plain diction, close to jigging and banality, are redeemed by the playful irony of self-satire. To understand Frost the reader notes the tactics of his lightheartedness, using devices like paradox, antithesis, and irony and releasing them in couplets and quatrains, riddles and parables. He inverted the obvious with paradox. Perception, not acrimony, sharpened his irony. He spun riddles, he scored points in parables; and meaning is in the texture of the rhymes, for example, in "To the Thawing Wind," "Nothing Gold Can Stay," "A Peck of Gold," like a body in a swing, swinging. In "The Objection to Being Stepped On" monosyllabic language imposes a stringent containment of decorative imagery. Bare functional images of garden (implied) and hoe are integer with tone (ironic), diction (simple), and subject matter (rural).

As Frost ruminates on the complexity of good and evil, the large issue is reduced to the simplicity of an anecdote. "When the mathematician would solve a difficult problem," says Thoreau, "he first frees the equation of all encumbrances, and reduces it to its simplest terms." Here the simplest terms are a garden, a hoe, and the poet. Inadvertently the poet steps on a hoe blade whose handle snaps up and strikes him a sharp blow on the head. The reader, reminded of similar incidents, is self-advised to pay attention to the tools of husbandry or, by extension, look where he walks and beware! A closer scrutiny proves the initial impulse, albeit involuntary, is the poet's. Autistically he is not set upon in dudgeon by activated spectral hoes in a fantasy world. The reasonable man knows "It [the hoe] wasn't to blame"; nevertheless, reacting humanly, he vents anger. In his human reaction the poet is our equal.

Yet there is a hint of a subtler suggestion—a moral one—that recalls the biblical injunction to turn swords into plowshares. "But *was* there a rule / The weapon should be / Turned into a tool?" How effectively these lines anticipate the limitations in the Plowshare Project of 1957, headed by Dr. Gerald W. Johnson, when the Atomic Energy Commission decided to use nuclear explosions for peacetime purposes. Frost's hoe, like the nuclear explosions, thus turns out to be a potential weapon, since in no way have the scientists who were responsible for nuclear fission been able to minimize the devastating hazards of human exposure to radioactivity. But when, rhetorically, we ask, "Is there any rule the tool should be turned into a weapon?" is it possible we find an answer in Emerson's contention in "Uriel" that "evil will bless and ice will burn"? When extremes of evil occur we do, on occasion, get an equal and opposite reaction.

Frost's deceptively simple parable, moving from a particular incident to a general idea, operates on three planes, first as a personal incident, second as a moral analogue, and third as an intellectual paradox. The latter is what Charles Feidelson, Jr., in *Symbolism and American Literature* calls "the most exciting quality of modern symbolism," that is, "the tension between opposite meanings in paradox and the tension between logical paradox and its literary resolution." This tendency toward logical paradox and its literary resolution is found in Frost's *Complete Poems,* early and late, in both "Mending Wall" and "The Egg and the Machine," in both "West-running Brook" and "To a Thinker." Frost likes to give equal play to opposing positions, an idiosyncratic reticence in commitment that has left him wide open to the charge of "spiritual drifting." Yet the detachment we find in such speculative neutrality should not be confused with indecisiveness.

Frost is not inside Kafka's Castle—"the secret sits in the middle and *knows*"—but outside where all of us are gathered, I expect, if we are genuinely humble. In this sense the important thing is one's *point d'appui*—*how* to take what is seen and felt in our protean experience. Like an equilibrist who contains rather than contests the contraries of good and evil, war and peace, chaos and order, violence and security, reason and passion, Frost balances and counterpoises the ambivalences in a dynamic equilibrium, as he made clear in another parable entitled "The Armful." This is the token of *his* Negative Capability which differs from that of Keats in its active confrontation and extrication rather than in "any irritable reaching after fact and reason." In "The Objection to Being Stepped On" the meaning is implicit in the embodied paradox, which is good art. The last two lines—"The first tool I step on / Turned into a weapon"—point up an awareness of the activated force of evil in the supposedly harmless implement of husbandry that dealt "a blow that I felt / Like malice prepense" and of good in a farmer's hoe. The poem eases, it does not torment. It is not obscure, only playfully simple. When the poet refines the problem of encumbrances, as he has in this poem, his materials suggest a perfectly fathomable profundity—a verifiable truth (good from evil) that does not exclude its opposite (evil from good).

•

Another short dramatic parable, "A Cabin in the Clearing," is, in form, a dialogue between the personifications, Mist and Smoke. Mist, one of two voyeuristic eavesdroppers contemplating the enterprising pioneers who live in a cabin in a wilderness clearing, is gently skeptical about the cabin's occupants, while Smoke is the attorney for the defense. The poet's vantage ground is external to, yet observant of, the natural forces. This opportunity for dramatic give-and-take is the kind of play in which the poet delights. Mist, while not unsympathetic, is pressing. As "the damper counterpart of smoke" it owns an honest doubt whether the day will ever come when these American people will know who they are. They have got an answer from neither the Red Man nor philosophers, nor from religion and history. Smoke thinks the way to understand destiny is by self-awareness. Only a historical perspective will enable these people to judge themselves. When the lamp goes out in the cabin, Mist believes thinking continues. In the dark times, in the epochs of anxiety, it is implied, thought persists. Man has his intellect at least and this is a big resource, the poet suggests here, as he did in "Riders."

This parable succeeds because the poetic dramatist absorbs the commentator, embodies an idea not of alienation but of identity, and releases it through personified natural forces. The dialogue closes with Mist and Smoke continuing the eavesdropping on an inner haze. The reaction to national destiny suggests a possible application to personal destiny. Nor has the parabolist succumbed to solemnity. A climactic couplet ironically ribs all the principals.

> Than smoke and mist who better could appraise
> The kindred spirit of an inner haze.

This colloquy demonstrates the effectiveness of Frost's original theory of speech tones, in which voices of people are overheard talking naturally as from behind a door.

> Let us pretend the dewdrops from the eaves
> Are you and I eavesdropping on their unrest—
> A mist and smoke eavesdropping on a haze—
> And see if we can tell the bass from the soprano.

"The poet," Frost says, "expects to leave the poem more felt than said," and this is the measure of his success in "A Cabin in the Clearing."

Both Frost's virtues and his limitations are pointed up in this parable. Its touch of reality shows in his perception of the visual world; his handling of a complex idea—man's destiny—with simplicity is *sui generis*. Moving cautiously and shrewdly from the data of the senses, he appeals to the head as well as the heart. The idea comes to a crisis *in* the poem and not in a statement about the crisis. Natural insight suffices, which is, as some think, a major limitation in the poet's view. His flights are linear, his range terrestrial, his virtue courage, his religion self-dependence. In Blake and Yeats natural insight is not enough. Blake's "Epistle to Thomas Butts" exalted a four-fold vision. In Yeats, for example, at a point beyond reality vision is concretely embodied, but one must wear an embroidered coat of myth to grasp this vision. It would be unfair, however, to contend that Frost is unaware of other levels, other ranges, other virtues, and other religious awarenesses. He does take things "as they come" and while it is a basic animal faith which leads him to believe in "playing to win," there is another level, a higher one, a pinnacle, where, as he says, "You've got to have that fear of some ultimate judgment beyond yourself to make [your] life acceptable in [your] sight. That's what you mean by the fear of God. However, you work at it."

4. The Darkling Plain: "The Night Light" (1946); "Design" (1922); "Bereft" (1927); "The Draft Horse" (1962)

Once, three years before his death when Frost was ruminating about "ultimates," he wondered "how far down into the terribleness of things you go" as a poet. "My great interest, I think, is to be among those things," he said. "You get among them and then you play with them like pieces." If we except his couplets and quatrains, his play was about as innocent as Faustus chivvying with the devil. But if the commentaries he makes and tne allusions he scores are a poet's way of avoiding being one more mirror in a universe whose intentions are at best equivocal, Frost is of the modern contemporary. His innovation—and his defense—was play.

For a long time what Melville said of Hawthorne seemed to apply to Frost. "You may be witched by [Hawthorne's] sunlight . . . ," wrote Melville; "but there is the blackness of darkness beyond." Lionel Trilling, in one brief, darkly-shadowed ascription—"a terrifying poet"—on the night of March 26, 1959, shattered the spell which enthralled those whose perceptions had heretofore been blinded by the bewitching sunlight of, say, "The Cow in Apple Time," "Brown's Descent," and "A Blue Ribbon at Amesbury." So it was Professor Trilling, not Frost, who scared the modern generation of Frost readers. The poet, who had long been writing of terrible episodes in the human condition—"A Servant to Servants," "The Housekeeper," "The Hill Wife," "Out, Out—," "Acquainted with the Night," "The Vanishing Red," "Home Burial," among other tragic and terrifying possibilites—was himself not quite the neurotic and paranoid figure of despair Trilling's words seemed to imply. The poet, who writes often of fear, contained it. Moreover, the poet could take a homely little incident like "The Night Light" and, gloom-shot as it might have been, suspend a no less bewitching gloom on a run of graceful rhymes.

She always had to burn a light
Beside her attic bed at night.
It gave bad dreams and broken sleep,
But helped the Lord her soul to keep.
Good gloom on her was thrown away.
It is on me by night or day,
Who have, as I suppose, ahead
The darkest of it still to dread.

What brings the reader up sharply are those last three boldly assertive lines. Without capitulating to an unknown future and without
any posturing, Frost refuses the self-indulgent luxury of gloom and
goes about his business.

"The terribleness of things" that Frost contemplates is dual. The
cosmic situation of man who finds himself in an alien but not necessarily hostile universe is evoked forthrightly in "An Old Man's
Winter Night" and unsettlingly in "Design." In his relationship to
this alien universe, man can be callously indifferent toward it, feel
ignored by it, fearfully seek sanctuary from its baleful onsets; or he
can respect it humbly and, without awe, confront it unblinkingly.
Man, in the cosmic situation, aware of his fallibility and of the uncertainty if not downright perversity of the interplay of history, destiny,
fate, or providence, has to face what Emerson called "the odious
facts," like famine, disease, suicide, nuclear warfare, genocide.

"Design," whose effectiveness as a speculative poem Randall Jarrell demonstrated brilliantly in "To the Laodiceans" (*Poetry and the
Age,* New York: Alfred A. Knopf, 1953), has long been a target for
explication. Isadore Traschen, for example, summed up its argument in contending "that the universe is a design of darkness," and
Irving Howe in "Robert Frost: A Momentary Stay" (in *A World More
Attractive*) represented it as "a dumb-show of purposeless terror."
One thing is sure. When Frost read the poem publicly (not often), he
made no disclosures, did not tip his hand on the ambiguities, but said
revealingly, "This is a kind of poem that I am never sure of because
[I think it's] too observing." What he meant was that his observations
in this instance took him into darker areas than was customary,
like Thoreau on the memorable occasion when he examined a repel-
ling fungus—*Phallus impudicus,* or stinking morel. "Design" was,
Frost thought, "a very special piece of observation," which leaves a
reader about where he came in.

One morning on his travels in the South, William Bartram,
gathering specimens of flowers from shrubs, discovered a large
spider *(Araneus saliens),* whose body was the size of a pigeon's egg,

stalking a bumblebee *(Apis bombylicus)*. While the bee was preoccupied with the flowers, the spider drew near and suddenly sprang on the bee, artfully trapped it in a web, fatigued the struggling bee in about fifteen minutes, and took it under cover of the leaves to devour. Bartram, conceiving all things as following "the vital principle of efficient cause of motion and action, in the animal and vegetable system" in the Creator's "wondrous machine," was not disturbed at what he saw. He might have quoted chapter and verse from William Paley's *Natural Theology* (1802).

> Nor ought we to feel our situation insecure. In every nature and
> every portion of nature which we can descry, we find attention
> bestowed upon even the minutest parts. On spiders and bees,
> for example. The hinges in the wings of an earwig and the joints
> of its antennae, are as highly wrought, as if the Creator had had
> nothing else to finish. We see no signs of diminution of care by
> multiplicity of objects, or of distraction of thought by variety.
> We have no reason to fear, therefore, our being forgotten, or
> overlooked, or neglected.

One day Frost found a fat *white* spider on a *white* heal-all *(Prunella vulgaris)* holding up a *white* moth, and speculated inquisitorially. But his mood and tone are different from Bartram's. Although, like Bartram, he too is surprised, he is surprised into a metaphysical question. Bartram is only surprised at the aggressive spider "taking on" such a formidable antagonist as the bumblebee. To Bartram, as to Paley, there is apparently a design, and for spiders to conquer bees is acceptably in the order of things. In *The Voyage of the "Beagle,"* Charles Darwin found evidence *against* Paley's argument for design. The finches which fascinated him on the different islands of the Galapagos were distinguished from one another because of no special providence. They were not, as Eiseley said, "instantaneously conceived at the moment of Creation." They were what they were —some with small beaks like warblers, others with thick, massive beaks—because of adaptation to environment, hence variations with which special providence had nothing whatever to do.

Frost subtly takes the position of naturalistic science in opposition to the argument for design in terms of special creation. With a flick of his wit—it is in the ironic question—he turns us away from Paley's static "natural theology" and *heads* us in the direction of Darwin's organic evolution in which "design" has as many facets as a prism. So in his ironic commentary on the argument for design he searched for evidences of God's tenderness with no evidence that man, any more than moth, spider, or heal-all, stands at the center of the universe. For haven't we as much reason to fear "our being forgotten, or neglected" as these humble phenomena of the natural universe? If "Design" is instructive, what is its point of edification? Is it that the power, wisdom, and goodness of God is somehow directed in favor of man? I think not; rather, they are being exercised in ceaseless struggle, possible variation of species, and toward inevitable extinction. If power, for example, or wisdom or, for that matter, goodness are being exercised, for whose benefit?—the moth's, the heal-all's, or the spider's? In effect, who is responsible for this tripartite complicity?

A larger view of design is also suggested; one that suggests life as radiating into divergent forms—flower and insect—and, at times, fortuitously converging in a little dance of death on a sterile flower stalk. In this view Frost transforms an eighteenth-century static concept of design into a dynamic one—design here includes the negations as well as the blessings, where all is part of the process. What Frost therefore might be calling in question in the last two lines is a dogmatic assertion; hence his concluding question. He may not doubt purpose in the universe—an overarching design as it were —only the dogmatism of a fixed position in a universe where evil as well as goodness has its place in the order of things. Hence Frost, rather than arguing for validity of ultimate design, only implies the narrowness and restrictiveness in its application. For there is no more assumption of preordained evil than of preordained goodness implied in the inquiring tone of the poet's searching question. He accepts Hardy's hostile universe no more readily than Emerson's benevolent one.

Frost called "Design" "a set little sonnet. And it's a kind of design." In artistry it has a consistent logic, moving from spider to flower to moth; its mode is exploratory, not expository; its statements direct and concrete, not general and abstract; its tone interrogative; its imagery natural; its manner teasingly serious; its scale cosmic; its form tightly held within conventional metrical limits. The triad of natural objects—a lethal spider, a dead moth, a blighted flower—assumes an ominous symbolic significance as "assorted characters of death and blight" in the octet. Wryly, they are "Mixed ready to begin the morning *right*" (italics added). The repulsive suggestion in the similitude "Like the ingredients of a witches' broth" evokes *Macbeth*. The "ingredients" could just as credibly be root of hemlock, toe of frog, a fenny snake. The summarizing line in the octet identifies imagistically each of the objects—"A *snowdrop* spider, a *flower like* froth, / And dead wings carried *like a paper kite*" (italics added). This is an ironic pleasantry; the killer and the killed are transformed from dreadfulness to innocence.

But the sestet is not typical; it does not resolve the situation as in a conventional sonnet. It inquires rhetorically, first, why was the flower white—"The wayside blue and innocent heal-all"? Secondly, what was the *white* spider doing at that height? And thirdly, why was a moth to be found *there*? Suggesting a provisional conjecture, the poet inquires: "What but design of darkness to appall? / If design govern in a thing so small." Obviously the necessary factors in an argument are provided; now we draw our inferences.

In viewpoint Frost is also designing. The element of chance intrudes both from without and from within in an otherwise necessitarian design. From without, it intrudes in the color of the heal-all, which normally is blue while this particular flower is white, an anomaly among heal-alls, and an inverted reading where dread, menace, and woe replace the customary beneficence and purity attached to white. And it intrudes *within* the context of the event for, if chance fatefully brings spider, heal-all, and moth together, then at least for the moth it is a malefic design. But is there an arbitrary, fixed design? "*If* [italics added] design govern in a thing so small." Or is the particular conjunction of white spider, white heal-all, and white moth only happenstance? Was the spider acted upon, or did it act according to its nature?

If design is universal, it will prevail everywhere, on every level, animal and human, and at every plane, from physical to metaphysical. Yet here there is no reenactment of the mystery of the Fall, since no such reenactment takes place in nature when design is amoral, not moral. The creatures—spider and moth—behave like creatures. The moth, for example, is the spider's natural prey, a trophy earned by its being what and where it was. The spider's act is not against but within nature. Under the necessity of securing food for self-preservation, it would accept a moth any time, white or black, brown or gray.

Frost alone considers these emblems "Assorted characters of death and blight." In a world of fixed design a spider acts by agency of its natural mechanism and feeds on moths. Similarly, blue heal-alls are blasted just as naturally; and although atypical, the white heal-all is not unexceptional in a world where albinos are to be found. The Fall is therefore *not* universal; it is not inherent in nature. It is an invention of man to account for the mystery of evil, which in the world of nature is an unambiguous power exercised directly and decisively. There is no religious significance here since no secular crime has been committed against God, man, *or* nature.

Although nothing offensive has happened, symbolically the little drama is dismayingly provocative. For, if the drama happens like this *in* nature—and surely no one doubts the verity of the poet's observation—is there any justification for, let alone explanation of, its happening within the microcosmic world of man included in the macrocosmic world of nature? Can such malefic things be, we exclaim—only to know they very well do happen. Frost contemplates without commitment the validation of an all-powerful universal force which does govern in things both large and small, then and now, waywardly, and with purpose, if any, beyond our ken, like Hardy's "knitter drowsed" whose "fingers play in skilled unmindfulness."

Evil is in the ruck of things, and its effect *is* appalling—to the cogitating poet. For it is he who suggests the unanswered questions in the dramatically wry *if* in the closing sentence. And the terror —the bogeyman—in this sonnet is the transference of a potentially appalling situation from insect and flower *to* the human plane. If not a sparrow falls without God's special providence, how then can this inimical little drama be justified? Typically, Frost's imagination fastens empirically on the small and concrete details and follows them into the large and abstract generalization: that reality (insect *and* man) is one and that design is fused oneness. So appalling is design! So natural is activity outside of design!

The real question is, therefore, *not* whether "design govern in a thing so small." If so important a matter as universal design governs in large, it also governs in little things. The real question is: Is there an original design? And, if the answer is that design does exist—as we surely find it in the calendrical progression of the seasons as well as in six-rayed snow crystals, from the coordination of moon and oceanic tides to sun and climatic response—then what the poem discloses is not the presence or absence of design but rather operative evil within the design. Why, in effect, is there this "design of darkness to appall?" Why do we find even in the small world intimations of evil? "Is He willing to prevent evil, but not able?" asks Epicurus of deity. "Then He is impotent. Is He able but not willing? Then He is malevolent. Is He both able and willing? Whence then is evil?" No poet is obligated to resolve the nature of evil so long as he can dramatize an awareness of the essential appearance, and "Design" does precisely this.

But there is also the dark aspect of the cosmic situation of man in a hostile universe. "Bereft" illustrates this aspect. How bereft can a man feel in a universe where he is at the mercy of unleashed natural forces? Beyond solitude there is isolation, and beyond isolation there is bereftness. But beyond bereftness there is desolation and beyond desolation despair. Frost's bereftness is beyond isolation but well this side of despair. Word that the poet is in the world alone is not word that he is unable to endure what has to be faced.

The world of natural forces outside the restive door—the world he encounters on the sagging floor of the porch—is personified by a wild and rampant wind, unloosed to do its worst. The aroused hostility of the wind is dramatized by two vocal images, the first of which suggests the menacing roar of a featureless jungle animal. And the second vocal image of an aggressive snake with its hiss is a clincher. The leaves coil and strike and miss in a familiar whirling thrust. In the observer's mood nature is hostile. Even exanimate objects—the dead leaves—simulate animate ones.

The outside world is indeed kicking up; the wind shakes the door, froths the water, sounds ominous, and the somber clouds mass portentously. Summer is at an end and the day is done. The solitary man in the house has been discovered, the attack is beginning, and he is exposed in a threatening universe. Word has gotten abroad that man in his aloneness is just short of being God-forsaken. His only succor is in that transcendent suggestion—"Word [he] had no one left but God." What a slight terrifically important shift it is from God-dependence to God-forsakenness.

There is also a psychological darkness in the moral condition of man. This "blackness," identified by Melville in Hawthorne's writings, is an inherent evil or essential depravity. Albert Camus identifies it when he states "the worm is in man's heart." It is the depravity of the miller in "The Vanishing Red," and "The Draft Horse" is its most startling example in Frost's poetry.

If I say this five-stanza, twenty-line poem ("The Draft Horse") emphasizes the finality of the inexplicable, the comment inadequately accounts for innocence (the unquestioning pair to whom the traumatic incident occurs) and the mystery of motivation. Since the innocent pair encounters a malevolent, destructive, and inexplicable action, the focus of our interest is not only on *why* this traumatic incident occurs but on *how* the unquestioning pair reacts to it. Tone of voice is important, but does it imply that the innocent pair who unquestioningly accept an act of unreasoning destructiveness *ought* to have reacted vigorously to the offensive act? Why does the pair accept the act so passively? Isn't there just a note of incredulity in the tone of voice?

Both the mysteriously motivated assailant and impersonal nature are involved. Yet the assailant who strikes the blow is not identified as operating directly under his own authority. The poet's voice says: "We assumed that the man himself / Or someone he had to obey." No identification is made, no honorific capitalization of someone raises the unidentified to godhead. Yet "obey," in biblical context, implies that we are enjoined to obedience by an authoritarian God. So whether the man is principal or agent is left as open and ambiguous as whiteness in *Moby Dick.*

Frost's parablelike poem embodies a disturbing acceptance of a demonstrable malice in the nature of things ("The night drew through the trees / In one long invidious draft"). We are reminded of "one strain of guilt," which identifies mankind in Hawthorne's "Young Goodman Brown." The hatred-at-large in the world is italicized by the passivity of the unquestioning pair who might have been expected to react self-defensively.

In "The Draft Horse" fate is less cosmic than anthropomorphic; it is personified in the man who comes out of the trees like a primitive force and whose gesture is as inexplicable, assertive, and destructive as the more impersonal frightful force in Melville's natural world. The man's actions represent a directed hatred, which is more outrageous than the display of a nonhuman impersonal fate since the power of intelligent will should be a civilized acquirement of man. Hardy's "Hap" underscores this fact.

> If but some vengeful god would call to me
> From up the sky, and laugh:
> . . .   .
> Then would I bear it, clench myself, and die,
> Steeled by the sense of ire unmerited;

In "The Draft Horse," as in "Hap," there is no consoling or vindicating, let alone explanatory, voice. Yet in spite of its obvious ambiguities, I hardly think "The Draft Horse" is a Frost put-on. Perhaps, like the king in *Through the Looking Glass,* we only wish we had such eyes "to be able to see Nobody! And at this distance, too! Why it's as much as we can do to see real people, by this light." Like Hemingway's "A Clean Well-Lighted Place," which is a parable *for* our time, "The Draft Horse" is a revealing parable *of* our time. It suggests that the things that are done to man and woman —the unquestioning pair—under the assumed dictates of others have an irrational imperiousness. And it exhibits a similar irrationality at the behest of unconscionable dictatorial power.

5. Light and Variable

Frost was one of the most naturally, not professionally, humorous poets in our literature. If the essence of his humor was play, in what sense was he playfully humorous? A key to another side of the "terrifying poet" is in Johan Huizinga's *Homo Ludens* (Boston: Beacon Press, 1950), where the spirit of play is related to a social impulse; "older than culture itself" and pervading it, he thought, "like a veritable ferment." To play was to play *freely:* to step outside ordinary life into a sphere of activity "with a disposition all of its own," and to play as it were "within certain fixed limits of time and place." Which is precisely what Frost did in the play-sphere of poetry when order, rhythm, change, movement, tension in the metrical form intensify the spirit of the context. In "Opposition," Sidney Lanier illustrated the spirit of the contest in the image of the lute.

> The lute's fixed fret, that runs athwart
> The strain and purpose of the string,
> For governance and nice consort
> Doth bar his wilful wavering.

In "How Hard It Is to Keep from Being King" Frost described the tension between the irregularity of the accent-stress and the regular beat of the meter as though they were equally matched contestants.

> Regular verse springs from the strain of rhythm
> Upon a metre, strict or loose iambic,
> From that strain comes the expressive *strains of music*
> The tune is not that metre, not that rhythm,
> But a resultant that rises from them.

In "The Silken Tent" Frost played seriously with rhythm and meter through a single metaphor and, as he said, "in one sentence that doesn't break in the middle." In "Departmental" he played craftily with end-rhymes, "just for the fun of it." He warned his listeners to watch the rhymes: "cloth, moth; size, surprise; such, touch." In his particular play, no less than in the play-sphere of a chessboard, a sacred circle, Loki's "great place of peace," or the Woolsack where the Lord Chancellor sat, he played within the conventions of form by entangling speech-tones "for the ear of the imagination."

Wherever riddle making, soothsaying, ritual, persuasion, entertainment, and artistry appear some aspect of poetry is found. "Men make poetry," Huizinga thought, "because they feel a need for social play." A vital function of man, poetry in turn vitalizes a community. As Emerson wrote: "It is frolic health." In Frost the *facultas ludendi* was so activated he constantly sought to amuse and delight by the natural play of his mind. We recall how he emphasized that his aim was to entertain by making play, which he did by deploying the resources of language, by strategy in metrical patterns, by "feats of association." Sometimes the play showed in *le mot juste* like "fading" in the superb line, "The flowers fading on the seed to come"; in the allusive "And so to roost" in "A Blue Ribbon at Amesbury," which is Pepysian; in euphemisms like "toga-togs" in "On our Sympathy with the Under Dog"; or inflected voice-tones of his mind, expressed, as he writes in one of his letters, "in pensées thrown together like the heads of Charles the Bold's army after it was defeated and slain in Switzerland." Frost belonged to a native tradition which included Franklin, Thoreau, and Emerson, Holmes and Lincoln, Josh Billings and Mark Twain, Finley Peter Dunne and Calvin Coolidge, and even, in its succinctness, our Indian culture. The sophisticated Frost, however, scores his epigrammatic points teasingly, while the Indian spokesmen differ from him in tone and mood. Playing with the contraries *good* and *evil*, Frost epigrammatized in a couplet: "It is from having stood contrasted / That good and bad so long have lasted." He said: "They stand up and support each other just the same as two playing cards do, you know, when you stand them up just right." On seeing the lump of purest iron ore in the United Nations building in Manhattan, he epigrammatized its doubleness in tools *or* weapons. "Nature within her inmost self divides / To trouble man with having to take sides." But when a Sioux is dying and wants to make clear how greatly offended he is by the misguidance of tutelary spirits, he says flatly, "Large Bear / Deceives me." The Indian is only laconic; Frost is laconic *and* witty.

The play of his humor is reflected in the edged verbal exchange called stichomythia which we find in the give-and-take between Tityrus and Meliboeus in "Build Soil," and also in the person to whom he addresses his answer in this monostich:

> But Islands of the Blessèd, bless you, son,
> I never came upon a blessèd one.

> ["An Answer"]

We see his humor also in the agility with which he made "unexpected connections" in the relationship of disparate things in acceptable puns as in the title, "In Divés' Dive," or in the use of "clear" in "Voice Ways":

> Some things are never clear
> But the weather is clear tonight,
> Thanks to a clearing rain.

And note in "Clear and Colder" the word "above":

> Human beings love it—love it.
> Gods above are not above it.

Or the masterly "light-natured" in "The Gold Hesperidee":

> But when he came to look, no apples there
> Under, or on the tree, or anywhere,
> And the light-natured tree seemed not to care!

"Cutting up a little, I always am," he explained, lightly self-deprecating. His "cutting up" assumed several forms. In the said-in-jest poems, it is a banal-seeming couplet of end-stop lines:

> The old dog barks backward without getting up.
> I can remember when he was a pup.
>
> ["The Span of Life"]

In "Waspish" he cuts up like a comic moralist in three couplets, and in "One Guess" he plays lightly in easy riddles. But in "Departmental" his *jeu d'esprit* stabs satirically, in "The Bear" ironically, in "Paul's Wife" whimsically, in "A Blue Ribbon at Amesbury" with restrained raillery; and in "Riders" the humanist's play-spirit surfaces braggingly when he boasts, "We have ideas yet that we haven't tried." This reminds us of Remus's "contemptuous gesture" in jumping over Romulus's wall "in the dawn of Roman history," a moral analogue of the Chinese warrior who rode up to his enemy's gate and calmly counted the planks with his whip. But Frost's boast has typically his taunt of truth.

"We get our effects on a tension," he believed. Consequently, one of his most fertile forms of play appeared in paradox, what Charles Feidelson referred to as "the tension between opposite meanings." That paradox went deep in Frost, not only in the temper of the art but in the character of the man, few would doubt; in a New Englander with a California birthplace; in a southern name, Robert Lee, in one who thought Grant a greater general; in the simplicity of his rural up-country life juxtaposed with the society of cities; in the rebellion from the rigidities of formal education, yet "barding around" in educational institutions; in the sanguine views of a "terrifying poet"; in the publicly bantering but privately serious complicated man.

In his poetry the paradoxes are omnipresent.

> The fact is the sweetest dream that labor knows.
>
> ["Mowing"]

I would not go in till the light went out;
It would not go out till I came in.

["The Thatch"]

"Men work together," I told him from the heart,
"Whether they work together or apart."

["The Tuft of Flowers"]

One aged man—one man—can't keep a house,
A farm, a countryside, or if he can,
It's thus he does it of a winter night.

["An Old Man's Winter Night"]

It is this backward motion toward the source,
Against the stream, that most we see ourselves in.

["West-running Brook"]

And below roared a brook hidden in trees,
The sound of which was silence for the place.

["The Generations of Men"]

Something we were withholding made us weak
Until we found out that it was ourselves
. . .   .
And forthwith found salvation in surrender.

["The Gift Outright"]

The bird would cease and be as other birds
But that he knows in singing not to sing.

["The Oven Bird"]

From "Into My Own" through "Directive," to paraphrase John
Dryden's apt comment on Ben Jonson's devotion to the ancients,
"You track him everywhere in their snow," so we track Frost everywhere in the paradoxes, whose key is resistance to dogma and orthodoxy. In an open-ended universe, truth forevermore must be "a
dialogue." He said in serious playfulness:

I love to toy with the Platonic notion
That wisdom need not be Athens Attic,
But well may be laconic, even Boeotian.
At least I will not have it systematic.

["Boeotian"]

Nor will he be systematic in the trial and testing of ideas in the open
forum of speculation. He took his place with the seer (vates), the
Arabic knower (sha'ir), and the sagacious old man of early Norse lit-

erature *(thulr)*, ruminating on the eternal conflict of opposites—the Chinese yin and yang, Heraclitean strife, which is the father of all things, and the Empedoclean principle of attraction and discord. The twist he gave the root-principle of existence was a theory of conflicting goods rather than the conflict of good and evil, right and wrong, virtue and vice.

> But even where, thus, opposing interests kill,
> They are to be thought of as opposing goods
> Oftener than as conflicting good and ill;
> Which makes the war-god seem no special dunce
> For always fighting on both sides at once.
>
>   ["To a Young Wretch"]

In an epoch of atomic reaction and guided missiles, computerization and automation, nuclear warfare and space exploration, he was like a Hellenic throwback whose Epicurean Garden was the back-country north of Boston and whose Aristotelian Porch was now a farmhouse at Derry, New Hampshire, or South Shaftsbury, Vermont, and now a cabin on the Homer Noble farm in Ripton. Something also of a Greek sophist, his performance, or *epideixis*, was an exhibition at the public lectern. Something of a street philosopher, Socratically he salted his conversation neatly with speculative rebuttals. Something of a rhetor, he triggered his ideas within the lecture halls of the universities. Who doubts, for example, that in "The Bear" or in "To a Thinker" Frost sophistically gave himself "up to play" as Theaetetus admitted of the sophists to the Stranger from Elea in the *Sophist?* Not a falsifier of wisdom, surely, but a sophisticated player with ideas, idiomatically "out on the town," exposing the limitation in the political right as in "Precaution" and the political left in "A Case for Jefferson."

All knowledge, Johan Huizinga contended, was polemical. And polemics, he thought, could not be divorced "from agonistics." The chief agonistics of our time are science, religion, and politics, and Frost hardly backed away from them. "I joke about science," he would say. "People misunderstand me sometimes. They think I'm antiscientist." When he read "Why Wait for Science," he emphasized the fun in it. "See," he said, "how much fun there is in science."

How readily we infer Frost was callously flippant because of his strong tendency to treat lightly the origin of planetary life. Svante Arrhenius and Lord Kelvin thought, for example, the spores of life came originally from outer space, driven across the earth orbit by light pressure or riding into our atmosphere on meteoric dust. The pointedness of Frost's last six lines in "Why Wait for Science" not only supported a theory of meteoric impregnation, it made a kind of joke of it. Meanwhile, the scientists go venturing on, and Prof. A. I. Oparin in *The Origin of Life on the Earth* (New York: Macmillan, 1938) has proposed an acceptable geochemical theory that the first living things appeared several billion years ago, not in transit from another planet or yet *ab ovo*, but developed in a kind of "organic soup." Professor Oparin conjectured that in the earth's early atmosphere organic compounds gave rise to life and ultraviolet light from solar radiation helped convert a mixture of organic compounds into life-originating organic soup. The thrust in Frost's play is directed at the theorizing tendency of scientists, but Professor Oparin could be right and Frost lightly irrelevant.

In the two *Masques* Frost was interested in "bandying about a little theology," which certainly amounted to handling sacred subjects with a secular touch. In *A Masque of Reason,* for example, the Frostian angle is the twist he gave the Jobean story, "that God was just showing off to the Devil," a twist that had its inception in the idea, as Frost said, that "there wouldn't be any evil if there wasn't any good. 'The one thing God can't make,' a countryman used to say, 'is a stick with only one end.' " He portrayed Jehovah as Blake's God and patient Job as "the great injured man," his wife Thyatira as a "Yankee character," a housewife full of having done what she thought right in taking care of Job but bored by philosophical discussion, and the Devil as the conventional Adversary of Old Testament theology. Underneath the humor is seriousness, beneath the seriousness is humor. Just as the ambiguity of Plinlimmon's horologicals and chronometricals interested Melville in *Pierre,* so the inability to reconcile human affliction with heavenly wisdom fascinated Frost. But the rusticity of his comedic humor is disaffecting to some readers. Hard to take was the flippancy of Job's wife in her reference to deity ("I'd know You by Blake's picture anywhere") or her irreverent reproachfulness: "God's had / Aeons of time and still it's mostly women / Get burned for prophecy, men almost never"—or Job's corny play on Kipling's invocation, "Lord God of Hosts": "She'd [i.e., Thyatira] like to know how You would take a prayer / That started off Lord God of Hostesses."

A Masque of Mercy, companion piece to *A Masque of Reason,* has as its countertheme to the latter that "mercy is only to the undeserving; only justice is to the deserving." In the second of his two "New England Biblicals," he gave the Gospels a double twist. He wanted, first, to dramatize Jonah's reluctance to trust God to be merciful to a fugitive like himself, and secondly, to indicate how the Sermon on the Mount was a frame-up to insure universal failure. In *A Masque of*

Mercy, we find corny punning (*Keeper:*"So you've been Bohning up on Thomism too"; or, *Paul:*"It's been a commonplace / Ever since Alexander Greeced the world") and barbed allusiveness (*Keeper:*"Oh, you mean *Moby Dick* / By Rockwell Kent that everybody's reading"; or, *Keeper:*"My friends and stokers, Jeffers and O'Neill"). No one is expected to be at the top of his form in the light and variable at all times, but Frost's exercise of self-criticism is notably more relaxed in the later than in the earlier poetry.

The poet's play, like the peripatetic on his porch or the sophist on the street corner, has its *point d'appui* in philosophic detachment. When we stand off just far enough from human or divine institutions, no matter how big, heroic, grand, imposing, and serious they are supposed to be, they *can* look funny. Obviously, this is the way the institution of religion looked to the poet.

CHAPTER 22
On a Field of Vision

Earth is still our fate.
"Kitty Hawk"

1.

Both *philosopher* and *philosophic* are awkward words when applied to a poet. If we describe a poet as a philosopher the term is loosely used. Frost, for example, has views about causation ("Why Wait for Science"), knowledge ("The Bear"), motion ("West-running Brook"), and change ("Nothing Gold Can Stay"), but his concern is in concretely embodying these concepts rather than in exploring them intensively as a philosopher would. *Philosophic* is a passive and facile descriptive term. It understates a poem's single vision and the design in the totality of a poet's experience.

If by philosopher and philosophic we mean sharply delimited and nontechnical speculation on the human condition, the terms as applied to Frost would be agreeable. Like Goethe, surely a philosophic poet in *Faust,* Frost sees contemplatively. Yet unlike Carlyle, who was a recalcitrant reformer writing a full-blown rhetorical prose, Frost's views of the joys and sufferings, the hopes and disillusionments, the great on-penetrations and the immedicable woes are embodied feelingly but not programmatically. How best, then, to characterize what is central to his vision and the method by which it is realized?

By definition a vision is individualized and charged with the dominant traits of temperament. It is more real because it is less general, to adapt one of Santayana's carefully phrased statements, and attains character because it trains our imagination into exclusiveness. However, a vision should not be confused with attitude. When Frost says "The fact is the sweetest dream that labor knows" or asserts "I had a lover's quarrel with the world," his attitudes are of course self-revealing. In the first instance, he identifies a relationship to his subject matter; in the second, he is objectifying a passionate introspective feeling. But when he says, in "The Lesson for Today," "No choice is left a poet, you might add, / But how to take the curse, tragic or comic," how can we doubt we have drawn close to a vision of the human condition? If this is not an apocalyptic *visio beatifica,* at least it has the compelling merit of a calm and unblinkingly realistic levelness of vision with which we associate self-restraint and endurance, courage and rationality. As a first glance in a vision it is more controlled and contemplative than the fierce and anguished passion of Yeats who cries out: "So like a bit of stone I lie / Under a broken tree. / I could recover if I shrieked / My heart's agony / To passing bird, but I am dumb / From human dignity." Neither, on the other hand, is Frost's vision infected by Hardy's somber resignation in "Hap," nor is it levitated by Browning's robust spiritual afflatus in "Rabbi ben Ezra."

In his single-minded exploration of the common realities of human experience uncommonly realized, Frost's non-Platonist vision contemplates the world within the context of limitary zones, enclosing barriers, and confining walls. That the impersonal forces of nature are no more uniformly benevolent than they are actively hostile, he had early learned. And that the humanities represented the book of the unworthies as well as the worthies he is quite aware. But, in one respect, he is invariably and wholly American, believing, as he did, in the capacity of men to shape their destiny in an open-ended universe. Reacting to the dramatic changes in our time, he refocused and revised his views without losing his humanistic sanguinity, no matter how qualified his meliorism or paradoxical his view of the human condition. He did it with scrupulous craftsmanship in a personal idiom, handling the tones of speech as an emancipated traditionalist with dryly ironic quizzicality and playfully bantering humor.

The way to Frost's vision, like the pathway to truth for Stephen Crane's wayfarer, is a hazard of singular knives, but it has to be made through what Philip Rahv calls "dialectical relation" of text and context. Critics are quick to take positions. The sentimentalist and moralizer make an uplifter of Frost, the poet of "Birches" and "The Tuft of Flowers." The Freudian finds "The Subverted Flower" and "The Lovely Shall Be Choosers" protective screens for a dark side. When Lawrance Thompson's man of many masks goes unrecognized, the interpreter is thought to be simplistic. If the darker side recognized by Lionel Trilling is not emphasized, the interpreter is accused of failing to recognize depth. Or if Frost's sanguinity is stressed, the interpreters are forthwith ridiculed "as a whole dunciad of babbling innocence." While sentimentalism will surely tab Frost as a Saint Valentine's-card poet, a cold-eyed scientific impersonality will only leave the poems as exercises in ingenious evasion. Once, late in life, Frost said in a public lecture: "There's a dispute as to how dark I am. Some think I'm too dark; others think I'm not dark enough." What is needed is the finer distinction to distinguish what is comic from tragic to tragicomic.

As a poet with a speculative interest in ideas, Frost is referred to as a metaphysical lyricist. I can only think it must mean that the mode of his imagination does not represent a recording of realities, such, for example, as Stendhal meant when he called a novel "a mirror carried along the highway." Instead, the mode of his imagination represents a way of seeing and feeling the reality of the world as well as discovering what is common in experience but obscured perhaps by what Coleridge called "the film of familiarity," until his insight and idiom put it in common possession. To borrow a provocative phrase from Wallace Stevens, Frost engages his world as "the spirit's alchemiciana." This is surely what Frost means when he says of the poet's subject matter: "It should have happened to everyone but it should have occurred to no one before as material." As in "For Once, Then, Something" and "All Revelation," the eye of his heart and mind is speculatively inclined and responsive to the detection of the unexpected and unanticipated. If this is true of Frost, is it not likely to be true of his poems? He thought so. "My poems . . . are all set to trip the reader head foremost into the boundless."

Yet in inhabiting a self-admitted naturalistic universe, as in "Storm Fear" and "Stars," he doesn't thereby accept the naturalistic view of man as wholly at the mercy of a mechanistic process, as "The Demiurge's Laugh," "Willful Homing," and "Sand Dunes" testify. Man, an image-making creature, creates the metaphors by which he identifies his relationship to things. In "The White-Tailed Hornet," an example of Frost's empirical common sense, he reverses the admonitory adage: "Go to the ant, thou sluggard, consider her ways and be wise." He makes out a sound case for the unwisdom of ascribing infallibility to nonhuman creatures. Not self-deceived, this guarded meliorist refuses to minimize the difference between human and nonhuman animal behavior.

Although speculatively he uses a strategy of options to leaves *or* flowers ("Leaves Compared with Flowers"), to govern *or* not to govern ("Design"), chaos *or* order ("The Aim Was Song"), boundlessness *or* limits ("The Middleness of the Road"), mind *or* matter ("The Bear"), harmony *or* strife ("On Looking up by Chance"), most commonly he exercises what might be called a dialectic of contained contradiction. This dialectic has its source in psychological tensions; in a passionate ambition to succeed as a poet ("Into My Own"); in recognizing the gap in human relationships ("The Tuft of Flowers"); in counterbalancing prospects of the living and the finalities of the dead ("The Vantage Point"); in the pathos implied in change and loss ("Reluctance"). One of his most searching containments is the tension between the exercise of his natural talents and the assured respectability of professional success. Another, more inward and aesthetic, is the extroversion of a storytelling love of the dramatic and a lyricist's introvertive intensity. Other contained polarities personal to Frost include political conservatism and a cultural universalism, the agrarian dream and scientific thrust, classical culture and other-worldly Christianity, nationalism and localism. One of the most poignant images in his poetry—the alluring dark woods—is counterpointed by the rational image of home and human promises. Some of his finest lyric poetry played variations on this containment in an otherwise unsettling and profoundly private world where ambiguities can only be properly contained on the elastic leash of paradox.

In an open-ended universe, as opposed to a locked-in one, stability consists not necessarily in reconciliation or unity of opposites but rather in a containment of them. In part, this is what John Keats's insight in his *locus classicus* on "Negative Capability" implies, and what Emily Dickinson surely intends when she contends: "In insecurity to lie / Is joy's insuring quality." Frost's dialectic is therefore not quite the same thing as we find in Emerson's great principle of Undulation in nature. In the same sense that it realistically confronts tensions and conflicts, it is no less dynamic. Yet it makes no attempt at reconciliation of these. Consequently, in "Bond and Free," he contemplates the suspended opposites of love and thought; in "In a Poem," of rhythm and meter; in "On the Heart's Beginning to Cloud the Mind," of heart and mind; in "Fire and Ice," of desire (lust) and hate; in "The Master Speed," of motion and rest; in "The Lesson for Today," of the tragic and comic; in "The Egg and the Machine," of the organic and the mechanical; and in the preface to *King Jasper,* of seriousness and humor. It was characteristic that he held opposing aspects of belief and opinion in a dialectical tension.

Precisely in this containment—not reconciliation—of opposites Frost is most idiosyncratic and possibly most American. In "The Bear," "The Thinker," and "Leaves Compared with Flowers," he refines Emerson's polarity theory in a seriocomic dialectic. He contains, he does not reconcile, Emerson's "shining abstractions." Armored with an ingenious and agile wit, he evokes a teasing image of the Secret that sits in the middle and knows. What the Secret knows is containment of passion and reason, alienation and sympathy, the irrationalities of life and Whitman's "primal sanities" of nature. Containment is the essence of his metaphysical lyric. He can barely resist the hypnotic spell of the dark woods, the beckoning tree branch, "the vague dream-heads," the thrush in the forest, and keep his eyes on the stars he looks for. How self-revealing he is when he tells a friend (Louis Mertins), "Maybe I'm one who never makes up his mind." Either on principle or from temperamental restlessness and intellectual curiosity, he was always taking and revising positions. Yet, fundamentally, his poetry does assume a posture—the sense sounds make. As a metaphysical lyricist he speculates on the realities of the world, he doesn't try to reform it.

He made little bits of clarity out of a familiar north-of-Boston world, a performance which constituted an evocation of a psychic situation and an imaginative order. Like a gray worsted thread, his poetry—especially the ecologic monologues and dialogues—stitched into the Joseph's many-colored coat of native literature a gum-gathering "isolato" from "higher up in the pass," locked-in codists of the hayfield, warped back-country survivors of a grim upland existence often broken by solitude and loneliness. But the world he received was not refracted in "views."

Where traditional life consists in memory, custom, and expectations, the problem is how to handle disjunctive contraries without temporizing. Inclined naturally to dialectical play among distinctions and options, as a shrewd equilibrist he shied away from trying to impose a facile resolution or effect an easy reconcilement. Just as dramatic dialogues and monologues swing on a dialectical axis of equilibration, so also do the lyrics, except that in the latter the give-and-take is commonly within the poet and not, as in the former, between people. Yet facile finality appears in neither dialogue nor lyric. Unlike the eupeptic Browning's *sursum corda* in "Prospice" and the "Epilogue to Asolando," Frost adjusted to the uncertainties of a complex world and said empirically: "But the strong are saying nothing until they see." Frost balances the contraries not only in poetic content but also in the formal tension between cadenced language and metrical beat, as he wrote in "How Hard It Is to Keep from Being King": "Regular verse springs from the strain of rhythm / Upon a meter, strict or loose iambic."

Containment implies a relational rather than a conflictive stance. When, for instance, consciousness divides into separable categories of good and bad, he preferred a unitary consciousness in which states of good and bad were distinguishable *within* the individual or context of the event. In "To a Young Wretch," he called this concept "opposing goods." Who, for example, shall say in "Home Burial" whether it is the husband *or* the wife who is good or bad? In "The Death of the Hired Man," who is to say that Silas is the responsibility of Warren and Mary any more than he is of his well-to-do-brother—"A somebody—director in the bank"?

Examples of equilibration appear frequently in his personal reactions. When F. D. R.'s four freedoms rallied a New Deal, Frost satirically magnified the freedoms to two and twenty, as though he could contain all of them. When Sandburg published *The People, Yes* (1936), he tartly countered, "the people, yes *and* no," in acknowledgment of differences which he could contain. When informed that virtue favors rural life, he curtly corrected the balance: "I'm city and country," yet acknowledged, "I'm a little more country than city." Quick to assert the right to be his own man—a revisionist of conventional approaches, orthodoxies, and inflexible commitment—he contended: "I'm not answerable for anything," which hardly seems to be the stance of a disequilibrist. He believed in wisdom and counterwisdom. "Truth," he stated emphatically, "is a dialogue," a perspectival position different from that of the dogmatic adherent of revealed truth.

Finally Frost's position is not remotely related to Emerson's or Whitman's or T. S. Eliot's in this respect. In his "Ode to W. H. Channing," Emerson assumed a position above the demands of a specific group, believing he could not leave his "honied thought" either for "the priest's cant" or the "statesman's rant." Frost did not associate himself metaphysically, like Whitman, with a "float forever held in solution," or as claustrally seek sanctuary in Eliot's mystical "still point." Least of all would he have supported a position of cancellation where differences are annulled. Equilibration, as a counterview to a closed universe where tomorrow would be predictably an extension of the present, rejects the fixed position as inflexible. Among options and alternatives, the virtue of an equilibrist's position is its flexibility. Where acceleration and change are in the order of things, where everything slips or cracks or fades rapidly in the general flux, the main thing as a humanistic equilibrist is not to lose one's balance. "It's well to have all kinds of feelings," Frost told his friend Sidney Cox, self-revealingly summing up the nub of human relationship, "for this is all kinds of a world."

2.

To illustrate the spectrum of Frost's containment, "A White-Tailed Hornet" serves as an example of one extreme of his speculative spectroscopy. In this case, say, at the infrared extreme, his exercise of logic in a revisionary empiricism in testing Fabre's thesis in *Souvenirs entomologiques* of the remarkable adequacies in the instincts and habits of insects is briefly summarized. This represents a containment of two positions and the repudiation of one. He inherited an old wives' tale, that insect instinct is infallible, man's is not, but after observing a white-tailed hornet mistake a nailhead for a fly and even a little huckleberry for a fly, he thought "this whole instinct matter" might bear revision. The point of the poem is, however, not so much the containment of two positions as it is, speculatively, a calling in question of the tendency of homo sapiens, time out of mind, to ascribe unerring certainty to instinct.

In another, shorter, sixteen-line poem, "Our Doom to Bloom," Frost is himself exercising a poet's instinct for generalization—in this case, on the function of the state. In this serio-lighthearted comment the method is to release through the medium of the prophetess—the wise old Cumaean sibyl—the generalization that "the state's one function is to give." The analogical object lesson is from the world of nature when growth and its ensuing ripening and fruitage are in the order of things. "Our Doom to Bloom" is an effective illustration of the envelope of containment. It reads:

> Cumaean Sibyl, charming Ogress,
> What are the simple facts of Progress
> That I may trade on with reliance
> In consultation with my clients?
> The Sibyl said, "Go Back to Rome
> And tell your clientele at home
> That if it's not a mere illusion
> All there is to it is diffusion—
> Of coats, oats, votes, to all mankind.
> In the Surviving Book we find
> That liberal, or conservative,
> The state's one function is to give.
> The bud must bloom till blowsy blown
> Its petals loosen and are strown;
> And that's a fate it can't evade
> Unless 'twould rather wilt than fade."

Although the origin of "Our Doom to Bloom" is anyone's guess, whether a historical anecdote or a contemporary event directly observed and comtemplated, it satisfies the poet's notion of making "a generalization that's a little concatenation of things you picked up from God knows where."

In the second century B.C., the Sibylline Books arrived in Rome from Cumae, an ancient city a dozen miles west of Naples. Founded by the Greeks as early as the eighth century B.C., it was celebrated particularly for its oracular cave, where, as Virgil wrote in *Ecologue 4*, the old sibyl prophesied. Her bundle of nine Sibylline Books was left in Rome where several were purchased and buried for safekeeping in the temple of Jove. Much consulted, these books finally perished in the fire of 82 B.C. So when the Roman citizen visits the sibyl to learn from her the facts about progress, he has turned, as it were, to a well-established arcane authority, not to an experimental one like, say, Aristotle in his *Politics* or Thucydides in the great history of the Peloponnesian War. The little parable raises the question of authority, but as a "positional" prophecy it gives an unequivocal direction. The democratic principle, based on the general welfare and blessings of *vox populi*, is that of *diffusion*—"Of coats, oats, votes, to all mankind." Now these are the services of the welfare state, whether liberal *or* conservative, whose principle is supported by doctrinal Christianity's advocacy of the abundant life.

This poem suggests the containment of the implied opposite. No matter how confirming the natural life cycle of the flower may be as an analogue for the functioning of our man-made political organization, if the doom of the flower is to bloom and then fade, or else, in sterility, wilt, a similar fate irrevocably confronts the state—except that to give or to shrivel, diffusion or aggrandizement, are in the natural order. As a poetic anecdote, Frost's little parable might be read as a justification of the Marshall Plan, when in 1947 our secretary of state, George C. Marshall, announced a foreign aid program, which advanced over thirteen million dollars to help the war-ravaged nations of western Europe. This generous and unsordid democratic gesture enabled postwar Europe to make a more rapid economic recovery. Yet in another sense Frost may be playing slyly with another view. His parable may also contain the opposite of the wise old Cumaean sibyl's suggestion: the state which operates, not with the generosity of social security, medical care, old-age compensations, but with a stern Puritan work ethic and a *realpolitik* of power politics in the totalitarian state.

As we move from infrared to ultraviolet on the spectrum, "Take Something Like a Star" (originally, "Choose Something Like a Star") is illustrative of the stabilizing of a positional containment so that gyroscopically "we may take something like a star / To stay our minds on and be staid." Frost's containment is dynamic, not in the sense of resolving contraries but in the sense of stabilizing the contraries *within* the human condition in an open-ended universe. For those who like Ivan Karamazov want not millions of rubles but answers to their questions, Frost's containment may seem to be at best only a holding action and not a resolving of issues. Yet it may well be a cybernetic solution in a changing world of shifting values, not because of any self-compensating resistance to the stresses in contraries but simply because of his ability to contain these stresses without inducing neuroses or paranoid complexes. I also think Frost's containment shows the honesty of writers who refuse to succumb to easy answers and who thereby do not fail us by a mindless mirroring of reality.

For his key idea in "Take Something Like a Star" Frost found an objective correlative for fixity where everything is in motion in the content of science. Once, he referred to a pendulum he had seen swinging back and forward under a tall dome, "and so sort of almost detached from the earth that it fell behind the movement of the earth." Then he made his conjecture. "You know," he asked, "what they're going to do in the end? They're going to find some way of leaving something behind while the world whirls under it, to get more force in the world than they've ever had before. . . . Out of little things like that, you know, the future comes. It's coming out of that, I'm sure; I don't say how." Frost was referring to the Foucault pendulum, when Jean Foucault first demonstrated in 1851 the rotation of the earth by means of a graduated disk which was seen to turn while a pendulum freely suspended maintained its plane of oscillation. In clarification, when Frost suggested getting more force in the world, what he really meant was not so much force as a better reference. In other words, in the future man will establish, as the scientist did for motion, some basic reference in historical or ideological terms.

"Take Something Like a Star" is a most revealing illustration of his containment, both ideologically and allusively. For example, he was certainly as concerned about the convergence of science and poetry as he was about their divergence. The ground on which they met was the area not only of form where numbers were common to both but also, allusively, of subject matter. "Take Something Like a Star" is a case in point. In its twenty-five lines it manages to refer to Keats's "Last Sonnet" ("Bright star, would I were steadfast as thou art—") and to include Shakespeare, Horace, and Catullus. In "Let me not to the marriage of true minds," Shakespeare's "ever-fixèd mark" is as steadfast as Keats's sleepless Eremite, and sonnet 116 in this great sequence was often quoted by Frost. The close of "Take Something Like a Star," Frost admitted, had "a sort of Horatian ending"; and once he said "the last part is almost the same as though it were out of

Horace—certain lines of Horace, I think." The "certain lines" were probably in the *Odes*—for example:

> Defeat true manliness can never know:
> Honors untarnished still it has to show.
>   Not taking up or laying office down
> Because the fickle mob will have it so.
>   [3.2; trans. Hugh Vibert MacNaughton]

or,

> To me, just Fate has granted one small farm,
> The tender spirit of the Grecian muse,
> And pow'r to shun the malice of the mob.
>   [2.16; trans. Enola Brandt]

or,

> Flee extremes, and choose thou the mean all-golden,
>   Treasure all priceless.
>   [2.10; trans. Margaret M. Fitzgerald]

"Neither Out Far nor In Deep" is at the ultraviolet extreme, where the containment of ambiguities is illustrated. It highlights the error in critical judgment which follows any attempt to make reductive in his philosophic position what was essentially pluralistic in an open-ended universe. For it was a universe wide without being vague, unpredictable without being absurd, and continuous in its ramifying process without being mechanical. But what *is* "Neither Out Far nor In Deep" saying? It seems to suggest affirmation. The last two lines—"But when was that ever a bar / To any watch they keep?"—appear to confirm the belief in the stamina of human effort. Is there anything to match human determination to meet trials and endure ordeals, even those not easily understood?

It was, however, Frost's habit to say, not recite, his poems, so the "voice tones" could be heard. The meaning in "Neither Out Far nor In Deep" should in part come from the way it is heard. For instance, isn't the voice speaking ironically in the last stanza? "But when was that ever a bar / To *any* watch they keep?" might be considered negative in tone. It might imply that even with our scientific instruments what, indeed, can we *see* either out far (with telescope) or in deep (with microscope)? Interpreted affirmatively "look" would be stressed. "They cannot *look* out far. / They cannot *look* in deep." Interpreted negatively "cannot" would be stressed. "They *cannot* look out far. / They *cannot* look in deep."

"All the fun's in how you say a thing," Frost wrote emphatically in "The Mountain." All the meaning is in how you *say* a poem. I am not contending the poem implies distrust of the staying power of human nature. But I am contending it implies the strictly limited aspect of both man's *senses*—note the use of the indefinite "look" rather than the definite "see"—*and* his *intellect* (in "far" and "deep"). How more circumscribed can man be than in his inability to see deeply into as well as far out?

Yet this is not a pessimistic poem. It faces the dual facts of human limitations and destiny unblinkingly. No matter how formidable the situation, the poet withholds judgment as to the ultimate outcome. Man may yet make the best of a difficult situation. When someone asked the cleric-politician, the Abbé Sieyes, what he had done during the days of terror in the French Revolution, he replied, "Ah, Monsieur, I survived." One can at least learn to accommodate to one's limitations and one can still make further attempts to understand who and what we are. "But as far as we can and as deep as we can," Frost said in a Bread Loaf talk, "still we penetrate into matter, further into matter."

This is a second possible interpretation of the poem—not to imply it is the more accurate one. But there is an ambiguity in the last stanza—the possibility of unforced choice. If the reader wants to take the words affirmatively, that is his affair. If he wants to take them negatively, that, too, is a matter of opinion. Yet he cannot dodge one haunting fact: the poet fulfills his obligation as poet by suggesting possibilities, not by nailing down a statement like Luther hammering a thesis to the court door at Wittenberg. "The poet expects," Frost has said, "to leave the poem more felt than said." So it is here.

In form and texture this poem does exactly what a poem is expected to do. By suggestion it evokes meaning. It does it simply and naturally in a trinity of sound, image, and idea: these three in conjunction, not in isolation.

By definition a poet is a craftsman just as he is a sensibilitist with a particular vision of human experience. In this deceptively simple lyric, Frost, the craftsman, communicates a vision of experience. His lyric begins with familiar objects—people sitting on the beach and looking seaward. While looking, these people sight a distant offshore object—a passing ship. They observe close by a standing gull reflected on "the wetter ground like glass"—certainly a fresh image and valid in circumstantial detail. Here is the evidence of a telescopic view, the offshore ship, and here too is our microscopic view, the nearby gull. These two views encompass the far-and-near view of dimensional man.

In the third stanza the poet plays with the variousness of land *and* sea.

> The land may vary more;
> But wherever the truth may be—
> The water comes ashore,
> And the people look at the sea.

He uses the prestigious abstraction "truth" to underscore mystery inherent in the variousness of land and sea. The land, which may vary more, evokes an image of the great, immeasurable, surrounding mystery of the natural universe. Both land and sea are significantly compounded in a symbol of implied boundlessness.

I note, too, that unremittingly the eternal tides keep at their work. "The water comes ashore, / And the people look at the sea." Natural processes are not affected by purblind human rumination or even by human interest and natural curiosity or yet by human perception; the large and important business of nature external to man continues uninterruptedly. Although an awareness of the natural process independent of man is not a remarkable insight, it is an apposite one. In the great range country of the Atomic Energy Commission test site northwest of Las Vegas, Nevada, where nuclear explosions have been made, the living things of the desert have returned. Where some of the bombs were exploded the atomized soil stimulated a resurgence of natural growth. Not only is the growth of the tumbleweeds extraordinarily luxuriant but the local reptiles and animals—the red foxes, snakes, and rodents—are doing all right. Frost is aware of the continuance of natural processes in "The Last Mowing," "The Birthplace," and "Sand Dunes."

The two superficially casual lines, "They cannot look out far. / They cannot look in deep," help to reinforce the point in the pregnant last stanza. For the land, which we assume we can control more readily than the sea, is just as opaque to human clairvoyance. In fact, land and sea represent a microcosm into which man with all his scientific and metaphysical pretension *cannot* look deeply. Yet, ironically, this limitation is no bar—nor should it ever be. The word *bar* is Frost's escape clause. As Goethe once said: "A man must cling to the belief that the incomprehensible is comprehensible; otherwise he would not try to fathom it." In his double way Frost is not only underscoring the limitations of the human intellect, he is also suggesting a humanistic position of containment. If I can look neither out far nor in deep—if both my reason and my senses are fallible—I can surely restrain myself within the limits of the comprehensible and by so doing find where the problems and principles of the universe apply.

"Neither Out Far nor In Deep" implies neither withdrawal nor denial of intellectual assertion. True, the vision is not exuberantly romantic, like Shelley's in the last stanza of "Prometheus Unbound," nor does it, at the other extreme, negate human effort. It represents, in effect, a vision of human enlightenment. The last stanza has what any good poem must have—inevitability. The use of "watch" is masterly since it evokes the connotative biblical image which haunted Thomas Hardy: "Watchman, what of the night?" (Isaiah 21:11). It implies at least a speculative trust. In the last go-down, Frost is saying people will still assert their courage and trust in their circumscribed senses, fallible intellect, limited energies, and conditional perceptions. They will stick it out, come volcanic or atomic hell *or* high Noachian tidal water.

In "Neither Out Far nor In Deep" the pathos of the human situation stands out. Just as this is not a cozy poem softening the blow of human inadequacy, neither is it a shrill one exhibiting the plight of man in a scornful way. As a matter of fact, the tone is so moderate the effect only gradually takes hold; but the implications in the effect are disturbing. Why? Because, despite the poet's sentiment in "Mowing," here it is not a sweet dream of which we become aware but a stern and stubborn truth that the vigil of the people on the beach —the human situation—is a blind and irredeemable trust of the heart. Evoked clearly, simply, and effectively is the contained image of human limitation—a truly searching one—but *without* despair, so what is seen is felt and what is felt is true. The human situation is not despicable; it is not a state of sloth; rather, it is a state of vigilance. You cannot look out far, you cannot look in deep. You would if you could but you can't; so you prepare to make the best of it. You trust in what you do see. You keep "watch," which implies vigilance, just as "bar" implies obstruction. Your acceptance is not, at least, a meek acquiescence.

3.

How does his vision relate to time and space? Frost had a sustaining past, a recognizable present, and a sensitive presentiment of the future. In "the trial by existence," before he could fulfill his passion as a

289

poet, he had to overcome self-doubt, find a poetic form and language for his subject matter, and attract an audience. Non-Cartesian in his relationship to time, he views its moments not as independent entities but as particular instants which are transformed into a continuous plurality. By shifting a spatial position, instants and views are multiplied. In time, Frost exercises the human prerogative of reflective detachment and his vantage point is a sunburned slope "and lolling juniper" where he could reflect on both "the white homes of men" and "the graves of men on an opposing hill"; and where, characteristically, he could in his spatial ambience turn on his arm and smell the earth and look into the crater of an ant. In "Neither Out Far nor In Deep," the people along the sand turn their backs on the land and look steadily at the sea. They are not, however, unaware of the land which "may vary more." If people are victims of an inflexible posture, looking outward in limited and depthless sight, it is by choice, not by a throw of chance. In "The Vantage Point," Frost guides the reflective mind in the implications of "wherever the truth may be," toward either land as empirical truth or sea as the focus of a speculative search for truth.

There is no sense in Frost as in Emerson of the eye trying to take in the whole field of spatial vision. This might suggest either, at one extreme, myopia or, at the other, native caution. In a complex, open-ended universe, with its contradictions and paradoxes, Frost, rather than trying to conciliate or enforce union, tries only to comprehend and contain variables and possibilities. In "The Armful," his pragmatic solution of trying to handle "extremes too hard to comprehend at once" is to drop the armful of packages in the road and restack his load. Variants of this view appear in "One Step Backward Taken" and "A Drumlin Woodchuck." Obviously he operates rationally within recognizable temporal and spatial limits, assuming what Joubert called "a temporal *perspective.*" In "The Middleness of the Road" the ton of car has nothing to do with "absolute flight and rest," which the horizontal sky and woods suggest. The self-restricted machine is grooved to its natural thoroughfare. What is true of the symbolic car in our technological era is equally applicable to the limits and bounds of the natural world in "There Are Roughly Zones" or "Good-By and Keep Cold," where nature's fruits, symbolized by peach and apple trees, are meteorologically restricted in their nature. Man, moved by this "limitless trait," can press his luck too far as orchardists often learn from experience.

The key to Frost's thought is the angle of vision from which the common in experience is perceptively seen. In the rhythm of duration he drew restrained transports—"favors," he called them—from the fugitive moments in present realities. Typical of his perceptiveness is a humorous playfulness, all the more disarming because often it hides a second space of interior reality. "A Winter Eden" has deceptive subtlety. In Frost's paradisal stronghold, where conies and birds consort in midwinter, the tender bark of a wild apple tree and last year's barberries "shining scarlet red" provide an ever-normal granary. Here everything is serene and reposeful. Since silence is uninterrupted by raucous cries or exuberant song, lassitude and sleep are in order. Detached, uncrowded, and identified by absence of frantic agitation, time, which encapsulates this microcosmic garden world is identified by short bursts of activity succeeded by pauses, rests, and terminations.

> This Eden day is done at two o'clock.
> An hour of winter day might seem too short
> To make it worth life's while to wake and sport.

There is, as Frost once acknowledged, "a hint" in "A Winter Eden" of an ulterior idea, which he did not identify but which seems to be calling in question the efficacy of the Puritan work ethic. The space-time images favor a prelapsarian Eden in an exclusively nonhuman environment. The reality of northern time (winter) transmutes a solid and credible space (an alder swamp) into a paradise. In effect, the real is transmuted into the ideal. But since the natural paradise of the world of bird and creature is not to be equated with the artificial world of the machine, it would do violence to attempt to humanize the ideal. However, a parabolic commentary is not precluded. After the Aesopian fashion, the natural world bears similitude to human behavior. Space is not a void and nullity but a condition of survival—for eating and sleeping—in a congealing environment. The temporal mode, vertical rather than horizontal, is an ascent by incremental snowfalls. In the frost, cold, and snow the meager solar light is compensated by the polar night with its additive of longer hours of diurnal sleep. In this earthly paradise, during the few available hours of winter light vivacious romps spell extended repose. "A Winter Eden" emphasizes a prevalence in Frost's poetry of the spatial concept which shrewdly makes a point of human prudence in keeping snug in the limitless; a concept exclusive of daring neither in space ("—on-penetration / Into earth and skies," says Frost in "Kitty Hawk") nor in time ("We have ideas yet that we haven't tried," he says in "Riders"). "A Winter Eden" hints much more in a spectrum of opposites of meteorological cold and heat, atmospheric light and dark, seasonal winter and memory of spring, ecological economy, sexual dormancy and seasonal mating, ideological ambiguities of natural and man-made worlds.

"Desert Places" expresses effectively the difference between spiritual and physical reality. When confronted with the expressionless vacuity of whiteness—not dissimilar from Melville's "heartless voids and immensities of the universe"—Frost experiences cosmic loneliness; he is included "unawares." Unlike the elderly protagonist in "An Old Man's Winter Night," who reacts restively to "All out of doors that looked darkly in at him," Frost contrasts psychological finiteness with the cosmic abstraction of spatial infinity in interstellar space, and, significantly, with no mention of divine immensity. He wrote:

> They cannot scare me with their empty spaces
> Between stars—on stars where no human race is.
> I have it in me so much nearer home
> To scare myself with my own desert places.

Just as Frost's relationship to time was non-Cartesian, so his relationship to space was non-Pascalian. Among his *pensées*, Pascal said, "le silence éternel de ces espaces infinis m'effraie." But the eternal silence of infinite space did not terrify Frost no matter how vividly he was aware of it. Without bravado, he contained the physical reality of space, but he was less assured about containing the spiritual reality of interior space. The terrifying vastness of exterior space was incomparable with the exacerbating intensities of interior space and the *angst* of our human condition. These two aspects of space—the exterior and the interior—are forever to be distinguished without accommodation and without trauma. The view in "Desert Places" is all the more arresting since in an earlier poem, "Stars," the separation between exterior and interior space was equated with isolation *and* alienation.

> And yet with neither love nor hate,
>   Those stars like some snow-white
> Minerva's snow-white marble eyes
>   Without the gift of sight.

"Desert Places" suggests that linear fall of time may have catastrophic historical consequences, but symbolically the psychological fall in space is not only vertiginous, it is also appalling. No more incisive illustration of this view can be found than in the closing lines of "The Impulse" in "The Hill Wife":

> Sudden and swift and light as that
>   The ties gave,

292

And he learned of finalities
Besides the grave.

Such a fall—such a "crack-up"—in interior space is summed up in Victor Hugo's aphorism in *The Man Who Laughs:* "All that is in the abyss is in man."

"Carpe Diem" succinctly states Frost's relationship to the remembered past, the perceived present, and the possibilities in the future.

But bid life seize the present?
It lives less in the present
Than in the future always
And less in both together
Than in the past.

But why not the present?

The present
Is too much for the senses,
Too crowding, too confusing—
Too present to imagine.

The poet's reaction implies the present moment can be overly dilated and in its exaggeration tend to boggle the mind. In relationship to the past, Frost shows no particular Proustian awakening of the emotions which the senses extract from time as in the memorable scent of hawthorn, sound of footsteps upon a gravel path, sight of a water bubble formed at the side of a water plant by the current. Instead, there is accessibility to a prehistoric past whose ancients, through archaeological diggings, send to the poet across the million years of the Ice Age a little ocher pebble wheel—"Two round dots and a ripple streak / So vivid as to seem to speak." In "Desert Places," the terrors of outer space are displaced by interior space. Similarly, in "A Missive Missile," the meaning in a stone age is muted into incoherence by the temporal distance. An "aeon-limit" precludes communication. "It cannot speak as far as this." Once again the world of bounds and limits appears prominently in time or space.

How does Frost envisage the future? Not, certainly, with Whitman's anticipatory imagination. In "It Is Almost the Year Two Thousand," "A Case for Jefferson," and "An Answer," he skeptically exposes the fantastic hopes of social thinkers and sentimentalists alike who envisage "the true Millennium" and the Isles of the Blessèd. Frost might even find himself agreeing with Freud in *Civilization and Its Discontents.* "Men are proud of those achievements," wrote Freud of an extraordinary advance in natural science, "and have a right to be. But they seem to have observed that this newly-won power over space and time, this subjugation of the forces of nature, which is the fulfillment of a longing that goes back thousands of years, has not increased the amount of pleasurable satisfaction which they may expect from life and has not made them feel happier." Although Frost is no soothsayer presuming to see across voids and over obstacles into unknown futures, he is sanguine. In "Kitty Hawk" the promise in the future is given a reverse twist; it is translated from spiritual terms into material.

> But God's own descent
> Into flesh was meant
> As a demonstration
> That the supreme merit
> Lay in risking spirit
> In substantiation.

This is "our instinctive venture." The homely imagery of spire and belfry in "A Steeple on the House" confirms Frost's reading of future time, at one level at least, as spiritual.

The linkage of the three aspects of time emphasizes his reading of temporality, not as an aggregation of successive instants, but as the transformation of particular instants into poems, which, taken together, contribute to the coherence, persistence, and continuity of design in his poetry. Two prose analogies illustrate this thrust. In "The Figure a Poem Makes," he said: "Like giants we are always hurling experience ahead of us to have the future with against the day when we may want to strike a line of purpose across it somewhere." In this highly enlarged motile, space-time image, the emphasis is on acquired experience and self-determining decision. Man can know, man can decide what to do with what he knows, Frost thinks. And the second analogy occurred when, speaking of a poet's insights, he borrowed the metaphor of the constellations from astronomy. "It is like the stars coming out in the early evening . . . ," he said. "It is later in the dark of life that you see forms, constellations." To illustrate, the reader sees how the poet reacted to boundaries early in life in "Mending Wall," and how later in life he reacted to them in "An Answer," and "Triple Bronze." Separately the poems represent flashes of stellar insight; together, they constellate.

In writing, as Graham Greene once said, there is a moment of crystallization "when the dominant theme is plainly expressed, when the private universe becomes visible even to the least sensitive reader." Graham Greene's assumption is predicated on the idea that in the part as well as in the sum of the parts we find an essential design. Yet may not the design be in the whole which, in its complexity, is greater than the sum of the parts? "The separateness of parts," Frost said, "is equally as important as the connection of the parts." Ten years later he asserted that "every single one of the poems has its design symbol," which confirms a continuing awareness in the beautiful similitude of insight. Frost did not compose his poems to fit a prearranged plan, but, like the separate stars, they finally constellated. A compelling force—a calling—may have "predestined" the constellations, and indeed seems to have done precisely this, but the constelled patterns were "unforeseen."

Surely Frost's metaphor, which suggests unconscious intent and fortuitous combination of variant themes in constellated clusters, supports Graham Greene's crystallizing moment. He did not resemble Zola who, at an early age, sat down and wrote the history of the Rougon-Macquart families with great thoroughness and exactitude of detail. On the contrary, from the beginning there was an unconscious, even if vague, ambiguous, and tentative thrust toward an ultimate design of which the poet was not completely aware. It is even possible to identify the unconscious, subtle, and reticent motivation with what the poet called "a passionate preference" for those atomistic facts in human experience which are the solid substance of his poetic vigil. What we as readers feel, and Frost as creator felt, is, in Emerson's words, "the ravishment of the intellect by coming nearer to the fact." The painful and shattering experiences, as well as the deeply lovely and abiding ones which Frost felt, charge with meaning the constelled designs of trees, flowers, webs, walls, and stars.

The metaphor of the constellated sky must not be pressed too hard. "I know," the poet admitted in "Education by Poetry," "the metaphor will break down at some point, but it has not failed everywhere." Although he was referring to the metaphor of evolution, his comment is generally applicable. The Whole—that is, the *Gestalt*, or design—is not really prior to the parts. Frost wrote poems, as he says, to resolve problems. "You know I've always said: every poem solves something for me." There are, in consequence, groups or clusters of poems on fear and loneliness, on death and escape, on nature and self and limits to knowledge which thematically constellate.

The climactic point in reading Frost originates in the simultaneity of the vision of separability and inseparability, of part and whole, of specific and general, of fact and implication, of distant and near, of star and constellation. This *is* the Grand Design. Becomingly, it gives us a sense of mystery of stellar space where the poet projects a human identity. In the psychological struggle with experience Frost gradually discerned a clarification of order, and an association of one poem with another. It is indeed like the stars coming out; only in the dark of life are the forms patent. The constellated sky—*Complete Poems*—at last will hold them all.

Finally, how does Frost react to the negative time of destruction and absence? In "The Times Table," the farmer associates time with the straining sigh of his mare when it stops at a watering trough after the long uphill pull. "A sigh for every so many breath, / And for every so many sigh a death. / That's what I always tell my wife / Is the multiplication table of life." However, the poet is unwilling to accept this fatalistic observation on the inevitability of death. He prefers the more affirmative image of the stream in "West-running Brook," where, in the movement of the white wave running counter to itself, Frost sees a "backward motion toward the source, / Against the stream"; a token of what "most we see ourselves in"; a tribute of the current to the sources. This sanguine image and its variants appear often in the poems, whether in "On a Tree Fallen across the Road," "Willful Homing," "Directive," or elsewhere. Not fecklessness or renunciation or lassitude but energy of will—drive, thrust, purposefulness—keynotes the tonality of time in his poetry.

CHAPTER 23
A Reviewal

You have me there, but loosely as I would be held.
"Not Quite Social"

In this reading of Robert Frost, it is the man as poet, contributing importantly to a native literature who has chiefly interested me. Consequently, I have rallied my points of clarification wherever possible from his own statements and tried to give these a critical perspective and a close examination. A man's respect for art is detectable in the high place he gives originality and initiative in the order of things. The originality and initiative which Frost asked for his country are tokens of his own claim to a place in literature. Yet exactly how original and unique is he?

Throughout this extended essay I have been aware of at least two qualifiers. First, the only justification of an interpretive statement is in its enabling us to understand and enjoy more fully the fruits of genius. And secondly, although it is unlikely any interpretation, no matter how convincing, will ever satisfy one who has already a fixed image of the poet in mind, it should help to quicken a reader's interest in testing the validity of parallel views.

In the twentieth century, isolation and estrangement from an indifferent public are stubborn realities when we recall Eliot's early life in London and how finally in *The Waste Land* he impressed upon his time the central image of alienation from a cultural past, and Yeats at Thoor Ballylee, estranged from the society of his time in a ruined Norman tower, near the Gregory estate in Ireland.

That similarly isolation and alienation clouded Frost's career is not as certain despite the rough journeying to poetic success during the first forty years of his life. This fact is certainly one of the most publicized in his career. Isolation must have been often felt by Frost. Yet how much of a factor was it in retarding his acceptance? Stoically, he learned to live with what had to be faced, but surely "back in those lonely days" at Franconia and Derry isolation compensatorily provided a necessary if protracted interval in which to acquire self-discipline, practice technique, and deeply reflect. But Frost's New Hampshire farmhouses are hardly the symbolic equivalent of Yeats's Thoor Ballylee, any more than a library at a chateau near Bordeaux or a chateau at Ferney represented an enforced isolation for Montaigne and Voltaire, respectively.

As long as a copy of Francis Palgrave's *Golden Treasury,* one of Frost's favorite books, was available, isolation, enforced or voluntary, was endurable. In *The Golden Treasury* the presence of the great poetic tradition of the past was experienced, not like a turbulence in the charged air but inwardly and deeply like a current in a broad stream. Palgrave's companionable book Frost later described as "almost without animus" and one that contained "the top of poetry." It was, in fact, "a gem of a little book of poetry." Palgrave, however, was scarcely a substitute for a responsive cultural public or for the fellowship of practitioners of a highly specialized craft. Not until the Little Iddens days in Gloucestershire in 1914 did Frost experience anything comparable to Yeats's Rhymers' Club. Yet, in Yeats's case, to be in the company of Lionel Johnson and Ernest Dowson was only to share the company of fellow Melvillean "isolatoes." While, at Little Iddens, Frost, who was in the company of congenial independents like Lascelles Abercrombie, W. W. Gibson, and especially Edward Thomas, did not then suffer the whims and exacerbations of "isolatoes." Unlike Yeats, who was not in the Dublin gunfights, Edward Thomas fought in the British army and died in combat on Easter Monday at Vimy Ridge in 1917. Thomas seemed no more than Frost to be isolated or alienated. This is not to say Frost had not realized the indifference of a reading public. But in England, thanks to Ezra Pound, he made his original breakthrough in book publication; and later, in the United States, made a similar breakthrough with a generous assist from Amy Lowell in the *New Republic.*

Why was Frost not alienated from his country? Is the answer not found in the man, in his pedagogic gift, and also partly in luck which enabled him to catch on as a teacher at Derry and Plymouth, at Amherst and Michigan, with the frailest of formal requirements and the realest of natural talents? Gifted with a rare talent for putting unorthodox ideas effectively in circulation, he avoided an entrapment which might have resulted in prolonged isolation and insufferable alienation. The essential point to be made is that while teaching, Frost, sharply aware of isolation and alienation in human nature during "those lonely days," turned these outward to his advantage in his poetry. A compassionate sympathy, albeit objectively controlled, enabled him to intensify the psychological effects of environment, especially in the back country north of Boston. In the mental suffering of the protagonist in "The Housekeeper," there is a sense of the common tie, just as there is in the more obvious expression of sympathy for "the Broken One" in "The Self-Seeker." In "An Old Man's Winter Night," as we watch the elderly protagonist go through the ritual gestures of an evening, we experience the sharp shock of recognition in the juxtaposition of an indifferent cosmic solitude and personal loneliness. The imaginative significance of Frost's poetic insight is inward and psychological, not external and behavioristic.

Frost's kind of truth is to be distinguished from, say, Pound's in the Cantos in several ways, but especially in kinds of people. The rural mower, for example, in "The Tuft of Flowers" is no Renaissance condottiere like Sigismundo Malatesta, no shaper of historical events like Jefferson. He is indeed as close to anonymity as it is possible to get without loss of felt recognition in his humanity. What the companion to the mower feels in "The Tuft of Flowers" is sheer morning gladness, a private experience. Pound's Sigismundo Malatesta gave the orders, and horsemen and footmen went into action. He is a powerful condottiere, a devotee of art, and an adversary of Pope Pius II, who excommunicated him. Jefferson is the national leader, who, in a stroke of genius, acquired the Louisiana territory and masterminded the Lewis and Clark expedition. Pound is thus more historical and Frost is more psychological and autobiographical in context.

What Frank Kermode in *Romantic Image* has written of our changing times, Frost saw clearly. "All that has happened . . . is that the wicked have discovered the lost intensity of the good," writes Kermode, "the world has become, as no one could foresee, more murderous as well as darker." Yet I do not think a sense of either personal isolation or alienation contributed to Frost's recognition of this view. In "Once by the Pacific" he anticipated a "darker" world where darkness is fatefully felt as a presentiment in the human heart. His perception of an essential darkness in life in "Acquainted with the Night," "Design," "The Hill Wife," or "The Housekeeper" has a long foreground in biblical literature, in Greek tragedy, in *Lear*. Yet to call Frost "a terrifying poet," as Lionel Trilling did, does not make him less acceptable to the readers of "Birches." James Dickey, following Randall Jarrell's "other Frost" and Trilling's "terrifying poet," asserts the best of Frost has to do with "darkness, confusion, panic, terror." But an equable interpretation can only add that the best of Frost not only effectively contained, in Emerson's phrase, "the odious facts" of experience but also effectively showed sanguinity, order, courage, sanity. To show this to be valid there are exemplary poems like "Directive," "Sitting by a Bush in Broad Sunlight," "Willful Homing," "The Onset," and "Riders," among others.

If we are asked how Frost's poetry should be taken, the answer is deceptively simple. Take it easy; don't read it hard. Almost in the same breath we must add, we only read it accurately when we understand what it communicates. Paradoxically, a poetry so simply read confounds by its complexity, judging by the differences in critical views. Some critics discriminate between the early and the later poetry in favor of the former. Those who read him as a regionalist rather than as a "realist" identify him as rustically oriented. His avoidance of emphatic commitment provoked an accusation of "spiritual drifting" and evasiveness. The absence of any big piece of resistance suggests that he has failed to impose upon his time any commanding literary image like Eliot's "waste land" and that he has failed to come to grips with the decadence of his culture, as Pound is thought to have done, if fragmentarily and somewhat incoherently, in the Cantos. He has been attacked by the socially minded critics for his illiberalism and antiintellectualism. Perhaps, in his ambiguities, there is a measure of validity in all of these negative criticisms. It is also true that a poet can be the victim of misplaced emphasis. Disparagement and piety can be equally persuasive personal stances, but neither represents a strongly objective position from which to project convincingly a wholly valid criticism of a poet.

To approach Frost's poetry as though it belonged only to the nineteenth century is to be the victim of this fallacy of misplaced emphasis. To be hypercritical of the poet as a traditionalist because he used conventional rhyme and meter fails to recognize the uses to which he put language in the devices of dramatic and lyric form. To write him off as one who believed in simple values, like independence, stoical courage, order, clarity, and reticence in the changing scene of our pluralistic epoch is to ignore his unremitting attempt to link these values with a permanent tradition, searchingly, contemplatively, and undogmatically. "Directive," with its parabolic frame and secular journeying, is a semireligious morality play. The couplets, like "Quantula" included in *A Witness Tree*, are his Tudor interludes; and in their biblical subject matter and trade-guild air of performance, the two *Masques* are his mystery plays.

To neglect his revelations because they seemed less perceptive of his time and because they were expressed more directly than Eliot's in *The Waste Land*, or because he appears less evocative in the use of the image than Pound and Eliot, or because, unlike them, he chose, following his English sojourn, *not* to sever his roots from a national

300

culture, suggests to me an egregious misplacement of emphasis. The most important criterion in poetry, whether we have in mind the anonymous "O Western Wind" or the great speech in *Macbeth*—"Tomorrow, and tomorrow, and tomorrow"—or "The Death of the Hired Man," must still be how deeply the poet's experience has been felt and how intensely, according to his capacity, the reader is moved by it.

Frost should be read for the feeling in his "numbers." He is important in American literature because he was a poet and not because he was a sometime upland New England farmer, a public lecturer to large and enthusiastic audiences, an imaginative, original teacher at Amherst College and the University of Michigan. If we ask what it is he brought into existence which we did not heretofore have, what shall we say? It can hardly be the region north of Boston "up where the trees grow short, the mosses tall." For already this region, and its fadeaway aspects described in "The Ghost House," had been competently described by the New England local colorists. Nor will Frost's special quality consist in the identification of the Yankee in poems like "Brown's Descent," "The Black Cottage," "The Gold Hesperidee," and all the others. This native breed of New Englander had long been recognized in the writings of Seba Smith and James Russell Lowell, in Sarah Orne Jewett and Mary E. Wilkins Freeman. Frost's innovation will be found precisely where we expect to find it in a poet, that is, in the words and the way they are renewed in idiom, image, and tone, where they communicate a "thought-felt" vision of human experience. A clue to this innovation is in the fact we do not generally recite his poems, we "say" them, borrowing a phrase from Yeats, with "the coming and going of the breath." How different, for example, is the Frostian conversational sound track from the traditional rhetorical one! Dramatically, Emerson writes in "The Snowstorm":

> .Announced by all the trumpets of the sky,
> Arrives the snow, and, driving o'er the fields,
> Seems nowhere to alight . . .

In "Desert Places," Frost "says":

> Snow falling and night falling fast, oh, fast
> In a field I looked into going past,
> And the ground almost covered smooth in snow,
> But a few weeds and stubble showing last.

301

Both Emerson and Frost write within the conventions of poetic form. What identifies Frost's stanza is not, as in Emerson's lines, the grandeur of metaphor that elevates a snow storm into universality, it is the simplicity of an image realized through the loosening and relaxing of metrical convention. The falling snow and drawing in of the evening take place directly and immediately before us in some familiar upland New England pasture. In the deceptive simplicity of such consummate art, language is one with felt experience.

What Frost has accomplished has been in part premised on luck and, in his case, the luck to endure far beyond the proverbial three-score years and ten. He endured from obscurity to recognition, sharpened his initiative on adversity, nourished his imagination on what is common in subject matter, like the back-country New England people and upland farms, the stretches of dark woods and the maple orchard, brooks and back meadows, stone walls and stars, birches and thrushes, and also, lest we forget, artifacts and Easter Island heads and Niels Bohr's atom. A reflective poet, he focused on a single-minded exploration of these common realities to be uncommonly realized through the resources of a craftsmanship refined to highly idiosyncratic style, and himself deeply moved he searched us with the poignant emotions of awkward sympathy, gnawing anxiety, and agonizing resignation as well as with the more familiar feelings expressed in a conversational idiom, sharp visual and auditory imagery, and rhythmic tone. In evidence, I cite the following examples.

> [Awkward sympathy]
> What good is he? Who else will harbour him
> At his age for the little he can do?
>   ["The Death of the Hired Man"]

> [Gnawing anxiety]
> I've been away once—yes, I've been away.
> The State Asylum.
>   ["A Servant to Servants"]

> [Agonizing resignation]
> Ah, when to the heart of man
>   Was it ever less than a treason
> To go with the drift of things
>   To yield with a grace to reason,
> And bow and accept the end
>   Of a love or a season?
>   ["Reluctance"]

[Familiar idiom]
What I like best's the lay of different farms.
    ["A Hundred Collars"]

[Visual imagery]
And now he comes again with clatter of stone,
And mounts the wall again with whited eyes
And all his tail that isn't hair up straight.
    ["The Runaway"]

[Auditory image]
She had no saying dark enough
    For the dark pine that kept
Forever trying the window-latch
    Of the room where they slept.
    ["The Oft-Repeated Dream"]

[Rhythmic tone]
Winds blow the open grassy places bleak.
    ["Atmosphere"]

Although the justification of Frost's claim on our attention as a major poet because of his use of language in a particular way has not gone unremarked upon, it deserves amplification. When, on May 10, 1961, a couple of years before his death, Frost read at Pierson College, Yale University, Prof. R.W.B. Lewis distinguished between what "The Silken Tent" meant and what Frost emphasized. Lewis, for example, in the Frost script for the Yales Series of Recorded Poets, stressed the subject of the poem—a lady—as "a moral type" while Frost stressed "the elaboration of a single conceit over the fourteen lines of a sonnet." When Lewis stressed the influence of Eve in "Never Again Would Birds' Song Be the Same," characteristically the poet stressed the appositional syntax. Once again the reader finds Frost's references to "Neither Out Far nor In Deep" as "a rhymy little thing," "a joke on microscope and telescope," applicable as they may be, still a bit of dust thrown in the eye.

Properly, however, the poet kept his eye on the form. Of "The Silken Tent," he said, "that's the free spirit," which is as much as anyone needed to say. Of "Away!" he said a little more, indicating what seemed important to him. "You know," he remarked, "the double interest in that ["Away!"] is those little stanzas; the same shape of stanzas but with different sentences in the vowels, posturing their way through, you know, squirming through. That's what I am interested in—taking the rhyme as if it wasn't there. As easy as that, you see. That's the game." Indeed, it was *his* game. He believed the poem existed in and for itself. This was the game, you *see*. The poem as a living thing was at the core of his reiterated definition of it as "a thought-felt thing."

When we ask further what the poet has added to the American imagination, it would hardly suffice to say "the sound of sense" because this has long been heard in the poetry of James Russell Lowell and in Whitman's "rasping speech of men." Nor would the social realism of his dramatic Yankee monologues and dialogues take temporal precedence over the reticent social realism of Howells and the far more candid naturalistic realism of Dreiser. Critics, often in obscure publications, have pointed out quietly and astutely that the "secret" of Frost is not to be penetrated by analysis of his temperament or of his ideas and the manner of his expressing them. Personally, I have been impressed by the capacity of Frost's art to embody the reality of things. When he stated, "The fact is the sweetest dream that labor knows," he was contending that things are neither less nor more than what they are, hardly a reductionist's view and not at all a hyperbolic one. A decaying woodpile, a rapt moment by dark woods on a snow evening, an old worn-out hired man, an incident in a haying field, the sight of rose pogonias, a spruce-gum gatherer appearing in a village street, a mood evoked during a midwinter sunset—these are his "facts," which as facets are not so much to be seen through as seen into. For example, in "Looking for a Sunset Bird in Winter," what is the essential reality—a remembered bird recognized in summer, and in midwinter an imagined bird glimpsed in the identical spot? This explication is only to say the remembrance is casual and trifling. His awareness encompasses the reality of an illusion evoked by the literal image of a crooked stroke across a sundown sky. Climactically, the absolute reality is of the "piercing little star" observed against the uncertainly defined "crooked stroke" in the closing stanza.

> A brush had left a crooked stroke
> Of what was either cloud or smoke
> From north to south across the blue;
> A piercing little star was through.

As elsewhere, the simplicity is deceiving. The solitary leaf is the only direct evidence for the observer's momentary illusion of a remembered bird. The last vivid image therefore evokes the reality of an earlier illusion or the mistaken identity of leaf for bird. Since poetry is form as well as content, Frost's poetry includes play of irony and paradox, intoning and vocal images, literal and rhetorical language, explicit and implicit statements, rhyming and iambic pentameter lines.

What is assumed to be ambiguity in Frost's vision and evasiveness in his attitude, I read otherwise. The center of this vision, deeply rooted in the principle of reality, will consist in his answer to whatever the problems of his time appeared to be in the terms by which he understood it. Frost recognized experience as a continuous and changing process, which, in its resultant complexity, constantly initiated new options and fresh choices. His personal relationship to this complexity was one of containment. "As to the conflicts of our age," he said, "I *am* the conflicts. I *contain* them but the society I've grown into takes care of most of it." In view of "The Armful," what Frost meant by containment is that he not only included the conflicts of his time but tried to stay on top of them, hold them together, and, by extension, present them with clarity. Obviously, to contain the polarities, fears and anxieties, alienation and estrangement of one's time is a sure measure of strength, and to contain anarchic polarities like barbarism and civilization represents a feat.

If we ask whether Frost's containment of contradictory forces and attitudes, impulses and concepts, is only an apologia for a deeply entrenched evasiveness, I should think rather that it was exemplary of a subtle understanding of and response to complex experience and that it represented refusal to accept easy reconciliations. Frost was fond of two relevant quotations. He quoted approvingly Gray's, "And be with caution bold," which indicates a proneness toward rational exercise of courage this side of imprudence. And he quoted appealingly Horatio's statement in *Hamlet:* "So have I heard and do in part believe it," which implies a wary detachment. In fact, the core of Frost's apparent ambiguities seems to me to be subtlety, not evasiveness; a subtle recognition of the complexity in experience, not the inability to accept confrontation.

An effective criticism of polarized containment might be launched against its potentially static position in irresolution and indecisiveness. The failure to keep open and progressive the exercise of options in an open-ended universe is as seriously an obscuration as dogmatic rigidity. Frost, a devotee of paradox, used this device to hold contraries together and then made them function actively by transforming opposites through metaphor into new unities: the coordinated enterprise of men who work together "whether they work together or apart"; the paradox of the oven bird who in "singing not to sing" gives us "talk-songs"; the paradoxical countercurrent which is the "backward motion toward the source," a natural motion of self-revelation *"that most we see ourselves in"* (italics added); the paradox of possession and its ultimate unity in federalism implied in "The Gift Outright"; the paradox of spatial geography reflected in "America Is Hard to See" ("Finding the East by sailing West"); the paradox of time, place, and person suggested in "Directive" ("a house that is no more a house / Upon a farm that is no more a farm / And in a town that is no more a town"); and a guide who "only has at heart your getting lost." In "Two Tramps in Mud Time" the contraries of vocation and avocation are metaphorically united—"As my two eyes make one in sight." Consequently, the new unity of love and need in work becomes paradoxically "play for mortal stakes."

However, those who view poetry mainly in the perspective of cultural history will seek in vain among Frost's unities for an Arcadia like Jacopo Sannazaro's in 1504 or Sir Philip Sidney's in 1590. Instead of Arcady, we have Frost's "An Answer": "But Islands of the Blessèd, bless you, son, / I never came upon a blessèd one." Instead of an age of gold, we find the temporal impermanence of "Nothing Gold Can Stay." Instead of the Forest of Arden we enter the dark woods. Instead of maypoles and festive dancing, we encounter "Home Burial" and "The Hill Wife." Instead of shepherds and shepherdesses, we observe in "A Case for Jefferson" the antics of the Marxian Muscovite by day and the Freudian Viennese by night. Indeed, the route through the poetry of Robert Frost leads neither to the quixotic nor to outlawry; neither to city nor greenwood. Instead, as noted, it leads away from the Great Chain of Being to an exercise of options in an open-ended universe. In fact, the point behind Frostian phrases like "strategic retreat" and "momentary stay" is a world where no ethos like Dante's faith in a god-centered universe is discoverable but where experience suggests Emerson's emphasis on life as activity and power residing "in the moment of transition from a past to a new state, in the shooting of the gulf, in the darting to an aim."

Frost, like Emerson, believed in the resources of man, but while Emerson's wellspring was a transcendental oversoul, Frost's resource was illuminated empiricism. The source of the ideas in "Riders"—"We have ideas yet that we haven't tried"—is hardly superterrestrial. Nor does Frost's view of nature resemble Emerson's "great apparition." And despite ruminating among the ultimates, he does not contemplate matter as spirit or, as Emerson did, see in natural things overt symbols. In a Bread Loaf talk, he made it clear that he wasn't particularly interested in Emerson's transcendental thinking. It was Emerson's "living line" in "Monadnoc," beginning with "Fourscore or a hundred words" and continuing for eighteen successive lines, and poems like "Uriel," "Brahma," "Berrying," and some of the quatrains that characteristically interested him as a confirmation of his own theory of voice tones. "The lines," he remarked pointedly of Emerson's poems, "all look the same lengths—funny thing—and they're all *said* differently" (italic added).

During the years in England (1912–15), Frost had remarked that "all a man's art is a bursting unity of opposites," and later (in 1936) he said significantly: "I have seen art make the change from form to content and back to form. We people who are given too much freedom sway between freedom and discipline." Then he asked: "Where would one like to exist?" He replied: "I would like to exist, alive and in motion, between those two things, swaying a little with my times." The "momentary stay," now on content, now on form, represented a polarization of conflicting opposites. This polarization is not unlike Albert Camus's Sisyphus, who, in toiling at his stone, has a moment of relief before the stone again rushes downhill. "That hour like a breathing-space . . . is the hour of consciousness." Or, in Frost's own "West-running Brook," the polarization is witnessed in the "backward motion toward the source" where the white wave runs counter to itself. It is here "that most we see ourselves in." Why? Because it represents a synthesis of polarized tensions. For example, at the United Nations building in New York City, Frost saw the symbolic lump of iron "that was," as he noted, "supposed to be perfectly pure and meant to be the oneness that we could all attain—the purity." His couplet "From Iron" is a comment on the synthesis of polarizing opposites. He wrote: "Nature within her inmost self divides / To trouble men with having to take sides." Reflecting on the lump of iron, Frost said: "It's tools and weapons right while you're looking at it. Everything's like that."

How will Frost's poetry be received, say, fifty years from now? Probably not with the enthusiasm with which an earlier generation in the present century first approached *North of Boston* or *New Hampshire*. The advent of the New Criticism with its emphasis on explication des textes, the appearance of fresh personalities like Robert Lowell and Theodore Roethke, James Dickey and John Berryman who emphasize the autobiographical, and the tremendous effect of technological changes in so many different ways are bound to affect the response of later generations to Frost's poetry.

Take, for example, Frost's relationship to his material in a changing time. The little horse stopping by snowy woods while its driver nostalgically contemplates the wintry scene already seems temporally remote. Aware of such a change, Frost unsentimentally pointed out during one of his Vermont readings that people, as he said, "think about horses though they don't see them on the streets any more. They are back here in the back hills and on the back roads." In "The Mountain," he wrote of the incurious ox driver with a yoke of white-faced oxen and a heavy cart, who moved so slow "it seemed no harm to stop him altogether." And in "A Star in a Stoneboat," he referred to the sledlike stoneboats upland Yankee farmers once commonly used to clear their rocky fields of drift boulders. Big powerful tractors have now replaced horses, oxen, and stoneboats.

The importance of intimate scientific knowledge notwithstanding, we experience pleasure in reading a poem like "Design," not because Frost is an expert arachnologist like Fabre, but because he is an extremely competent poet who moves us by the use of language, image, and cadence. No matter what the superficial external condition, there will always be the inner human condition where inconsolable grief for a dead baby (in "Home Burial"), delight in the attractiveness of nature (in "A Young Birch"), elation in the buoyant spring (in "To the Thawing Wind"), the conjugal impulse (in "Putting in the Seed"), or the unutterable loneliness of the back-country woman (in "The Hill Wife") supersedes a preoccupation with place. Catullan thoughts and feelings like a common thread stitch together "Into My Own" and "In Winter in the Woods," and *A Boy's Will* and *In the Clearing*.

To contend that poetry diminishes in interest because of special subject matter is beside the point, as every reader of Chaucer or Shakespeare knows. The changing rural New England scene has little to do with Frost's ulterior poetic purpose. The natural scene and its identities are only the background. "Some people have called me a nature poet, because of the background, but I'm not a nature poet," Frost declared pretty emphatically. "There's always something else in my poetry."

While the views and context in poems change with climate of opinion and technological advances, Frost's "something else" remains. His survival value consists in the old intuitive knowledge and the simple truths of the human heart, which Catullus called *mens animi*, because these have a deep and abiding hold on the human imagination.

Index to Frost Quotations

Key

The references to Ripton and Middlebury, respectively, except where otherwise indicated, note visits with Robert Frost either at the Homer Noble Farm in Ripton or at my home in Middlebury, Vermont. In referring to the English School and the Writers' Conference at Middlebury College's Bread Loaf Campus at Bread Loaf, Vermont, the abbreviation BLES represents the former, and BLWC the latter.

The Poetry of Robert Frost, edited by Edward Connery Lathem (New York: Holt, Rinehart and Winston, 1969), is the standard text and reference used throughout. I have also found helpful *Interviews with Robert Frost,* ed. Edward Connery Lathem (New York: Holt, Rinehart and Winston, 1966), and *Selected Letters of Robert Frost,* ed. Lawrance Thompson (New York: Holt, Rinehart and Winston, 1964).

The Poetry of Robert Frost	PRF
Personal conversations with Robert Frost	C
Robert Frost, formal lecture-readings	R
Robert Frost, informal talks	T
Interviews with Robert Frost	I
Selected Letters of Robert Frost	SL

The numerals which appear at the left refer to the pages of the book. The words of each quotation indicate the beginning and end of the passage in the text.

1. Introduction

6   "the silences," C, Middlebury, May 9, 1952

2. Four Meetings

9   "A . . . far," I, p. 270
10   "performance," C, South Shaftsbury, July 28, 1935
14   "It's . . . tone," R.F. quoted in Guy Davenport's "First National Poetry: A Report," *National Review,* Jan. 15, 1963
15   "You . . . friend," C, Middlebury, Sept. 17, 1947

"Cut . . . therapeutic," Ibid.
"Well . . . woods," C, Cambridge, Mass., Dec. 13, 1947

16 "What . . . lot," C, Bread Loaf, August 8, 1953

3. A Sense of Place

17 "Did . . . you?," PRF, p. 114
  "a . . . sand," Ibid., p. 5
18–19 "I . . . had," Ibid., p. 6
19 "The healed," Ibid., p. 6
  "The . . . field," Ibid., p. 5
  "thought-felt," C, Middlebury, May 10, 1952
  "All . . . him," PRF, p. 108
19–20 "Always . . . inside," Ibid., p. 127
20 "Back . . . days," R,BLES, July 3, 1961
  "The . . . bones," Quoted by Harvey Breit, *New York Times Book Review*, Nov. 27, 1949
  "It . . . beauty," PRF, p. 375
  "I . . . me," R, Ripton Community House, July 23, 1955
  "not . . . now," R, Middlebury College, May 10, 1950
  "snow . . . alders," R, BLES, June 30, 1955
21 "We . . . are," PRF, p. 49
  "Sun-shaped . . . small," Ibid., p. 13
  "as . . . place," Ibid., p. 18
  "shakes . . . breeze," Ibid., p. 17
  "shadowy presence," Ibid., p. 41
  "To . . . snow!" Ibid., p. 237
  "For . . . wept," Ibid., p. 242
  "The . . . field," Ibid., p. 5
  "The . . . trees," Ibid., p. 265
22 "The . . . things," Ibid., p. 70
  "Yankees . . . were," Ibid., p. 139
  "finalities . . . grave," Ibid., p. 129
  "nothing . . . hope," Ibid., p. 38
  "my . . . poem," R, Middlebury College, Sept. 17, 1943
  "a realmist," C, Ripton, July 3, 1949
  "a pursuitist," PRF, p. 421
23 "thought-felt substance," R, BLES, July 6, 1937
  "that . . . New England," T, BLES, July 27, 1960
  "I . . . New England," Ibid.
24 "Because . . . New Hampshire," PRF, p. 166

4. Viva Voce

29 "Outraging the poem," R, BLES, June 30, 1955
31 "I've . . . next," R, BLES, June 29, 1959
32 "There's . . . anchor," R, BLES, June 30, 1955
  "The . . . anywhere," Ibid.
  "The . . . better," Ibid.
  "And . . . have," Ibid.
33 "You . . . beyond," Ibid.

34   "They're . . . indulgence," R, BLES, June 30, 1958
        "that . . . days," T, BLES, Aug. 2, 1954
        "heroism of magnanimity," R, June 30, 1955
        "great stuff, insubordination," R, July 3, 1957
        "And . . . left," R, BLES, July 3, 1957
35   "all . . . thing," PRF, p. 44

16.   The Masking of a Poet

199   "I'm . . . teacher," R, BLES, June 28, 1951
200   "There . . . there," SL, p. 98
        "Maybe . . . mind," Quoted in Louis Mertins, *Robert Frost: Life and
        Talks–Walking* (Norman, Okla.: University of Oklahoma Press, 1965),
        p. 378.
        "I . . . young," PRF, p. 308
200–201 "That's . . . voting," R, BLES, July 3, 1961
201   "My . . . Madison," R, BLES, June 29, 1959
        "that . . . book," T, BLES, July 27, 1960
        "that pretty . . . book," Ibid.
        "one . . . great," R, BLES, July 2, 1962
        "cant . . . criticism," T, BLES, July 27, 1960
        "Them . . . cream," R, BLES, July 3, 1961
        "I . . . stove," T, BLES, July 27, 1960
        "barding around," T, BLES, Aug. 2, 1954
202   "I'm . . . well-mixed," I, p. 185
        "I . . . hardtop," Louis Mertins, p. 354
        "I . . . day," R, BLES, July 3, 1957
204   "a . . . synecdochist," T, BLES, July 27, 1960
        "*how* . . . say," T, BLES, July 20, 1936
        "Out . . . together," Gorham Munson, *Robert Frost* (New York: George H.
        Doran Co., 1927), p. 127
205   "I'm . . . people," R, BLES, June 30, 1958
        "my . . . teaching," Ibid.
        "all . . . fact," R, BLES, July 20, 1936
        "They . . . poems," R, BLES, June 30, 1958
        "I . . . poems," R, BLES, June 30, 1955
206   "not . . . know," R, BLES, June 30, 1958
        "to . . . say," Ibid.
        "I've . . . narrative," R, Middlebury College, May 10, 1950
        "It's . . . see," R, BLES, July 3, 1957
        "The . . . too," Ibid.
        "I . . . there," Ibid.
        "Thinking . . . material," T, BLES, July 27, 1960
207   "It's . . . it," Ibid.
        "There's . . . low," Ibid.
        "Feeling . . . thinking," T, BLES, Aug. 1, 1957

17.   The Sayer

208   "Now . . . talking," PRF, p. 48
209   "There . . . that," T, BLES, Aug. 1954

"What's . . . anything?" Ibid.

"Always . . . alive," Ibid.

"There . . . composition," Ibid.

"It's . . . books," Ibid.

210   "Just . . . same," R, BLES, July 4, 1960

211   "It's . . . see?" Quoted in Elizabeth Shepley Sergeant, *Robert Frost: The Trial by Existence* (New York: Holt, Rinehart and Winston, 1960), p. 411

"Numbers . . . poetry," BLES, July 27, 1960

"Science . . . inclusive," I, p. 196

"I'm . . . science," I, p. 209

212   "Very . . . attractive," T, BLES, July 28, 1955

"a . . . scientists," R, BLES, June 30, 1955

"Lost . . . betterness," R, BLES, June 29, 1959

"a . . . flight," Ibid.

"domestic science," Ibid.

"our . . . planet," Ibid.

"a . . . tourism," Ibid.

"But . . . greatness," Ibid.

"God's . . . substantiation," PRF, p. 435

212–13   "But . . . matter," R, BLES, June 29, 1959

213   "Through . . . pages," Ibid.

"the . . . Emerson," Ibid.

"I . . . own," Ibid.

"the . . . mind," I, p. 209

"the . . . humanities," Ibid.

214   "pretty . . . trio," T, BLES, July 28, 1955

"I . . , farm," R, BLWC, Aug. 26, 1954

"Whether . . . garden," T, BLES, July 28, 1955

215   "Back . . . days," R, BLES, July 3, 1961

"Glory . . . days," T, BLES, Aug. 2, 1954

"Let . . . way," Ibid.

"Let's . . . love," R, BLES, June 29, 1959

"See . . . neighbors," Ibid.

"Seems . . . five," R, BLES, July 4, 1960

"It . . . lasted," Ibid.

"a . . . deal," Ibid.

"about . . . know," T, BLES, July 27, 1960

"a . . . myself," Ibid.

216   "See . . . together," R, BLES, July 4, 1960

"After . . . mine?" T, BLES, July 27, 1960

"beyond . . . it," PRF, p. 225

"a . . . confusion," *Complete Poems of Robert Frost* (New York: Henry Holt and Co., 1949), p. vi

"What . . . me," T, BLES, July 27, 1960

"It's . . . that," Ibid.

"I . . . source," Ibid. The source of the quotation is to be found in Lawrance Thompson's *Robert Frost: The Early Years*, p. 427. The quotation originally appeared in the untitled pocket notebook which Frost kept in England, 1912–15.

217   "a . . . thing," T, BLES, Aug. 2, 1954

218   "Perhaps . . . mean," PRF, p. 78
220   "with . . . down," Sergeant, pp. 410–11
       "this . . . writing," R, Middlebury College, May 10, 1950
       "I . . . all," Ibid.
       "just . . . it," R, BLES, July 20, 1936
       "Shape . . . parts," Ibid.
       "the . . . forms," Ibid.
221   "You . . . do," R, BLES, June 30, 1955
       "seems . . . you," T, BLES, July 27, 1960
221–22 "I . . . it," Ibid.
222   "lucky snatches," T, BLES, July 25, 1949
       "I . . . command," R, BLES, June 30, 1958
223   "I . . . done," SL, p. 88
       "I . . . art," Ibid., p. 228
       "I . . . inquiry?" T, BLES, July 28, 1955
       "And . . . poetry," Ibid.
       "Because . . . got," PRF, p. 50
       "You . . . you—" Ibid., pp. 54, 55
       "She . . . see," Ibid., p. 155
224   "I . . . window," Ibid., p. 112
       "Vocal images," Sergeant, p. xxv
       "renewal . . . words," C, South Shaftsbury, Vt., May 1931
       "I . . . stung," PRF, p. 226
225   "art . . . soul," Ibid., p. 353
226   "As . . . woods," Ibid., p. 334
       "those . . . gloom," Ibid., p. 5
       "Whose . . . know," Ibid., p. 244
227   "from . . . pocket," R, BLES, July 5, 1954
       "to . . . time," SL, p. 79
       "the . . . music," T, BLES, July 27, 1960
       "feat . . . association," "Robert Frost," USIS film
       "That . . . that," Writers at Work, 2nd ser. (New York: Viking, 1965),
       p. 30.
       "By . . . be," PRF, p. 223
228   "We . . . knows," Ibid., p. 312
       "Out . . . hissed," Ibid., p. 251
229   "To . . . rows," Ibid., p. 17
       "I . . . sun," Ibid., p. 22
       "And . . . grass," R, BLES, June 30, 1955
       "leastways," PRF, p. 64
       "daft," Ibid., p. 36
       "dite," Ibid., p. 80
       "tote road," Ibid., p. 208
       "windrows," Ibid., p. 69
       "shooks," Ibid., p. 95
       "swab," Ibid., p. 72
       "jag," Ibid., p. 71
       "water bar," Ibid., p. 263
       "stoneboat," Ibid., p. 172

"hugger-mugger," Ibid., p. 176

"beholden to," Ibid., p. 35

"stint," Ibid., p. 77

"dunnow," Ibid., p. 80

"mebbe," Ibid., p. 80

"We . . . enjoy," Ibid., p. 62

230   "So . . . hayfield," Ibid., p. 62

"I . . . off," Ibid., p. 71

"But . . . it," Ibid., p. 87

"A . . . said," Ibid., p. 48

"They . . . of," Ibid., p. 66

"See . . . maybe," R, BLES, July 5, 1954

"Pushing . . . ahead," PRF, p. 338

"Do . . . myself," R, BLES, July 5, 1954

"You . . . it," Ibid.

"And . . . See," Ibid.

231   "terribly . . . me," R, BLES, July 2, 1956

"And . . . after," Ibid.

"this . . . nature," Ibid.

"From . . . brim," PRF, p. 23

"I . . . things," R, BLES, July 4, 1960

"I . . . that," R, BLES, July 2, 1956

"The . . . have," R, BLES, June 30, 1955

"I . . . cry," PRF, p. 14

"The . . . ceiling," Ibid., p. 117

"The . . . still," Ibid., p. 12

"Fresh . . . black," Ibid., p. 55

"The . . . nails," Ibid., p. 56

"to . . . about," Ibid., p. 5

231–32   "You . . . wood," Ibid., p. 94

232   "feats . . . association," "Robert Frost," USIS film

"The . . . *chops*," PRF, pp. 5, 6

"That . . . flowers," Ibid., p. 13

"The . . . go," Ibid., p. 27

"And . . . trees," Ibid., p. 12

"this . . . forbid," R, BLES, July 5, 1954

"I . . . poem," Ibid.

"I've . . . somewhat," R, BLES, June 25, 1953

232–33   "Too . . . sing," PRF, p. 334

233   "I . . . then," R, BLES, June 25, 1953

"One . . . for," Ibid.

"Over . . . eve," PRF, p. 102

"When . . . mire," Ibid., p. 225

"Now . . . there," R, BLES, July 4, 1960

"And . . . stanzas," Ibid.

"self-surprise," "Poetry as Prowess," Charles Eliot Norton Lecture, Cambridge, Mass., March 25, 1936

234   "I . . . material," R, BLES, July 4, 1960

"feats . . . association," "Robert Frost," USIS film

"But . . . dust," PRF, p. 386

"But . . . dough," Ibid., p. 378

"Clematis . . . bundle," Ibid., p. 102
"The . . . bullets," Ibid., p. 217
"hangs . . . parakeet," Ibid., p. 411
"put . . . night," Ibid., p. 38
235   "brushed . . . Garden," Ibid., p. 188
"Those . . . sight," Ibid., p. 9
"Every . . . suppose," R, Middlebury College, May 15, 1950
"a . . . it," Ibid.
"one . . . taken," PRF, p. 376
"The . . . metaphor," R, BLES, June 29, 1950
"The . . . game," Ibid.
235–36   "He . . . world," PRF, p. 419
236   "You're . . . it," R, BLES, July 27, 1960
"words . . . deeds," Gorham B. Munson, *Robert Frost*, p. 98
236–37   "Our . . . know," R, BLES, July 5, 1954
237   "By . . . apex," Ibid.
"I . . . it," R, BLES, July 27, 1960
"the . . . worlds," Ibid.
"You . . . am," Ibid.
"ultimate things," R, BLES, July 4, 1960

19.   The Act of Taking

238   "The . . . hear," PRF, p.78
"Poetry . . . you," R, Middlebury College, May 27, 1936
239   "strategic retreat," Ibid., p. 282
239–40   "There . . . that," R, BLES, July 4, 1960
240   "I . . . else," R, Middlebury College, May 28, 1936
"cavalierly," C, Ripton, July 13, 1948
"Poems . . . meaning," T, BLES, Aug. 6, 1945
"The . . . poem," Frost quoted in Stallman and West, *The Art of Modern Fiction* (New York, 1949), pp. iv, 449
"I . . . in," Frost quoted in *College News*, Bryn Mawr, March 23, 1960
"These . . . write," Frost quoted in Mertins, *Robert Frost: Talks–Walking*, p. 372
241   "Mr. Frost . . . competition," T, *Meet the Press*, March 22, 1959
242   "This . . . wild," Chester Morrison, "A Visit with Robert Frost," *Look*, March 31, 1959
"I . . . appertaining," SL, pp. 343, 344
"She . . . learn," PRF, p. 257
243   "the . . . school," R, BLES, July 5, 1954
"Most . . . scholars," Ibid.
"in . . . hard," T, BLES, Aug. 2, 1954
"Now . . . it," R, BLES, July 5, 1954
"poesy pure," Ibid.
"That's . . . for," Ibid.
"My . . . me," R, BLES, July 2, 1956
"They've . . . home," R, BLES, July 5, 1954
"But . . . studied," T, BLES, Aug. 2, 1954
243–44   "Now . . . you," Ibid.
244   "The . . . it," Ibid.

"Any . . . note," Ibid.

"taking . . . poetry," Ibid.

"there . . . all," Ibid.

"It . . . it," Ibid.

"All . . . up," Ibid.

244–45 "Well . . . it," Ibid.

245 "I . . . fooling," R, BLES, June 30, 1955

"the . . . God," Ibid.

"[Einstein] . . . Newton," Ibid.

"of . . . way," Ibid.

"that . . . poetry," Ibid.

"The . . . concerns," Ibid.

246 "to . . . symbolism," R, BLES, June 25, 1953

"We're . . . beside," Ibid.

"a . . . besides," Ibid.

"And . . . that," Ibid.

"let . . . symbols," Ibid.

"People . . . them," Ibid.

246–47 "And . . . them," Ibid.

247 "It's . . . art," Ibid.

"The . . . that," R, BLES, June 30, 1955

"Poetry . . . you," R, Middlebury College, May 27, 1936

"Some . . . times," R, BLES, July 4, 1960

"I . . . you," Ibid.

"too observing," R, BLES, June 30, 1958

248 "This . . . observation," Ibid.

"It's . . . on," Ibid.

"No . . . there," Ibid.

"Those . . . meter," Ibid.

"It's . . . abandoned," Ibid.

"Again . . . me," Ibid.

"For . . . there," PRF, p. 415

"He . . . alone," Ibid., p. 338

"strikes . . . note," R, BLES, June 30, 1958

"O . . . mild," PRF, p. 27

"I . . . prayerful," R, BLES, June 30, 1958

"All . . . everything," R, BLES, June 29, 1959

"See . . . see," Ibid.

249 "all . . . things," R, BLES, July 4, 1960

"My . . . pieces," Ibid.

"a . . . sentence," Ibid.

"Wonderful . . . form," Ibid.

"the . . . poem," Ibid.

"the . . . merit," PRF, p. 435

"This . . . in?" R, BLES, July 4, 1960

"There . . . there," Ibid.

250 "Look . . . delicacy," Ibid.

"always . . . quite," Ibid.

"Symbol . . . things," Ibid.

"I . . . that," Ibid.

"these . . . people," Ibid.

317

"They . . . right," R, BLES, July 4, 1960
"Nature . . . sides," PRF, p. 468
"But . . . one," Ibid., p. 363
"unexpected connections," C, Ripton, June 30, 1950
"Some . . . rain," PRF, p. 301
"Human . . . it," Ibid., p. 304
"But . . . care," Ibid., p. 284
"cutting . . . up," C, Middlebury, Vt., May 10, 1952
272   "The . . . pup," PRF, p. 308
"We . . . tried," Ibid., p. 267
"We . . . tension," R, BLWC, Aug. 18, 1951
"The . . . knows," PRF, p. 17
"I . . . in," Ibid., p. 252
"Men . . . apart," Ibid., p. 23
"One . . . night," Ibid., p. 108
273   "It . . . in," Ibid., p. 260
"And . . . place," Ibid., p. 76
"Something . . . surrender," Ibid., p. 348
"The . . . sing," Ibid., p. 119
"a dialogue," Quoted in *Time,* Oct. 9, 1950, p. 80
"I . . . systematic," PRF, p. 362
"But . . . once," Ibid., p. 349
274   "I . . . anti-scientist," R, BLES, July 3, 1961
"See . . . science," Ibid.
275   "bandying . . . theology," T, BLES, July 10, 1957
"that . . . Devil," Ibid.
"there . . . end," Ibid.
"the . . . man," Ibid.
"I'd . . . anywhere," PRF, p. 476
"God's . . . never," Ibid., p. 478
"She'd . . . Hostesses," Ibid., p. 480
"mercy . . . deserving," R, BLWC, Aug. 18, 1945
"New England Biblicals," Quoted in *The Atlantic Monthly,* Nov. 1947, p. 68
"universal failure," C, Cambridge, Mass., Dec. 13, 1947
"So . . . too," PRF, p. 505
"It's . . . world," Ibid., p. 54
"Oh . . . reading," Ibid., p. 495
"My . . . O'Neill," Ibid., p. 516

21.   On a Field of Vision

277   "Earth . . . fate," PRF, p. 437
"the . . . knows," Ibid., p. 17
"I . . . world," Ibid., p. 353
277–78 "No . . . comic," Ibid.
278   "book . . . unworthies," I, p. 209
279   "There's . . . enough," R, Middlebury College, Oct. 7, 1959
"It . . . material," SL, p. 426
"My . . . boundless," Ibid., p. 344
281   "the . . . dream-heads," PRF, p. 251

"Maybe . . . mind," Louis Mertins, *Robert Frost: Life and Talks–Walking,* p. 378

"higher . . . pass," PRF, p. 140

"But . . . see," Ibid., p. 300

"Regular . . . iambic," Ibid., p. 460

"opposing goods," Ibid., p. 350

282 "A . . . bank?" PRF, p. 39

"two and twenty," C, Middlebury, Vt., May 28, 1943

"the . . . no," C, Ripton, June 1, 1948

"I'm . . . city," "Robert Frost," Holt, Rinehart, and Winston film

"I'm . . . anything," C, Middlebury, Vt., May 10, 1950

"Truth . . . dialogue," *Time,* October 9, 1950, p. 80

"It's . . . world," Sidney Cox, *Robert Frost: Original Ordinary Man* (New York: Henry Holt and Co., 1929), p. 20

283 "This . . . matter," PRF, p. 279

"the . . . give," Ibid., p. 450

"Cumaean . . . fade," Ibid., pp. 449, 450

"a . . . where," R, BLES, June 30, 1959

284 "of . . . mankind," PRF, p. 450

"We . . . staid," Ibid., p. 403

285 "and . . . earth," R, BLES, July 3, 1961

"you . . . how," Ibid.

"a . . . ending," R, Middlebury College, April 29, 1957

285–86 "the . . . think," R, BLES, June 28, 1951

286 "But . . . keep?" PRF, p. 301

287 "All . . . thing," PRF, p. 44

"But . . . matter," R, BLES, June 29, 1959

"The . . . said," C, Weybridge, Vt., Sept. 28, 1957

289 "the existence," PRF, p. 19

290 "and . . . juniper," PRF, p. 17

"may . . . more," Ibid., p. 301

"wherever . . . be," Ibid., p. 301

"extremes . . . once," Ibid., pp. 266, 267

"absolute . . . rest," Ibid., p. 388

"limitless trait," Ibid., p. 305

"favors," C, BLES, Summer 1928

291 "shining . . . red," PRF, p. 254

"This . . . sport," Ibid.

"a hint," R, BLES, July 4, 1960

"on-penetration . . . skies," PRF, p. 435

"We . . . tried," Ibid., p. 267

292 "all . . . him," Ibid., p. 108

"They . . . places," Ibid., p. 296

"And . . . sight," Ibid., p. 9

292–93 "Sudden . . . grave," Ibid., p. 129

293 "But . . . past," Ibid., pp. 335, 336

"The . . . imagine," Ibid.

"Two . . . speak," Ibid., p. 326

"It . . . this," Ibid.

"the . . . Millenium," Ibid., p. 361

294 "But . . . substantiation," Ibid., p. 435

"Our . . . venture," Ibid.

"Like . . . somewhere," *Complete Poems of Robert Frost*, p. vii

"It . . . constellations," Quoted in Lawrance Thompson, *Fire and Ice*, p. 135

295   "The . . . parts," R, BLES, Aug. 6, 1945

"every . . . symbol," R, BLES, July 2, 1956

"predestined," Thompson, *Fire and Ice*, p. 133

"unforeseen," Ibid.

"a . . . preference," PRF, p. 425

"I . . . everywhere," *Selected Prose*, pp. 38, 39

"You . . . me," "Robert Frost," USIS film

296   "A . . . life," PRF, p. 263

"backward . . . in," Ibid., p. 257

22.   A Reviewal

297   "You . . . held," PRF, p. 306

297–98   "back . . . days," R, BLES, July 3, 1961

298   "almost . . . animus," R, BLES, July 2, 1956

"a . . . poetry," R, BLES, July 5, 1954

299   "the Broken One," PRF, p. 100

300   "realmist," C, Ripton, Vt., July 2, 1949

301   "numbers," T, BLES, July 27, 1960

"up . . . tall," PRF, p. 210

"thought-felt," T, BLES, Aug. 2, 1954

"Snow . . . last," PRF, p. 296

302   "What . . . do?" Ibid., p. 35

"I've . . . Asylum," Ibid., p. 62

"Ah . . . season?" Ibid., p. 29

303   "What . . . farms," Ibid., p. 49

"And . . . straight," Ibid., p. 223

"She . . . slept," Ibid., p. 127

"Winds . . . bleak," Ibid., p. 246

"a . . . type," "Robert Frost Reads from His Own Works," May 19, 1961, Yale Series of Recorded Poets (YP 320)

"the . . . sonnet," Ibid.

"a . . . thing," Ibid.

"a . . . telescope," Ibid.

"that's . . . spirit," Ibid.

"you . . . game," Ibid.

304   "a . . . thing," C, Middlebury College, May 10, 1952

"The . . . knows," PRF, p. 27

"piercing little star," Ibid., p. 233

"a . . . through," Ibid.

305   "As . . . it," Elizabeth Shepley Sergeant, *Robert Frost, Trial by Existence*, p. 406

"whether . . . apart," PRF, p. 23

"singing . . . sing," Ibid., p. 120

"talk-songs," Elizabeth Shepley Sergeant, *Fire Under the Andes* (New York, 1927), p. 295

"backward . . . stream," PRF, p. 260

"that . . . in," Ibid.
306 "Finding . . . West," Ibid., p. 416
"a . . . town," Ibid., p. 377
"a . . . lost," Ibid.
"As . . . sight," Ibid.
"play-stakes," Ibid.
"But . . . one," Ibid., p. 363
"strategic retreat," Ibid., p. 282
"momentary stay," *Complete Poems*, p. vi
"we . . . tried," PRF, p. 268
"living line," T, BLES, Aug. 2, 1954
307 "The . . . differently," Ibid.
"all . . . opposites," Thompson, *Robert Frost: The Early Years,* p. 427
"I . . . times," R, Middlebury College, May 27, 1936
"backward . . . source," PRF, p. 210
"that . . . purity," R, BLES, June 29, 1959
"Nature . . . sides," PRF, p. 468
"It's . . . that," R, BLES, June 29, 1959
308 "think . . . roads," R, Middlebury College, April 9, 1957
"it . . . altogether," PRF, p. 41
"Some . . . poetry," I, p. 114

General Index

329

330